The Strait

Book of Obenabi

His Songs

from the pen of Fredy Perlman

THE STRAIT

Book of Obenabi. His Songs

Black & Red
Detroit
1988

Available from:

Black & Red
P.O. Box 02374
Detroit, Michigan 48202

B & R expresses gratitude to
Dumont Press Graphix, Kitchener, Ontario
for making their typesetting equipment available.

NOTE TO THE READER   v

A Note to the Reader:

An early death kept Fredy Perlman from finishing the two-volume account of Robert Dupré's forebears who lived on the Strait and in the surrounding woodlands. In both volumes, "Book of Obenabi. His Songs" and "Book of Robert Dupré. His Tales," narrators recount familiar historic events as individuals indigenous to the region might have experienced them.

Fredy intended to present *The Strait* as texts written down by Obenabi's nephew, Robert Dupré, in the 1850s. In 1851 Obenabi presumably told (or sang) his narrative to Dupré in Detroit's prison hospital, uncle and nephew having been jailed as conspirators who opposed construction of a railroad across Michigan.

In addition to Obenabi's songs, Robert Dupré was to be credited with preserving the tales of his aunt Wabnokwe. This history purports to be based on journals Obenabi's sister kept throughout her life, and it constitutes Book II of *The Strait*. As a French-speaking resident of Detroit, Dupré wrote both narratives in French.

Fredy planned to present himself as the translator of Dupré's manuscripts. His ostensible link to the text was through Ted Nasibu, a twentieth-century "rememberer" who was a fellow-printer at the Detroit Printing Co-op on Michigan Avenue. Both Ted and his friend Tissie appear in an earlier Black & Red publication, *Letters of Insurgents*. Through Tissie, Ted became acquainted with Robert Avis, Tissie's cousin and Dupré's great-grandson.

The Prologue situates Avis in a hospital bed in 1984. The surroundings combined with his anguish transport him to his great-grandfather's side as the latter listens to his uncle Obenabi in 1851. At the beginning of Chapter 1, Obenabi, who also carries the name Jacob Burr-net, is recounting the experiences of his thirty-second year, events which occurred in 1826.

This volume of *The Strait* was essentially complete at the time of Fredy's death in 1985 but a few minor changes were appropriate. In Chapter 9, I used Fredy's outline to write some missing paragraphs. A few inconsistancies remain, but I hope they are minor.

With some misgivings, I have added the chronological dates on the right-hand pages. Although each page of Fredy's manuscript mentions the year in which the events occurred, I doubt that he planned to include them when publishing the book. I feel they aid the reader in situating the story so have retained them.

Fredy did intend to append a glossary, but the rudimentary one provided here is mine, not his.

John Ricklefs designed the cover.

The photos are by Frank Jackson.

Lorraine Perlman
March 1988

Contents

A note to the reader v

Prologue 1

Chapter 1. Obenabi's first journey 5
    Journey to the Beginning 5
    Descent to the Water 14
    Reemergence 22
    The Mask 30

Chapter 2. Obenabi's grandmothers 39
    Yahatase's children 39
    Wedasi 49
    Nangisi 60
    Binesikwe 69

Chapter 3. Miogwewe 81
    Kukamigokwe 81
    Shutaha 93
    Chacapwe 106
    Sagikwe 117

Chapter 4. Miogwewe continues 129
    Ubankiko 129
    Ozagi 141
    Wagoshkwe 153
    Menoko 164

Chapter 5. Katabwe 175
Lenapi 175
Miní 184
Lókaskwe 195
Oashi 206

Chapter 6. Katabwe continues 217
Namakwe 217
Aptegizhek 228
Sigenak 240
Nanikibi 251

Chapter 7. Obenabi 263
Birth and journey 263
The Strait 273
Puritan school 284
Fire and departure 293

Chapter 8. Obenabi's guides 305
Obenabi's dream 305
Topinbi and Shabeni 316
Song of Udatonte 327
Separation 335

Interlude 345

Chapter 9. Obenabi's second journey 347
The last council fire 347
Meteya's Village 355
Adoption of Wimego 368
Suicide of Wimego 383

Epilogue 397

Glossary 399

Prologue

Early morning's undone dream pulls me back to its activity, makes waking seem death, gives reality a fearful aura.

"It's time for your surgery, Mr. Avis," says Madge May the nurse. I'm here as object for treatment, there's nothing to fear, nothing supernatural; diagnosis and remedy are determined by procedures accessible to all, and what is each of us but a product at a different stage of processing, transformed by labor into a more finished if not more perfect product?

Orderlies Gabe Godfroy and Bill Wells prepare the bed on wheels, as Tom Williams the intern notes schedules and circumstances on his pad, while elsewhere the various specialists—bookkeepers, administrators, technicians, surgeons, nurses—are activated by the commander-in-chief, Dr. Cass, like an army, like meshing gears of clockwork, with an efficiency in stark contrast to my malfunctioning, inefficient bodily organs, defying death and disease with Organization and Confidence. It's impressive what they can do nowadays.

All I ever feared was failure to sell myself on the labor market, and this fear was dispelled by qualifications acquired in school, experience in teamwork gained in military service, and finally the benefits, good money and insurance earned in industry. My self-assurance grew with my confidence in the solidity of my environment, in its unbounded power to capture unprocessed raw matter (whether rock or tree or bodily organ, or a shy street kid like me, Robert Avis), define it with a fixed concept that holds under all conditions, reduce its inessential qualities to mathematical entities in order at last to transform it by technological processes into a product freed of its primal imperfections and shaped for insertion into the process that produced it.

Alongside my self-assurance grew a secret pride, not of a mere impressed spectator, but of an active participant who had mastered a machine anyone with drive can learn to handle, the pride of a product and agent of the machine determining destiny.

Procedural indications following the diagnosis of my abdominal discomfort strengthened my unshaken confidence in the organization that encompasses occupational hazards as part of the original intention, removes a diseased colon as easily as birdsnests and trees from the path of a highway, banishes death to the company of dragons in the museum of curios. Someone with drive doesn't succumb to nature's caprices.

My heart, weakened by the colon removal, was revived by an electric stimulator, a marketable replacement pump being unavailable as yet.

A clean and efficient mechanical filter is an improvement on the kidneys that followed my colon. As for my hair, driven out by radiation—of what use was it?

So when the neurosurgeon told me there was something on my brain and nothing could be done, I smiled right through him, piercing him with my confidence. I've never actually worked as a buyer for a firm, but with schooling and earning, I've been one all my life. When I pay good money, lots of it, and hear, "That's the best we can do," I smile. "Come now, you can do better than that."

I know people die, but people are poor, lack confidence, have no drive, and can't operate the machine.

The fear that grips me in my half-waking state is new to me; long-repressed urges seem to be devouring my sense.

In response to surgeon's assistant Bill Conner's cold explanation of the coming procedure, I grab the bedpost and curl my lip upward like one suddenly gone rabid, like a paranoid protester. I behave as if by waking I'd slip into a frightful dream, as if the long-familiar staff people were bent on doing me ill, as if they were jailers bent only on walling me in, as if they were teachers bent only on breaking my spirit, as if they were police agents bent on capturing me, as if they were demons bent on destroying me.

Guards McCloskey and Washington leer at me from the doorway. My eyes insanely return the leer and then go wildly wandering in search of fellow-feeling, kinship, solidarity, but find only the annoyed expressions of salaried employees. Nurse Ann Kanish smooths my pillow and urges me resume my sleep.

PROLOGUE 1984

Is it shock, drugs, early morning weakness, or the obstruction on my brain that turn objective reality into a nightmare and flood my mind with spectres, long-forgotten moments that played no part in my development, instants when time stood still? I felt only a twinge when I read about Ted Nasibu being killed by a car near the bridge; the article called him a printer (rememberer, preserver); I'd known him during the war as a thief. Yet now the twinge becomes a spasm, and I feel myself running alongside Ted and my cousin Tissie on the riverbank below the bridge toward Grandfather Avis dipping his fishline into the water of the strait, a fish skeleton, arrowhead and bundle neatly arranged on the concrete beside him.

Now we're walking up the embankment with a bucketful of fish to the brick and shingle rowhouse of Brenda Avis née Dupré, my and Tissie's grandmother. I pretend to be listening to the old woman, but I'm savoring the smell of frying fish, glancing at the floorplan of a slaveship on the kitchen wall, fingering a copper pendant she hands me. "Get yourself ready, Robert," she says, singling me out to accompany her to a gathering of dee pees in a house on the boulevard, where in a huge plain room I'm surrounded by chanting and gesticulating skeletons.

The chant cuts like a peeling knife through my identities as patient, technician, veteran, student, removing successive masks as so many layers of an onion, leaving no core, only a weak voice which, when it joins the chanters, causes the room's plain walls to turn into barbed fence of Treblinka surrounded by endless stretches of cotton fuzz of Louisiana bordered by oak openings on Michigan's lower peninsula.

Three songs, each with distinct melodies and rhythms, at first clash dissonantly, then companion each other in counterpoint, finally fuse in a harmony of sound that like a tidal wave upsets the dikes set up against this very flood, overwhelming the years of schooling, service and labor, lifting the singers beyond range of the obscene shouts of uniformed Virginians removing forest dwellers, of whiparmed overseers abusing field workers, of swastikad guards harassing the expropriated.

My urge to remain myself, to regain wakeful sanity, fights my desire to plunge yet further into dream's or death's illusory light, but my will is limp, all fixity is gone. I run from waking rather than from sleep, sensing myself not as responsible law-abiding Robert Avis, but as thief Nasibu before the fatal blow rushing from the bridge; as emaciated Treblinkan before the fatal roundup rushing to festivities in a tree-surrounded Polish village; as Grandfather Avis's grandmother before the fatal kidnapping, moving ecstatically to drumbeats by the shore of a bluegreen lake in Westafrica; as Grandmother Brenda's father Robert Dupré escaping from the anguish of a decomposing village to lean on a tree by the riverbank (perhaps on the very spot where Ted was killed), long before there was a bridge across the Strait.

    A needle in my vein rouses me to leer at the whitefrocked figures writhing on white walls of tile, cement and plastic, but the smooth surfaces quickly change into familiar walls of apartments, locker rooms, barracks, schoolrooms, and then crease and shrivel, until I'm surrounded by walls of plain, cracked, poorly fitted wooden boards, while the figures are metamorphosed into a museum of period costumes, some in tuxedos dangling their watch chains, others in wool, at least one clad in animal skins and moccasins, all swearing like ruffians, but some with pistols in their waists.

    I finger the pendant suspended from my neck, my free hand clasps a column which I experience as living tree and indispensable support, my eyes wander from face to face, pausing at the pimp responsible for my arrest, and resting at a blanket-wrapped old man who clutches a bundle; soon I'm beside him, entranced by his chant....

Chapter 1.

Obenabi

Journey to the Beginning

  It was fear of the manhunters who killed my uncle Topinbi that roused me to travel on the path toward the morning sun from the Bison Prairie on the long lake to the beaverlodge village on the strait.
  Though companioned by a horse weighed down by dead beavers, like Topinbi used to go, I did not follow the trail in search of objects but of knowledge. I went as a scout, to learn if the angry sun would continue to warm the lodges of his grandchildren in the Bison Prairie. As I went further east, the wide trail, its bushes removed, its trees felled, was like a scar gouged by some unfeeling beast that destroys all life on its path. I thought that by scouting I could learn why such a

powerful creature insists on following paths of deer and of Rootkin who did not scar the forest.

The sight of so many beings deprived of life for no reason filled me with sorrow, and at a crossing with a familiar deer trail I strayed from the wide path and guided my horse northward toward a lake once far removed from the paths of unfeeling Invaders, where deer play among sparse trees on green ground that surrounds water as still and blue as the sky.

The moment I saw the great tree that had witnessed my love fifteen springs earlier, all the pain flowed from my heart, all the sorrow from my mind. I let the horse roam, sat near the root of the tree, took a lock of black hair from my bundle, and sang.

For two days my voice roamed over the water between the grassy shores singing of birds who returned when the snows melted and the trees birthed new leaves, singing of Rootkin who had wandered here from the land of ice and would wander no further, singing of Udatonte who took winter's cold from me by guiding me to the spring warmth of this tree.

And as I sang my body filled with joy, my limbs grew as light as the limbs of a weightless deer hopping among the trees, a deer running to the grassy shore to lap the lake's blue water, suddenly startled by the reflection of another deer lapping beside him, startled by Udatonte alongside me in the shape of a young deer nudging my side with her nose, singing me her dreams by touch. My mind, very far from the dead beings along the widened path, suddenly knew it was not a deer, nor any living being, that was nudging my side.

The barrel-end of a rifle was pressed into my arm. The man who pointed it held my horse's reins in his other hand.

Tears came to my eyes, not so much from fear as from deep sorrow, for the coming of this man put an abrupt end to all the beauty, love, joy. I sensed the question on the lips of the birds, of the trees, even of the water and the grass: Why, in the midst of this green where all forms of newborn life trustingly wrapped themselves with air's warmth and joyfully absorbed earth's moisture, why was this smirking creature with his killing-stick here at all?

But the question stayed mute, as if it were not he who had to answer but we, as if the birds, trees, lake, grass and I existed only on the suffrance of this man, as if the sun could warm the living only with his consent, as if the great mystery had come to depend on one's distance from the end of his killing-stick.

"Git up off the grass," he ordered, pointing the rifle at my heart as I rose shaking like a leaf in the wind, with a fear I had not felt since my separation from Udatonte. What I had learned from uncle Topinbi's death was being confirmed: in the vicinity of such a person, all life became a hunted animal. "I'll pay for whatever harm my horse done," I offered weakly, knowing that he, without a trace of greatness or valor, without even a show of excellence, but simply by moving a finger, could take all the money, the furs and the horse.

"What do they call ye, Yaller-face-in-the-sky?" he spat, laughing.

"Burr-net," I answered, pronouncing carefully. "Jacob Burr-net."

"Barnets of Noo Jersey?" he asked, and lowered the rifle when I nodded. "You rangers gonna have your heads blown off trespassing on property looking like redskins." He dropped my horse's reins and walked quickly toward the forest.

I silently thanked Wimego my father for giving me this second life, and pulled cloth pants and a cotton shirt from the fur stack, masking myself before proceeding toward the beaver village.

Long before my path reached ancient Shutaha's trail, I was greeted by axe-marked stumps, mortally wounded trees, detritus-surrounded camp spots. When I heard piercing shouts in the language of Scabeaters and their Scalper kin, I quickened my pace, circling the outskirts of the village of dams built on land, at last reaching the woods behind the great lodge that stands on the graves of our ancestors and pausing among trees to watch children playing.

My tired horse's neigh betrayed my presence to a silk-clad youngster playing scout who shouted, "Look, it's chief Topin-a-bee with the fur shipment!"

Four girls, three in dresses and one in deerskin, ran toward me after the boy. "Mais ce n'est pas Topinbi, ce doit être l'oncle Jacques," exclaimed a tall, thin girl with eyes as green and hair as yellow as my sister's.

Whereupon the youngest girl danced around the boy singing, as if to reproach him, "It's not Topinbi but uncle Jack," a refrain the boy interspersed with, "But I'm the one who saw his pack."

"Besides, he's not your uncle," the boy declared as he leapt out of the circle, "and he's Ben, like me, not Jack."

"Bienvenue," said the tall girl smiling, walking toward me extending her hand. "Je suis ta nièce Marti et voici ma soeur Molly."

The boy was judge Jay-may's son Benji-may, Marti explained; the youngest girl was not the boy's sister but his niece, Margít's granddaughter Marianne Brooks, and the black-braided girl in deerskin who studied me from her post between two trees was Mendideti from Karontaen, "mais ici on l'appelle Anne; elle est notre préceptrice."

Mendideti glared with burning eyes at the fur load on the horse and chanted, in Udatonte's tongue, "They say Obenabi the son of Nanikibi does not swim in the blood of his beaverkin."

I tried to keep my eyes fixed on hers, but shame forced mine toward the braid of wavy hair and then toward the ground— shame of what she saw, of all I was impersonating.

My thoughts were drowned by the voices of Benji-may and Marianne who raced each other toward the great lodge shouting, "Father, Maman! It's uncle Ben avec les fourrures du parque aux vaches!"

Soon aunt Margít was embracing me, "Bienvenue, Jacques, mais quelle surprise!" Tears flowing, all her emotions worn externally like clothes.

A younger woman, undoubtedly Greta-may Brooks, ran behind Margít, avoided glancing at me, grabbed Marianne by the hand and hastily disappeared.

As I moved hesitantly toward the back entrance, judge Jay-may shouted for someone to take charge of the horse and its load, then patted me on the back and called me prodigal son, his eyes shifting between me and the peltry.

At last Wabnokwe emerged, thin, frail, unchanged but for the hint of grey further lightening her yellow hair. "I thank the rising sun—" she began in the tongue of our Rootkin, but speaking it nasally, like the habitants, and then she too threw her arms around me and wept, "Mon petit frère." I sensed she already knew why I had come.

I explained to Wabnokwe that I would feast and sleep only after smoking and counciling with my kin of the Strait. Walking away from the afternoon sun toward the riverbank, I was struck by a sound and sight more hideous than all the stumps and injured trees. An ominous screech filled the air and smoke blackened the sky as if the Strait's water were boiling and rising in grey steam, its banks shrieking from pain. Looking past intervening trees toward the water, my eyes saw something my mind rejected: an island was floating in the strait, moving upstream, cinders and smoke emerging from its tallest lodge. So intrusive, so unnatural a sight can be described only with the habitants' word *barbare*. Yet I felt it was I who was out of place and, reflecting on my earlier shame, I wondered if it was shame over my being here at all, or shame over my feeling out of place on ground where my grandmothers lay buried.

Wabnokwe and Jim-may led me to the house and restored my calm by making the wondrous sounds emerge from their music instruments. When the music ended, the councilroom of the great lodge was crowded with kin I hadn't seen for eleven springs. Several of the May children were in the circle: of course playful young Benji-may, his slightly older sister Carrie-may, who seemed to wish she were elsewhere, and young Jim-may, a physical replica of his father, but with pensive eyes.

Cousins Beth Lion, Lisa Will-yams and Likét Kampó sat next to each other and whispered, as inseparable as they had been. The former fourth corner of their world, aunt Monik unaccompanied by her husband Kuyeryé, sat alongside and whispered with the other three. Aunt Margít's twin Jozét sat next to her husband Wit-nags across the circle from me.

I prepared a pipe and aimed the smoke toward the opening behind me and carried the pipe to Wit-nags, who passed it directly to Jay-may. The pipestem had barely reached the judge's mouth when Wit-nags burst with impatience. "We already know all about your uncle's death, if that's what you're hiding behind this smokescreen."

Mumbling to aunt Monik, "La démocratie de tes beaux-frères est une tyrannie," Likét rose, ready to leave.

Angry eyes of Monik and Margít sought their sister's, until at last Jozét whispered to Wit-nags, "Mais tais-toi, mon vieux, et laisse-le fumer et parler, puisqu'il est venu jusqu'ici." Likét sat down, and all eyes turned to me.

I thanked the life-giving powers for preserving so many of my kin for this gathering. While Wabnokwe was translating for Wit-nags' and Jay-may's benefit, Wit-nags shouted, "You're wasting our time, Burr-net. Come to the point! And speak American. We all know you're as conversant with it as your sister."

Jay-may then told Wabnokwe, "If your kinsman insists on using his own language, please refrain from translating until he starts talking sense."

I went on to describe the circumstances of uncle Topinbi's death, just as cousin Shandó had narrated them: the nightlong torture, the fatal weakness, the final fall.

Although Wabnokwe, on the verge of tears gave an abbreviated summary of my account, Wit-nags interrupted before she was done, and furiously asked me, "Who told you this fairy tale, Burr-net? Chief To-pin-a-bee's ghost? We learned the facts from people who saw, with their own eyes, how and why the chief died. He died because he fell off his horse. He fell because he was too drunk to ride."

Aunt Margít, visibly irritated, said quietly to her husband, "Mais Shandó était avec Topinbi!"

It was Wit-nags who answered, "Is Burr-net setting drunkard Shandó's veracity above a surveying crew's?"

Wabnokwe, biting her lip from frustration, urged me to disregard the intrusions.

I told her I had not come as the voice of our Bison Prairie kin, but only as a scout; that our kin were not of one voice; some were already preparing paint; others wanted the killers turned over to Topinbi's village, still others insisted not only that the killers be brought to justice by those who engaged them, but also that torturers and manhunters, if they had to be nurtured, be encouraged and guided to practice their arts among each other and not among our kin. Our girls were no longer sent to the forest to fast. Our boys go to fasting lodges without being told that their isolation is continually protected by armed scouts.

I then said that Shandó was preparing to accompany a man in search of a land beyond the Long River far from the settlements of the Invaders, and that I had come to the Strait to learn if my sister and cousins could dream of accompanying their western kin to such a land if it were found.

My last statements hit the gathering like a sudden thunderstorm.

"Quelle horreur!" said Likét.

"Mais tu es fou, mon frère!" Wabnokwe exclaimed.

Aunt Monîk and even aunt Jozét glared at me with indignant disbelief.

We're like hunted animals; we cannot live in constant fear, I tried to explain, but was cut short by Mendideti, whose near-whisper in Udatonte's tongue was like wind shaking fall leaves. "It is said the earth and sun gave your grandfather strength, rain quenched his thirst, and the great trees protected him. Yet

OBENABI'S FIRST JOURNEY   1826   11

you speak of wandering to prairies and plains with little rain and few trees. You speak of a land with few rivers and no lakes for your canoes. Once there, will you give chase to the bison hunters who live there as you're being chased? Whose protection will you seek when Invaders follow you across the Long River?"

The unanswerable questions posed in Udatonte's musical tongue made me see myself as I was seen, and I was horrified.

"La fille a raison," Lisa said, admonishing me.

Likét said, "La belle presqu'île privée de ses arbres, de ses animaux, et maintenant de ses gens—c'est l'enfer!"

Aunt Margít was in tears, as was my sister. My head felt like a rattle, empty yet banging.

Cousin Beth, ready as ever to give all of herself to the unsheltered, took it on herself to defend me. "Nous n'avons pas le droit de le juger. Mendideti connait l'horreur, mais nous n'en sommes pas les victimes. Qui sommes-nous sinon les institutrices, les femmes, les servantes des envahisseurs?"

At this point Jay-may apparently guessed the subject of our discussion. "Do I understand that your brother wants this matter brought before the headman?"

Wabnokwe answered, "The way a hunted animal would wish to reason with his hunter."

Wit-nags responded with, "If he wants government protection, is he willing to talk about relocating to premises where such protection is feasible?"

Jay-may said, "He made some reference to that preacher's New Caynin across the Long River."

"If you'd said this in English, it would have been the most sensible thing you'd ever said," Wit-nags said to me. To the judge he added, "That preacher is doing God's work out there."

Mendideti extended her arms winglike. "The carrion birds have sighted raw flesh." All but two smiled.

Jay-may rose as if to strike her. "I'll not have that heathen casting spells at my expense!"

Benji-may, Molly and Marti pulled Mendideti outside. Margít kept the judge from following. Wabnokwe told Jay-may, "My brother is here to see that our uncle's murderers are brought to justice."

"We would all like to see justice done," Jay-may said. "But let me be blunt. The official report of your uncle's death was submitted by several people of substance. Does your brother wish to challenge this report in court with a story he heard from a certain Monsieur Shandoné?"

Aunt Margít pleaded, "Mais tu es insupportable! Shandó est mon neveu!"

"Your relative Shandó is not a stranger to the court, having been convicted . . ." Jay-may spoke on.

But I rose from the circle, suffocating. The air was like the grey smoke I had seen over the strait, the voices merged into a deafening din above which I heard Udatonte's musical voice like a distant hum. I stumbled toward clear air, to a spot overlooking the now calm river. The sun had set behind the great lodge. I longed to be with the children playing among the trees separating me from the water.

In the darkening light the children appeared to be reenacting the scene inside: Benji-may was sitting uncomfortably, like his father, while Mendideti, her arms extended, sang of greedy vultures circling high above their prey. Benji-may rose, stick in hand, freed himself from Marti's restraining grasp, and rushed toward Mendideti.

The two girls hid behind trees, and when Benji-may stopped to look, he was caught in an ambush. Now it was Marti who rushed toward him, nearly exposing herself to a blow from his stick, when Mendideti leapt from behind a bush and downed him, sending the stick flying. Marti held the boy's feet, Mendideti his shoulders, as they carried him to a spot behind two trees.

The boy's free hand flailed violently in the air until it embedded itself in the long braid, loosening a curtain of black hair while Mendideti struggled to tear off his shirt and tie up his hands with it. All I could see through the narrow opening between the two trees was the boy's heaving chest and the black hair above it, his legs, presumably still held by Marti, being hidden from me by the tree on the right, his head by the tree on the left, so that the boy's body appeared like a convulsing, beheaded torso.

As the curtain of hair descended toward the torso like a sheet of black rain, a high-pitched, sad voice rose above the treetops with the song of a girl celebrating the return of her sister's beloved while mourning the absence of her own young love among the victors.

My head, no longer a rattle but more like a bucket heavy with tree sap, fell back to rest on the tree trunk behind me. In the moonless dark, I could barely distinguish the human figures from the intervening bushes shaking in the wind, yet still I raised sleep-heavy lids and kept my eyes fixed on the torso, for I had become entranced by the game and intoxicated by the melody. The hair hung over the boy's chest like drooping branches of a willow or like the rounded poles of a circular lodge suspended above sleepers.

The song, though now only a hum barely audible above the rustle of shaking bushes, nevertheless drowned out the noises that had come from the lodge behind me, the continual comings and goings, the multi-lingual shouting.

Suddenly even the hum ceased, the chest stopped heaving, no wind shook the bushes, the world was perfectly still.

A gentle breeze from the west shakes the bush before me ever so slightly, turning the black hair beyond it into shimmering drops of rain that fall along intermittent strands, encircling the headless torso like transparent walls of a circular black tent.

While all else stays motionless and silent, the black tent slowly descends until the ends of the strands touch the region near the torso's neck; here the tent begins to sweep along the torso's length, hovering above the heart before proceeding toward the navel, stopping, returning toward the heart and neck only to resume the first course yet again, stroking the torso rhythmically like a curtain of rain caressing a newly planted field, like waves of ocean water sweeping over sand and then receding, like flocks of birds flying southward in fall and in spring returning.

Now the torso's heaving resumes, no longer resisting but responding, its rises and falls converging with the rhythm of the waves stroking it, like the earth when it pushes up shoots in spring and reaches upward toward the sun and clouds that caress her, uniting herself and the sky into a single pulsating being.

All at once my stomach heaves and my whole body starts trembling, for out of the corner of my eye, to the left of the tree that hides the head from my view, I see four gushing streams of liquid, each shaped like an arch. The gushing ceases when the transparent tent reaches the torso's neck and then resumes when the black tent again sweeps toward the navel. Further to the left, on the spot where one of the gushing arches reaches ground, a sapling emerges, and grows larger with every shower of black rain; where a second stream hits ground an egg cracks, a tiny bird emerges, stands facing the stream, fills its beak with black liquid and extends its wings; a third jet lands on a worm and elongates it into the writhing body of a snake; while the fourth stream showers the body of a furry animal that rises on its hind legs like a bear, exposes its chest to the stream and heaves in rhythm with the onrush, like the torso beneath the tent of hair.

Shaking with repulsion, I circumvent the arches and crawl toward the strait's shore.

Descent to the water

I stumble toward a split tree at the water's edge and lean against a roundish rock below its overhanging branch as fog settles over the strait.

Suddenly the rock moves, as if it were alive. I quickly realize it's I who jumped at the smoking island's screech. My ears continue to buzz with threatening sounds: railing laughter that seems to come from the great lodge, the melody accompanying the gushing of the arch-shaped streams. Enveloped by fog at the strait's edge, trapped between the smoking island, the mocking lodge and the horrid gushing, I feel like a stalked animal in a field of forces it cannot grasp. Longing to flee, I remove my bundle's lock of hair and clutch it in my right hand.

There's a sound in the fog, which I first take for water lapping the shore but soon identify as the swish of a paddle. I fill with joy as I distinguish the outline of a canoe as it glides to shore. A hand gropes toward mine, grasps, pulls me in. I enter, gratefully kneel behind a silent figure as she paddles toward the middle of the strait. Soon we're gliding past land which must be the Isle of Fruit Trees across from Udatonte's Karontaen, away from the cramping alternatives of forced escape or death, toward a place where seeds and dreams can grow unhindered. "New corn grows only where the old plants are destroyed," the paddling figure chants in Udatonte's melodious tongue.

OBENABI'S FIRST JOURNEY 1813

The voice is strange. Leaning forward, I make out waves in her braid's hair! Fear sharpens my awareness of my whereabouts, and I realize with dismay that the land we're passing is too short to be the Isle of Fruit Trees, that the previous island was the Isle of Serpents where habitants once kept their hogs, that the land we're passing is the fisher's isle, that we haven't been moving toward Karontaen at all, but rather northward toward the gate where the Clear Lake empties into the strait, and that we're heading directly into the mouth of the Morningland River.

By the dim light of fogged sunrise I make out floating objects; when near one I see it's a corpse! Now I hear shouts and gunshots. The paddler banks the canoe near the river's bend, leaps out and runs toward the din.

I start to tremble when a voice near my canoe drawls: I'll skin this yaller chief fur me yunguns. Another shouts: cant ya see sur t'ant no cheef but a yaller skwa—nuthin but a yaller skwa?

A rifle shot deafens me; my arm burns with pain; my right hand's tightly gripped contents are gone! Distracted by the pain, I look up only when the canoe moves. The fog has lifted. Along the back of the girl paddling falls a long braid of straight black hair. Udatonte! I extend my left hand toward her shoulder, but can't reach it, as if she were gliding in a different canoe directly ahead of mine.

We return to the rivermouth, pass the Clear Lake's shore, enter the strait and head toward the shore with the roundish rock and the double-trunked tree. Where Jay-may's rectangular lodge stood, there's a long bark mound consisting of several connected round lodges with open tops and south-facing entrances.

Masked figures emerge from the long lodge, dancing to a drumbeat, humming a melody sung at the planting of cornseeds. The first dancer carries an object. I cry out from horror when I recognize the object as a hand.

She who brings me to this, never showing her face, cannot be Udatonte. I slide to the canoe floor, weak from pain and dismay, yet still longing to be taken to the healing blue water of the lake surrounded by grass. The canoe moves. As if my longing had been heard.

But when I look out I realize with returned dismay that we're not heading inland toward the Grass Lake nor westward toward the Long River but northward across the Clear Lake and through the upper strait beside the Peninsula's thumb. Day and night she paddles, now across Sagi Bay between thumb and forefinger, now toward Mishilimakina at the tip of the long fingers, now south again past the village of the leaning tree, across the bay to the little finger, down the length of Mishigami, not once pausing to alleviate my pain, and instead of heading toward sunset and Long River at the Lakebottom's portage, completing a circle by turning toward Bison Prairie at the wrist's crease, carrying the canoe over the Kekionga portage to hurry back—when suddenly she stops by a shore where the lodges are flattened, the cornfields burned, and runs toward a field of fallen trees which resounds with the derisive laughter of village-destroyers.

I lose consciousness when something sharp crashes into my head—and regain it stretched out on the canoe floor, shivering from cold, head splitting, arm burning, trying to remember what I was fleeing and where I was rushing. Powerful arms lift me, and I look up at an ancient face, wrinkled like bark.

I'm carried into a circle of sitting women and placed on the ground near the fire at the center. The bark-faced woman chants a melody I last heard when my cousin's son was born, others rise and begin to dance around me and the fire, each adding another melody, other words, some in harmony, others in dissonance with the rest. The volume rises, the pace quickens, the dance becomes frenzied and my head threatens to explode. I use up my remaining energy rising to my feet and stumbling out of the circle.

The dance stops. My captor rushes at me; she returns me to the center and sings me a riddle about a man who came from the Sunrise Mountains to the valleys of the Wabash looking for seeds. She tells how the man plucked her lover's courage in the forests of Kekionga, seized her brother's strength in the valley of the great Kanawha, filched her father's generosity at the crossing paths of Pickawillany, plundered her grandmother's vision on the shores of Mishigami, sowed his pilfered seeds, reaped their fruit, and grew fearful, weak, mean and blind, for he sowed only leaves, having destroyed the seeds, being a man who put last things first.

Her song done, she and the other women put out the fire and disperse with its ashes, leaving me shivering with cold and pain.

Redfrocked soldiers emerge from the forest, rail and kick me, poke my body with surveying instruments; a scalping knife cuts the sash that holds my bundle, moves toward my head—then pauses above my eyes, glistening, and withdraws as Redcoats and instruments return to the forest fleeing from a bear who ambles toward me carrying a stick.

I stretch my left hand toward my spilled pendant, but the bear picks it up and as she ties it around her neck I see below the bear's head the body of an ancient woman covered to the waist by white hair. Apprehensively I gather the rest of my bundle's contents, but can't find the fragment of bark scroll.

My fright grows when countless others approach; bodies of young and old women and men, short bearded men, children with heads of wolves, moose, bear, fox, deer, or topped by heads of turtles, herons, hawks, even sturgeons and watersnakes. The greatest number form into a large circle at the very fringe of the forest, others into a smaller circle inside the larger, while scores gather near my sides and feet.

The bearwoman unrolls over me a scroll which depicts a palm, its fingertips by my feet, its wrist by my neck. The figures nearest me pile up dry sticks which the bearwoman proceeds to light, abandoning her own stick in the third fire. Trapped between scalping Redcoats, masked captors and three raging fires, I struggle to shake off the scroll covering me and to rise—but a fox and a beaver rush to keep my feet down, while the bearwoman replaces the scroll.

A song with words of ancient Riverpeople begins in the outer circle behind my head, another is sung on my right in the language of Turtlefolk, a third below my feet and on my left in the tongue of Rootkin. Those in the middle circle dance, the path of their movement forming the outline of a hand. My anxiety grows when the innermost figures whirl and leap with unrestrained vigor around each fire, those on my right repeatedly naming Tiosa Rondion, those by my feet Mishilimakina, those on my left Bison Prairie.

The chanting, dancing and whirling grow ever more frenzied—when all at once the circles become an inchoate multitude as a hare with a stick chases the group on my right, extinguishes its fire, repeats this by my feet and proceeds to extinguish the fire on my left. Here the whitehaired bearwoman blocks his path. The hare tries to chase her. But when bears from every quarter, all armed with sticks, encircle him, the hare slips his mask over my head and flees to the fringe as a beaver. Now the enraged bears close their circle around me, poking me with their sticks.

My feet suddenly freed by my captors, I leap away from the sticks and trip headfirst into the fire! The bearwoman extinguishes my burning hair as well as the fire and then vanishes with her scroll and all her throng.

Alone, cold, writhing with pain, I'm horrified by the thought that the grey moon on the horizon is the rising sun and that I'm nearly blind. Something cold touches my injured arm, sending a shudder down my spine. On my right lies a body I must have looked over to see the horizon. Apparently a young woman, she seems to have been pushed up from the earth like a flower. Weakly pulling me, she's trying to rise and make me rise with her.

Turning my head, I make out bodies everywhere and the figure of a man removing robes, cutting pendants, taking earrings. Looking up I see agitated black shapes whose excited cries identify them as ravens waiting for the scavenger to be done with his picking. Moving toward my companion and me, the scavenger roars with laughter—and stops abruptly when my companion rises and shouts a curse in the Turtlefolk tongue: May your children's children scavenge your grave and filch your bones for trophies!

She gropes toward my bundle, removes my arrowhead, places her hands under my armpits to help me rise, and aims the arrowhead at the scavenger as if it were a spear. Although unscathed, he quickly gathers up his trophies and flees.

My companion looks around as if in search of something among the plague's harvest of bodies, among the barren trees with spring buds swallowed by winter's return, and she wails, as if to give voice to the desolation.

She walks supporting me to the canoe on the strait's shore, paddles awkwardly across the strait, and although not herself strong, walks on, supporting me, over the length of Morningland to the Great Falls. Here she pauses, collects icy water in cupped hands, and applies it over my eyes. Neither the water nor her sad wail improve my sight but the weight of my head is lightened by the untiring determination with which she guides me along the bank of the Easternmost Lake to where the waters flow out of the land through the great Northern River.

My left hand with all the weight behind it resting on her supporting shoulder, she seems to become thinner and smaller, yet she trods on toward ancient Hochelaga, the island village. Here she rushes from abandoned round lodges to abandoned longhouses, then runs in desperation to the shore where bearded men carry bags from floating islands and she curses: Destroyers of seeds! May all you reap torture, poison and destroy you!

Both of us stumble from exhaustion as she pulls me on toward ancient Stadacona, the village on hills overlooking the river, where on the ruins of destroyed longhouses, bearded men gather and disperse, entering and leaving square lodges.

My guide leaves me and runs into a longhouse that still stands. I hear a child's voice scream with frustration, and in the distance an echo that for an instant resembles the scavenger's laughter.

My companion returns, still as death, in the arms of a tall woman in otterskin. The woman places the small body on the ground and my companion vanishes, as if swallowed by the earth that pushed her up.

I collapse from exhaustion and from my new and most painful loss. The otterwoman pulls my shell out of my bundle and fixes it over my right eye while singing in the tongue of ancient Oceanshore Rootkin of earth's exhaustion from swallowing so many corpses and of a new earth that will rise from the corpses' bones; and as she sings, floating islands crowded with bearded men from Hochelaga, pause by the shore to gather Stadacona's bearded men.

The otterwoman picks me up and carries me like a child yet further toward the sunrise, crossing streams by raft or canoe, never slowing her pace nor ceasing her song.

All the floating islands are congregating at the Northern River's enormous mouth where the Great Lakes' waters flow into the salt sea. Bearded men offer us knives and ropes while pulling on the otterskin. The woman rushes past them toward the southern entrance of a lodge at land's end. I vaguely remember having dreaded this lodge, but no longer know why.

The woman takes my feather from my bundle, rushes to a corner, returns with a large bag, removes a shell identical to mine and places it over my left eye.

I'm carried out of the lodge and deposited on something soft and yielding. Two hands remove the shells from my eyes. I'm astounded by the light! I can see—but too late to view the face of the tall Rootwoman; even her otterskin robe recedes in the distance as I rise in the air on the soft back of a raven. The bird swoops toward longbearded men who, on seeing us, gather up furs, ropes, knives, and flee to floating islands. The raven flies eastward over the land surrounded by salt sea, then southward over shores of eastern Rootkin and Lenapikin, eastward again over the land of stone giants and feathered serpents, and wherever she swoops down, horses rear up and throw off lance-armed riders; cows, sheep, horses, rats and men with guns race each other to crowded islands floating out to sea.

Raven and I chuckle over the simplicity of our stratagem: the bearded men take bird and rider for a single being, an invincible deity coming to reclaim her invaded land.

Returning northward, I forget my pains on seeing the great river's banks lush with leaves and multicolored flowers, teeming with animals, shimmering with the ecstatic motion of Talamatun dancers in myriad camps of longhouses.

At last I see the otterwoman, paddling upstream almost as quickly as the raven flies, the water in her canoe's channel seeming to be rushing upstream with her. Between each stroke she throws a shell, and where the shells land, birds hatch, trees bloom, village fires are lit, councilgrounds throb with orgies of renewal.

Strapping the canoe to her back, the otterwoman runs from the shore of the Easternmost Lake to the Sunrise Mountains and resumes her water journey where the body of the Beautiful River is fed by the outstretched arms of two rushing mountain rivers. Downstream at the valleys whose mouths kiss the Beautiful River, at the Muskingum, Kanawha, Scioto, Omaumek, Kentaki, Wabash, and then upstream along the shores of the Long River, she pauses to place shells on mounds shaped like mountains, breasts, bears, serpents, thunderbirds. Bones emerge from the mounds and bloom into bodies of Riverpeople, Tellegwi, who dance in masks of wolves, serpents and moose.

Throwing her remaining shells toward earthlodges in western prairies and stonelodges in distant canyons of the Sunset Mountains, she runs to the shore of Mishigami, fills her bag with stones, and walks over the hand-shaped Peninsula, sowing stones which become Neshnabek, the first people.

Scores of Neshnabek paddle from Kichigami toward the three corners of the hand, while Talamutun from Morningland

and Tellegwi from the river valleys rush to mingle with them. As the raven rises into moonless night, stars light up the great circles surrounding the Peninsula. The soothing up and down rhythm of her wings puts me to sleep.

I find myself at the very edge of salt water where northern lands end, dancing alongside naked Neshnabek around a fire that wards off icy Digowin. I feel free, my head is clear, my feet strong, my right hand grasps a spearhandle and my bundle holds a packet of fishbones.

When our dancing slackens, Digowin extinguishes our fire and tries to hold down the rising sun, but we chase after him through thick forests along the paths he flattens disguised as a monstrous bison with serpent's face and bird's feet; we conquer the monster and celebrate a feast.

The monster's angry spirit causes earth to shake and flood, so we flee across a land of sand where our feet burn and our throats parch until at last we reach a world where we need neither fire nor spears, a world of perpetual lushness and warmth where we sing with birds, dance with bears, hop with hares and slither with snakes, where we bathe ourselves with sun, travel with stars and wrap ourselves with moonlight while we bed with beautiful earth.

Alone with the full moon, I dip my head to sip water from a still pond. A face rises, its lips kiss mine. In the shell-less turtle with beaver's head and glistening silvery-grey scales I recognize the one I'm seeking.

I lower my bundle into the pond but the water muddies and she vanishes. Slowly I crawl into the pond after her, waddling on turtle feet to the very bottom of the watery world. I sense myself becoming liquid, full, unbounded.

Reemergence

I dissolve. There's only water. Water with a dream in its depths, like moon's reflection, a liquid yolk wrapped in a watery blanket, a seed in a womb, a dream that's roused whenever sun's yellow hair caresses or moon's cool tongue licks the water's surface and makes it ripple.

Sun's warm strands penetrate, make the dream rise like a bubble and break through the surface as foam, which becomes a rainbow uniting water with sky while its moisture falls and dissolves.

Love-play of sun and moon on water's surface rouses the dream again, making it fly upward, fragment into myriad particles which dance frenziedly until, exhausted and amorphous, they fall back as slime and mud, only to rise yet again, intoxicated with desire, and heave upward in a gush that pulls up water's bottom and sends mud and slime dancing toward the sky.

Water rushes upward to reclaim the fragmenting mud, but its dominion is overturned. The mud dries in baking sun and hardens into mountains. Bottom is top.

Desire satisfied, the fragments relax, fall back, try to dissolve, try to become one again. But the unity is ruptured. Rather than lying naked and thirsty between water and sky, fragments who flew out on wings waddle back on paddles, but then return again, bodies in water, snouts sniffing air, oscillating between land and water like beavers, undecided.

Waves and torrents wash down all who try to waddle upshore, until earth starts to play with the water, to trap it between her rocky bones. Turning the water into her body's blood, earth decorates her moistened flesh with hair and welcomes the silvery-grey scaled turtle spawning on its surface. When reckless feasting by the turtle's children thins earth's lush hair, the parent turns on the children and, like the water that reclaimed risen mud, swallows the offspring.

They give themselves—but only when they can't avoid being eaten. Many fly into the air, others crawl under rocks, yet others walk to dens. Some of us join the fliers in their nests, the crawlers under their rocks, the walkers in their dens.

Some of us nurture a dream, which soon gnaws our depths. Hiding our dream, we wake the others on a moonless night and invite them to feast on a food that emerges only after dark, a food we name Digowin.

Our kin descend from trees, emerge from rocks and dens, and wait for our signal, when all pounce at once and tear off chunks of Digowin. Strengthened and intoxicated by what we eat, we dance frenziedly, circling the spot ecstatically, stretching out limbs toward the sky until we fall to the ground exhausted.

The morning after the feast, we wake surrounded by enormous fishbones which are all that remains of our parent, and by herbs pushing up from the ground, berries ripening on bushes, fruit sprouting on trees. Earth's hair is renewed! It grows out of the same dreaming slime we're made of!

Yet our kin turn from us, avoid us, some even run from us. We look at ourselves, at all those implicated in the deed, at the winged ones with curved beaks and claws, at the furry ones with fangs, and at the slow, weak shell-less turtles with silvery-grey scales, and we see what the others are seeing, we see the one we named Digowin, the unquenchable, the flesh-eater, the devourer of kin.

The moment we recognize ourselves, earth begins to shake, chasms open, prairies rise up into mountains, forests are drowned by brackish waters. We flee toward nests, under rocks, into dens, but our cousins refuse to shelter us. Even carrion birds and wolves, enraged at us for implicating them in our deed, turn against us and threaten to do with us what we did with Digowin. If only we hadn't implicated others!

The shaking, the hostility, the threats don't end until we agree to take ourselves and the remains of our parent away from our moist, warm home. With heavy hearts we trudge beyond forest's end to where earth's skin is scorched. To avoid burning all four limbs on the hot sand, we walk on hind legs only; our scales fall off our dried-up skins; only those on toes and fingers remain. Many despair and return to the land of our plant-eating kin.

Those of us who at last reach sand's end, averse to raw flesh since the morning after our deed, acquire a taste for roasted flesh when we find a giant burnt by a forest fire. Tying stones to tree stems, we stalk the giant's kin, and convince them to offer themselves to us by reminding them we're all Digowin's grandchildren.

We come to a lush forest on a tongue of land bounded by ice mountains and salt sea. Here generous water cousins attach themselves to our poles, fleet deer give themselves when we learn to deliver our stone-tipped stems from bows, even enormous bison occasionally pause in the path of our spears.

Covering ourselves with our cousins' skins during ever longer and colder nights, we recover the warmth we left only when we gorge and intoxicate ourselves on our cousins' flesh, and when we huddle around moistened hot stones in bison skin tents where reunited fragments dissolve into warm sweat.

But a fire blazes across the sky and melts the ice mountains, flooding forests with cold slush, washing our cousins and earth's lushness into the salt sea. On paddle-shoes that hold us above deep snow, we flee behind hares and deer to where great mountains rise.

Here we part sadly with sisters and brothers who take the slope facing sunset and we wander into woodlands bounded by seas of sweet water. We know the moment we arrive that we will wander no more. Our first home could not have been more lush, more beautiful.

The cousins who welcome us to Kichigami, this land of great lakes, seem to have forgiven or forgotten our deed. As in ancient days, bear, beaver, deer, muskrat and marten whisper to us in the forest, sparrow and gull sing to us, sturgeon visit us in dreams. They show us the paths, guide us to an island with red stones, lead us to roots, berries, tree nectar, water rice, and on a windless day take us to a birch grove where the very bark sings of lodges that hold warmth, of containers that hold tree sugar, of canoes that float on sweet water.

Yet some of us again grow restless with a dream that gnaws our depths. We set out, unexpectedly reach Boweting, the cataract where Kichigami's waters flow out, smash our canoes, and return to our camp on foot. Setting out again in new canoes, which we carry past the cataract, we come to an island at the center of the lakes. Following one and then the other side, we learn the island is a giant's right hand. After sleeping and feasting on the giant's palm, we carry our canoes up the giant's body, follow a stream, and reach a beautiful river that flows from the sunrise.

Walking toward a camping spot, we come to tracks made by two-legged walkers. A sister tells us that these tracks were not made by Neshnabek, and we grow fearful, since we, the Neshnabek, the Rootkin, are the only upright walkers in all Kichigami.

The tracks must be Digowin's. We prepare to flee. But our uncle stops us by saying that Neshnabek do not flee from Digowin; then he tells us his dream: I saw a hare who told me he was Wiske, the giver. He told me he was once as weak as the first Neshnabek, until he instigated the slaying of Digowin. The deed made him potent. When the fleeing Neshnabek grew hungry, he gave a tree stem the pointed shape of his long member and so made the first spear. When we grew cold, he rubbed his member on dry sticks and made them flame. He guided us to the land of ice and made our first arrow, bow and snowshoe. When we reached Kichigami he gave us the canoe and the bark lodge. He commands the deer to offer themselves to our arrows. He even speaks to the wind and the rain. When I begged for his powers, the hare vanished.

Emboldened by his dream, we name our uncle Wiske and follow him, by the light of the full moon, toward the source of the tracks made by people who are not Neshnabek. We come to a brushless field cleared neither by storm nor by fire, then to a camp of round, breast-shaped mounds surrounded by a mud embankment. Climbing a hill, we reach a gathering more numerous than several camps of Neshnabek.

Horned men leaning on spears suck reeds attached to bowls and emit smoke. Women wearing bison robes dance, wail and shout incomprehensible sounds. At the center of all is a monstrous serpent with several coils and gaping jaws.

Tellegwi, one of us whispers, naming the strangers Serpents. All at once a naked girl runs up the hill, past horned men, past wailing women, straight into the serpent's jaws. We notice three other naked girls dancing in the field below the hill. Rushing down, we ambush each in turn as she begins to run uphill, and we carry them to the river's shore, far from the serpent's jaws. Wiske promptly impregnates all three virgins with his large member.

Only the forethought of a nephew who had brought the canoes from their hiding places saves Wiske's member from being cut to pieces by the spears of pursuing horned men.

On our return journey Wiske alternately boasts of our exploit as a second victory over Digowin, and vows to return with a canoe caravan of armed nephews to achieve such a victory. He says the Tellegwi, even the three brides, are not people but embodiments of Digowin, whose spirit abandoned our parent's body just before our deed, and came here to wait for our coming.

The journey is long. We stray from our path to seek bison for the strange women. One of them learns to speak, and even to dispute with Wiske: We have flesh from earth, life from the sun and blood from the sky, like you.

Wiske says: If the Tellegwi were cousins of the Neshnabek, they would have had to devise the spear, flee over the land of ice, and arrive in Kichigami before us, all without the hare's guidance. That's unthinkable. You are Digowin.

The bride responds: Cousins or not, our grandmothers were camped on the Beautiful River before there were any Neshnabek, when a mountain-sized white serpent descended from the north and swallowed people, animals, trees and land. No Wiske stopped the serpent, and we had to flee to the south, where we acquired the seed-scattering powers of the wind. When we returned the serpent retreated, for which we thank him whenever we give our seeds to earth.

By the time we reach our Rootkin's shore, Wiske, like the rest of us, wears a bison's head and robe, emits smoke from a pipe, and waves a spear.

Our surprised kin don't greet us with welcoming laughter. They shower us with arrows and come after us in swift canoes. We flee more quickly than we fled from the Tellegwi.

Wiske removes his bison coverings and swims toward our kin shouting obscenities. The rest of us paddle without pause to a spot halfway between hostile kin, a place on the palm, by the thumb and wrist, by a beaverpond next to a strait.

Our new kinswomen give birth to daughters and a son.

Before long, bison hunters from the Beautiful River as well as deerhunters from the north hear us learning each other's songs, approach our camp, and at last smoke with us. From the visitors we learn that Wiske, having vowed to defeat Digowin for the second time, led a caravan of armed nephews, not through the strait to where Tellegwi warriors waited, but toward the sunset and down a long river. They found a camp of strangers and promptly attacked, convinced that the strangers were Tellegwi, even though their lodges stood on ground and not on mounds, men wore no bison heads, youth carried bows and not spears.

The strangers' discernment was no greater than Wiske's, for they hastily revenged themselves on the Neshnabek by attacking a band of Tellegwi bison hunters.

On hearing this, we send a peace party toward sunset in search of the strangers. After a long absence, the peacemakers return with a strange youth who tells us, in broken Rootspeech aided by signs, that his kin are not monsters, man-eaters or serpents; on the contrary: We fled from a land far to the south where stone giants, man-eaters and great-horned serpents pursued us.

The stranger learns to dispute with us more quickly than he learns our speech, and when he hears our account of the first Wiske's victory over Digowin, he protests: Wiske did not slay the great turtle, since earth still rests on the turtle's back.

Laughing, we name him Turtleperson, Talamatun, somewhat unfairly, since Neshnabek trace their descent to the turtle, whereas the stranger claims to descend from a woman who fell from the sky, for whose sake a beaver and a muskrat nearly burst their lungs diving to the bottom of the sea for earth to place on the turtle's back.

The youth tells us: When your Wiske attacked us, we thought the man-eaters were after us again, so we broke camp and crossed the Long River on rafts and logs. But the closer we got to the sunrise, the more our scouts spoke of the things we feared, of earthen giants, of horned serpents, of spear-armed men whose very tongue resembled the tongue of our old pursuers. When your party reached us, we were relieved to learn our attacker was a mere hare, and we stretched our memories to catch every familiar word spoken by the Riverwoman among the peacemakers, our tongues being anciently related. We were enraptured by your kinswoman's description of a vast woodland with beaver and deer, and without bison to trample our cornfields.

We expect the Talamatun's numerous kin to arrive any day from their sunset camps, but canoes of deerhunters from the north arrive instead and invite us to a great fish feast at the cataract of Boweting.

Our guest accompanies us to the north, fearful that something terrible happened to his kin.

At the council, a one-armed warrior speaks of Wiske's second and larger caravan of armed nephews: Finding no camps on the Long River, we paddled up the Beautiful River and attacked villages with and without mounds. At first the besieged took their revenge by turning on each other. But when they began to make common cause with each other and against us, Wiske fled. The rest of us appeased our pursuers by offering protection from the monster Digowin, some to one camp, some to the other. Now all are suspicious of Neshnabek; every village sings of war;

bands of fratricidal manhunters roam the woods and indiscriminately attack bison hunters, deerhunters, travelers, even vision seekers. Rumors grow ever more terrifying. Each village thinks its mortal enemy lodges in the village at two removes. Yet I return home only to find our uncle recruiting still another armed caravan!

A newly painted youth rises and asks indignantly: Where would we be without our uncle's guidance, his gifts, his protection from Digowin, his striving . . .

Before the youth is done, an old Rootwoman pulls Wiske into the circle by the ear and asks: What guidance? What gifts? What protection? Was it this hare or our great-grandmother who pulled a dead bison from a rockslide and placed a sharp rock in her son's hand; who saw lightning strike dead brushwood and ever after kept a firestick; who followed a duck to where rice grows, a bee to where sap oozes, a bear to where berries ripen; who heard from a sturgeon about the canoe and went with a whitefish to find the red rock? What's this one's gift but to turn our youth into hollow reeds filled with his wind? Who is the Digowin we need protection from if not this boaster?

Wiske's eyes look to the sky, as if inviting the clouds to strike us with lightning and to drown us, but when several women approach him with sticks in their hands, he slinks away toward the forest.

The clouds suddenly release a torrential storm, and through the lightning and thunder the women shout: Go to a land of ice, or of rampant floods, or of sand where no rain falls, no rice grows, no sap oozes. There find nephews who need your gifts!

After the storm, peace parties set out in four directions. But by the time the peacemakers reach their destinations, the whole world is changed.

Most Talamatun are heading toward the sunrise, many Tellegwi toward sunset. Some are joining each other in villages north of the Beautiful River.

Rootkin who joined with Tellegwi are moving to valleys south of the river; those who joined with Talamatun are heading toward sunrise and the salt sea.

When we return to our encampment, we find Talamatun lodged in the Morningland across the strait; they name the strait's shores Karontaen.

Tiosa Rondion, place of the beaverdams, is the name the Turtlefolk give our village. It is no longer a mere camp. We, the beaverchildren, peacemakers of northern speech and southern ways, maintain three ever-living fires on the triangular councilground of Tiosa Rondion. Around these fires we sing and council with Rootkin, Riverpeople and Turtlefolk from the four directions of the circle surrounding the hand in the lakes.

Our main disputes are with each other, and on cold winter nights these never end. A youth who returns from a deerhunt ridicules his sister for running naked in a newly planted field.

The girl retorts: I'm not like those who fool earth by eating the flesh and giving her the bones, nor those who fool the sky by burning the tobacco and giving him the smoke.

Who leads you to it, your own dream or your grandmother's? the boy taunts.

Their bison-horned cousin asks the boy: And who leads you? Grandmother or the sly embroiler? I've seen you place beaverteeth and hawkfeathers on the rock by the split tree you think no one recognizes, one trunk leaning over water, the other over land like a giant hare's ears.

When the snows melt, the three leave Tiosa Rondion and go sharpen their own ways, the boy accompanying his uncle to the fish feast at Boweting, the girl accompanying her father to the strawberry festival in Morningland, their cousin accompanying his mother to the festival on the Beautiful River where Tellegwi from every quarter merge the bones of their dead in a common grave under a rising mound that bonds the descendants in renewed kinship.

Disputes resume the moment the three return, and continue through the meal of squash in maple syrup, deermeat with corn, bison chunks in bean sauce. The disputants pause when the girl fills a pipe and passes it to her cousin, when tobacco fragments reunited by a flame emerge from the bowl as smoke and rise to the sky like the bubbles of longing that once pulled upward from ocean's floor.

We're still learning each other's ways and songs, and embellishing our own, when canoes arrive from the north and, with an urgency we've sensed once before, invite us, not only to a fish feast, but also to the first bone festival held by Neshnabek.

At Boweting we hear of great whales swimming to earth from where the sun rises in the salt sea. We hear this, not from a protection-offering long-eared hare, but from a tall Rootwoman covered by an otterskin robe decorated with oceanshells.

Many of us start to shake; cold sweat drips down our faces.

The Mask

Something of vast importance is about to slip out of my grasp. I reach out to hold on—but it's already too late. There's a flapping of wings.

I wake leaning against a roundish rock by a split tree at water's edge; the night is moonless; fog licks the water of the strait.

How did I get here? There's a packet of fishbones in the bundle beside me. I faintly remember having been under the water. Did I climb out by the tree's roots?

I feel light, as if I were floating; I find myself sitting on a bed of down. I remember falling asleep on a raven's back. Was it she who just flew off? Raising a feather toward my eyes, I can see its outline, but not the hand that holds it.

Feather and bundle are here. But I'm not here. Yet I'm able to put the feather into the bundle. It's as if I were a dream without a mind or a body.

I hear the swish of a paddle in the water. A figure approaches through the fog, each hand extending something. I reach out; my left hand grasps a shell, a small ocean shell; my right tightens its grip on a mask with a face as wrinkled as the shell's.

I lift the mask to where my face should be. I'm suddenly elsewhere. I'm the person whose mask I wear.

The mask is smooth now, I have a young woman's body. The afternoon sun is in my eyes, but I cast no shadow.

I faintly remember having emerged from a place under the ground, or from a cave, or a womb.

Looking behind me I remember I've just come out of the long medicine lodge. An ancient woman, my grandmother, emerges after me, her hand extending something. It's a shell.

She bids me sit next to her, unrolls a disintegrating scroll which depicts four aligned circles in a long rectangular enclosure, like the lodge I've just been through, and pointing to a tiny shell-like form at the western edge of the rectangle, she starts to sing.

She sings of the love-play of sun and moon that roused a dream to rise from ocean's floor. Moving her finger from the shell to shapes inside the circles, she sings of the time when the first people feasted endlessly on earth's sumptuous fruits and sky's sweet nectar, of the time of the separation from kin, of the journey to the land of ice, and of the fourth age when the people reached the shores of Kichigami and recovered the kinship, the beauty and the abundance they had lost in their wanderings.

Carefully rolling and tying the first, Grandmother unrolls a second, newer scroll, with lines and ovals and the outline of a hand in the center. I recognize the paths from oceanshore to sunset. She chants in a mournful wail as she guides my eyes from the shell-like shapes by the sunrise edge toward the turtle- and bear-like shapes along the river and the lakes.

She sings of the time of her first fish feast at Boweting, when an oceanshore Rootwoman brought shells from the sea and a message from the otter: great whales had come from the sunrise to the shores of the island beyond the mouth of the Northern River and had swallowed the island's people, chipmunks, squirrels and rabbits.

Tears come to Grandmother's eyes as her finger follows a line along the bottom of the scroll, pausing at spots where black wings of carrion birds hover over skulls, each spot designating a Tellegwi mound village on the Beautiful River, where Grandfather's people witnessed more deaths than when the white serpents had descended from the north.

She sings of the time of my mother's birth in Tiosa Rondion, when Grandfather went to the last bone festival on the Beautiful River and never returned, when Tellegwi from every quarter arrived with the bones of their kin and wailed of deaths so numerous that even the carrion birds were repelled: Tellegwi from the oceanshore chanted of whales that disgorged short-statured manlike creatures with covered bodies and the pallor of death on their faces; every direction in which the faces turned, healthy men and women grew feverish, red spots appeared on chests and stomachs, blood ran from every orifice, bodies became wasted.

Tellegwi from the south chanted of giant dogs with men's heads that spat fire and killed all people and animals in their path. Angry villagers danced and sang, then ambushed the monsters and killed them, only to succumb to fatal tortures sent after them by the monsters' ghosts.

Survivors carried the bones of their dead kin to the Beautiful River, raised a mound over them, and while they built and chanted, they became delirious and chilled, their groins swelled and turned dark, they disgorged a black poison. In a few days the half-raised mound was surrounded by corpses; the dead had swallowed the living.

Southbranch Rootkin who visited Tiosa Rondion said all the mound villages of the Muskingum, Scioto, Omaumek and Wabash valleys were abandoned.

The few surviving Riverpeople had taken the bones of their kin to the village of Cahokia on the Long River, where surviving Tellegwi from every quarter congregated for their last bone festival, raised a great mound, buried large gifts, pleaded with the dead to spare the living, but all to no avail.

When the plague broke out in Cahokia, many fled to western plains and mountains, determined to forget bone festivals, river villages, mounds, ancestors, as well as their last mound-building kin who perished while raising the greatest of all their mounds.

The bone festival ceased to be celebrated in Boweting. After Grandfather's death, Grandmother became keeper of the second fire in Tiosa Rondion, and she went to the Boweting fish feast every spring to take part in the doings of the medicine lodge.

The year of my birth a second messenger from the east arrived in Boweting and sang of islands that floated from the sunrise and collided with the land, of manlike beings wearing glistening knives who came off the islands spitting fire, of a fever that attacked all Eastbranch Rootkin who had contact with those beings: hearts raced, skins bled and turned yellow; suddenly the fever retreated, only to return more violently; people vomited blood and then black sand.

Of every ten Rootkin in the coastal villages, only one survived. Some of the survivors sought refuge in the joint villages of Turtlefolk and Rootkin along the banks of the Northern River, but the strange islands had already entered the river's mouth, their sorcery had already attacked Neshnabek and Talamatun villagers.

People who had never seen the sea monsters lay writhing on the ground, their skins swelled, blistered and oozed; the healthiest felt the greatest pain and died first; in a longlodge of thirty people, two survived: a grandmother and a baby.

The villages along both banks of the Northern River became desolate. At the beautiful hill village of Stadacona, numerous men from the sea spat fire at the few surviving Turtlefolk, and then swallowed the yellow corn and the squashes and beans of their mangled victims' lush fields.

OBENABI'S FIRST JOURNEY 1560

Survivors fled into the woodlands by the Eastern River; others fled westward, but the sorcery flew ahead of them faster than canoes.

No sea monsters had reached the island village of Hochelaga, yet it was a burial ground. Its lodges held unburied corpses of Turtlefolk, Rootkin and newly adopted refugees. The few who survived were tormented by blisters which crusted, itched and pained; when the crusts fell off, the skin stayed marked by pits. Many marked survivors accompanied Rootkin to the Bay of Rolling White Sands in the northern Morningland, and a few even to the Boweting cataract and the shores of Kichigami.

The year of my first bleeding I accompanied Grandmother to the spring doings at Boweting. The refugees from the east who hovered around the medicine lodge repelled me. Some had swollen tongues and distrusted people, animals and earth; some had no memory of kin; some had swollen eyes and were vengeful, gloomy, indifferent to everything.

In Tiosa Rondion, a young and healthy deerhunter began to give me songs. I longed to go with him to a hunting lodge in the northern forest. But the Oceanshore Rootwoman visited my dream: she was short and old, her sightless eyes and her tongue were swelled, her skin was broken by pits.

I did not answer the hunter's songs, but continued to gather Grandmother's herbs and to accompany her to the spring doings in Boweting. I stayed away from the somber and irritable refugees from the east, and mingled with Kichigami Rootkin and with Peninsula cousins who burned three fires in Mishilimakina just south of Boweting and in Bison Prairie at the opposite corner of the Peninsula by the wrist's crease.

When Grandmother asked if I felt ready, I followed her into the crowded medicine lodge. I fell to the ground when hit by the shell thrown by the Oceanshore Rootwoman and rose again when she sang; she was exactly as I had seen her in my dream.

Grandmother emerges from the lodge after me, gives me the shell that hit me, bids me sit next to her as she unrolls her scrolls and sings her songs, those of the four ages and those of the great changes. When her songs are done, she rolls the scrolls, ties them, and gives them to me.

A few days later I and the lodge women throw earth over Grandmother's grave.

I wait for the doings to be over and seek out the Oceanshore Rootwoman. I confess to her that my mind is on a young deerhunter, that I'm repelled by the medicine lodge, by her, by the otter and the shell and everything that comes from the salt sea, and that I'm not a worthy keeper of Grandmother's scrolls. I unroll the scroll that shows the changes and migrations and I tell her I learned only one thing: whatever comes westward from the ocean brings desolation.

The old woman can't see the scroll I hold before her. She tells me to join the deerhunter and bear him children, to keep the scrolls, to forget the medicine lodge until the shell and the otter visit my dreams.

I return to the village by the beaverdam and answer the deerhunter's song. I go with him to hunting lodges in the northern forest. I bear him a son and a daughter. I replace Grandmother as keeper of Tiosa Rondion's second fire and I see to it that the flame never dies. But it burns for no one. No Riverpeople ever council or smoke around my fire; the nearest Tellegwi are in a bay beyond the Long Lake on the other side of the Peninsula.

I go north with the hunter less and less frequently, preferring to paddle alone to the small isle at the entrance to the Strait, where I fish, or to the long isle across from Tiosa Rondion, where I grab turkeys, or to the large isle downstream, where I gather fruits and berries.

I most enjoy paddling to the beautiful Isle of Rattlesnakes where, all alone under a full moon, I sing the songs Grandmother taught me about my silvery-grey scaled ancestors during their first age; or paddling to the Isle of White Trees at the very end of the Strait where, dancing alone among the trees, I feel the joy of the foamlike beings who flew up from water toward sky and slid back down along the rainbow.

My pensive daughter watches a Tellegwi aunt dance to the growing corn and listens to a Neshnabek aunt sing to herbs and roots. My son wanders with his father in the northern forest; they return with deermeat on their dog-drawn travois, sometimes with bear. But the year the boy's uncle prepares a dream lodge after the snows melt, neither the boy nor the man returns.

Birds fly south, then north, then south again, but neither boy nor man returns.

The son of the woman who keeps the third fire gives my daughter a pendant; she grows blind to one aunt's dances, deaf to the other's songs, and accepts the gift.

Only then does her brother return, in a canoe laden with objects that are not of this world, with a band of men whose skins are gouged by deep pits.

My son avoids me. I find him hovering around the first fire, listening to stories about Wiske, giving the young narrators objects from his canoe, and telling the youth of the longbearded men from the salt sea who are raising stone lodges in all the Northern River's abandoned villages, from the mouth to Hochelaga.

It is said that some of them hold contests at killing people with their firesticks. When told we war only to avenge dead kin, they laugh at us for calling petty feuds wars. Their bearded faces beam when they're near the skins of dead beaver, mink or marten. Those are the things they war over. They kill the living and hoard the dead. The more dead things they hoard, the more their power grows.

My son's eyes gleam with pride, as if the powers he described were his own.

Yet this boy who'd once helped track moose in midwinter winds sits close to the fire wrapped in fur and shivers, coughs and drips. I stay close to him after the other youth disperse. He's somber and irritable. He tells me: Father and I were returning by way of the Morningland. We paused at a festival. The plague broke out. Bodies lay on the ground writhing with pain. Certain men moved among the dead and dying and stripped them of robes, pendants, belts. I crawled to those men. I was alive! I helped them strip corpses. I found a cache of furs in a lodge. The men gave me gifts. They adopted me. They took me with them to Stadacona to deliver the animal skins. I saw the bearded men who laugh when we talk of our kinship with animals. I saw their faces beam when they sighted our bundles of fur. They gave me shimmering knives and axes sharper than stone.

I say to my son: Those who deny their kinship with animals deny people as well. In our songs, the powers you praise are powers of the devourer of life, the unquenchable Digowin.

He says: I sang our songs. I prepared to dream. I kept bones intact. But I saw a whole village succumb even as they danced and sang. My father whispered to animals, dreamed of them. He always kept their bones intact. He was one of the first to perish after two days of indescribable pain. The animals didn't protect him. They mocked him. They betrayed him. I writhed helplessly alongside him. But I crawled away from that field of corpses. I no longer wanted to dream of animals. The power that devoured so much life so quickly was greater. I understood this after I met the Longbeards. Why do they thrive and multiply while we die and dwindle? Because they're not guided by our dreams. They scatter bones and throw them into campfires. They know how to squeeze power over the living out of the skins of the dead. But their power is not in the animals or in earth. Their power is in axes and knives sharper than stone, and in firesticks that kill at short and long distances. This is the power that protects and guides me.

Scavengers who reap plague's harvest have twisted his pit-marked spirit. I say nothing; I walk, almost run away from my son. In his understanding, it is not the earth-claimer and kin-devourer, but earth and kin, who are monsters, and his killing missions make him Wiske, the world-changer, the slayer of Digowin.

I paddle to the Isle of Rattlesnakes. There, among the trees behind the sandy beach, I see the otter emerge from the strait and walk toward me with a shell. The shell touches me. I fall to the ground. When I rise I hear the songs I've sung all my life with melodies and words I've never heard before.

When I return to the village, my son and his band have left to refill their canoes with skins; none of the Strait's youth accompanied the band; none have pit-marked skins.

I rush to my daughter's lodge; she has given birth to a son. I take the baby in my arms, carry him to all the lodges, and invite his grandparents, aunts and cousins to gather by the fires.

I place the baby on his back at the center of the council-ground, arrange the masked dancers in circles within circles and sing the melodies and words as the otter sang them, no longer repelled by otter, shell or salt sea, for I suddenly know that the shell is not death, that the otter's message is beautiful, that the great water is the source of all that emerged from it, not only of monsters reclaiming life, but also of a dream that rose toward the sky.

Singing of the life that first emerged, I feel the water heaving and retreating in my chest, rushing like rivers among my bones, lodging like lakes in my flesh. I feel myself and the baby and the kin around us transported to the lush warmth of the first age, or to Kichigami when we first arrived.

Life rose up from the ocean floor, this baby emerged from my daughter's womb, I rose from the ground on the beach of

Rattlesnake Isle, Tellegwi will rise again in the valleys that kiss the Beautiful River and Talamatun in the villages along both banks of the Northern River.

No change is final. When the prearranged hare breaks through our circles and extinguishes the fires, I place a stick in my grandson's hand. The baby restlessly waves arms and legs toward the sky. I name him Wedasi, fighter, when he shakes the stick at the hare. I fall in ecstasy alongside the child and at last dissolve in sleep.

The following spring I take my daughter, her husband and their child to the fish feast at Boweting. I reenter the medicine lodge. A generation has passed since my previous visit.

We renew our visit every spring, but only four times.

Returning to Tiosa Rondion from our last visit to Boweting, we see our kin on shore gesticulating frantically, some pointing northward, others to the ground. They want us to flee. The ground is crowded with corpses; the plague has crossed the strait and reached the place of the beaverdams.

I press the child to my breast; his mother and father paddle with all their strength. We're joined by canoes rushing out of Sagi Bay. Grandchildren of Turtlefolk, Riverpeople and Rootkin are all fleeing from the Peninsula that had been their home since the fourth age began.

At the top of the thumb we separate from Talamatun cousins who guide their bark canoes as gracefully as Rootkin toward the Morningland's northern Bay of White Sands. As we glide past the tips of the fingers and enter the long lake Mishigami, we're joined by survivors from Mishilimakina, and as we cross Mishigami, canoes from Bison Prairie approach us. The three fires are extinguished in every corner of the Peninsula.

Many rush to the carryingplaces, determined to cross the Long River and wander past the prairies toward the plains and mountains beyond the sunset.

We find refuge on an island in the green bay on the sunset shore of Mishigami.

I unroll the scroll with the changes and etch into it the beaverchildren and all their Peninsulakin migrating from the center to the periphery.

Visiting Neshnabek from Kichigami smoke at the first fire of our new councilground. I light the second fire, and the green bay's Tellegwi share their songs with us, but these last Riverpeople in the Great Lakes do not sing of mounds or bones or the

Beautiful River. The third fire remains unlit; its keeper lies unburied in Tiosa Rondion and her son, my daughter's husband, cannot bring himself to replace her.

Soon after my daughter gives birth to a second son, a canoe caravan arrives with my son and with good news from the east: our Talamatun cousins invite us to renew our kinship by celebrating a festival of bones at the Bay of White Rolling Sands in the Morningland.

Together with my son and my daughter's family in one canoe, heading toward a festival of renewal with the cousins who complete us, I joyously anticipate life's reemergence.

I am not ready for the fever, the cracking skin, the blisters. Did I fail to hear the otter's message in its entirety? Was it necessary to reenact the murder of Digowin as well?

I tell my daughter: Your husband is dead. Take the children and the scrolls and flee to the sunset. I can no longer teach you the songs.

The pain is unbearable. I tear off the mask.

Chapter 2.

Obenabi's grandmothers

Yahatase's children

    I find myself leaning on the roundish rock by the Strait's edge, wondering if this is the same moonless night, or the sixth since my journey began. The shadowy figure before me gives me an arrowhead and a blistered mask. The mask burns my face and I try frantically to remove it. But my arms fly wildly in front of me and reach for the arrowhead a young hunter extends to me. My mind floods with memories.
    I shudder remembering the corner where I huddled with my baby sister, my embracing arms protecting her from the spectacle on the longhouse floor, the frightful dance so different from any I had seen before, altogether lacking the joy and mirth I so loved in the planting and strawberry festival dances.

Sister trembled and buried her face in my neck, but I looked fearlessly, attentively, at mouths twisting into the grimaces of false faces and vomiting black sand. I knew that, after the dance, aunts and grandmothers would tell me why their bodies had writhed, why their groins had turned black, why their mouths had discharged sand; they would tell me what part of earth was renewed and made beautiful by this dance. And I would have to remember, for one day I would have to renew earth's beauty for the others.

When the writhing and vomiting and groaning stopped, two ghosts in long black robes entered the longhouse. One took my sister; the other offered me his hand. I understood the ceremony wasn't over.

Outside, people of other longhouses lay motionless on the ground.

Carrion birds hovered above the village, their excited cries replacing the groans and shouts of the stilled villagers. I made out the figure of a man removing cloaks, cutting pendants, taking earrings.

I pulled my hand free, ran back to our lodge and screamed to wake my mother, uncles and grandfathers, but none stirred. My scream was answered only by an echo that sounded like laughter coming from the carrion birds or the scavenging man.

Vomiting on the longhouse floor, I wished earth who'd pushed me up would swallow me, but the robed ghost returned for me and carried me far from my longhouse and my village. Hooded ghosts with crosses came and went during my interminable night of aching and vomiting. They didn't tell me why they had arranged the fearful ceremony I had seen.

When I stopped vomiting, the blackrobed ghosts named me Anne and took me to another part of the stone cave. Here girls with covered bodies sang in the tongue of the ghosts and repeatedly crossed themselves.

I kept on asking Why? I refused to eat until they told me that Le Dieu, the grandfather of all the Blackrobes, had arranged the death dance because he didn't like the songs or feasts or ceremonies of the longhouse people, and they said he would make me vomit sand if I didn't cross myself and sing and bow to his mother, La Sainte Marie.

They also told me that Le Dieu made all the decisions in the councils in the sky just as our grandfathers did in our longhouse councils. But I knew that longhouse grandmothers made the decisions, so I knew it was La Sainte Marie who had killed the people in our longhouses. I refused to sing to her.

The Robes always watched us. They named my sister Marie and frightened her into singing their songs. I went on singing the longhouse songs and they called me a child of Satan. When I called them disease-bringers, the Robes said war had killed the people of my longhouse, and they spoke of eastern enemies whom they named Serpents and Wolfpacks.

But there were days when they admitted killing my people with the plague. On those days they'd say the plague was a bane only to the children of Satan but a boon to the children of Dieu and Sainte Marie. I knew what they meant. The plague left cloaks and pendants for scavengers of things, like the one I'd seen, and it left kinless Annes and Maries for the scavengers of souls.

When the Robes thought we had forgotten the people of our village, they told us the plague could not have killed forty of our people to every one of theirs. Since only a few of their people had died, all the people I remembered couldn't have existed. I grew up doubting there was any truth in their Word.

But my sister grew up believing their truth, believing that their Word came first. She grew up forgetting that first came the earth and the sun and the sky, that next came the seed from which came plants and flowers and people and their Word, that the children of the marriage of earth with sky, the children of the seed, came last.

When we weren't watched, I took my sister to the garden or to the edge of the forest where it was all so plain to see. She looked, but she didn't see. She returned to the stone cave to bow to crosses, kneel to statues and sing to the bringers of plague.

When I was watched, I too bowed and kneeled and moved my lips. I too learned the Robes' languages, the one they spoke to each other and the one they spoke to their statues. I too would have grown up forgetting.

But when I was with the pelt dressers, I stayed close to a woman who remembered the dreams of the original people. The Robes called her a witch.

She told me: I wasn't a witch before I came to the mission, although I had known several witches in my village. My cousin had learned from a Tellegwi how to speak to a dead ancestor who asked for gifts the earth wanted. My aunt dreamed of things to come, and then we had to make them come, just like the Talamatun. My Neshnabek grandmothers dreamt of animals and were guided by them. I wanted to be a witch. I fasted. But I couldn't concentrate because I was afraid. My fear came from my uncles who carried dressed pelts to the Longbeards of Stadacona and returned to our village with metal pots, hatchets, knives, crosses and sometimes rifles. Only those who learned Holy Mary songs were given rifles. Many learned the songs so as to be given rifles. Those who returned with rifles called my fasting cousin, aunt and grandmothers witches and said the wrath of God struck down villages with witches in them. What my uncles foresaw came to pass. Talamatun from across the river burned our lodges and carried off my cousins, aunts and grandmothers. The witchcraft had provoked the raid, I then believed, and I let my uncles bring me to Stadacona where I'd be safe from raids and witches. I still wanted to speak to a dead ancestor or dream of things to come or have an animal guide, but the Robes said dreams that weren't in their Book were false, so I stopped fasting. I was afraid of God's wrath. My fear made me listen carefully to everything the Robes told me: the earth where my ancestors lay was hell, the forest was the Devil's lodging and animals were his creatures, festivals to regenerate the earth were orgies; enjoyment of earth's fruit was evil, we originated in sin, our lives were a painful burden, our salvation was death, and after death we would be regenerated, but not all of us, only those who had believed the Word—that's why we had to seek guidance only from the carriers of the Word, the Blackrobes. The year of the plague, when you and Maní came, I listened even more intently to the Robes, and I also listened to the children and to an old Turtlewoman. And then I fasted. I learned witchcraft by myself in a corner of the Blackrobes' lodge. After several days of fasting, a bear came for me. Taking large strides, he carried me to the outskirts of a Talamatun village on the other side of the river. I heard shots. Men who had been repairing longhouses, women who had been harvesting corn, fell to the ground. I heard a Longbeard urging my uncles to shoot again. I saw what had provoked the wrath that had destroyed my village. The robed and bearded men had implicated us in their feuds. It was their dreams that were evil. From that day, whenever the Robes speak to me of Satan, sin or evil, I fast, for now I know that my dreams come from the same depths from which earth, life and joy emerged.

•

I listened to the woman in the pelt lodge, but I didn't want to dream; I wanted to put seeds into earth and see corn plants grow, as my grandmothers had.

I joined the seed planters and clung to an old woman who secretly sang the longhouse people's planting festival songs. The Robes called her a sorceress because she sang of a time they wanted us to forget, a time when there was no mission or trading post in Stadacona, a time when both banks of the Northern River were solid green with corngold openings. And she sang of the time when it all ended:

We lodged and fed the longbearded men who disembarked from the ships, and then we lodged and fed the plague that disembarked with them. We were crippled by the plague, yet we protected our guests from the fury of those among our kin who did not feel the obligations of hosts toward the plague-bringers. Soon we were feuding among ourselves. Peacemakers went from lodge to lodge to repair the breach. Our robed guests gave rifles to their protectors. The carnage that followed made the breach irreparable. People of a single tongue who had been spared by the plague attacked each other and separated. Those who refused to be hospitable to the robed strangers went into the forests south of the river. The rest of us went west to join people of our tongue on the island called Morningland by the people of the Lakes. The Northern River's abandoned fields and villages filled with bearded and robed strangers. Two Robes followed us to Morningland, gathered children deprived of lodge and kin by plague, and taught them to sing of Sainte Marie and to speak of our eastern kin as fierce Serpents. Youth who grew hot and fearful at the thought of serpents were given rifles, and the feud sped over the distance that separated us from our kin. Each raid was followed by a counter-raid. Peaceful emissaries from both sides eloquently denounced the fratricide, but to no avail. The easterners named our youth Holy Marys and said that users of the alien killing-sticks were neither good hunters nor brave raiders, but were mindless destroyers of the tree of life. They warned that we, a mere branch, would fall if the tree fell. The eastern branches gathered at a great council and put an end to feuds among themselves. They sent emissaries to beg us to bury our crosses and join them under the shade of their long-leafed tree. We sent peacemakers, but even as our emissaries counciled with the other branches reunited around the tree, our firespitting Holy Marys attacked the council and put an end to all talk of reconciliation. The Robes' converts did not attack the easterners to adopt them under our tree, for we weren't nursing a tree, nor to avenge dead kin, for that was sinful, but to vanquish paganism. The rest of us thought of the easterners' warning and started to nurse a tree. We counciled with the Ehrye people of similar language who lived in the valleys of the Beautiful River. They had inherited a festival from grandfathers of different speech. We begged them to arrange this festival in Morningland. We invited all the people of the lakes and valleys to bury the bones of their dead in a common grave, and to embrace each other as children of common ancestors. Blackrobes came and brought the plague with them. We and our Ehrye neighbors were devastated. Our tree was stillborn.

The old woman's eyes filled with tears. I told her I was born in the village where that festival was held, and asked why she had followed the plague-bringers to Stadacona. She said the Robes took the children to make them forget. She wanted the children to remember. She gave me a grain of corn and taught me to sing of the great turtle, of the woman who fell from the sky and of her twins.

I sang of earth mating with sun and sky to make seeds generate food, life and joy, and I translated into the Robes' language so as to hear them rail against orgies, sodomy, evil and sin.

I had been in the mission for six winters and was ready to leave, if only my sister left with me. But my sister thought there was nothing but plague outside the mission, and the plague was Hell. When I took her to the pelt lodge, she smiled at the northern woman's pronouncing her name Maní, but heard nothing else. After listening to the old seed planter, she ran to cross herself before a statue.

One day new Blackrobes visited the mission. A few days later I heard groans of pain from every direction. Then the pelt dresser called my sister and me. She shouted to us not to enter the lodge: Maní! On the shores of Kichigami you'll lose your thirst for the Robes' Paradise.

To me, she said: Ankwe! Keep singing your songs; life is unlivable without them.

My eyes were so full of tears I could barely see the swellings, the oozing blisters on so many bodies. Robes pulled us away as they had earlier, but I freed myself and Maní from their grasp and became the sorceress they thought me: Destroyers of seeds! I shouted at them, May all you reap poison and destroy you!

They who disfigured our bodies with their plagues and our spirits with their songs responded with: Heretic! Savage!

Maní and I ran out of the mission. She no longer feared the Hell outside. It was Hell inside.

We found the old seed planter gathering others who ran out. She gathered enough of us to fill a longhouse and took us past Stadacona's square lodges to the harbor, where we saw bearded men carry bags from ships to shore. She had me ask a band of northern men, fur carriers, to take us to the Bay of Rolling White Sands in Morningland.

Maní trembled from fear of a pagan place but I was happy with anticipation. I was at last leaving Hell and traveling to the center of the world.

But my heart broke when we reached our destination. The disease hadn't only visited the Stadacona mission, it had almost depopulated Morningland's remaining villages. We joined people from large villages with many lodges in a small village with a few lodges.

The old woman wanted to go east and be adopted by the people nursing the long-leafed tree. Maní paled at the thought. She knew the easterners loved crosswearers as dearly as the Robes loved fierce Serpents, and she knew the easterners did not think it sinful to avenge dead kin.

I told the old woman that Maní and I wanted to start our new lives in Morningland, and I went to seek a dream by a stream near the edge of the village on a night when the moon was full.

I had been fasting since the day the fur dresser had given her life. I sat by the stream and waited. Soon a beaver came to me and told me he was going to drown the world. He raised a dam so high that the water swallowed the village and the forest. When I saw the beaver again he was carrying mud to a turtle's back. He winked at me and the mud became a field where laughing children ran among stalks of yellow corn caressed by sun and wind.

I told the old woman my dream and she scolded me. She called me Yahatase, serpent who changes her skin: You were born a longhouse granddaughter. Then you spoke like a Holy Mary. You've just begun to sing like a seedkeeper. Yet now you dream like a northerner of different speech and reject your own people.

It occurred to me that a serpent sheds an ugly old skin and grows a beautiful new one, unlike the Robes who never change their skins. Anne was drowned by a beaver. Yahatase be it! I liked my new skin.

Some of our people who had gone east returned as emissaries of the eastern league and told us to bury our crosses, stop singing to life-hating spirits, and join the branches surrounding the living tree. A few rifle-armed youth, incensed by the presence of fierce Serpents in our midst, murdered the emissaries.

Soon after this deed, the fur carriers who had brought us to Morningland came to warn us that a large band of easterners was heading toward us and that these Serpents from the sunrise were armed with rifles given to them by Oceanshore strangers whom the Robes considered more evil than pagans. The old woman insisted on staying in the village, thinking the warriors were rushing toward us to adopt us.

I was convinced they had good reason to kill us all. I fled with Maní to the forest. In a few days we were lost, hungry and cold. I understood why Longbeards and Blackrobes feared the forest: they didn't know how to enjoy earth's gifts any better than my sister or I did.

We smelled roasting meat and thought we were in Paradise. We followed the smell to where the northern fur carriers were camped. We overflowed with gratitude, even when they told us they hadn't lost sight of us since we had left our longhouse, and that we had confirmed what they'd heard about the powers of mission people in the forest.

When the carriers told us the war was over, we followed them through the forest past a neighboring village which was completely desolate. Maní cried. I rushed from abandoned roundlodges to abandoned longhouses, then to a spot where a square lodge had stood. The Robes' lodge was burned to the ground. But there were no corpses.

Maní clung to me and trembled when we glimpsed our village. Nothing and no one remained. Every lodge was a mound of ashes; even our fields were burned.

Suddenly the old woman walked toward us from a bark lodge by forest's edge. She told us our village had been attacked by children of people who had lived in Morningland: The easterners begged us to join them by their tree, but our Holy Marys responded to the invitation by pointing their rifles. Then the easterners pulled hidden rifles from cloaks and bundles, more rifles than there were in all Morningland. Everyone went east.

Our crosswearers and gun carriers went bound, tied to each other like dogs to a travois.

The old woman, who so longed for the songs and dances, the names and meanings of the longhouse festivals, had stayed and waited for our return, knowing that Maní would not have been adopted.

The fur carriers offered to take us to a distant island in a beautiful green bay where neither plagues nor raiding Serpents would reach us. Thinking of my dream, and of what the fur dresser had told Maní, I couldn't wait to step from a canoe to the shore of that beautiful island. But the old woman didn't want to be adopted by people of different speech and ways. She wanted Maní to bury her cross, learn the longhouse songs, and go to where the leaves and branches were connected to a living tree.

Maní wouldn't part with her cross, and I was too far removed from our mother's ways to let myself be guided by the longhouse grandmother. The old woman talked in signs to one of the carriers; she rejected my offer to translate. At last she told us we would go together to a green bay, to a lake called Mishigami.

During the journey, Maní and I were speechless. We hadn't imagined there was so much beauty in the world. But when we reached our destination, I was disappointed and felt betrayed. I didn't see the playful and vigorous people the fur dresser had led me to expect, nor the gorgeous field my dream's beaver had promised. I saw the same thing I had seen since my fifth spring: a gathering of plague's survivors. These had fled from a place they named with our tongue, Tiosa Rondion; perhaps that was the beaver village of my dream.

The person who adopted us was the carrier I liked least of the entire band, a somber, irritable man who coughed and shivered even though he kept his pockmarked skin covered with fur. He made me think of the man who had moved among the corpses of my first village removing cloaks and pendants. I was sure he never dreamed. He spoke mainly of the Longbeards of Stadacona, and he spoke of them with the same mixture of pride and reverent humility with which my sister spoke of La Sainte Marie.

This man and his two nephews lived in a square lodge on the fringe of the island village. They helped us raise a small longhouse. The man brought meat to the old woman. The younger nephew brought beads and quills to Maní. The older nephew kept his distance from us and said nothing; he seemed hostile to our presence in his village.

My disappointment gave way to hope in spring, when several men cleared a field, and women with corn, squash and bean seeds joined us in a planting ceremony. We were enchanted that women of northern speech were familiar with the songs and dances of Turtlefolk, as they called us. While I danced, I felt the seeds germinating in earth, the plants pushing through, and I knew the seeds germinating in me would also push through.

But my hopes didn't last a season. The canoe caravan returned from the east with the trophies gotten for the scavenged furs. The carrier came to our lodge, deliberately avoided the old woman, and with an ugly smile frozen across his face, handed me beads, cloth, a pot, a knife and meat.

Something in my head burst. I dumped the gifts into the pot and threw the entire offering at the man's face. I remembered the old woman talking to this man with signs. I could almost hear them: she wanted to complete her longhouse with a man who would bring meat and father children, even if he spoke differently. He wanted to swell his power bundle with a many-tongued companion who would help him speak directly to the Longbeards, even if she changed her skin like a serpent. Perhaps he wanted the Longbeards to name him le chef des gens du lac. I shouted to him: Take the old woman and father her children! And may your children scavenge your grave and filch your bones for trophies!

I fled to a spot on the shore and looked out on the bay. The old woman would have to make do without meat. I felt sorry for her. When I returned to our lodge, Maní embraced me; she was proud of my chastity! I wished she'd had the mind and heart to embrace the old woman instead.

I ran daily to my spot on shore. Soon I became aware that someone was spying on me. One day a canoe floated into my view. The older nephew stood in it with his back to me and speared fish. Some days later I found the canoe abandoned near my spot; the spear was in it. I paddled out, tried to spear fish, and at last succeeded. I sensed that my whole performance was watched. But I used the canoe whenever I found it, and danced back to our lodge with the fish I speared.

Then I found a bow and several arrows. I sent arrows toward leaves and branches until I lost them all. The next day the arrows were all retrieved and I shot them again, a little more accurately. One day I saw a deer. I aimed. The deer fell to the ground. I ran towards it and froze. I cried in the face of the beautiful life I had taken. I turned to walk away. At that moment the youth, the hostile older nephew, appeared from nowhere, walked past me and knelt by the deer. He removed the arrow and broke off the stem.

He gives me the arrowhead. His gift, his shyness, his way of providing our lodge with meat, make me cry harder. He carries the deer to my lodge, walking several steps behind me. I turn and ask Why?

Wedasi

Why was he so hostile when we first came? Why is he so generous now? The youth places the deer at the entrance to my lodge and leaves, answering no questions.

Now it's I who follow him, one day to a forest opening, another to the edge of a stream, then to the island's shore, at last to the spot where I first sensed him watching me.

He tells me gradually, not all at once, the things he's never before told anyone.

His grandmother named him Wedasi, warrior, but he doesn't know what feats she expected of him. His first memory is of returning to his village Tiosa Rondion, of his kin on shore shouting and waving their arms, and of his father paddling furiously away from his village. He tells me the canoe didn't stop until it reached this island in the green bay where more people were gathered than he thought existed. He says he didn't know how few they were.

As a boy of five springs, he didn't know why his people had left Tiosa Rondion, he didn't understand the talk of a plague that had visited his Peninsula.

He said he often followed his mother to the forest when she gathered herbs. She sang of Tellegwi kin and of great Serpents that descended from the north. She mixed herbs in certain combinations but Wedasi was too distracted by the sounds of birds and the motions of animals to concentrate on the characteristics of the herbs or the meaning of the songs.

The third winter in Greenbay, Wedasi's father gave him a bow and took him along when he went into the forest. The youth's father often sang of his mother, Wedasi's grandmother, the keeper of the Talamatun fire in Tiosa Rondion. When Wedasi asked if she was still there, tears filled his father's eyes. Wedasi was ten when his brother Nangisi was born. He tells me: Grandmother let me help arrange the naming ceremony. We had visitors from every quarter. Her older son, my mother's brother, had come from the east with canoes full of gifts; and Neshnabek as well as Tellegwi from the Greenbay shores had come to smoke at our fires and see the gifts. Grandmother called my uncle a scavenger and a pit-marked spirit; she said he gave skins of uneaten and unburied animals to men who gave him objects he didn't need. She told me the Greenbay Tellegwi who counciled at her fire were people whose memories had been washed away by the plague, and that's why they hovered around Uncle's gifts. She showed me the scrolls from which she never parted, but I was distracted by the objects I recognized: the shells, birds, trees, and they were all I saw. When she sang of four ages, a land of ice, a feud between Neshnabek, Tellegwi and Talamatun, I heard only words. I told Grandmother none of it meant anything to me, and asked if my memory was washed away or my spirit pit-marked. She said I'd remember everything after the ceremony, when I fasted in my dream lodge.

But before the ceremony ended, Wedasi's uncle spoke of a bone festival to be celebrated by my mother's and grandmother's people in my own village in the Bay of Rolling Sands in Morningland. Wedasi's grandmother no longer spoke of his dream lodge. She sang of the three fires and of the fourth age and of an otter who would come from the sea and bring the dead back to life by throwing shells on their bones.

In Morningland, Wedasi was filled with wonder by the number of people gathered, by the extent of our corn fields, by the bison heads worn and the skeletons carried by the Ehrye people of the Beautiful River's valleys. He tells me his father seemed angered by the Talamatun who wore crosses and muttered, by the blackrobed figures who hovered on the fringes like silent crows, and by the bearded men with covered bodies to whom his uncle gave their pelts.

Soon after they arrived, his father rushed him and his brother from the festival ground and set up a tent deep in the forest. Wedasi wanted to be with his grandmother who had stayed at the festival; he wanted to see the three fires and the otter who brought skeletons to life.

When his father left the tent at night, thinking the youths were asleep, Wedasi followed him to a councilground where one fire burned. He says he lost sight of him in the multitude gathered around the fire. A bison-headed Ehrye stood in the center and told that a spirit had visited his dream and warned that the Blackrobes traveling two by two through the land were carrying the plague to all the villages. Then he heard his father say the strangers' very gifts weakened those who touched them, killed the healthy, and turned the sickly into submissive, chanting scavengers.

At that point, people began to move about, grumbling angrily. Afraid he'd be discovered, Wedasi ran back to the tent. But his father didn't return. His mother said nothing; her eyes begged Wedasi to stay by her side. But he knew something was about to happen; he returned to the councilground. Several Beautiful River people were vomiting. They told him to stay away from the cursed place.

He went into the village. In every lodge he found people writhing from pain. He found his father, who was angry when he saw Wedasi and told him not to enter but to run, like the people on Tiosa Rondion's shore who had waved at their returning canoe seven years earlier.

When he ran back to the tent, he was terrified. He thought Blackrobes, Longbeards and crosswearers were running after him. He found his mother arguing with her brother. His uncle was urging her to leave Morningland, saying Wedasi's father and grandmother would come later. But his mother already knew something terrible had happened.

Carrying Nangisi, she had Wedasi guide her to the festival ground. Before reaching the lodge where his father lay, the youth's grandmother walked toward them. She seemed old and withered; she vomited sandy blood. She said Wedasi's father was dead. She gave his mother the scrolls from which she'd never parted and told them to flee.

Wedasi's uncle, his bundle filled with new gifts, paddled his sister and her children to their Greenbay island, perhaps at the very moment when two Blackrobes took Maní and me from a corpse-filled longhouse to the mission in Stadacona. Wedasi tells me that during the journey his mother was as silent as a stone. His uncle kept repeating that the youth's father and grandmother would come later until Wedasi told him he knew they had died of the plague brought by the Blackrobes. His uncle grew angry. He said beavers, racoons and deer had brought the plague. He said the Longbeards laughed at us for loving animals and wanting to speak to them in dreams. He said the Longbeards spoke to animals with firesticks, and loved only dead animals.

Soon after Wedasi's people and other survivors had returned to Greenbay, his mother told him to take Nangisi and go elsewhere. She tried to scatter the people his grandmother had gathered on this island during her last years. His mother looked as withered as his grandmother had looked in the Bay of Rolling Sands. She gave him everything that was hers: her herb bundle, the pendant his father had given her, his grandmother's scrolls, all without ceremony. She said nothing; her eyes begged him to leave her alone.

The plague was on this island. Some people ran from sweat lodges to the bay's water to heal but they never came up. Wedasi went to the forest and untied his grandmother's scrolls, hoping they would help him understand. But all he saw was the same shells and birds and figures he had seen before, and he couldn't remember the songs. He tells me he had been distracted and too young to concentrate. He hadn't known he'd inherit the scrolls. He rolled his grandmother's scrolls with his tears inside, and tied them.

When he got back to their lodge, his uncle was carrying his mother's wasted body to a burial spot in the forest. He placed the herb bundle and his grandmother's scrolls alongside his mother, keeping a bark fragment that broke off; then he helped his uncle cover her body with earth. He says his insides were dead.

Wedasi's uncle was shunned by the surviving villagers, many of whom feared his gifts. He built a square lodge for himself and his nephews on the outer fringe of the village of roundlodges.

Wedasi's grandmother had tried to make a whole out of fragments. His uncle took fragments out of the whole. The plague left many youth without kin, without names, without dreams, without guides, and some of these youth accompanied the carrier and admiringly called him Wiske the gift-giver.

The youth's uncle taught him to use his firestick and to hunt animals not for eating but for the caravans that took dressed skins to Boweting, where Longbeards had set up a post. The carrier said his nephew was well named because his aim was good, and he gave Wedasi a firestick. For a time, Wedasi was proud of his powers, like the other carriers. He no longer felt empty. He had a quality: good aim. He felt stronger than the animals who cringed from him; his firestick had greater powers than the dances and herbs and other medicines.

One day he tracked a moose deep into the forest; he became distracted and kept following the large animal long after he sighted it, watching where it stopped and what it did. He got so close he could touch it. The moose turned to look at him, and then went back to eating flowers. Wedasi raised his firestick and waited. The moose turned again and looked into the young hunter's eyes, trusting, unafraid, and then proudly walked away. It was Wedasi who cringed. He didn't feel strong or brave, but weak and cowardly and stupid; his powers were not lodged in himself but in a contrivance he had not made.

Wedasi buried his firestick behind his uncle's lodge; he hunted with his bow, but only when he was hungry, and he took care to express his gratitude to the proud and generous animals he hunted.

One day he returned to the spot where the moose had looked at him and he built a fasting lodge. He didn't know what to expect. Those who could have prepared him were dead. He hoped the trusting moose would come and help him. Instead, a bear came, looked at him and went on. A wolf walked near his lodge indifferently, not once looking up, though he must have smelled him.

After a few days he felt sick and weak, but still nothing came, neither a spirit nor a moose. He started thinking of the bone festival where his father and grandmother had died. He couldn't get it out of his mind. He thought of the Ehrye warrior saying that Blackrobes carried the plague to the villages, and of his father saying that even the gifts of the strangers weakened and killed the Rootkin.

Wedasi wondered why his father had said that since Wedasi's uncle had carried those gifts to every corner of the Peninsula. And suddenly he understood. He understood his mother's silence and his father's anger. He remembered their last day in Tiosa Rondion. They had left to go with Wedasi's grandmother to the fish feast in Boweting the same day his uncle and the caravan had left to take their fur bundles to the east.

When they returned to Tiosa Rondion, his father's mother and others were spitting sandy blood and dying. Wedasi's uncle must have known that they had all fled to Greenbay, but he didn't show his face here for seven years. When at last he came, it was to invite them to resume their kinship with Talamatun cousins. The carrier's invitation made the youth's father dream of sitting at a fire with his mother's ancestors; it made his grandmother dream of resuming life as it had been before the plague, and it made Wedasi dream of an otter who would revive people with shells.

Wedasi thinks it must have become clear to his father as soon as they arrived at the Bay of Rolling Sands that his uncle's sole aim had been to lure the Greenbay furs eastward and to lure the Longbeards' gifts westward. Even more must have become clear to his father. Some survivors must have remembered that a plague had ravaged Morningland seven years earlier when Wedasi's uncle had gone east to fill his canoes and then returned to Tiosa Rondion before them; he had carried his gift to every corner of the Peninsula.

In his dream lodge, Wedasi saw that his uncle was as heedless of consequences as the makers of firesticks. He wondered what dismal beings in dark caves devised killing-sticks they didn't themselves wield; and said no herb collector gathers poisons to murder distant strangers who never wronged him, whom he doesn't confront, whose death he doesn't see, for a revenge he doesn't seek.

Wedasi thanks the earth and trees and animals for helping him see clearly. He saw something his grandmother had called Digowin, something that scavenges, something that swallows life without intending to, something that's stupid but proud of strength and intelligence which are not and never become its own. He saw that the men called Longbeards wielded his uncle the way the carrier wields a firestick, and that the colorful cloth and the pots and hatchets are what his father thought they were, objects that weaken and kill.

Maní and I and the old woman arrived in a canoe laden with pots, hatchets, knives and cloth; a cross hung from Maní's neck, and she muttered like people Wedasi had seen at the Bay of Rolling Sands. Wedasi didn't welcome us; he thought we were his uncle's, or even the plague's, accomplices.

But when he saw me throw his uncle's gifts in his face, Wedasi saw that he had made a bad mistake: With that single act, you did more than I've known how to do since I've lived in uncle Wiske's lodge. I followed you to your clearing to repair my mistake.

I ask him why he chose such a strange way to give me fish and meat.

Looking at the arrowhead I carry around my neck, he tells me it was because he was sure I wouldn't accept those gifts from the hand of that man's nephew. But when he gave me the arrowhead, I looked at him with eyes as trusting and unafraid as the moose's, and saw that he had made another mistake. He laughs shyly.

I want him to say more, but I know he won't, for he's told me all. I know that the trust in my eyes reminds him of the trust, not in the moose's, but in his grandmother's eyes. I know his grandmother expected something from him, and although he doesn't know what it is, it's what he wants to give me, as if I too expected it from him. How can I make him stop seeing his grandmother's expectant eyes behind my loving eyes?

I know how. By bringing about what his grandmother expected from him. Then I'll be able to give him what he'd like to give me. What his grandmother wanted is as clear to me as if she'd told me herself. I may not know all the right words or melodies, but neither does Wedasi nor anyone alive.

Until now I've avoided the people who have visited our island in the green bay. Now I have reason to mingle with the newly arrived longhouse people who have been to the Sunset Mountains. I beg them to stay with us, for my sake, for the sake of Wedasi's grandmother, and for the sake of the old woman who was forced to this island by Maní's and my unwillingness to join the people of the long-leafed tree.

Our guests say they are glad to rest after having wandered to every corner of the world. They tell us they were still numerous enough to fill a large village after the plague reduced them on the Northern River. They fled to Morningland and sought protection in the Blackrobes' crosses and chants. Disenchanted by the Robes' powers after being further reduced by a second plague, the survivors returned eastward and sought adoption among the people of the long-leafed tree.

But they would not abandon brothers and cousins who refused to bury their crosses, just as I had refused to abandon Maní, and so had to flee from those whose refuge they had sought. Shunned by one side for stubbornness and by the other for inconstancy, they then retraced the original migration of the longhouse people, following the Beautiful River to where it flows into the Long River of the sunset.

They continued westward over prairies and plains until their path was blocked by mountains with craters and volcanos. Returning eastward to dry plains, they found no familiar berries, roots or fruit, and hunger killed many more. They gave earth seeds, but their half-grown corn was destroyed by stampeding bison and their camp was attacked by bison hunters who rode animals similar to the Longbeards' horses. The survivors thought their last reduction was an omen and they returned toward the sunrise, for their rememberers said horselike animals did not exist in the western plains.

While Maní chants with the crosswearers among the guests, the old woman and I and Wedasi listen to what the wanderers tell us of the eastern longhouse people leagued around the long-leafed tree. Wedasi asks if it's true that the easterners use Wiske's weapons to reconstitute their tree. Our guests tell us the easterners do use firesticks, but only against Holy Marys, and not always against them, for the concern of their longhouse grandmothers is to regenerate the world, not to depopulate it. Themselves reduced by plague and harassed by Northern River Longbeards and Oceanshore Invaders, the easterners have filled their longhouses and villages by adopting people of eleven different tongues, among whom are captured children of three tongues spoken by the Invaders from the sea, and all of the adopted bear ancestral names, wear masks in the festivals, sing the songs and understand the meanings.

Our guests' words bring tears to the old woman's eyes, for she contrasts what she hears with the incompleteness of our lives. But their words fill me with hope and clarify my task.

Although the wanderers are barely numerous enough to fill a single longhouse, on my insistence we raise two new longhouses, leaving space for visitors of different tongues, and we help our new kin clear a field, Wedasi alongside me, his brother Nangisi alongside Maní.

Soon more guests arrive, people from Wedasi's Peninsula who had fled southward to the valley of the Beautiful River, where they were attacked and reduced by the plague that devastated the Ehryes. The newcomers stay. The old woman is taken up with adoption ceremonies, instructing me in the arrangements, teaching Peninsula people and northerners the rhythms and melodies of longhouse dances, listening attentively when old northerners sing of their origins. She seems younger.

I too feel light inside as I hop from a naming ceremony to a planting festival. People of five languages, some with crosses, form a circle around a councilground surrounded by long and round lodges. At the center Wedasi has drawn a triangle and lit a fire at each of its points.

In the field of our three plant sisters, the tall yellow corn embraced by intertwining bean vines and adored by heavy squashes shakes its hair in the wind and generously offers its fruit to us. The rhythm of feasts and festivals is undoing the ravages we've undergone. The wounds are healing without the aid of firesticks or bands of warriors or a league covenant or even a council of grandmothers.

Peninsula people are dancing around a newborn child and singing of the time when their ancestors first came to the shores of the Great Lakes. It's the third summer since we helped raise the new lodges, and the child newly named Chacapwe is surrounded by trees with strong branches; the island looks more and more like the land a beaver once promised me in a dream.

My eyes seek Wedasi's. I know this village is a beginning toward what his grandmother wanted, and I wish he'd attach himself to it and let himself be supported by it; I wish he'd rise with me out of his anguish as the corn rises out of the ground, as our new lodges rose up. But the eyes that greet mine are not filled with joyful celebration of the plants that grew from the seeds we planted.

Wedasi's eyes are sad, almost morose; they're searching for something, anxiously, as if his life depended on it. I wonder if he's contrasting my fulfillment of my dream with his own, as if we'd been racing. I wonder if he's reproaching himself for having failed to grasp the message of his grandmother's scrolls, for having failed to grasp what his grandmother had wanted him to reconstitute.

I take to spying on him to see if I can leave a helpful canoe somewhere on his path, as he did for me. I soon learn that he devotes all his energy to a very small field: his uncle's lodge; and that, if he makes contrasts, he surely contrasts the rest of the village with the square lodge that stands on its fringe, the lodge from which his uncle leads a rifle-armed band to murder our furry forest neighbors.

Perhaps Wedasi feels that whatever he retained from his grandmother is needed most in this lodge. He takes his fourteen-spring brother Nangisi to the forest with a bow and arrows; he tells Nangisi that the original people killed their animal kin only to satisfy hunger, not to fill their uncle's eastbound canoes. He shows his brother that neither bears nor wolves conspire to exterminate weaker animals; he urges Nangisi to fast and builds him a dream lodge deep in the forest. Nangisi wants to be liked by his older brother. He uses every occasion to express his love and gratitude to Wedasi, except when their uncle's canoes return from the sunrise. Then he's the first person on the landingplace.

I realize I can't help Wedasi wean his brother away from his uncle. I wish he'd leave Nangisi in his uncle's lodge and come to my longhouse. I prepare to tell him that he's distracted again, that he's wasting himself to no purpose, that a beautiful flower grows on a healthy bush or out of fertile soil and not in isolation or out of sand, that his uncle's lodge is as isolated from the other lodges as the band of carriers is from the life of the village, that his grandmother had devoted herself to people who could grow to a fourth age and not to those stunted in a second or third age, that a poisonous plant can serve as soil for healthy plants but can't itself be made healthy.

My love for Wedasi feeds my resentment of Nangisi and blinds me to a spell that originates in the core of my own lodge, a spell that binds and twists Wedasi's brother Nangisi out of shape.

My first glimmer comes on the day Nangisi returns from his dream lodge. Maní and I are in the field. Knowing he's tried before, Maní asks him if he saw anything this time.

Nangisi, assuming I'm in on the secret, answers her: Exactly what you said. When I got tired and hungry, I saw lots of animals. They all spoke to me. That should make Wedasi happy.

Roused by this exchange, I seek my sister's eyes and ask: Did you tell him that is what he'd see, Maní?

The world's most innocent eyes, a child's eyes, look back at me. She thinks I suspect her chastity! Silly sister! The whole village laughs at the chastity that loves all equally but can't see the one who wants the love. My anger melts.

I run from Maní to the clearing to which I ran from the uncle's gifts. Wedasi is there before me. He already knows how Nangisi dreamed, what guidance he found.

I sit next to Wedasi but say nothing; all I'd prepared to tell him is as dead as last year's leaves. Did Wedasi know what I'm just starting to understand? Would I have believed him if he'd told me?

I know why I've been so blind. Innocent, lovable Maní is so good, so generous to everyone, especially to the crosswearers, always sharing their woes and teaching their children to share them. I've never listened, but I know what woes she shares and teaches.

I too was taught to wail heartrendingly of our depopulation by the fierce Serpents, the Wolfpacks who banded together against helpless rabbits. I too was taught to think little and speak less of plagues, yet to thank Dieu for sending a boon to his children and a bane to the serpentine pagans who tried to reconstitute their villages without his Word. I too was taught that the Lord who subjected this world and its creatures to his will was not of this world, that I was his sister and not the sister of deer or beaver or trees or lakes or earth or sun for my spirit was like unto his, that my respect for earth was submission to the Devil and my gratitude to animals was idolatry, that it was my task to subject myself and earth and all her creatures to his will.

No wonder the crosswearers to whom Maní is so good are the carrier's most reliable hunters. No wonder the children with whom she chants are on the landingplace beside Nangisi when the canoes return with their trophies. No wonder Nangisi can agree with Wedasi that beaver are not hostile to people, that strong animals don't spend their lives killing weak ones, that their uncle's reasons for slaughtering beaver are senseless.

Maní helps Nangisi agree with everything Wedasi tells him, and to stand Wedasi on his head even while agreeing, by giving Nangisi far better reasons than his uncle's for the slaughter. Maní is helping Nangisi become everything Wedasi opposes. She's helping Nangisi see himself as a proud firestick, as a local incarnation of the outside power that subjugates the world's creatures to its will, as a bane to the Devil's kin and a boon to the kin of the Lord, as a foe to fierce Serpents and an ally to the plague.

Nangisi

Wedasi wants his brother to know of their grandmother; he wants Nangisi to know of three fires around which four peoples gathered and began to live their fourth age.
Nangisi smiles like one whose memory has been washed away by plague. He nods like one whose spirit is pitmarked; after smiling and nodding, he joins hunters who war against the forest's furry inhabitants.
Yet Wedasi persists. He blames himself for failing to give his brother what their grandmother had given Wedasi. I understand why Wedasi persists. Nangisi is not like their uncle. He's not outwardly pitmarked; he's neither somber nor irritable. Nangisi is healthy, open and ingratiating; he chooses his every move with others in view, like those Maní calls saints.
Nangisi takes part in the village festivals, he knows the words of the songs and the steps of the dances. He hunts with a bow and shows respect for the bones of animals. And he does it all the same way that he dreamed, seeing nothing and feeling nothing, but concerned that his gesture make Wedasi or Maní or someone else happy.
When Nangisi leaves with his uncle's caravan to take furs to the Longbeards in Boweting, it's not because he has at last rejected the grandmother's way and chosen the uncle's, but because he wants to enhance his grandmother's way with the gifts he brings.
Wedasi, alone in his canoe, takes frequent journeys away from the island. The few times I see him, I remind him there's a place in the longhouse intended for him. Part of him wants to come, I know; but another part is ashamed, as if he were to blame for his brother's choices.
Wedasi waits. At last, what he's waiting for seems to arrive. Nangisi and other carriers return in empty canoes. Nangisi's uncle is dead. The carrier band breaks up. Wedasi hopes his brother will immerse himself in the life of the village and grow to his fourth age. But after questioning other carriers, Wedasi and I anticipate Nangisi's immersion with trepidation.
The uncle fell ill at a place called Shequamegon in a bay of Kichigami, the great northern lake. On his deathbed, this depopulator of forests urged his band to kill without restraint and gather a veritable mound of furs. He sent word to the Longbeards of Boweting that he would part with his fur load if

they warded off his death, as if life were a gift conferred by a trading post for a large enough load of furs. He thought death killed only his singing, dreaming, bow-armed kin; he thought rifle-wielders who burned animal bones and carried furs to Longbeards would live forever. He clutched his rifle to the very end. Believing himself invulnerable, he chose no heir.

As soon as his uncle was dead, Nangisi showed his respect by arranging an unusual ceremony. He urged the carriers to go to their villages and return with the bones of dead kin. He sent word to the Boweting Longbeards to continue their westward journey.

In Shequamegon, Nangisi had the carriers enact a festival of bones like those Wedasi had described to him, binding the carriers in kinship with each other, with the uncle, and with the nephew. Nangisi bound the visiting Longbeards to himself and to the band by giving them the entire mound of furs gathered to make the uncle deathless.

Wedasi and I know that Nangisi has not returned to immerse himself in village festivals and naming ceremonies; we know that Nangisi is only waiting for the snow to melt.

When the snow does melt, Nangisi and the other carriers head toward Shequamegon to rejoin the band.

The carriers return during harvest moon with a fully reconstituted caravan. Nangisi is in the central canoe, waving his uncle's rifle. A girl wearing Stadacona cloth is beside him. Two Longbeards disembark from the last canoe. The village children and youth can't decide which to idolize: the girl in cloth, the Longbeards, or cousin Nangisi. At last they circle like flies around Nangisi, for he's everything Maní told them about an earthly being who incarnates otherworldly powers.

The girl Nangisi calls Binesikwe, birdwoman, is as proficient as Maní or I in the Longbeards' tongue. Nangisi no doubt expects her to do for him what I refused to do for his uncle. A cross dangles from her neck in memory of the Blackrobes who helped her forget the kin their plague carried off.

The cross should delight my sister. But I see that Maní is in tears and flees from my glance. Maní is jealous; she wanted to be Nangisi's companion. She hid her love, even from herself, for too long.

Nangisi invites all the villagers to a ceremony, something his isolated uncle never did. He even sends runners to invite the kin of all the beaverkillers along the green bay's shores.

I run to my clearing before the ceremony begins. If Maní has reasons for not looking at the gifts brought by Nangisi, I have reasons for not looking at what Nangisi is doing to our village.

Wedasi comes to tell me what's happening, which I don't want to hear; he doesn't tell me what he will do about it, which is all I want to hear. He tells me the ceremony is taking place, not on the councilground in the center of the village, but by the square lodge on the fringe. Longbeards and carriers are the center, villagers the fringe. Nangisi showed the depth of his gratitude and understanding by throwing tobacco to the earth spirit who provides beaver, and by blowing smoke to the water spirit who threatens Neshnabek fur carriers with drowning.

Then Nangisi parodied the calumet ceremony by passing a pipe to the older Longbeard. Villagers chuckled, knowing that Nangisi could commit and impersonate no one but himself. Nangisi wanted the Longbeards to think that by smoking with him, they were forming a bond with the entire village. This was Nangisi's self-naming ceremony; he named himself, in the Longbeards' eyes, le chef of our village.

Wedasi tells me the carriers arranged themselves around three fires. Nangisi led the Longbeards to the center of the triangle. Binesikwe translated Nangisi's explanation of the proceedings.

Nangisi spoke of the Firekeepers, the Peninsula people who welcomed their kin from the four quarters, and he pointed to his uncle's original carriers, the kinless, dreamless men who had taken the plague to the Peninsula. He spoke of Neshnabek and pointed to the axe and bead seekers he had gathered at Shequamegon. He spoke of Tellegwi and pointed to the bayshore people whose memories were washed away by plague. He spoke of Talamatun and pointed to the crosswearing youths whom Maní had taught to chant.

Wedasi bites his lip with frustration; he now knows that Nangisi heard and absorbed everything Wedasi told him, for he now sees Nangisi putting it all to use and probably thinking Wedasi is happily proud of him. Nangisi heard of four peoples and three fires with the same ears with which he heard of dreams and bone rituals. Severed from oneness with earth, animals and kin by my sister's wisdom, he learned from his uncle that animals give themselves to his rifles when he performs a bone ritual and also when he doesn't.

Nangisi learned on his own that villagers accept him and make much of him when he does perform a bone ritual, and when he lights three fires and sings of four peoples. Nangisi didn't tell the Longbeards which of the four peoples he spoke for. He had the Longbeards see him at the center; he had them see the world lit up by the fires, not the dark world of amused, surprised or angry villagers watching from the fringes. The Longbeards must have been confident that Nangisi was showing them our world, for they saw it with their own eyes.

In the Stadacona mission I had wondered how the Blackrobes had acquired their self-confident understanding of le gouvernement parmi les sauvages, with its chefs and councils of men. Now I know. If the Robes were here now, they would be counciling with le grand chef des peuples du lac.

Wedasi bites his lip, but I take his hand and rush back to the village with him, determined to act.

When we reach the place of the three fires, children already encircle the iron knives, axes kettles, cloth, beads and metal arrowheads the Longbeards carried from their canoe. I know that the Longbeards didn't come from Boweting to make children happy any more than to see Nangisi's parody of the ceremony of three fires. These are people who distribute gifts so as to create obligations. They view our youths the way travelers would view a pack of dogs: to determine if they're strong enough to pull a travois.

Wedasi's grandmother made a whole out of fragments; her son pulled fragments out of the whole and put them into his power bundle; I won't let her grandson Nangisi repeat her son's feat. I rush with Wedasi into the longhouse. The old woman is consoling Maní by scolding her. I tell the old woman we seek her advice about the two Longbeards in our village.

Maní says she'll go help Chacapwe's mother birth her second child; my sister looks at me with fear as she leaves, probably guessing what advice I've come to seek. It's the first time I've sought the old woman's advice. I ask her to remember the day when the longhouse people of the Northern River began feuding over whether to lodge or dislodge the strangers.

She sends Wedasi to gather all the rememberers he can find on both shores of the bay. She sends me to all the longhouses and roundlodges on our island.

Late that night, while Nangisi and the Longbeards are still distributing gifts by the square lodge on the fringe, the old woman speaks to the fourscore tense people gathered in our longhouse. She says that for three generations the seasons have been good to carrion birds, and it's not due to the birds. She reminds her listeners why we're all here, in a green bay on the sunset shore of Mishigami: Strangers came through our land two by two, in the guise of gift-givers. Wherever the strangers went, the inhabitants died. She asks: Where are the elk and beaver who were once as numerous as sands on a beach? Where are the people of the Northern River, of the Beautiful River, of the Morningland, of the Peninsula?

The gathered people become agitated. An old hunter tells that the elk were able to defend themselves from predatory wolverines by running to water, but that nothing protects the elk from the power of the Longbeards. A longhouse woman says such power is a poisoned mushroom that grows on dung. Another adds that the gift-givers should more properly be named life-takers or worldeaters.

The old woman then says that there were some among our kin who did not feel the obligations of hosts toward the plague-bringers.

Everyone is silent. The same thought must be on everyone's mind, just as it must have been on everyone's mind at the council in the Bay of Rolling Sands to which Wedasi followed his father.

The following night, Nangisi and the Longbeards wait by the fires while the carriers and their kin bring all their furs, even their worn cloaks for which the Longbeards have a special liking. The darkness surrounding the three fires grows larger as the green bay's other fires are extinguished. The dark circle closes in on the lit triangle, which diminishes as the prudent slip out of the light.

Drums and hundreds of murmurs generate a rumble that seems to come from under the earth, and the lit-up faces appear to be looking into the crater of a volcano. The Longbeards seek an explanation from the translator.

Nangisi, undaunted, tells them his brother has prepared a special ceremony for their benefit.

Now Wedasi leaps into the center and asks Binesikwe to translate his words: The rumble is the voice of all the plague's victims. Turning to Nangisi he adds: The voice of our grandmothers, our mother and father, our kin of Tiosa Rondion, our cousins of the Peninsula.

Nangisi has Binesikwe tell the Longbeards that the ceremony is a celebration of a gift-giving hero who saved the original people by slaying a monster called Digowin. Either Nangisi is fearless and uncannily clever, or else this is not the first time he's been threatened by his brother, and he knows how Wedasi carries out threats. It dawns on me that Wedasi, misnamed warrior, as fierce as a moose, learned from his grandmother how to expel a monster, whether it be a worldeater or a trickster.

Wedasi raises his arms and postpones the deed decided by last night's council. He rushes to the square lodge and reemerges with his bundle, his bow and a captive hare. He walks through the outer circle, then past the lit figures, to the center.

Wedasi holds the hare and waits. He's waiting for me! He's holding the gift I've been waiting for, the gift he's wanted to give me for ten years. I wish he hadn't chosen this moment. My mind races, my heart thumps.

My head tells me not to sacrifice the wellbeing of the village, not to go to the man who forces this choice on me. My head tells me I'm a child of a longhouse, and last night the longhouse council decided, so there's no going back. My head tells me the poisonous mushrooms should be buried deep in the ground, the mushrooms and dung should merge with earth and water and should nourish seeds, protect shoots, embrace roots of healthy plants, sustain a tree with strong branches and long leaves.

But my heart tells me the world is regenerated by love, by the union of earth with sky. My heart goes out to the man of Tiosa Rondion, the grandchild of peacemakers, the hunter who buried his firestick after looking into the eyes of a moose.

The drumming deafens me. Unable to hold back my tears, I leave the outer circle and walk past the carriers, past Nangisi and the Longbeards, toward Wedasi's gift. I take the hare, kneel, and hold the animal on the ground. Wedasi's knife beheads the creature; its last convulsions reverberate through the inner and outer circles.

Suddenly the tension vanishes. The drumming stops. The rumble ends. The circles disperse.

Wedasi waits for me to raise up the animal and walk beside him. He beckons the Longbeards to accompany him. He abandons his brother's lodge and guides the strangers to the longhouse where their death was decided, but where no harm can reach them now.

The old woman cooks the monster and feeds it to the Longbeards. Wiske is expelled. Digowin is eaten. I ask Wedasi if he's satisfied. I ask him if this is the wedding feast he wanted. He tells me that the death of these two bearded men would not revive the dead, nor heal the lame, nor restore the fourth age.

Wedasi's adoption of the bearded men does not add permanent leaves to our tree, for the Longbeards don't stay the night. Maní guides them to Nangisi, and Nangisi hastily paddles them and all the furs away from the island in the green bay.

My ears fill with a drumming and a rumble whenever I think of the cruel men who give trophies to children who scavenge and to youths who slaughter our forest neighbors, who justify the slaughter by saying the animals are of the flesh but their hunters of the spirit, who push hunters to murder unconverted kin because such people are, like the animals, of the flesh.

Yet the northerners were satisfied that the Longbeards were expelled, and the old woman would even have adopted them into our longhouse.

I wonder if my hatred is excessive, if it comes from the Blackrobes' mission, if it's a child of their desire to purify the world of evil.

I accept Wedasi's love and give him mine. But I don't feel our love reflected in the world around us. This is no longer the village his grandmother hoped he'd reconstitute.

Nangisi hasn't brought any more Longbeards since the hare was slain, but the Longbeards' gifts have penetrated into every lodge. Now all the village children, and not only the crosswearers, look for the return of Nangisi's gift-bearing canoes, and too many youths are willing to scavenge among corpses for worn fur cloaks.

My ears hear the drumming whenever I cross paths with Nangisi's little birdwoman, Binesikwe. She was born in Boweting soon after Longbeards set up a fur post and Blackrobes a mission. Her kin died the year Maní and I left Stadacona, of the same disease that killed the fur dresser. She was only two, younger than Maní had been when the Blackrobes took her to their mission. She was given a cross to hang from her neck and taught to forget her past, her songs, and her people. She saw Blackrobes turn children and youth against their own kin. She saw Longbeards feed people a poisoned water that made them lash out at each other like sick dogs. But she expresses no hatred. She thinks killers and deceivers who wear crosses are saved. She sews their brightly-colored beads into bird patterns on her cloth skirt without a thought, or maybe thinking the gifts come from a cloth-bearing tree and a bead bush.

She grows big with Nangisi's child, yet hops around as lightly as if she were one of the beaded birds on her skirt, with no thought of the ground on which she'll lay her burden down.

I carry Wedasi's child with all my thoughts on the ground. I know the ground is poisoned. It's the same ground on which my first longhouse stood, the ground on which I saw a shadowy figure scavenging, removing scabs from dead bodies. I can't hop. My child is too heavy. I hobble in search of ground on which a healthy plant can grow to full stature and bear all its fruit.

The pains grow more frequent. I carry the child to a mat in a longhouse on an island that rests on a great turtle's back, but the turtle is ill. Disease is sapping the turtle's strength and she can no longer support her load. She's let the creatures on the eastern part of her shell slip into the sea; she's dying. Her shell is blistered, it's as full of holes as a rotting fallen tree trunk.

My child wants life, blindly confident that its beginning is the world's beginning, that its emergence will revive the dying turtle.

My kind sister rubs me; she's pained by my pain, relieved by my relief. She's undergoing her third birth. On the night of the longhouse council she suffered through the long and painful birth of Chacapwe's brother Nopshinga. A moon ago she rubbed Binesikwe until Nangisi's daughter Kukamigokwe emerged from under the bird-decorated skirt. Thrice a mother and still virgin, Maní seems reconciled to her lonesome chastity and to Nangisi's crosswearing bride, to whom she gladly gives refuge from my hostility.

Wedasi beams after my pains end, but neither my son nor I beam back. I see my child's eyes asking: What mask has my father carved for me? The mask of a scavenger, or a beaver-killer, or a manhunter, or a beaded bird with a long beard? Do you expect me to regenerate the world better than my mother or father have?

At my son's naming, there's joy everywhere except in me. What am I turning into? The dancers avoid me. None dare name my son. They see the rage in my eyes. I, Yahatase, the happiest of the longhouse singers and seedkeepers, have changed my skin again. Ever since Wedasi saved the lives of the Longbeards, I've been the bitterest person on the island. I think only of Nangisi, who is in Boweting again with his load of scavenged furs. I'm afraid he'll grow a beard on my son and turn him into a scavenger. I show my fear by shunning his birdwoman and by cursing her moon-old Kukamigokwe. I seem unable to remove my rattling skin even long enough to smile to a child.

Yet Binesikwe is the one who dares offer a name to my son. She whispers: Chebansi, duckling, the name as meek as the voice that offers it.

I snap: Nadowe, fierce serpent. I try to drown out the meek whisper. I accept what I'm affirming: blood feud, endless war, sacrifice if necessary to renew this poisoned ground.

But the old women hear Chebansi and resume the dance. I wonder if my son is better named than his warrior father, than I, than his aunt, the mother of God. I wonder if he'll be Chebansi, a bird like his namer, but awkward, too heavy for his feet, flying only reluctantly, preferring to sit on water's surface letting waves raise and lower him. But the duckling's father already expects the child to soar like an eagle.

Wedasi helps clear fields, he repairs lodges, and he leaves on lonesome journeys to prepare a gift that will help his son see what the father couldn't see in his grandmother's gift.

He journeys upriver and down, he goes north and south along Mishigami's coast seeking storytellers, scrollkeepers, medicine women, rememberers. He returns with neatly tied scrolls and with disintegrating bark fragments. He spreads the fragments before him, his eyes filled with hope and anticipation. He compares the fragments with others gathered on earlier journeys, and before long his eyes have the same tortured expression they had when he told of his inability to understand his grandmother's scrolls. He arranges and rearranges the fragments, he gazes at the figures on them long and intently, but he sees no more than he already knows; he sees figures that describe a beginning followed by three ages and an interrupted fourth, when events took place which are no longer possible. But he doesn't see the sequel, the strangers from the sea, the plagues, the scavengers. The only sequel he sees is that the scrolls describing the four ages are disintegrating into fragments.

Gathering up and storing the fragments, he then unties and examines the complete scrolls, but cursorily, without patience or interest, as if he'd rather not see them, as if he wanted to destroy them. These scrolls show what's lacking on the fragments. They show the path of disease from the seashell coast to the sunset, but they're not continuous with the earlier, disintegrating scrolls. They don't show a fourth or any other age. There's a breach. The two sets of scrolls seem to be made by beings as different from each other as beavers from people, and like beavers and people, they're no longer able to speak to each other.

I try to share Wedasi's interest and his anguish, but on the day when Nangisi returns from Boweting speaking of fierce Serpents infesting the northern Woodlands, the sound of drumming returns to my ears and I lose all patience with the scrolls.

While Wedasi has been trying to reconstitute birch fragments, our village of adopted kin has been disintegrating. While he's been seeking the memory of life, our living and seemingly healthy tree with strong branches and growing leaves has been sending its roots ever deeper into sand.

Nangisi and his carriers are the center of the gathering by the square lodge that was once the village's shunned fringe. They speak of eastern Wolfpacks who slipped past the Boweting cataract and now slink hungrily toward Shequamegon. All the village crosswearers and all the short-memoried, headed by Maní and Binesikwe, beg the rifle-armed carriers and beaver-killers to turn into manhunters and protect us from the Wolfpacks.

Wedasi's brother Wiske beams with pride, eager to fill hollow reeds with his wind, eager to embroil Neshnabek in war against the monster Digowin.

Binesikwe

Enraged that memories can be so short, enraged that our center is so easily dislodged, I shout that Wolfpacks and fierce Serpents are the names Blackrobes give my kin, Maní's kin, our eastern cousins, the longhouse people of the long-leafed tree.

But my voice is drowned by the noise of the excited youths around Nangisi and by the wails of the crosswearers.

I run toward my clearing by the shore, blind to where I'm stepping. I stumble; my head crashes against a tree.

I find myself sitting in a shallow pond with an island in its center; a tiny longhouse stands on the island. A little figure waves to me from the longhouse entrance; I recognize the figure as my son of two springs, Chebansi. The pond empties, the longhouse turns into a beaverlodge and the figure at the entrance is a beaver I've seen before. He waves to me, but sadly, as if he were pleading, begging for something. Suddenly there's movement all around me. Rifle-armed men run toward the lodge, poke their sticks in and shoot into it. The beaver leaps from his lodge into the dry pond. Shots ring out from every direction.

Wedasi kneels beside me on the ground of my clearing. He places leaves on my bleeding head. He carries me back to the village and calls for a council. He has me tell my dream. An old longhouse man, one of the people who returned from the Sunset Mountains, says he'll go scouting to the north to determine if the Wolfpacks are indeed our kin. I insist on going with the old man, even though I'm carrying my second child and my head bleeds.

Wedasi, knowing he can't dissuade me, decides to accompany me. When Maní learns of the scouting party, she too insists on going. She says she knows that the people she loves most are going to their death, and she doesn't want them to die unredeemed.

The four of us leave Greenbay as quickly as the canoe will take us, paddle up the river that traverses the northern land, run across the carrying places, and turn eastward when we reach the Kichigami shore. A hunter tells us where to find not one, but two bands of walking easterners, one pursuing the other.

We bank our canoe, but just as we turn to begin our search, we find ourselves surrounded by rifle-armed youths who wear crosses. The youths lead us to the center of their camp, face to face with several grandfathers and two Blackrobes.

Maní's necklace and her endless crossings and mumbling save us from harm. The Blackrobes and their converts are delighted to learn we're from Greenbay. They've already met Nangisi whom they take, no doubt from his own claim, for a crosswearing refugee from a Morningland longhouse.

I look around the camp until I spot a one-armed warrior who wears no cross. I approach him and ask if he's afraid to talk to a group of pagans. He tells me he recently threw his cross into the lake to be rid of its weight. I take Wedasi and the old man to the warrior and ask if the Blackrobes and their converts have long ears. He assures us they're too occupied looking for Serpents to pay any more attention to us.

After hearing why we've come, the one-armed warrior tells us: We, as well as our pursuers, were once a large village of Robe-led plague survivors in central Morningland. We frequently raided the longhouse people of the sunrise because the Robes convinced us the eastern Serpents intended to destroy us. The Serpents captured one of our raiding parties; we formed new parties and went on raiding. This spring many of the captured raiders returned with gifts, told us they'd been adopted by the easterners, and urged us to kill the Robes who lied to us. They told us disease was ravaging the eastern villages, and they were determined to end our fratricidal raids. Most of our people accepted the easterners' gifts, but a hundred of us slipped past our encirclers with the Robes and fled in search of crosswearing longhouse kin who, the Robes assured us, were very numerous in the land of the Sunset Lakes. More than five hundred of our kin set out after us, so that we grew dizzy from constantly looking ahead while looking behind. Our pursuers could easily have captured us, but disease reduced them at the very outset, allowing us to increase our distance from them. We fled past the cataract. Our kin were still after us, but our scouts saw that they had been reduced to two hundred and were still declining. The Robes spoke of the disease as a stroke of heaven and said it was reaping an abundant harvest for eternity. Many of us began to have doubts about eternity. But at this point the Robes made contact with your kinsman Nangisi, who promised to send a war party against our pursuers. We saw that our new allies were neither numerous nor longhouse kin. And then disease broke out among us. Some of us, deceived once or twice too often, are ready to send a peace party to our pursuers. What keeps us from doing this is the knowledge that the Robes would not hesitate to urge your kinsman Nangisi to attack our pursuers while we sit with them counciling for peace.

Wedasi and the old man, yellow as autumn leaves from the tale, assure the one-armed warrior we will not pause until we cut off Nangisi's war party.

I grab Maní, and the four of us rush unobstructed to our canoe. There's no time for Maní to nurse the ill or pray for the dying; there's no time for the old man to build a sweat lodge in which we can purify ourselves; there's no time to sleep. As soon as we reach the canoe, I slip to its bottom from exhaustion.

I see my beaver standing at his lodge entrance vomiting black sand. Rifle-armed warriors rush past me, shoot, pull off the skin, and then eat the diseased flesh of the beaver who once showed me a field where laughing children ran among stalks of yellow corn caressed by sun and wind.

Wedasi helps me from the canoe to the longhouse. He cries when I tell him my dream, but he doesn't have me tell the others. It's too late. The old woman and Binesikwe tried to restrain Nangisi's warriors. But the warriors painted themselves and they danced and they would not let Nangisi wait for the return of our scouting party.

My child grows heavy inside me and I'm exhausted all the time, but after my long sleep in the canoe, I'm unable to either sleep or wake. I hear a constant drumming.

One day the earth shakes, trees fall on each other and slide into the bay; a mound of stones flattens, a stream changes course and flows to the opposite shore of the island, and a burning star flies across the sky.

The day after the shaking earth, the warriors return from their victory over the monster. They and their Shequamegon allies killed two hundred fierce Serpents. They must have ambushed Serpents who were sitting at a peace council with crosswearing kin, but Nangisi's warriors are as proud of their deed as dogs who defeated a rabbit, their tails high in the air.

I wander into their midst and aim Wedasi's arrowhead at Nangisi as if it were a spear. I expect to see his mouth bloody and foul from devouring the flesh of my kin. I want to shout: Who is the Digowin we need protection from if not this boaster?

But my shout gags in my throat when I see one of the manhunters fall to the ground, his face contorted with pain, his skin covered with blisters. I reel and vomit at the sight and feel myself sinking to the ground. Thoughts writhe inside my head like copulating snakes.

Suddenly the whole world becomes silent. I fall through a hole and I keep falling and falling, but the abyss has no bottom, there's no earth, the great turtle is dead, she was exhausted by too many corpses from too many plagues.

I keep falling during an interminable night of aching and vomiting longer than the night after the plague that emptied my first longhouse.

When at last I stop falling, I find myself in a miniature lodge next to a miniature child. Surely she's Shutaha, the girl-child who lodged the woman who fell from the sky, Shutaha the plague's child, Shutaha the new beginning. I sing to Shutaha of the destruction of the old that precedes the birth of the new. I remember one who said: Ankwe, keep singing your songs, life is unlivable without them.

I crawl off my mat to see the sky, but a carrion bird tries to stop me, a bird with a cross dangling from its neck, a bird whose claw raised a spoon to my mouth while I fell. I push my hand into the bird's beak and crawl out of the tiny lodge. I wade through mud and I look. There's no longhouse, no village, no island. The world ended. The beautiful field the beaver gave me perished with him.

This must be the other shore, the one that survived. It must be resting on another turtle, one who survived. And those staring faces—they must be the people who survived. They're building lodges, small ones, there's no need for longhouses.

I recognize two of the survivors, the brothers, the bad twin who hides from me and the good twin with the anguished eyes who runs toward me to raise me out of the mud. I sing to him of Shutaha the new beginning.

His tears sing to me of all those who died. They didn't vomit sandy blood, as in my dream; no, their lives oozed out through blisters.

The man from Tiosa Rondion returns me to the side of my daughter in the miniature lodge.

The peaceful man's arrowhead hangs from my neck again, as it did before. He didn't put it back; she did, the carrion bird with dangling cross who spoons potions toward my mouth.

I knock the spoon out of the bird's claw and sing to her of the people I once lodged on an island. I sing to her of longhouse people who had been to the Sunset Mountains and Peninsula people who had been in a Beautiful Valley, all of whom I had invited to my island. I sing of an old woman who longed to go to the sunrise, whom I pulled to the sunset so that she could die nursing my sister. I sing of my blistered Maní who went with me to the shore of Kichigami because she thought I would die, my kind, dead sister who couldn't see well because a cross blocked her view. I hear the bird sob faintly, but the sound of drumming drowns the sob and I return to night.

The ground is hard when I leave the miniature lodge on my feet. I reject the bird's claw and find support on the shoulder of a young woman who only yesterday was a child, the Peninsula people's daughter Chacapwe, who guides her little brother Nopshinga with one hand and my Shutaha with the other.

Who are the others, the staring ones whose eyes turn to the ground when mine seek them? They're survivors from elsewhere. I learn that Wedasi invited them to stay. So he's still gathering fragments, the man with the anguished eyes, Chacapwe's only surviving Peninsula uncle. The lodge to which she guides me is small and round, but the place is beautiful and the lodge will withstand earth's shaking. I must remember to sing of this lodge to uncle Wedasi.

I'm able to walk unsupported among the roundlodges of the small village on the bay's shore. I can even reach the small field and give earth a seed.

Chacapwe comes to tell me her dream. The others have already heard and spoken, but she wants me, her aunt Yahatase, to hear her dream and sing to her. She dreamt of a beaverlodge. I sing to her of a place on the other side of the world where there are still beaverlodges, a place I dreamt of called Tiosa Rondion.

My son Chebansi comes to me. He wants to show me his game. He's awkward, big for his age. Looking into his eyes, I sing to him of a moose, and I remove the arrowhead from my neck and place it on his. He has a trickster's eyes. He guides me to the shade of a tall, broad tree and bids me sit by his wide-eyed sister Shutaha and her life-enamored cousin Miogwewe.

Chebansi runs off to hide behind a square lodge whose occupant is away. Girls gather twigs and place them in three mounds, around which they form a circle; I recognize the village. Boys emerge from behind the square lodge doing paddling motions with sticks, some carrying stones; I recognize the gift caravan. In the center of the caravan Chebansi impersonates his uncle with uncanny accuracy, waving the stick above his head and shouting victoriously.

The shout deafens me and the sound of drumming returns to my ears. I crawl toward him intending to shriek: May all you reap destroy you! But I see that he's not the other, he's not bearded, he's the duckling, my son.

My vision blurs. A girl lights the fires. She glances toward me with hatred; she's Wiske's firstborn, Kukamigokwe. I feel something pulling me back. It's Shutaha hanging on to my skirt. I crawl toward a boy carrying gifts, grab the stones from his hands and hurl them with all my strength at the square lodge.

Suddenly the sun burns itself out and it's night, yet I still hear the crackling fires, I hear the boys dancing, Chebansi at their head. I hear Kukamigokwe carrying screaming Shutaha into the third fire. I feel a claw on my arm trying to raise me off the ground. I fight the bird with all my strength.

Two hands pull me by the hair. A voice shrieks: Crazy, ungrateful Serpent witch, you're hurting my mother! If only the plague had devoured you!

The raspy, cutting, hate-filled voice of the bird's firstborn Kukamigokwe pierces my head.

I vomit and my head clears. I sit up. The sun hasn't burnt itself out. The mounds of sticks are not lit. My daughter is not on fire. She sobs near my feet and buries her face in my brightly colored bird-patterned skirt. Binesikwe's younger daughter Miogwewe strokes Shutaha's hair with one hand and her mother's with the other.

Binesikwe lies next to me, trembling and sobbing. No cross dangles from her neck. I raise her hand to my lips to tell her I know it's not a claw, to tell her I heard her during my interminable night, to tell her I know she tried to propitiate my rage with the two most precious gifts she could bring me. I know she abandoned Nangisi's square lodge and came to mine to replace my blistered sister, I know she gave me her joy-spreading second-born to replace my wandering son, I know she buried her cross when she saw it made me vomit, I know she's not a carrion bird but a clawless, soft, helpless little woman who loves me with no good reason.

I try to shed the skin of the ungrateful serpent. I try not to hear the drumming. I see that flowers bud and bloom, new shoots spring from the ground, rivers flow. I try not to see beyond. I try to keep myself from singing the longhouse songs, the songs no women in the village remember. I give earth seeds of life-sustaining corn and see the stalks come up straight and strong without a planting festival.

I try to smile to the woman who gave up her lodge, husband, daughter and cross for me, but my mouth only stretches to the side and gives me the twisted grin of a false-face. Binesikwe smiles to me with tears in her eyes; maybe she knows I'm trying.

My son is away on a journey. I try not to think of the poison that weakens him. I try to forget the scavenger I saw moving among corpses picking off cloaks and pendants.

I look into my daughter's wide eyes and see that she'll grow straight and strong. I see her eyes penetrate through mine to my gnarled thoughts seeking whatever strengthens and completes; she loves the moon and the straight tree, the serpent and the phallus; she loves whatever nourishes life.

In her cousin Miogwewe's scheming eyes I see a power that will plot and intrigue to keep life's circle from breaking. I try not to think how small that circle has become.

But the noises that make me reel and vomit don't all come from inside my head. A piercing shout reaches our cornfield. It's Kukamigokwe's intrusive, mocking, cutting voice announcing the arrival of the gift caravan. The women and children run toward it. I walk toward the village slowly; Binesikwe stays behind with me.

When we arrive, the carriers are already unloading their gifts. The mock three fires are being prepared. Wedasi and Binesikwe urge me to rest in my lodge or return to the field, but I insist on seeing the carriers' doings; I feel myself strong enough. I already know that Nangisi's parody of his grandmother's ceremony is the only center of this village on the world's fringe, and I don't expect to learn anything worse.

Nangisi stands at the center of the fires and boasts of the unprecedented size of the caravan and length of the journey. Thirty canoes bypassed Boweting and made their way to Hochelaga on the Northern River, the newest gatheringplace of Longbeards and Blackrobes and fur carriers who don't know of Hochelaga as an ancient place of longhouses and fields.

Nangisi smirks as he lays out pots and axes, knives and cloth. I wonder if the same smirk was on the faces of the Blackrobes who brought the Word and its companion to my first village.

Now the youths, my Chebansi and Chacapwe's brother Nopshinga foremost among them, begin to reenact the voyage so as to immortalize it in their and our memories.

The chanting boys emulate the swoosh of thirty paddles pushing on one side, then thirty on the other, their bodies rocking like trees bending and straightening in the wind. Their snakelike procession winds across the councilground as they sing of gliding past the cataract toward the Bay of Rolling Sands, over rivers and carryingplaces, to their distant destination.

The moment the boys pretend to disembark and walk up the embankment, Chebansi and others, with masks and coverings, arrange themselves into the squares and circles that constitute Hochelaga. Their poses, motions and coverings remind me of the Stadacona where Maní and I spent the years of our childhood. The censitaires on road-building corvée are more ragged than I remember them, the cloth- and frill-clad habitants more ostentatious, the uniformed soldiers more aggressive, but the black-hooded figures are exactly as I remember them, hovering on the outer edge like birds of prey over carrion.

At the very center, Chebansi in a plumed hat with cords and ribbons dangling from his brilliant uniform and surrounded by his court of similarly clad boys, impersonates le chef of Hochelaga, the Seigneur, the mind and will of the Longbeards.

Now Nopshinga, impersonating Nangisi, leads the carriers toward le chef, and the rifle-armed uniformed men stiffen, ready to kill at le chef's command. The censitaires drop the axes with which they were scarring the forest, the smirking habitants leave off caressing the furs brought by the carriers, and I imagine the habitants' women greedily peering through the slightly opened doors of their post and clay lodges.

Le chef raises his arm and the whole crowd of Longbeards move in response, as if they were his limbs.

Chebansi winks to me. His gesture reminds me of a beaver I saw in a dream. He wants me to watch attentively. He wants me to know he's not what I think him. I feel my face smile for the first time in many seasons. I realize he's mocking what he's impersonating.

Chebansi as le chef accepts Nopshinga's belt and hastily puffs the offered pipe while the carriers deposit the furs at le chef's feet. Twisting his face into a mask of greed which makes all of us laugh, Chebansi tells Nopshinga and the carriers: Le roi cannot give you all the gifts you ask for, because le roi already has too many furs.

Pausing to adjust his smirk, Chebansi then says: Is this all you brought? This is not enough. Le roi needs twice, thrice as many pelts. Tell your hunters they must cease hunting for food, they must hunt only for l'état and for our sun, le roi. They must devote themselves entirely to his growth, they must not be distracted by animals, lazy kinsmen or dreams, they must learn to subdue all obstacles that turn them from this supreme goal.

Chebansi prepared all this for me! He has heard not only his uncle's and my sister's songs, but also Wedasi's and mine! As the villagers rearrange themselves around the fires for Nangisi's gift-giving ceremony, storm clouds move across the sky.

I run toward my son to tell him of my delight from his beautiful gift. But before I reach him, I hear several shrieks and see a circle that is not part of the ceremony. Running towards it, I see Binesikwe raising up a man covered by ugly lumps.

Binesikwe shouts to Wedasi to take me and the children to the forest; then she shouts to Nangisi, who rushes away with Kukamigokwe and Miogwewe. I help her support and half-carry the dying man to the lodge furthest from the councilground. When we return we find another, and we remove him. But then we see yet another.

The people gathered around the fires disperse in every direction, toward lodges, toward the field, toward the water. Only those unable to move remain in the circles.

Chebansi and Shutaha run toward me. Binesikwe and I scream to them to stop. We turn and run toward the lodge with the diseased men. When I look out, I see Wedasi pulling my children slowly away from this village he raised on the fringe of the world.

When they're gone, I seek in the darkness of the lodge and see that the woman in the brightly colored bird-patterned skirt is no longer able to raise me up from mud. Her lips move. Putting my ear to them I hear she's singing longhouse songs. She must have learned them from me during my long night of aching and vomiting. She left her lodge and buried her cross so as to sing alongside me. And she must have sung my songs to Chebansi, she whom I suspected of filling my son with Maní's and Nangisi's wind.

I take her in my arms and sing with her. My speaking voice returns to me: I don't fear you or hate you, Binesikwe, I trust you.

Surely she knows now. She looks just like my sister, all blister and ooze. I leave her for a while. The storm has turned our village into a mud pond. Everyone is gone except the corpses. My feet slip on the muddy ground. There's no one left to raise me up. Earth is shedding tears. She's crying from pain. She's being violated and tortured. I have no seeds to give her, but one. I give myself. I slide into the mud, letting her who pushed me up swallow me: Thunderspear, split my skull, not the strongbranched tree! Muddy earth, swallow me, not life!

My hand shakes when I remove the beautiful but blistered mask that still oozes after I set it on the ground.

Chapter 3.

Miogwewe

Kukamigokwe

    I find myself alone by the strait's edge. I expect someone to come with a mask and a gift. No one comes. By the light of early dawn I make out a pendant hanging from a low branch. Reaching for the pendant, I make out the outline of a mask by the tree's base. It's the mask of an ancient woman with long white hair. I put on the mask.
    Suddenly I recognize the pendant. It's the greenstone pendant Shutaha left hanging from a low branch, the pendant she made for me to replace uncle Wedasi's gift to me. She knew how I loved my first pendant. Uncle Wedasi gave it to me soon after Chebansi returned from his first journey to Boweting with my father. He wanted to tell his mother about the journey, but she

didn't let him. She wanted to show him she loved him. She removed the arrowhead that hung from her neck and gave it to Chebansi. Then Chebansi enacted the journey for her. Aunt Yahatase thought her son had been to the end of the world, had fallen off, and had come back up twisted. She was sad beyond bearing. She tried to make the world open up. She wanted Chebansi to go back down and then come up the right way. Chebansi couldn't see what she wanted.

My mother dried aunt Yahatase's tears. She took me to aunt Yahatase's lodge to replace Chebansi. Uncle Wedasi sang to me of the Beginning. And then he gave me the greenstone pendant, his mother's gift to him. He made me Shutaha's sister.

Uncle Wedasi tried to help Chebansi see. He built a fasting lodge. Nopshinga and Chebansi went to it together. But Chebansi let hunger be his guide. He speared fish and roasted them while telling stories.

Chebansi's stories excused him in everyone's eyes but his mother's. He was full of stories whenever he returned from Boweting. He told us there was a man in Boweting whose member was so long it raced across a pond to impregnate a woman. Shutaha said she wanted to see such a member. I shuddered. Nopshinga told us that the man's member had chased a chipmunk into a tree hollow and gotten chewed up.

Chebansi was very funny when he returned with the thirty canoes from Hochelaga, the spring when uncle Wedasi was building Shutaha and me a fasting lodge. Kukamigokwe announced the arrival of the canoes. Shutaha and I were dropping fish into my mother's cornhills while aunt Yahatase sang. We left our two mothers and ran to the shore. Chebansi prepared his impersonations. He made my father and the Hochelaga men look like the man he'd described.

But our laughter was cut short. Suddenly my father was yanking Kukamigokwe and me toward an unfamiliar clearing. Chacapwe was already there, keeping the little children from wandering back to the village. The others came later. They had burned the lodges and father's gifts and uncle Wedasi's scrolls. They had buried the bones and raised a mound over them. I would never again be with my mother or aunt Yahatase.

Uncle Wedasi brought only his otterskin bundle and his bow. He said the green bay had not been good to us. He walked toward the canoes. Shutaha and Chebansi, Chacapwe and Nopshinga went with him.

Kukamigokwe held on to my arm. She had wished the plague would devour aunt Yahatase. She had hated aunt Yahatase more than she had loved our mother. She thanked the plague. Kukamigokwe always sought the most powerful ally. She told me Mishigami would swallow uncle Wedasi and all who went with him.

I concentrated on the tree behind her and begged it to drop a branch on her. She became afraid and let go of my arm. Filled with gratitude, I hung the greenstone pendant on the tree's branch.

I ran to shore. The canoes were almost beyond my voice's reach.

I trembled when Shutaha pulled me in. I didn't look back into the bay. I knew Chacapwe and Nopshinga were in the canoe behind ours. Chebansi shed tears. He had wanted to please his mother. But she had turned from him and gone to die with my mother.

Uncle Wedasi dried Chebansi's tears by asking him to name the islands and shore points. Chebansi brightened as he talked. He told us of the northern land and the cataract he'd visited. He pointed to the Isle of Beavers, the Bay of Sturgeons, and the abandoned village by the leaning tree on the hand-shaped Peninsula. He pointed to Mishilimakina on the tips of the long fingers when we passed through the Northern Straits, the meetingplace of three great lakes.

Uncle Wedasi caught whitefish with a net and said we were moving toward the center of the world. I thought we had moved from the world's center toward its eastern edge and were about to fall off. But there was another world beyond the straits. There was an island full of white trees, and a bay called Sagi between the thumb and forefinger, and then another strait.

At last we reached uncle Wedasi's place, Tiosa Rondion, the place that linked the lakes and bays with the Northern River and the Ocean, the place that linked Kichigami's forests with the Beautiful River's valleys. Deer, bears and swans along both shores seemed to be urging us to end our journey and stay by their strait.

Chacapwe, Shutaha and I ran from groves of fruit trees to vines heavy with grapes. We ran across a meadow to the edge of a beaverpond and saw four lodges surrounded by oak trees. Beyond the oaks we saw bubbling fountains and the sand hills of an old burial ground. Chacapwe had dreamt of such a place.

Aunt Yahatase had named the place of her dream Tiosa Rondion. The people of the place came out of their lodges to greet us. They prepared sweat lodges, danced with us, fed us. They were people who had survived the great plague. They lit the three fires for us. They hadn't lit them since the death and exile of the others. But they wouldn't join uncle Wedasi in the dance enacting the expulsion of Wiske.

A stocky man named Raccoon, Ahsepona, said Wiske was the founder of the village on the Strait. Wiske, shaped like a split tree by a roundish rock, had watched over his village. But a spring ago, two Blackrobes came through the Strait. The villagers hid in the forest. The Blackrobes made ugly noises, smashed the roundish rock and cut down the tree. The man of the Strait said the Blackrobes had broken the link between earth and sky.

Chacapwe said a new tree would grow, as the sun rises after night, as birds return after the snows melt.

Uncle Wedasi said we would move on. He didn't want to stay where Blackrobes had been.

All but one of us returned to the canoes. As we pushed off the Strait's shore, I and those in Nopshinga's canoe looked back at the four-lodge village called Tiosa Rondion. Chacapwe stood proudly on shore alongside the stocky man named Raccoon.

Uncle Wedasi was sad when he left his birthplace. But he wanted us to grow far from Blackrobes.

We glided through the Strait's mouth into the lake of the vanished Ehryes. We were rounding the hand. We turned into a river along the wrist. On its banks we saw forest-reclaimed remains of Kekionga's fields and villages.

We found people at the carryingplace near the river's source. They were kin of Nopshinga's and Chacapwe's mother. They had recently come back to Kekionga from western prairies.

We danced and feasted with the Prairiekin. But we didn't stay in Kekionga. We carried our canoes to the river that flowed further westward along the wrist.

While we glided past forests and flowers and tall grass, Shutaha shaped a greenstone given to her by the people of the Strait. I made out the outline of the pendant I had hung on the tree in Greenbay.

Suddenly uncle Wedasi paddled more quickly. There was impatience, even joy, in his eyes.

I saw a moose looking toward us from an opening on the northern shore.
This is the place, Shutaha said, as if she recognized the exact spot uncle Wedasi was seeking. Across from where we landed, bison grazed at the very edge of the river.
Chebansi and I ran behind Shutaha gathering multicolored fruit and picking ripe grapes from heavy trees and vines waiting for us to accept their offerings. We paused at terraces where vanished villagers had once planted corn and beans and squash.
This was the Bison Prairie where people from four directions had once danced around three fires.
Uncle Wedasi saw a spot on which four lodges could rise between earth and sky. The men left to hunt.
When they returned, uncle Wedasi prepared us for the founding ceremony. He re-lit the long-extinguished fires. Wearing a moose's head, he did the dance of the Firekeepers. I wore a bear's head, Nopshinga bison horns, and Shutaha a turtle's shell. Chebansi as a hare tried to put the fires out. Chebansi was a funny hare—fat, awkward and slow. Shutaha and I beat sticks on the ground. The hare tried to flee from our sticks but nearly tripped into one of the fires. He knew how to impersonate tricksters. But he couldn't be one.
After the expulsion, uncle Wedasi took a bark fragment from his bundle. He drew the outlines of four lodges on the ground. He told us our great-grandmothers had gone through the four lodges. In the first, the mother had swallowed her children. In the second, the remaining children swallowed their mother. In the third, the children became embroiled in fratricidal feuds and swallowed each other. In the fourth, they expelled the embroiler and made peace.
We raised our four lodges. Soon Prairiekin from southern valleys raised lodges alongside ours. Other Firekeepers from Greenbay joined us. Rootkin came from the northern forests.
Shutaha learned the secrets of women who shaped bowls. I watched women who stretched the skins of muskrat and deer on drying frames. When we joined planters in the fields, Shutaha and I sang her mother's songs.
Uncle Wedasi built us a fasting lodge. The bear came to my dream. Shutaha fasted but didn't dream. She said her dream would come when she needed it.
Chebansi grew restless and lean. In Greenbay he'd floated between his father Wedasi and his uncle Nangisi, imperson-

ating one to the other. In Bison Prairie he had to stand on his own spot and be himself. But he couldn't stand, he could only float.

Nopshinga found a band of hunters heading northward. The two youths floated to the mouth of our river with the hunters. They returned from Mishigami's north with a canoe caravan. My father Nangisi and my sister Kukamigokwe came to Bison Prairie with them. Five winters had passed since my father and uncle had separated.

My father told us the gathering of peoples at Greenbay had dispersed after our departure. The disease that killed my mother and aunt Yahatase had attacked all the people of the bay. Most of the bay's Riverpeople had fled to the Plains west of the Long River. Rootkin had fled to Kichigami's forests. Firekeepers had returned to the Peninsula. Turtlefolk had gone to Mishilimakina on the tip of the hand. An Invader had come from the Northern River to set up a fur post in Greenbay. Falsetongue is the name Nopshinga gave this Invader.

Kukamigokwe boasted that this Falsetongue considered our father the center of the bay's Peninsulakin. Shutaha reminded Kukamigokwe that we had just learned there were no Peninsulakin left in Greenbay. Kukamigokwe glared at Shutaha with the same hatred with which she had looked at aunt Yahatase.

I was not sad when my father and sister returned to their Falsetongue and his fur post.

But Chebansi soon followed them. Chebansi was floating again. He and Nopshinga had learned how to cross Mishigami. As soon as the snows melted, they left Bison Prairie.

When they returned, Chebansi was fat with stories. They had accompanied my father and Falsetongue to Boweting. They had seen a great procession. Chebansi reenacted it for us. Falsetongue in a blue cloak and four Blackrobes with crosses and plaques led the procession. They were followed by bearded boatmen with colorful sashes and hundreds of chanting Turtlefolk.

Chebansi, impersonating blue-clad Falsetongue, pretended to reach a summit, where he planted a plaque. Nopshinga, in a black robe, placed a large cross beside the plaque. Then Chebansi sang in the Invaders' tongue. He harangued the skies. He linked the Invaders' Sun with the lakes, rivers, forests and animals of Kichigami.

Nopshinga told us Falsetongue's harangue was followed by a thunderburst of firesticks discharged into the sky.

After hearing Chebansi's translation of the harangue, uncle Wedasi told us a story. He told of a man who ate a scab. This meal gave the man a great hunger. He ate all the food in his lodge. Then he went to other lodges and ate all the food. When he had eaten all the food in his village, he sought the food of neighboring villages. Uncle Wedasi said the Invaders were like the Scabeater. They had insatiable appetites. After having eaten all the food on their side of the salt sea, they had come to eat all there was on our side.

Uncle Wedasi no longer withdrew the bark fragment from his bundle. He said he was learning to see without it. When he scratched on the ground, he drew only a line and a point, the wrist and Bison Prairie. He did not draw the Oceanshore or the eastern Woodlands or the Northern River. He did not draw the paths followed by my father and Chebansi and Nopshinga. And he no longer hunted. He was going blind.

Uncle Wedasi wanted our village to be far from the Scabeaters. But his brother and his son brought them close.

Chebansi and Nopshinga came to tell us that my father had brought distant Rootkin and numerous Scabeaters to our river. My sister had taken one of these Rootkin, a man named Winámek to her lodge. We were invited to take part in the celebration.

As we floated toward the Rivermouth, Chebansi told us we would meet a Scabeater who had built a great boat. This boat had been pushed from the Easternmost Lake to Greenbay by wind. Chebansi was overawed.

But Nopshinga warned us that this Boatmaker was also a weaver of nets. He was an embroiler even craftier than Falsetongue. Boatmaker was an enemy of Falsetongue and the Blackrobes. He travelled with barefooted Greyrobes. He had turned Nangisi's head with gifts, praise and poisoned water. My father and his carriers had put all their furs into the great boat. The furs had been gathered for Falsetongue, who would be very surprised when he returned to Greenbay. Boatmaker had sent the boat and all the furs to his allies in Hochelaga. But he had stayed. Scabeater that he was, he wanted more. My sister had told Boatmaker the center of the Peninsula's Firekeepers was not in Greenbay but in Bison Prairie.

Kukamigokwe wanted to trap fish of her own with Boatmaker's net. She had brought him to the Rivermouth to help him enlarge his net. She wanted to put our father and her new man at the real center of the Peninsula's Firekeepers.

Shutaha and I laughed at Nopshinga's warning. I knew my sister wanted the moon in her lodge, but she hadn't the strength to hold on to me. Shutaha said she'd always wanted to see the man with the long member. Now she could see two such men at the Rivermouth.

We saw bearded men pushing logs over rolling logs. They were building a palisaded enclosure on the hilltop that overlooked the Rivermouth and the lake. We saw firesticks everywhere, as well as a large device which, Nopshinga told us, could hurl thunderstones to a great distance.

When we reached the council fires, we saw that the linking ceremony was a pretext for another ceremony. My father and sister sat between a short bearded man with quick, suspicious eyes and a fat, flabby beardless man. Shutaha's curiosity must have vanished. If these men had long members, they did not carry them between their legs. Their members came in the form of firesticks, of pointed logs surrounding the hilltop enclosure, of devices that discharged thunderstones.

The two strangers offered uncle Wedasi a calumet and welcomed us as if we were the guests, they the hosts.

Boatmaker wore a bloodred coat trimmed with yellowstone. He didn't listen. He harangued. Chebansi translated, mimicking the red and yellow man's gestures so accurately it seemed two Boatmakers were haranguing us. Boatmaker had come to protect us from our enemies the eastern Serpents, as he referred to aunt Yahatase's kin.

It seemed to us that Boatmaker had raised his picketed enclosure to protect himself from nearer enemies. He seemed to fear blind uncle Wedasi. Kukamigokwe must have neglected to tell him Firekeepers were peaceful. Perhaps he expected Falsetongue and his Blackrobes to come after the furs he had taken from them.

Boatmaker told us he would leave armed men in the enclosure to protect us during his quest. He was seeking the mouth of the Long River. He spoke of it as something he had lost. I wondered if he intended to take it back east with him if he found it.

Kukamigokwe beamed when the big man from the east rose to harangue us. Winámek spoke a quaint Rootspeech none of us had ever heard, the tongue of ancient Oceanshore Rootkin.

Uncle Wedasi asked the easterner if his first kin had reached the seashell coast by way of the northern forests at the time of their arrival in Kichigami, or by way of the river valleys at the time of Wiske's war and the great dispersal. Winámek knew nothing of the arrival or the dispersal. The earliest Rootperson he knew of was his great-grandfather, who perished of the plague soon after great whales swam to earth from where the sun rises in the salt sea. The flab in Winámek's limbs was not in his voice. His strength was in his tongue. His story entranced us.

He told us Invaders occupied villages made desolate by the plague. They ate all they found in abandoned fields and storage places. After filling themselves with what the plague granted them, the Invaders starved. They knew nothing of cornplanting or tree-tapping, and they feared to enter the forest even though armed with firesticks. Winámek's grandfather took them meat and taught them planting and tapping. They grew stronger. The yearly births of their women and the frequent boats from the sunrise increased their numbers. They gave the grandfather a metal knife for their lives and a hatchet for his teachings. This absolved them of love and gratitude.

Winámek told us they did not regard anyone as kin, even each other. Their world contained only enemies.

They offered Winámek's father a pot for his cloak. Playing with their firesticks, they gave him some beads and a few hatchets and demanded the ground his village stood on. Winámek's father did not feel compassionate toward them. He sharpened his arrows.

The face behind the gifts revealed itself. Armed gangs of Invaders arrived in the dark of night. They set fire to the entire village. They burned warriors together with their grandmothers and children. Villagers who fled the flames were killed by firesticks. Winámek and another boy escaped both fires unharmed.

Winámek found refuge on the Eastern River, among Rootkin who had survived similar massacres. Threatened from downriver by the Oceanshore Invaders and from upriver by Serpents, Winámek's name for Turtlefolk, the Eastern River Rootkin learned to sleep with their weapons. But to no avail. The Invaders and the Serpents ganged up with each other against the Rootkin. The Invaders gave Serpent warriors trophies for the scalps of dead Rootkin. They broke the spirits of those they captured and used them as dogs.

The Invaders despised the lame and respected the strong, Winámek said. They respected the Serpents. The Serpents knew how to gang up with each other. They treated all others as enemies. They also knew when to gang up with their enemies' enemies. Winámek's next refuge was Hochelaga, which he found full of his enemies' enemies. In Boatmaker, Winámek found a Scabeater who was eager to gang up against the common enemy. Winámek said the Oceanshore Invaders were numerous but cowardly. The eastern Serpents were brave but few. The Rootkin of the Great Lakes were as brave as the Serpents and as numerous as coastal sands. He spoke of a league of western Rootkin.

Uncle Wedasi rose and said suffering was an affliction to be pitied, not kindling with which to feed fires of hatred. He said Winámek knew people only as hunters and prey. Then he turned his back on Boatmaker and my father and sister. Shutaha and I guided him to the canoes and returned to our village.

Uncle Wedasi told us a fox lay on his back doing antics until ducks waddled up the bank to watch him. Then the fox kept still, moving his tail ever so slightly. When the silly ducks pecked his tail, he sprang on them.

We were to have listened to Winámek's sufferings until our tears moved us to stroke his back. Then he'd spring on us. His league would no longer be confined to my father's carriers camped outside Boatmaker's enclosure. It would embrace the Firekeepers of Bison Prairie and the Rootkin and Prairiekin who counciled with us. We would all become Wiske's nephews. Our minds would empty when he dreamt. Our tongues would become paralyzed when he spoke. Our bodies would go prone when his member went prowling. Our warriors would perpetrate the monstrosities of the Oceanshore Invaders. The monstrosities would be heroic feats when perpetrated by Winámek's league.

Kukamigokwe neglected to tell her fox that we weren't ducks.

We didn't only walk out of Winámek's circle. We warned our kin of the trap. Nopshinga carried the word from the Strait to the Beautiful and Long River's valleys. Winámek's league remained confined to the three fires lit by my father at the foot of the hill with the enclosure.

Kukamigokwe and her big man did not give up their hunt. On my father's bidding, Chebansi came to invite us to the naming ceremony for Winámek's and my sister's son. Chebansi also told us Winámek expected me to find a place in my sister's lodge. Chebansi mimicked the big man mouthing this request as something modest, almost trivial. Chebansi laughed with us. Shutaha told her brother to urge Winámek to protect us from the armed Scabeaters in the enclosure. They were the only Serpents we would see in the western Lakes. They had already helped themselves to four canoes we had not given them.

Kukamigokwe grew desperate. Unable to enlarge her net by embracing uncle Wedasi, she decided to isolate him. She joined a medicine lodge. Uncle Wedasi had told us about his grandmother's medicine lodge. Its people had used medicine to restore the powers of the afflicted. The people in Kukamigokwe's lodge used medicine to enhance the powers of the healers. They were mainly carriers and they concentrated on poisonous powers. She and her lodge spread the word that there were Serpents in Bison Prairie. She didn't identify the Serpents yet. She had a scheme. She wasn't surprised by my refusal to join her in big Winámek's lodge. She knew I was close to Nopshinga. She spoke to my father of this closeness.

Chebansi came to tell me that Nopshinga had consulted my father about taking me as his companion.

I knew Nopshinga was far, and I knew he would have spoken to me first, so I knew it was Kukamogokwe who had consulted my father. Chebansi should have known this too.

Kukamigokwe expected me to leave uncle Wedasi and Shutaha and move to Nopshinga's lodge. Then she and Winámek would make themselves at home among Nopshinga's kin. Nangisi would be the father and Kukamigokwe the sister of Firekeepers from Tiosa Rondion to Bison Prairie and of Prairiekin from the wrist to the valleys. And then my sister and her medicine people would identify the Serpents in our midst. They would point to the husband and daughter of the Serpent witch Yahatase.

I knew how to frustrate her scheme. I remembered that uncle Wedasi had not enlarged his brother's lodge when he had taken aunt Yahatase for his companion.

I told cousin Chebansi I looked forward to the linking.

He paddled and waddled to my father with the message. That settled it. The event could no more be stopped than a river's flow. My father and sister amassed gifts. Prairiekin prepared masks and dances. They sent runners to invite cousins from every direction. Poor Nopshinga was the last to learn of his coming linking. He was near the Long River hunting bison when word of it reached him.

On the night of the event, I trembled as I hadn't done since the day I'd left Greenbay. I hoped Shutaha had found the occasion to tell Nopshinga my intentions. I wondered if he remembered uncle Wedasi's linking ceremony.

Kukamigokwe rocked her cradleboard and beamed. She expected me to leave the Serpent lodge and rush to her big man's great league. She thought my reasons would be the same as hers. She was as narrow as a knife's cutting edge.

My father beamed too. Playful Nangisi was looking forward to the new kin who would dance around his three fires. His betrayal of Falsetongue had reduced the number of his followers more than the plague had. His son by marriage, big Winámek, puffed and grinned as he watched a chipmunk run into the hollow of a tree.

Nopshinga left the corner of his Prairiekin and walked toward me with his gift. Both of us faced my father and sister and their big man. I took Nopshinga's gift. Then Nopshinga turned—away from my sister, away from his Prairiekin, toward uncle Wedasi's lodge. As I turned, I saw the smile on my father's face freeze like a mask's. He had seen all this before.

Shutaha patted Nopshinga, took the meat from me and, unable to contain herself, burst out laughing. Soon everyone was laughing except Nangisi, Kukamigokwe and Winámek.

Through the lodge opening I saw my sister rush away with her cradleboard, her face livid with rage. I told myself that even the sharpest knife could cut only something softer than itself. I saw Winámek strut after her toward the canoes. His face was pale, his finger pointed eastward, the direction from which Serpents were to come. I thought that if he sent his shortened member into yet another tree hollow, the little that remained would get chewed up.

Nopshinga hadn't needed Shutaha's instructions. He had no desire to strengthen either Winámek or Boatmaker the Scabeater. Neither he nor Chebansi trusted Winámek. Boatmaker was hated even by his own bearded followers. Instead of enlarging Winámek's ailing tree, Nopshinga and I had girdled it. Before long the tree fell.

Chebansi told us the enclosure's armed men were demented from drinking poisoned water. They were celebrating Boatmaker's death. They were no longer obliged to keep each other inside the enclosure. Boatmaker had found the mouth of the Long River. There one of his kinsmen had murdered him.

Shutaha accompanied her brother to the Rivermouth. She wanted to see demented Scabeaters. She also wanted to see what remained of the great league of western Rootkin. She hoped Kukamigokwe would see her examining the remains. With Boatmaker gone, even my father and his carriers would turn their backs on Winámek. Kukamigokwe and her big man would shine only for their infant son.

Shutaha returned with the young Scabeater who had taken our canoes.

Shutaha

Shutaha said the enclosure overlooking the Rivermouth was a mound of rubble. The armed Scabeaters had lost their fear and destroyed it. They had gone to seek adoption among those they had looked over.

The young Scabeater Shutaha brought to our lodge named himself Pyerwá. Shutaha told me she'd found him attractive after she'd drunk poisoned water. But when the poison wore off, the beard and the hair-covered body repelled her.

Soon the hair was all that remained of Pyerwá's former coverings. When he was out of food for his firestick, he watched Nopshinga fashion arrowheads. He watched blind Wedasi weave a basket by feel. He watched me dress an animal skin. He watched Shutaha shape a bowl. She gave it to him. It broke the first time he used it. He said he preferred metal pots; they didn't break. We asked him to make us a metal pot. He didn't know how to begin.

Shutaha was pleased with our strange kinsman. She said even her mother would have been pleased. Yahatase would have seen that Kukamigokwe and Winámek had beards on their hearts, whereas Pyerwá's heart was as hairless as ours. He was an unformed shoot who'd been stunted by growing in poisoned ground. Among us he would blossom.

Shutaha and I sang of repopulated villages filled with transplanted shoots guided by their own dreams.

The child inside me was eager to stretch out near my dream village, on the green prairie beside the blue water.

Chebansi had gone with my father to seek Falsetongue, with gifts of propitiation. Chebansi returned agitated and afraid. He said Falsetongue had refused to accept my father's gifts. Falsetongue no longer needed my father or his carriers. He had formed his own bands. He had turned Prairiekin of the Long River into scavengers and pillagers. Falsetongue and his Blackrobes had gone to villages in the valleys of the Wabash. They had told the villagers stories of monsters and man-eaters. These were stories Falsetongue had learned from my father. They referred to the age when Turtlefolk and Riverpeople had called each other man-eaters. But when Falsetongue told the stories, he referred to the Serpents he hated, the eastern Turtlefolk. His listeners heard him confirm barely-remembered fears. And when Falsetongue saw them afraid, he offered to protect them from the Serpents. He gave away hatchets and firesticks while he gathered furs and followers. He led bands of pillagers toward the sunset across the Long River. The pillagers attacked the ancient Turtlefolk who live in earthlodges in the Plains. They captured Earthlodge people and took them to Hochelaga as if they were furs. The Hochelaga Scabeaters broke the Earthlodge people's spirits, called them Panis, separated kin from kin. They made each other human gifts. But they considered the captives and not themselves man-eaters.

The Earthlodge people began to dream of a remedy, and Falsetongue began to fear them. The Earthlodge people learned of this remedy from people who lived in stonelodges yet further toward the sunset. The Stonelodge people had been similarly treated by Invaders who had come from the south. They had listened to a healer's dream. All the men, women and children of all the Stonelodges had armed themselves with arrows, spears and stones. They had attacked the Blackrobes' idol-lodges. They had chased every Invader from every corner of their land.

Falsetongue feared that the Earthlodge people were dreaming of a similar remedy. He feared that Rootkin would learn of the Stonelodge medicine. He feared that he and all other Scabeaters would be driven to the other side of the salt sea. Falsetongue sought to protect himself by turning all resentment of Scabeaters into hatred of Serpents. His pillagers ambushed a band of eastern Turtlefolk. The Turtlefolk responded by sending a scouting party westward.

When uncle Wedasi learned of this scouting party, he resolved to do what he had done once before, what Firekeepers had always done. If Turtlefolk were camped on the Peninsula, uncle Wedasi would go to their camp and greet them as a kinsman with a gift of love and a calumet of peace. Shutaha reached the same resolve as quickly as her father. We counciled with the other villagers. No one in Bison Prairie wanted to be embroiled in a war against Falsetongue's enemies.

We learned that the eastern scouts were not camped on the Peninsula but west of it, halfway between the Lakebottom and the Long River. We got as far as a village of Redearth Rootkin on the carrying place at the Lakebottom. Chebansi would go no further. Like his aunt Maní, he feared that the easterners would kill his father and sister. I, too, could go no further because I began to feel birth pains. Nopshinga stayed with me, as did Pyerwá, who feared the easterners would not know what to make of his beard.

My newborn daughter was absorbing the warmth of the spring sun when Shutaha, her father, and the accompanying Redearth kin returned to the Lakebottom. Shutaha spoke to me of a beautiful hunter as tall as a pine and strong as a bear with whom she had shared peace and love. He had whittled a stick and Shutaha had gathered the pieces. He had told her he would return to Bison Prairie after his scouting mission.

The Lakebottom village filled with Firekeepers from the Peninsula, Prairiekin from the valleys, Redearth kin from Mishigami's sunset shore. All danced with complete abandon celebrating the revival of a fire that had not been lit since almost forgotten days. Uncle Wedasi showed the peace belt and said the easterners' feud was not with us but with Scabeaters whose murderous raids had cut their tree of peace. Scabeaters had told the easterners to stay away from Rootkin of the Lakes. But the easterners were not the Scabeaters' dogs. They were free people who went where they pleased. They had come to see if the people of the Lakes let themselves be treated as dogs.

The celebrants returned to their villages when leaves began to fall. We remained on the other shore of Mishigami. We raised our winter lodge at a place blind uncle Wedasi remembered from his boyhood in Greenbay. But the peace we carried in our hearts existed nowhere else. We didn't know it had already been undone. Kukamigokwe preferred to die rather than live unrevenged for the mockery to which my linking ceremony had subjected her. When we left Bison Prairie on our peace mission, my sister learned that Falsetongue and his pillagers were desperately seeking allies. Eleven canoes of Oceanshore Invaders had broken through the Scabeaters' strongholds and reached Boweting. Numerous Rootkin and bearded renegades had smoked with the Invaders, accepted gifts and given furs. Falsetongue feared that Rootkin and renegades would unite with eastern Serpents and, armed with Invaders' firesticks, would apply the Stonelodge medicine to the Scabeaters. Kukamigokwe sent a messenger to Falsetongue. Her message was that renegade Scabeaters and Rootkin were conspiring with Serpents, and that his old ally Nangisi needed reinforcements to quash the conspiracy. While we had been celebrating, Winámek had been gathering an army of manhunters at the Lakebottom. The manhunters pursued celebrants returning to their kin, and murdered them on the outskirts of their villages. They scalped the corpses in the Serpent manner, and then entered the villages wailing that Serpents were ravaging the Peninsula. The homebound eastern scouts were followed by trees that spat fire and bushes that stabbed. If Shutaha's beautiful hunter reached the eastern Woodlands, no peace or love could have remained in his heart.

We returned to the Lakebottom village from our winter camp and found the whole world changed. We were told that Winámek's scouts had spotted a band of fierce Serpents rushing toward us to seek revenge. We knew nothing of Winámek having scouts or of Turtlefolk desiring revenge. But I knew my sister. And uncle Wedasi remembered the end of his earlier peace mission. Aunt Yahatase had dreamed of beavers exterminated by firesticks. My father and his carriers had murdered the Turtlefolk with whom the peacemakers had counciled.

Our Redearth hosts knew even less than we did. Falsetongue as well as Winámek were strangers to them. They knew Turtlefolk only from the peace council to which they had guided Shutaha and her father.

Suddenly eastern warriors arrived at the Lakebottom village and surrounded it. They entered from three directions. One of the warriors, in fluent Rootspeech, arrogantly demanded to see the false peacemaker who had lulled his brothers to sleep in order to pounce on them as they dreamt.

Pregnant Shutaha helped me guide her blind father toward the loudmouth. Uncle Wedasi extended the peacebelt he had received the previous spring from the arrogant speaker's brothers.

Powerful arms pulled me away from uncle Wedasi and threw me on the ground. I saw Nopshinga lunge forward unarmed. An instant later he was on the ground. I looked toward the spot I had reached with uncle Wedasi. The horrible deed was done.

Shutaha lay on the ground giving birth to the nephew of her father's murderer. Her wide eyes were fixed on the bleeding head of uncle Wedasi, murdered because he had sought peace.

Chebansi appeared from nowhere and lunged at his father's murderers, but he got no further than Nopshinga.

Winámek's armed band stamped through the village long after the deed was done.

Salty tears merged with the sweet milk sucked by Shutaha's son and my girlchild Mangashko during the burial at Bison Prairie.

Chebansi and Nangisi, Nopshinga and Pyerwá, Firekeepers and Prairiekin carried baskets of earth to uncle Wedasi's tomb. Everyone was at the burial except Kukamigokwe and Winámek, who were far away, counciling with Falsetongue.

Chebansi had warned us, but Chebansi had been so much in bark canoes, we'd thought he didn't recognize solid ground.

Nangisi had known of all the preparations: Falsetongue's, Winámek's and Kukamigokwe's. But he had sat at the Rivermouth, saying nothing and doing less, because he regarded Falsetongue his friend and Serpents his enemies. Yet he shed tears into the earth he carried to his brother's tomb.

Shutaha sat apart. She hadn't eaten or drunk since the deed. She had collapsed during our return from the Lakebottom. She had been starving her newborn son until I'd taken him from her. She was so thin she seemed all eyes. I feared she'd become like her mother. Her mother's kin had raided the Peninsula only once, and they had killed only her father.

Falsetongue had turned eastern Turtlefolk into what he called them: vipers, wolfpacks. Winámek acquired his league. He came to recruit warriors. He said he sought to revenge his uncle's death. Bison Prairie emptied. Firekeepers turned their backs on peace and joined him. Chebansi carried his father's otterskin bundle to war.

Chebansi painted himself and went east in order to avenge his father, Nangisi in order to regain the confidence of Falsetongue, and Winámek in order to place himself at the head of the Great Lakes army.

When the warriors returned to celebrate their victories, they brought their trophies directly to the murdered man's closest kin.

Chebansi came to tell us what Shutaha, Nopshinga and I already knew: that his father's death was a mere pretext for the raid. The raid's real purpose was to weave western Rootkin into a net with which Scabeaters could catch fish. Chebansi told us Winámek's manhunters had gone to the shore of the Clear Lake by the Strait. They had been joined by armed Scabeaters and by Falsetongue's pillagers. From this camp, Falsetongue had led plundering raids against Oceanshore Invaders heading toward Boweting for furs. Falsetongue embroiled Rootkin in feuds brought here from the other side of the world. Falsetongue's and Winámek's allied bands then went to infest the eastern Woodlands the way they said Serpents infested our woodlands. They killed men, women and children, they burned villages and fields as if life itself were their enemy. Chebansi told us he sickened of the wanton killing and plundering of his mother's kin.

Yet when my sister prepared a virtual pageant to propitiate the spirit of her dead uncle Wedasi, Chebansi helped prepare. He didn't see that the tears of the murdered man's children were a mere pretext for Kukamigokwe's pageant.

It was said that Nangisi had used his brother's death to place himself at the head of the carrier band. My sister was trying to use uncle Wedasi's death to place herself and Winámek at the center of the Peninsula's Firekeepers. She wasn't satisfied with Nangisi's three fires, which lit only the faces of his carriers. She wanted her three fires to light up all the people of the world's four corners. Her big man and his manhunters had returned with enough gifts to dry everyone's tears.

But Shutaha, still stunned from the murder, wasn't about to put plundered gifts in her father's place. And she wasn't about to thank these consolers for their kindness.

Shutaha, her eyes wide open, moved like a sleepwalker toward the mound of gifts. I knew her intentions. My father and sister must also have guessed them. Only Pyerwá tried to stop her. None else dared. She was the murdered man's daughter. She scooped up cloth, beads, blankets, hatchets and knives and carried them to one fire. She scooped up another load for the next fire. Her mother's spirit danced in the flames that leapt to the sky. The three fires brightened the four corners. Uncle Wedasi's bones could rest.

Shutaha looked defiantly at the pageant's arrangers. Her eyes accused them of the murder of her father.

I rose and proudly walked alongside Shutaha to our lodge. Nopshinga followed us. He said others—Firekeepers, Peninsula and Redearth kin—were also rising and leaving. Winámek and Kukamigokwe after the victories, as before, sat by three fires with Nangisi and his band of carriers.

Pyerwá came to the lodge with tears in his eyes. He said his people killed each other for the objects Shutaha burned.

Chebansi came last. He told us a story his father had told him after he'd returned from his fasting lodge. It was the story of one who had not resisted eating fish during his fast. Instead of seeing an animal, the fast-breaker had become one. He turned into a dog. Chebansi said he had been pulling Nangisi's travois while Nangisi had pulled Winámek's. The light from Shutaha's fires had shamed Chebansi; it had enabled him to see himself as his mother had seen him.

Winámek and Kukamigokwe were surrounded by indifference and hostility. Winámek's western army dissolved like snow in spring. We learned that a thousand eastern Turtlefolk retaliated against the westerners' raid by plundering Hochelaga, the Scabeaters' stronghold. No western warriors rushed to the Scabeaters' aid. The Scabeaters who before had urged their allies to slaughter the common enemy now made peace with the enemy without consulting the allies.

Winámek and Kukamigokwe failed to make their lodge the center of the Firekeepers. So they turned it into a center of Scabeaters. Their lodge replaced the Greenbay post. Furs from the Long River, Lakebottom and Mishigami's other shore passed through it on their way to Boweting. Two Blackrobes came from Greenbay and raised an idol lodge beside Kukamigokwe's medicine lodge. They sprinkled children with water and taught them spells. Nangisi wept shamelessly as he watched. The spells reminded him of aunt Maní. The only child who paid attention to the Blackrobes was Kukamigokwe's son Wabskeni. The other children quickly tired of the spells. The Blackrobes blamed Pyerwá for the children's indifference. They said his singing of our songs made the children hostile to theirs. Kukamigokwe blamed Shutaha. She said the Serpent entranced the children with her secret language and poisoned them. The gift-burner who had councilled with Serpents, kidnapped Nopshinga and housed a renegade Scabeater was now bewitching the children.

In her way Kukamigokwe saw further than the Blackrobes. It was true that the children around Shutaha, as well as those around me or Nopshinga, didn't feel any need for the Blackrobes' spells. They sensed themselves as branches of a living tree. They were strengthened by the songs we sang in our fields, by the stories we told while dressing pelts or shaping bowls, by the rites performed before the hunt, by the dances celebrating the return of the hunters, and by their own dreams. The Blackrobes' teaching was a wind that could carry only dead leaves. It couldn't stir a living tree.

The two Blackrobes returned to Greenbay, to children of disease who had lost their kin and their songs, to children who had no dreams.

Other Scabeaters replaced the Blackrobes. Identically clad armed men arrived. They destroyed a beautiful fruit orchard by the river's edge. They built a picketed enclosure similar to the one Boatmaker had raised at the Rivermouth. They came to protect Falsetongue from real and imagined enemies. A band of Falsetongue's pillagers had been defeated by Earthlodge people armed with firesticks. It was said that the firesticks had been brought by Redearth kin who had visited the eastern Woodlands. The Redearth kin were said to have councilled with the Earthlodge people about the Stonelodge medicine. Falsetongue feared for his post and his life. He expected the Peninsula's Firekeepers and Prairiekin to start counciling about the remedy applied by the people of the stonelodges.

Falsetongue's armed kinsmen liked Shutaha's medicine no better. The adoption of renegade Scabeaters in our village would undo the ravages of plague more surely than the

Stonelodge medicine. The armed Scabeaters seemed as hostile to this as to the remedy that turned their camps into fields of corpses. The headman of the enclosure, the one called Lekomandá by the others, sent his uniformed men out to capture renegade Scabeaters. Chebansi impersonated him as saying the renegades did nothing for him. He said they cared for nothing he esteemed, followed every inclination and avoided all correction.

To avoid being captured, Pyerwá fled from Bison Prairie. Nopshinga led him to Chacapwa's lodge in Tiosa Rondion.

Pyerwá's departure pained Shutaha. Kukamigokwe rejoiced. But even Kukamigokwe couldn't have been proud of the enclosure at Bison Prairie's edge. It was a substitute for Winámek's power. It was a reminder that despite all his raids he had failed to raise his league.

Kukamigokwe looked for power elsewhere. She gathered poisonous herbs. She filled her son with hatred toward Serpents. She was intent on bringing the war against Serpents into the heart of Bison Prairie. She began by spreading stories. Her medicine people spoke of Shutaha's mother as a demented sorceress who had tried to slaughter Nangisi. They said Yahatase had conspired to drive Firekeepers into Serpent captivity.

Nangisi said and did nothing. I was ashamed to be his daughter. Aunt Yahatase's tree and uncle Wedasi's fourth age were as strange to him as to Kukamigokwe. He only remembered that Yahatase had showed him no great love. Silent accomplice in his brother's murder, he let his daughter mutilate and spread stories he himself had told her.

Chebansi spoke to him. But Nangisi couldn't see that Kukamigokwe's stories really differed from his own, just as he couldn't see that Kukamigokwe's medicine lodge differed from his grandmother's.

Gradually stories told by Scabeaters and carriers were added. It was said that Serpents captured human beings in the western Plains and carried them to Oceanshore Invaders, who shipped the captives to Ocean islands as if they were cattle or furs. We all knew Falsetongue and his pillagers engaged in such raids. But in the mouths of my sister's allies, Shutaha's Serpents were the only raiders.

Accusing Shutaha of being a sorceress, Kukamigokwe herself turned to sorcery. One night Shutaha found a bear's claw on her mat. I resented my sister's using my dream animal so cruelly. Another night we found the mutilated body of a turtle on the floor of our lodge. Nopshinga and I and several Prairiekin spoke to Nangisi. He said we were making a great noise about children's games.

Kukamigokwe's game reached its climax when her enemies suddenly came to her aid. I was in the forest preparing a fasting lodge for my Mangashko. A band of revenge-seeking Turtlewarriors sprang from the trees and killed an unarmed Bison Prairie man. The eastern Turtlefolk strengthened their enemies and hurt their friends for the second time. Winámek set out after them, followed by manhunters, carriers and armed Scabeaters. Even Kukamigokwe's son Wabskeni painted himself, but the warriors left him behind.

After the war party left, Shutaha's eight-spring old son failed to return to our lodge. Carriers returning from the pursuit found him, scalped in the Serpent manner. His body was mutilated, not in the Serpent manner, but like the turtle we had found on our lodge floor. Children's games! Shutaha's eyes had her mother's look in them. Chebansi feared for his own and his sister's lives.

Nopshinga painted himself. When the war party returned, Prairiekin and Firekeepers confronted Winámek. Kukamigokwe and her Wabskeni were in the Scabeaters' enclosure. Winámek quickly joined them.

A council was called. Nopshinga said it was time to send a belt to Redearth kin of the other shore. Nangisi suddenly remembered his brother the peacemaker. He said he would go to Boweting to tell the Scabeaters to remove their armed men from our riverbank. Firekeepers urged him to go. They did not want more fratricide in Bison Prairie.

When Nopshinga and I returned to our lodge, I saw something hanging on a low branch of the tree by the entrance. Reaching toward the branch, I see that it's the greenstone pendant Shutaha had shaped in the canoe when we first came to Bison Prairie. It's identical to the pendant uncle Wedasi had given me when I'd been adopted into aunt Yahatase's lodge, the pendant I'd left on a branch in Greenbay.

I take the pendant, enter the lodge, and see that all other traces of Shutaha are gone.

I learn that, while we had been counciling, Shutaha and Chebansi had set out with a band of Prairiekin going to Boweting.

Bison Prairie without Shutaha is empty to me. I decide to leave Mangashko's fasting lodge to Nopshinga and to accompany my father to the Northern Straits.

It's my first long journey since my childhood, my first journey with my father, my first view of the sunset shore of the Peninsula. I complete the circle when we reach the Beaver Island halfway between Greenbay and the Northern Straits. We stop at the palisaded village on the Peninsula's northernmost point, Mishilimakina. Turtlefolk I had known in Greenbay greet us as Yahatase's kin. They caress us, feast us, make much of us. I had thought they were all crosswearers, but not all are. We learn that Chebansi and Shutaha are among our hosts.

As soon as we're alone with Chebansi, my father tells of his mission and asks if Chebansi knows Falsetongue's whereabouts.

Chebansi says Falsetongue is with the Blackrobes at Boweting by the northern cataract. He tells us the Scabeaters are divided, and have been since Boatmaker's time, as we had guessed. Their headman in Mishilimakina is a man called Lekomandá, like the headman in Bison Prairie's enclosure. He dislikes Blackrobes, surrounds himself with barefooted Greyrobes, and cares only to amass furs, which he accomplishes by making fur carriers foolish with poisoned water. The Blackrobes, Falsetongue's allies, are lodged in Boweting. Their aim is to amass furs as well as souls. They want to prohibit the flow of poisoned water because it makes souls unreceptive to their spells. The two parties war against each other by having messengers race each other to the Scabeaters' central lodge in Stadacona.

Nangisi prevails on Chebansi to accompany him to Boweting in search of Falsetongue.

My hosts lead me to Shutaha. She's ill. She seems demented. She has drunk the poisoned water. She barely recognizes me. She talks as if she were in a dream. She tells me she died when her son died. She says those who killed her son have bearded hearts. They love power and hate life. They want to bloat themselves by eating the world instead of fulfilling themselves by flowing out into the world.

She dreamt her own body was mutilated. She felt great pain. The pain stopped when she left her body. Shutaha wandered northward and on the way she met her mother. Yahatase told her she had been with the great Turtle. The Turtle was the world's support and the monster who ate the world. The two were one. The Turtle was all of life.

Shutaha went to her mother's kin in Mishilimakina and everything she saw confirmed what Yahatase said. Excrement was nourishment. Shutaha's death was her birth. The Scabeaters' poison was medicine. Shutaha sat among crosswearing Turtlefolk and uniformed Scabeaters and saw crosses and uniforms fall away like dead leaves.

She says the poisoned water helps people leave their mutilated bodies. Women and men as averse to carnal passion as her aunt Mani abandon themselves to orgies, dance with the phallus and flow out toward the moon.

Shutaha says the poisoned water brings dreams to those who never dreamt. She dreamt new songs and new rituals. She says she no longer needs her mother's medicine. She can replace her son without blood feud, endless war or sacrifice. She's Wedasi's daughter too. She's replacing her son with uncles, cousins and sons from among the Scabeaters. She already knows that Pyerwá did not have a bearded heart, like Kukamigokwe. He could shed his skin as easily as Yahatase. And once he shed his old skin, all he needed to grow and become a Turtle was our songs and the warmth of our lodge. She says the Scabeaters' water loosens the bad ground that keeps stunted shoots from growing. Once they're loose, all the shoots need is healthy ground, and the marks made by plague and Blackrobes fall away like scabs. She says she'll make Turtles of Scabeaters, right next to the largest Blackrobe mission on the Lakes, under Lekomandá's very nose, and with his own medicine.

Shutaha is not as empty without me as I am without her. I accompany a caravan of Rootkin and return to Bison Prairie.

Nopshinga tells me Winámek and his son haven't once dared leave the Scabeaters' enclosure. Our Mangashko tells me a turtle came to her dream. I tell her she couldn't have a better guide. I hang Shutaha's pendant around her neck.

When the ice thaws, Chebansi arrives in Bison Prairie with a young woman. He tells us that my father, the world-changer, brought havoc to his Blackrobed allies on the Northern Straits. Chebansi and Nangisi found Falsetongue in Boweting. They went with him and twelve canoes of Blackrobes and Scabeaters to Stadacona. My wily father hadn't gone to put an end to what Kukamigokwe started, but to complete it. In the Scabeaters' central lodge, Falsetongue composed a scroll with Nangisi's words. The scroll said women of the Lakes were using poisoned water to destroy young Scabeaters. It said our women enticed drunken Scabeaters into their lodges and turned them into renegades from the Scabeaters' ways. Falsetongue sent this scroll to the Scabeaters' Sun across the Ocean. Many moons later the Sun's response arrived in Stadacona. The Sun's scroll said Scabeaters were to stop hunting in the western Lakes. All fur posts and enclosures were to close. Only Blackrobes were to remain. That way there would be no Scabeaters in the Lakes for our women to entice. Nangisi and Falsetongue bit their lips. They composed another scroll to undo the effects of the first. Now they said the people of the Lakes could not live without the Scabeaters because they had forgotten how to hunt with bows and arrows, how to cook with bark and earthen pots. Falsetongue himself took this scroll across the salt sea. Nangisi waited for his ally's return, but Chebansi knew Falsetongue wouldn't return.

In Stadacona Chebansi had learned that the Scabeaters' Sun didn't only want to stop his young men from drinking with our women. He also wanted them to stop sending furs across the Ocean. The Sun's lodge was full of furs and he had no room for more. Chebansi tells us the Scabeaters gather furs for power, not for warmth. Just as Blackrobes get power from plague and not wellbeing, big Scabeaters get power from dearth and not plenty. The fewer the pelts, the greater the powers of the pelt holders. The Sun was burning the pelts he already had. Falsetongue was a great pelt holder. He would leave his ally Nangisi waiting for a long time.

Chebansi accompanied a Greyrobe rushing to Mishilimakina with the news. There he found Nopshinga's sister Chacapwe inviting Shutaha to Tiosa Rondion to celebrate the linking of her daughter with our Pyerwá.

On hearing Chebansi's news, not only Shutaha but all other Turtlefolk and most Scabeaters accepted Chacapwe's invitation and abandoned the Blackrobes of the Northern Straits.

Chacapwe

Chebansi doesn't want to be in Bison Prairie when my father brings Winámek the news from Stadacona. Nopshinga and I don't either, and we all look forward to being with Shutaha and Chacapwe and Pyerwá. Many of Bison Prairie's Firekeepers leave with us. We follow the deertrail used by ancient Peninsulakin to reach Tiosa Rondion and Sagi Bay.

The young woman Chebansi calls Sagikwe points excitedly to the sacred places along the way. My Nopshinga has walked the trail several times but knows nothing of the landmarks. Yet Sagikwe, who has never been here, recognizes trees, meadows, lakes. She heard her grandfather sing of them. She was born near the Sagi Bay to Rootkin who returned to the Peninsula several springs after we did. She had her first glimpse of Scabeaters and pillagers during her eleventh spring. She and her kin hid in the forest, and then fled, from the armed men gathered by Falsetongue and Winámek to pillage canoe caravans and raid eastern Turtlefolk. Sagikwe speaks of the armed men, especially the identically-clad, obedient Scabeaters, as an army of ants. She and her kin fled to rejoin Rootkin at the northern cataract, unaware that Boweting was a center of Scabeaters. She gathered herbs and tree sugars, remade the world in her quillwork, and sang at yearly fish feasts. From Rootkin she learned of the diseases brought by the Invaders.

Sagikwe wears uncle Wedasi's arrowhead around her neck. Something like aunt Yahatase's fire burns in her eyes. But unlike Chebansi's mother, Sagikwe thinks of Wiske as her ally. She says Wiske taught our Neshnabek ancestors to catch herring, sturgeon and whitefish. He made the first net by copying a spider's web. He'll show us how to catch the ant-men.

As we near the Strait, I too recognize sacred places, the ones so frequently described by uncle Wedasi, the meadows, rivulets and fountains, the vines and fruit trees Shutaha and I ran among.

We arrive in Tiosa Rondion during a great council and a naming.

Chacapwe and her Ahsepona, the Raccoon, remove our weariness by sweating with us and caressing us. Thirty springs have passed since Chacapwe stayed on the Strait when the rest of us went on.

She beams with barely disguised pride. The village of mounds and beaverdams is once again the center of the world. Turtlefolk, Firekeepers and Prairiekin council with Northern River Invaders. A new village of four peoples, the village of uncle Wedasi's songs, rises out of the council fire. Chacapwe's lodge is the navel of the village. Her newly-named granddaughter is its beginning. Chacapwe proudly displays her beautiful daughter Ubankiko, who welcomed our bearded Pyerwá to her lodge. Pyerwá names their newborn girlchild Maní, after Shutaha's cross-wearing aunt who helped birth Nopshinga.

There's one who doesn't celebrate the renewal of Tiosa Rondion. He's Ahsepona, the stocky, solitary grandfather who in his youth saw Blackrobes destroy the sacred tree and rock that had stood at water's edge. He had not welcomed Pyerwá when Nopshinga brought him. Ahsepona had accepted him as Ubankiko's companion only after hearing Pyerwá chant the songs Shutaha and I taught him.

The lone hunter keeps apart from those counciling with the Scabeaters.

Shutaha urges me to hear the counciling orators. Her enthusiasm is more guarded than Chacapwe's. But she doesn't share Ahsepona's forebodings. The Scabeaters are not yet Turtles, but Shutaha is convinced they can be.

A hundred of them abandoned the Blackrobes of the Northern Straits. The Blackrobes were celebrating their Sun's closure of the Lakes to all Scabeaters but themselves. They were left to celebrate by themselves. The others accompanied Shutaha's Turtlefolk to Tiosa Rondion.

Their spokesman, called Lekomandá Kadyak, is beardless. He's flanked by two barefooted Greyrobes who pour and drink poisoned water as freely as he.

Shutaha says Lekomandá's generosity with the liquid poison shows his weakness, not his strength. The villagers depend on him for little else. He depends on them for everything else. Shutaha and the planting Turtlewomen supply all his corn, beans and squashes. Neshnabek hunters provide his furs. Chacapwe, Ahsepona and the Tiosa Rondion hosts give him space on which to raise his lodge.

At the council, which is an adoption ceremony, the Scabeaters bind themselves in kinship with the people of the Strait. The pledges of the new cousins are on belts to be kept in a lodge of

Turtlefolk. Shutaha thinks the Scabeaters will, in time, sing our songs as easily as Pyerwá. And when they do, a long-leafed tree will extend its branches in four directions. Her father's fourth age will resume.

But Nopshinga raises doubts in my mind. To him, Lekomandá Kadyak is a weaver of nets, like Boatmaker and Falsetongue. Nopshinga urges me to listen carefully to Chebansi's translation of Lekomandá's acceptance speech.

The headman's words flow with gratitude, but there's a cataract along the stream's course. He speaks as if he were the host and we the guests. He assures the gathering that his Sun will shelter and protect all the kin of the Strait.

Nopshinga thinks Lekomandá Kadyak understands the bond and the belts as Winámek would understand them. Boatmaker's heir is another long-membered trickster founding another league.

Chebansi translates the Scabeater's words as if they were his own. But I can see he shares Nopshinga's fears. Since childhood, Chebansi has expressed his fears by mirroring, by impersonating those he fears.

When Sagikwe gives birth to a son, the second child of the Strait, Chebansi decides to do more than to mirror. He asks Shutaha and me to help him prepare for his son's naming ceremony. He wants us to arrange the expulsion ceremony his father failed to complete in Tiosa Rondion thirty winters earlier. I ask him to show me the reminder, the sole survivor from the fourth age, the scroll fragment in his bundle.

Everyone takes part except Sagikwe and Ahsepona.

Chacapwe and Ubankiko, the hosts who light the three fires, wear beavermasks. Mangashko as a deer and I as a bear are Rootkin. Nopshinga and other Prairiekin are Riverpeople. Shutaha and the Turtlefolk complete the circle, which forms the outline of a hand. Pyerwá is the hare who disrupts the fires until we chase him. Chebansi stands on the fringes and interprets the ceremony for curious Scabeaters.

Sagikwe names her son Ozagi. She returns to her lodge, hostile to our expulsion of the hare.

Ahsepona, the oldest of the hosts, observes the ceremony from the forest edge, as hostile as Sagikwe.

During the expulsion of Wiske, Nangisi and a band of carriers arrive from Bison Prairie. And then a disturbance puts an abrupt end to the ceremony.

Vigorously pursuing the hare, Mangashko runs into the forest. Several young Scabeaters, demented by poisoned water, surround her. They maltreat Mangashko even though she wears ceremonial garments. Ahsepona reaches the spot, an arrow poised in his bow. The Scabeaters run, but not before removing Shutaha's pendant from Mangashko's neck.

The deed confirms Ahsepona's hostility toward the destroyers and desecrators of Wiske's tree and rock.

When Shutaha and I arrive, Sagikwe is inflaming my daughter against the ant-men in Tiosa Rondion. Sagikwe, and now Mangashko, are hostile to the very presence of the strangers on the Peninsula. Sagikwe reminds me ever more of Yahatase. She's ready for war, blood feud, even sacrifice.

Ahsepona and other hunters bring out war paint and prepare an altogether different ceremony.

Chebansi and Pyerwá rush to the Scabeaters' camp to seek satisfaction for the ugly deed.

Nangisi sarcastically tells Shutaha that she leapt from the jaws of the fox Winámek into the jaws of a wolf. Shutaha tells my father her life is safer beyond the reach of his protection from either fox or wolf. But Nangisi isn't offering protection. He's trying to undo the unintended consequences of his plea to the Scabeaters' Sun. He's himself ready to leap into a wolf's jaws, if that will help him. Falsetongue has not returned. All Scabeaters have abandoned Bison Prairie. Winámek has no allies other than the Blackrobes in Boweting. Kukamigokwe gave away all her pots, ornaments and dresses, out of fear. Nangisi's carriers have been taking their furs to Oceanshore Invaders. Nangisi knows that the Strait's Lekomandá has been hoarding furs, waiting for the day when the Hochelaga fur gang becomes eager for them. Nangisi is here, not to insert himself in Chacapwe's village, but to make Lekomandá the heir of Falsetongue as well as Boatmaker.

Chebansi does not offer himself as mediator. He doesn't forget his father and his nephew. He doesn't forget that Nangisi could have stirred against the murderers, but kept still.

Chebansi no longer needs Nangisi. His first joy is his son Ozagi. His second is to run between Mangashko's defenders and attackers, impersonating each to the other. He's peacemaker Wedasi to the enraged defenders. He's furious Yahatase to the attackers.

Lekomandá Kadyak punishes the attackers by having them enclosed in a box, a man-sized bird cage.

Shutaha wants to transplant the quarrel. She pushes Chebansi and Pyerwá to beg for the attackers' release. The songs of Ahsepona's angry and armed kinsmen strengthen her plea.

The Scabeaters' beardless headman refuses to release Mangashko's attackers. He says he's the only one on the Strait with the power to punish them.

Shutaha gives Chebansi another message for Lekomandá Kadyak. Chebansi tells the headman that Turtlefolk will grow corn only for themselves and Rootkin will take their furs elsewhere. Shutaha is no longer as helpless as when she lay on the ground giving birth while her father was murdered. Lekomandá Kadyak has Mangashko's attackers released from the cage.

Shutaha wants the attackers to be punished by Mangashko, not by an outsider to the quarrel. Pyerwá advises the attackers to go to Mangashko with gifts.

The young strangers, no longer demented by the liquid poison, seem almost rational. They return the pendant and offer many other gifts. Through Pyerwá, they offer Mangashko whatever else she wants, even their lives. Mangashko laughs. She would like all Invaders to return to the Ocean, but she wants nothing more from these three.

Attackers as well as defenders drink liquid poison until they all become demented. The quarrel is all but forgotten. For the duration of a night, yesterday's enemies are the closest kin. Shutaha tells me the Scabeaters have long restless members. But they don't know how to use them. That's why they turn to firesticks and other devices. She thinks the liquid poison is like a medicinal herb. It can kill. But in the right combination and with the proper ceremony, it can cure. It loosens the ground and makes openings. The restless phallus can be guided into an opening. Its seed will germinate. With proper nurturing, healthy plants will grow. The monster will have been turned into a source of life.

At dawn, when the poison-brought dreams slip away with the night, Pyerwá wakes us with his explanation. He tells us the three Scabeaters were drawn, not to Mangashko, but to the pendant hanging from her neck. The firelight made the pendant glisten, and the Scabeaters thought it was not of greenstone but of yellowstone. Pyerwá says the strangers value yellowstone above their lives, they even kill each other to possess it. I

shudder. These beings who only yesterday seemed so reasonable are Scabeaters after all.
 Chacapwe thinks they're all healthy plants already. Sagikwe thinks they're all poisonous. Chacapwe beams too much, Sagikwe too little. Shutaha thinks the shoots can be transplanted. Chebansi drifts between Shutaha and Sagikwe, and I find myself drifting.
 Nopshinga says Shutaha takes crabs for sturgeon. She adopted me. She adopted Pyerwá. She thinks she can adopt a hundred Scabeaters. Nopshinga tries to see with Shutaha's wide eyes. But he sees neither the fertile ground nor the seedling that can grow into a long-leafed tree. He sees a stick without branches or roots.
 I see a gathering of fragments whose traces of the fourth age are as dim as the marks on Chebansi's piece of bark scroll. The newly-lit three fires of Tiosa Rondion don't light up the four peoples of Wedasi's songs. The places of Rootkin are taken by Nangisi's carriers. Most Turtlefolk are crosswearers from Mishilimakina. There are no Riverpeople. The only real host stays away from the fires. And the strangers watering the tree with poisoned water don't seem intent on making it grow, but on drowning it.
 Nopshinga longs for the Tiosa Rondion of the songs. But he thinks Shutaha's dream village was killed when Invaders and their diseases reached the Oceanshore. The real Tiosa Rondion is not in the sky but on a Strait where land and water paths intersect.
 Nopshinga helps arrange ceremonies, sings loudly and dances with vigor. But his attention is on the Redearth kin who carry furs from the other shore of Mishigami to the Oceanshore Invaders. The journeys of the Redearth kin make Nangisi's carriers restless. Nopshinga understands this restlessness. As a youth he had shared it.
 One of the carriers, a man known as Kendawa, the Eagle of Bison Prairie, at last breaks loose. He and several companions join a caravan of Redearth kin who take their furs wherever they please.
 Kendawa and his band return to the mouth of the Strait laden with gifts from Lekomandá's Oceanshore enemies. They are detained by an armed band of Lekomandá's uniformed Scabeaters. The Scabeaters give Kendawa a few more furs than he started with, and take all the enemy gifts. Then Lekoman-

dá's men bring the eastern blankets, cloth, powder, firesticks and poisoned water to Tiosa Rondion. Lekomandá Kadyak barters his loot for several times the furs his men gave Kendawa. The carriers become enraged at what they call Lekomandá's betrayal of his allies. Nangisi and Kendawa rush to Bison Prairie to council with Winámek and Kukamigokwe. Nopshinga helps me imagine what happens next. Kukamigokwe rants and rages about the den of Serpents camped at the gate to the western Lakes. Several members lengthen, harden, and become anxious to strike. Winámek's league comes back to life. The big man goes to the Northern Straits to council with Blackrobes, with the remains of Falsetongue's pillagers, and with his murderous son Wabskeni. Kendawa and his band join another eastbound caravan to seek new powder and firesticks. Nangisi, the peacemaker's brother, stays in Bison Prairie, lights three fires, and waits for the outcome. Kukamigokwe, no peacemaker, summons the powers of her medicine lodge to help her son finish the task she began. Winámek lets his member be carried from Mishilimakina to the Strait by Wabskeni and his pillagers.

Kendawa and his band are already camped at the Isle of Turkeys when they're joined by the pillagers from Mishilimakina.

The mutilator of the body of Shutaha's son leads the raid on Tiosa Rondion. The attackers burn Lekomandá's lodge. They burn the lodge of the Greyrobes as well as the lodge that holds their cross and idols. And then the raiders wait to be joined. It seems that Nangisi's appraisal had led them to expect Peninsulakin and even Turtlefolk to rise against Lekomandá.

Turtle and Prairie youth do paint themselves, but they stand alongside Nopshinga, Chebansi and Pyerwá against the raiders. Ahsepona and other Peninsulakin arm themselves, but not in order to place Winámek on a spot vacated by Lekomandá.

Kendawa and several other carriers fall ill.

Wabskeni, finding himself with a shrunken member, as isolated as the Blackrobes of Mishilimakina, rushes back to the Northern Straits.

Kendawa and other carriers break out in blisters. The smallpox is in Tiosa Rondion.

I see the disease that killed Yahatase and my mother in Greenbay thirty-five springs ago. I didn't see the blisters then; Nangisi pulled my sister and me away from the dying. Yahatase thought the Invaders placed the disease into the canoes of our gift carriers so as to empty the world of original people and to break the spirits of survivors. Those with broken spirits turn to Blackrobes for protection from a disease more powerful than our medicines. Smallpox makes people crosswearers. The plague that killed my mother and aunt must have been among the gifts Nangisi and Chebansi were given in Hochelaga. The blisters torturing Kendawa must have been given to him by the Oceanshore Invaders on the Eastern River.

Sagikwe tries to battle the disease. She recruits Mangashko and Chebansi to the task.

Shutaha urges me to help remove the healthy to the Morningland shore of the Strait. Her eyes have her mother's urgency in them. She wanted a poison that regenerated the Turtle, not one that killed her. She embraced a phallus that generated life, not one that ripped up the living.

Shutaha takes Sagikwe's son Ozagi across. Ahsepona and Chacapwe take their daughter Ubankiko and their granddaughter Mani.

Mangashko begs Nopshinga and me to help Sagikwe and Chebansi heal the ailing Eagle of Bison Prairie.

Nopshinga and Chebansi forget that Kendawa was yesterday's raider and remember him as the companion of their youth. They sweat with him. Chebansi invites a healer from among the Scabeaters. Nopshinga urges Rootkin to raise a shaking tent.

I urge Mangashko and Sagikwe to help me arrange an enactment of the four ages of our ancestors. We dance as I sing of the time of the monster, of the children, of Wiske, of the three fires of Tiosa Rondion. I sing of the time before Invaders or their diseases reached the Oceanshore.

Kendawa's blisters become scabbed. He grows stronger.

Sagikwe rejoices. She thinks Kendawa and Wabskeni raided Tiosa Rondion in response to her wishes. She regretted the failure of the raid. She didn't want the long member to get chewed up in the hollow of a tree. She thinks Wiske is life itself, the great progenitor; his member is not to be guided to a hole in the ground, but to be raised high above the ground.

Kendawa grows stronger. But the father of Sagikwe's son breaks out in blisters. Chebansi doesn't die the way Yahatase had foreseen. She had seen him as a beaver shot by scavengers.

Before dying, Chebansi gives his father's otterskin bag to Sagikwe. He wants his son Ozagi to carry it.

Uncle Wedasi's kin had fled to save their children from the first plague in Tiosa Rondion. His son returned to succumb to the second.

My Nopshinga had often guided Chebansi. Now he follows his friend on their last journey. Weak and disfigured, he tells Mangashko and me to be wary of adopting Invaders, to take only their children into our lodges. He says all the others have blisters on their spirits. They bring our death. Even Pyerwá. Mangashko pours tears over her dead father. She joins Sagikwe in chanting that health is a world without Invaders.

Those of Kendawa's followers who could still walk in Tiosa Rondion accompanied Wabskeni to Mishilimakina. Many of them were prone before they reached the Northern Straits. Wabskeni accompanied his father to Bison Prairie. By the time they reached Kukamigokwe, their pillagers were blistered. My sister was one of the many who died of smallpox in Bison Prairie.

The news brings no joy to Shutaha. My sister's hatred had not planted hatred in the heart of Wedasi's daughter.

But the news weighs little now. Shutaha bites her lips to keep from crying for the brother who stayed so close to her during his last years. She bites her lips for Nopshinga and for all the dead among the Turtlefolk and Peninsulakin. Even some Scabeaters succumbed. Shutaha's eyes are joyless, her face mourns, until the day when numerous canoes arrive from Hochelaga.

Over a hundred Scabeaters, with horses and cattle and iron instruments, disembark in Tiosa Rondion, apparently determined to stay.

There's a glimmer in Shutaha's eyes. I remember the day in Mishilimakina when she told me she would replace her dead son with several from among the Scabeaters. But her enthusiasm is guarded.

Chacapwe, who also lost a brother, expresses her enthusiasm openly. She's ready to adopt bearded as well as beardless scavengers with all their beads and pots. Her daughter Ubankiko welcomes the beads and pots above all else.

Chacapwe is convinced we're strong enough to adopt them all. Sagikwe is convinced we're strong enough to get rid of them all. Ahsepona keeps apart. He, like my dead Nopshinga, thinks their spirits are blistered, even our kinsman Pyerwá's.

I long for Yahatase who had lived among them, for Chebansi who had understood them, for Nopshinga who had seen through them. But I'm alone now. I have to see with my own eyes. I can't see with Shutaha's. I'm as repelled by the strangers as Sagikwe. Nangisi and Winámek sought power by giving all they had. The Invaders seem to gain power by retaining all they have. They're all hoarders. Even Pyerwá seems intent on accumulating furs, knives, shells, anything. If they give, it's only with a view to enlarging their hoard. Pyerwá tells me they even try to hoard land. They pretend that land is like a medicine bundle or a pendant or a song. Lekomandá pretends that the land on the coast of the Strait is his hoard. The others pretend to believe him. Lekomandá pretends to give each a strip of the land. The others pretend to be so grateful for this gift of earth that they bind themselves to supply him with food and fur, to chop his wood, haul his water, build his lodge, flatten his path, and raise a picketed enclosure around him. Pyerwá takes this game so seriously that he rushes to Lekomandá to beg for his strip. He fears that without Lekomandá's word, there'll be no earth on which he can raise his lodge. Pyerwá carries the game to foolish lengths. When he grinds corn by wind, he carries gifts, not to the wind, but to Lekomandá. When he drinks the milk of cows, he takes his gifts, not to the grass or clouds or sun, nor even to the cows, but to Lekomandá, who pretends that the cows are his members. Pyerwá agrees that the game is absurd. He tells me the armed scavengers in the enclosure force all others to play it. But I don't see what keeps the armed men inside the enclosure. Pyerwá says they all hate Lekomandá. They outnumber Lekomandá fifty to one. Yet they impose his wishes on each other, as if each were Lekomandá to all the others. And they stay penned in like Pyerwá's companions in the Bison Prairie enclosure before the death of Boatmaker.

My Mangashko grows ever more hostile to the Scabeaters. She sees them through Sagikwe's eyes. And she grows ever fonder of Kendawa.

But the Eagle stays away from Mangashko. He's twice her age, and he's ashamed of his disfigurement. He takes Mangashko's fondness for pity. He stays with us and brings us meat. He thinks himself responsible for our Nopshinga's death. But Kendawa's every look and move tell us he longs to return to the remaining carriers in Bison Prairie.

Sagikwe quarrels daily with Shutaha. She even resents Shutaha's love for five-spring Ozagi. She says Shutaha will grow the boy a beard. Only Chebansi's vacillating and mirroring kept the two women in the same lodge. Sagikwe decides to remove Ozagi from Shutaha's reach. She rejects Chacapwe's invitation. She looks up to Ahsepona but she's repelled by Pyerwá. She responds to the invitation by ridiculing Ubankiko for using dead beads instead of living quills to ornament moccasins. Sagikwe comes to my lodge to be near Mangashko and Kendawa. She fumes about the ant-men, as she calls the Scabeaters.

One night Sagikwe wakes us to tell us her dream. She saw all the trees of the Peninsula girdled and dying. Wherever she looked she saw picketed enclosures. Inside the enclosures, cows wearing bead-ornamented uniforms ate all the shoots, bushes and grass. Suddenly Sagikwe realized she was herself inside a picketed enclosure, one barely large enough to hold her. She woke terrified.

The day after her dream, Sagikwe resolves to remove her son from the cows and ant-men of the Strait. She urges Kendawa to return to his carriers. She begs Mangashko to accompany her to Bison Prairie.

Their decision pains me, most of all Mangashko's. All three long to be near the embroiler Winámek and his son, the mutilator Wabskeni. When I try to see with Sagikwe's eyes, I feel my waking life to be a bad dream in which I move backward. I see myself moving from an interrupted fourth age to an earlier age. A monster emerges from the Ocean and begins to swallow everything living. Wiske, the hare, is the only creature who dares confront the monster. All is so clear in that age, when none see in Wiske the monster's attributes and appetites. It's as if Neshnabek had not lived four ages, or as if we had never heard their songs.

I suspect I'll be needed in Bison Prairie when the dreamers wake. I take my leave of Chacapwe and her kin.

And I take my leave of Shutaha. Neither of us speaks. We both know that I'm choosing the easier task. Shutaha isn't merely preventing fratricide. She's trying to bring new life out of death. She wants to draw health from disease. She'd like to carry cows, ants, and scabs from the first age to the fourth. She's paddling her canoe across a strait of disease and hostility whose every wave tries to swallow her and all she carries. If Yahatase was guardedly demented, her daughter is recklessly insane. The obstacles Shutaha faces make Kukamigokwe's sorceries seem what Nangisi called them: children's games. Mangashko carries Shutaha's pendant to Bison Prairie. I wait for the day when Mangashko hears the pendant speak.

Sagikwe

Shutaha dreams of the transformation of two hundred alien Scabeaters into kindred human beings. I face only my own kin. Nangisi is, after all, my father, Winámek my sister's husband, Sagikwe my cousin's wife, Mangashko my own daughter. Yet I don't know where to begin. The game was easy when all I had to do was to avoid Kukamigokwe's traps. But she's a ghost now. When her traps were visible, I needed Chebansi's or Nopshinga's eyes to see them. Now her traps are not even visible.

I beg young Ozagi to let me see the scroll fragment in his bundle. I seek out old Firekeepers and ask to see their scrolls. I find several medicine lodge scrolls that trace the path of the Invaders' diseases from the Oceanshore to the Lakes. But I find no scroll that contains the song of Ozagi's fragment, the song of the four ages. I wander and fast to stop seeing with my own eyes, to start seeing with earth's eyes, as Yahatase saw.

Kendawa has stopped resisting Mangashko's advances. Nangisi as well as Winámek urged him to bring her a gift.

Nangisi asks me to arrange the feast celebrating their linking. I see an opening. I beg Nangisi to help with the arrangements. I ask him to remember everything he learned from his brother about the three fires and the four ages. I beg him to be Wedasi for a day, to make Bison Prairie a center of Firekeepers, of kinship, of peace. I in turn agree to sing alongside Winámek as well as the mutilator Wabskeni. I assume I've nothing to fear. Wiske's member followed too many chipmunks into hollow trees and it's all chewed up. Winámek's league is as extinct as the scrolls from the fourth age. Even the Blackrobes of Mishilimakina abandoned it. After Wabskeni's failure to disperse the village on the Strait, the Blackrobes of the Northern Straits burned the lodges of their idols and returned to Hochelaga. The only surviving fragment of the league is Wabskeni himself, in a Scabeater's uniform, and a small band of similarly-clad crosswearing pillagers who trail behind Wabskeni as he oscillates between Mishilimakina and Bison Prairie.

Nangisi does what he promised, as he understands it. He lights the three fires and peoples them with guests. He sings without feeling and retires to drink. He's as indifferent to the spirit of the ceremony as a Scabeater.

The things he learned from Wedasi are turned against Wedasi, but Nangisi goes on drinking.

Winámek is the one who steps into the opening. Foxy Winámek puts the expulsion ceremony to his own use. He substitutes a dog for the hare. Instead of Neshnabek women chasing the hare, Wabskeni and his pillagers pounce on the dog. They disembowel the animal. They eat its flesh. It doesn't take me long to realize that the dog is the monster and Wabskeni is Wiske. The dog is Kukamigokwe's monster: Serpents of the eastern Woodlands, Yahatase, Shutaha. But Winámek is silent about the monster's identity. He has his eye on my daughter and her Eagle.

Sagikwe doesn't keep silent. She identifies the monster right away as the Invader, the ant-man. She doesn't know Wabskeni as the Scabeaters' most loyal ally in the western Lakes. She knows him as Wiske, the world-saver, the intrepid enemy of the monster, the slayer of Digowin. Mangashko and Kendawa join her in eating the monster's flesh.

Kendawa, unlike my Nopshinga, leads his bride and Shutaha's pendant away from my lodge and toward the square lodge of his grandfather Nangisi, his uncle Winámek and his cousin Wabskeni.

Nangisi did what he promised. He made a whole of our fragments. But a strange, illusory whole. Kendawa wants to go where he pleases. But Winámek would have all Neshnabek go only where he pleases. Mangashko, with Sagikwe, wants all Scabeaters to leave the Peninsula. But Winámek would have Falsetongue's Scabeaters return, and Wabskeni exists to remove all others from the Peninsula.

Sagikwe is pleased. She's so much like Yahatase, yet she embraces everything Yahatase hated. Sagikwe knows I share her antipathy toward the Scabeaters. She doesn't know I share Shutaha's hopes. She and Ozagi come to my lodge to replace my Mangashko.

Winámek comes to our lodge bearing gifts. He's no longer big and awesome. The inactivity, the many winters without fasting, are making him old and fat. His gifts are intended for me. He fears Sagikwe. He knows she'll put a knife in his breast the day she discovers he's not the one she thinks him. He wants to make his net a little tighter. He would like me to replace my absent sister in his lodge. He has less to gain from my acceptance than he did the previous time he made this request, twenty-seven winters ago. Some of his thoughts must be on me. He seems to think he can fill the chasm inside me.

I don't burn his gifts, as Shutaha did. I don't fling them in his face, as Yahatase is said to have done to his great-uncle's. I carry Winámek's gifts gently out of my lodge. I tell him I'm not Kukamigokwe. I don't want to be at the head of Falsetongue's pillagers. I don't want to install myself in the lodge of the Strait's Lekomandá. I don't want my kin to depend on Winámek's gifts. I don't want to see my kin become ants who carry furs to Winámek. I tell him the only gift he has brought us is fratricidal war. I sing to him of the desolation of the Oceanshore. He's the one who described it to us. Yet he'd have us bring this desolation on ourselves. I beg him to take what remains of his long member and offer it to people whose trees bear no sap, whose land bears no corn. I beg him to go among people who have no memory of world's beauty, whose past begins with the arrival of the Invaders and their diseases, whose dreams are drowned by Blackrobes' chants, who consider their own ancestors man-eaters while considering Scabeaters human. Such people seek his league. I don't.

The eloquent Winámek struts out of my lodge without a word.

Sagikwe praises my boldness. At close range she finds the large man less awesome and appealing than his name. But she remains convinced I should save my ire for those Shutaha wants to adopt. When she builds a fasting tent for Ozagi, she doesn't ask for my help.

The boy is fat, awkward and playful, like his father. But unlike Chebansi, Ozagi returns from his fast emaciated. He appears to have dreamed instead of eating fish. Ozagi and a friend named Mota hover around Kendawa, my daughter's Eagle. But they don't join the caravans yet.

Kendawa leaves Bison Prairie with Winámek and Wabskeni. During his absence he becomes a father, I a grandmother. Mangashko arranges the naming ceremony without me. She names her daughter Menoko. Winámek returns alone. He prepares another dog feast. He wants us all to celebrate the removal of Lekomandá Kadyak from Tiosa Rondion.

The dog is still being eaten when Chacapwe's Raccoon arrives from the Strait. He comes to shame those celebrating the dog's disemboweling. Winámek hastily names Ahsepona the dog's jaw, and all but I turn deaf ears to the Raccoon from the Strait.

Ahsepona tells me the reason for Winámek's hasty naming. He tells me things I could have guessed if I had concentrated as Nopshinga was able to do. Nangisi knew what was happening. But he wanted me deaf and blind.

The Blackrobes who abandoned Mishilimakina did not change their skins when they reached Hochelaga. They merely relocated the vantage point from which to weave the schemes familiar to me since Falsetongue's days. Nor did Winámek lose contact with their intrigues. His restless son kept him in touch with every unravelling scheme.

Lekomandá Kadyak was summoned to the Scabeaters' center Stadacona to explain his hoard of gifts that came from enemy Invaders. Winámek chose this moment to send Wabskeni and Kendawa on a second raid of the village on the Strait. The first had not brought enough desolation. Kukamigokwe's ghost hovered over the Strait. Wabskeni offered gifts to Turtlefolk and Peninsulakin. Then he turned to insult Pyerwá and other adopted Scabeaters. He called Pyerwá lazy, undisciplined, and a renegade from the true faith, insults that could not have meant much to Wabskeni's ally Kendawa.

Ahsepona, his face painted a raccoon's mask, faced Wabskeni, not to shield Pyerwá, but to confront those who had brought the plague to his village.

Kendawa harangued Peninsulakin and Turtlefolk. He said the Invaders intended to transform them all into dogs.

Youths painted and armed themselves. They remembered the plague that had followed the previous raid. They stood beside Ahsepona.

The tension drove Wabskeni's dog, an actual dog, to bite one of the youths near Ahsepona. The youth kicked the dog. Wabskeni's firesticks promptly murdered five youths.

The Scabeater temporarily replacing Lekomandá, hearing shots so near his enclosure, became as hysterical as Wabskeni's dog. Thinking that eastern Serpents were invading the Strait, he ordered the uniformed Scabeaters to kill. Shutaha, Chacapwe, Pyerwá and Ubankiko begged the killers to desist from the wanton slaughter. But thirty of Kendawa's and Wabskeni's armed men were dead before the smoke settled. Wabskeni fled, as he had done earlier.

Kendawa was injured. Ahsepona and Pyerwá carried their kinsman to Chacapwe's lodge. While the Eagle's daughter was born in Bison Prairie the father lost a leg in Tiosa Rondion. Kendawa cursed his hosts. He called Ahsepona a traitor and Pyerwá a bloodthirsty enemy.

Lekomandá Kadyak returned from Stadacona. Turtlefolk and Peninsulakin greeted him with a war council. Ahsepona and the youths and hunters spoke with painted faces and weapons in hand. They said they would make the raiders from the north answer for the death of the five youths, for the plague that had killed half the people, for the earlier plague, and for the destruction of Wiske's tree. They said Lekomandá would have to answer for the massacre of thirty of Kendawa's kinsmen.

Lekomandá stomped on Ahsepona's warbelt. He said the slaughter would not have taken place if he had not been called away. He called himself a peacemaker and said our quarrels invited Serpents and Oceanshore Invaders to the Lakes. He said the Strait's council had shown it could not maintain peace without him. He said he wanted justice, not vengeance. He said he had already dispatched the one guilty of the massacre. What this meant was that his murderous replacement had returned to Stadacona.

Lekomandá said he would aim his firesticks at anyone who settled grievances without his permission. He pretended to assume all the powers of the Strait's council.

Ahsepona and the other warriors remained painted and armed. They saw that the Scabeater would not answer for anything.

Lekomandá dispatched couriers to the north, to pretend to seek those guilty of the raid. The couriers returned from Mishilimakina with four emissaries, two of whom were Winámek and Wabskeni. The emissaries did not appear before the council. They went directly to Lekomandá's lodge.

Lekomandá did not reemerge from his lodge until the emissaries returned to the north. He then told the council that the one responsible for the raid was a man called The Heavy, and that the emissaries had returned to the north to root him out. He said peace had been restored, urged all carriers to bring their furs to him, and threatened to kill carriers who took furs to the eastern Woodlands.

It was evident to all that Lekomandá Kadyak had capitulated to those he had pretended to punish. The emissaries must have told the Scabeater to break his alliance with seed scatterers and dancing women, and to ally himself with Winámek's pelts and Wabskeni's arms. If he refused, Winámek no doubt told him, he would have neither pelts nor gifts nor peace, and he would lose his post.

The warriors were enraged. Kendawa was incensed by what he considered Wabskeni's betrayal of his allies.

Ahsepona called Firekeepers to prepare to resist the alliance of predators hovering above his village. It was the first time Firekeepers had painted themselves since Nopshinga had confronted Winámek after Wabskeni's murder of Shutaha's son.

Shutaha, Chacapwe and Ubankiko urged the warriors to lay down their weapons. Acceptance of the predators' alliance was preferable to fratricide. Corpses could not be adopted and turned into Turtles.

The warriors would not be restrained. They attacked the enclosure and killed three uniformed Scabeaters.

Lekomandá, heavily outnumbered, was willing to agree to anything. He even said he would welcome Redearth kin who came to the Strait to drink poisoned water with him.

But the occasion Winámek and the Blackrobes were waiting for had arrived. Lekomandá Kadyak had shown that he could not maintain peace on the Strait. He was removed from his post and summoned to Stadacona. A Scabeater amenable to Winámek and the Blackrobes' wishes was sent to Tiosa Rondion to replace him.

Winámek returned to Bison Prairie to celebrate. Ahsepona came to make us see and hear.

Sagikwe and Mangashko dance with Nangisi's carriers and help him make a mockery of the three fires. Both are deaf to Ahsepona. Sagikwe regards her one-time ally as an enemy. She takes him for an agent of ousted Lekomandá and a defender of the Strait's ant-men. I try to make Mangashko listen, but all she hears is that Ahsepona stood by the Scabeaters who injured Kendawa. She's convinced that Kendawa is being held captive by the Scabeaters in Chacapwe's lodge.

Ahsepona decides to take his news, as well as a warbelt, to the Redearth kin of the other shore and to the Prairiekin of the valleys.

A runner arrives from the Strait. Winámek and Wabskeni promptly prepare to depart, fully armed.

Nangisi decides to accompany the warriors to the Strait. Sagikwe urges her son to go with Nangisi. Eleven-spring Ozagi and his ancient granduncle are on the best of terms. At times Nangisi seems the younger of the two.

Mangashko decides to carry her Menoko to Tiosa Rondion.

I don't know what news the runner brought, but I do know that Winámek is rushing to place himself and his son at the head of the league of Rootkin of the western Lakes. Nangisi wants to reestablish the position he and his carriers lost when Falsetongue failed to return from across the Ocean. Mangashko intends to free Kendawa from his captors, Pyerwá, Chacapwe and Shutaha.

I'm left alone with Sagikwe. We've nothing to say to each other. We're both tense and owly. A whole age seems to pass before news from the Strait reaches Bison Prairie.

Wabskeni and Winámek return and engage their pillagers in a flurry of activity. Winámek speaks of a great victory, and warns that Serpents are about to attack the Peninsula. I realize I was wrong about the condition of Wiske's member. I had overestimated the sharpness of chipmunks' teeth.

I look to see how Sagikwe responds to Winámek's identification of his present enemies as Serpents, not Scabeaters. But she doesn't respond. The momentum of hatred and war cloud her mind. Winámek could tell her he was battling Rootkin and she would still remain convinced he wielded his weapon only against ant-men.

Wabskeni gathers men and youths willing to join his uniformed pillagers, and he departs in search of more victories.

We learn the destination of Wabskeni's army when a crowd of enraged villagers moves toward our lodge. At the head of the crowd, the boy Mota leads his friend Ozagi toward nearly distraught Sagikwe. Ozagi looks as wide-eyed as Shutaha. Both boys cry.

Mota excitedly tells us that Wabskeni's army murdered Kendawa and fifty other Rootkin returning westward from the Strait. The pillagers would have killed Mangashko, Menoko and Ozagi as well, if Mota hadn't cut the slaughter short.

Sagikwe is sure the boy is lying. She shakes Ozagi, begging him to deny his friend's story.

Ozagi confirms his friend's story. He says Wabskeni will claim he was hunting Serpents. But Wabskeni knew perfectly well that the people he ambushed were Rootkin, Firekeepers and Prairiekin.

Ozagi is less excited than Mota. He narrates in Chebansi's best manner. Despite the near loss of his life, he impersonates people and enacts deeds as if he were uninvolved.

Sagikwe guesses that he stayed in Shutaha's lodge. She thinks Shutaha bewitched him.

Soon after Ozagi and his cousins and uncles arrived in Tiosa Rondion, Redearth kin from the other shore reached the Strait. Many of them were carriers whom Kendawa had once accompanied to the Eastern River. They jokingly said they had come to the Strait to accept Lekomandá Kadyak's invitation to drink poison water with him. Actually they were responding to Ahsepona's call to help him oust Lekomandá's successor from Tiosa Rondion.

Ahsepona promptly went to them to greet them as brothers. Kendawa would have gone too if he could have walked.

The new Lekomandá, flanked by Wabskeni and Winámek, left his enclosure to confront the Redearth kin. The Scabeater asked them what they wanted in Tiosa Rondion.

One of the Redearth kin, a man called Lamina, asked what the Scabeater wanted on the Strait. He said his kin had been invited to drink poisoned water with the previous headman. The Redearth kin were the only people on the Lakes who had never shed a drop of Invaders' blood. They were eager to share the Scabeater's poison water while listening to his answer.

To this, the new Lekomandá said he did not want the Redearth kin to camp so near his enclosure on the Strait.

Lamina laughed. He said his kin did not like the Scabeaters' enclosure so near their camp on the Strait.

Lamina's laughter was answered by murderous shots. Prompted by Wabskeni, the new Lekomandá called out all the armed Scabeaters of his enclosure and told them to aim at women and children, to kill indiscriminately.

One of the first to fall was Ahsepona. He had not been able to deliver the Firekeepers' greeting to the Redearth kin. He was no longer able to take the greeting of the Redearth kin to the people of Tiosa Rondion. He had always known he would die at the hand of those who had cut his tree and destroyed his rock.

The killing was so quick, it seemed so well prepared, that Lamina concluded he had been led into an ambush by Ahsepona's invitation. He prepared to besiege the Strait's entire shore.

Kendawa sent runners to tell Lamina he had allies on the Strait. Shutaha sent runners to tell Lamina the Strait's council would make the Scabeaters answer for the murder of his kin.

But the ghosts of dead kin blinded Lamina. He saw only Scabeaters on the Strait. He heard only that Tiosa Rondion's people were all each other's kin, and therefore his enemies. The runners who returned said he was determined not to be led into an ambush twice by the same council of women.

Inside Tiosa Rondion, Pyerwá was recruited to defend the besieged village. Many of the Turtlefolk and Peninsulakin who had been ready to attack the Scabeaters' enclosure hesitantly turned against its besiegers. Winámek called the besiegers Serpents, and Wabskeni's pillagers burned to exterminate lifelong enemies.

Shutaha was repelled by the fratricide. Kukamigokwe's ghost was cutting down Shutaha's long-leafed tree. Ozagi stayed in Shutaha's lodge and absorbed her revulsion.

Tiosa Rondion was defended by the combined forces of Scabeaters, pillagers and most of the Strait's youth. The defenders were armed with the enclosure's inexhaustible stock of firesticks and powder and with the Scabeaters' device for hurling thunderstones. The besiegers' arms were limited, and they knew they were outnumbered. Lamina sent emissaries to ask for a truce which gave him time to smoke at the Strait's council.

Wabskeni had the emissaries murdered and their mutilated bodies hurled toward the besiegers.

The infuriated Redearth kin resumed their siege. They shot flaming arrows into the village and into the Scabeaters' enclosure. Fires broke out everywhere. Bearded hoarders joined with Firekeepers, uniformed Scabeaters joined with Turtleyouth to quench the fires. They filled hollowed-out canoes with the Strait's water and passed them from hand to hand in serpentine lines that moved from fire to fire.

The Redearth kin could neither defeat their enemies nor council with them nor burn them out. On the nineteenth day of the siege, the remnant of Lamina's force and his camp of women and children retreated from the Strait. On the same day, word reached Tiosa Rondion that numerous Prairiekin were coming from the Long River in response to Ahsepona's invitation. Kendawa prepared to dispatch runners. But Wabskeni had already set out to intercept Lamina's allies. Wabskeni told the Prairiekin that eastern Serpents and Invaders were besieging the Peninsula, and he convinced them to lend their power to his army. The combined armies of Scabeaters, pillagers and Prairiekin set out after Lamina's retreating kin. Hundreds of Redearth kin were slaughtered. Hundreds of women and children were captured and taken to Hochelaga to be treated as human cattle.

By the time the Prairiekin saw their deception, Wabskeni was already on his way to Bison Prairie to spread the deception further.

When Kendawa learned of the massacre, he had himself carried to the Prairiekin. Mangashko and Ozagi followed the Eagle. Ahsepona's daughter Ubankiko, together with Pyerwá, their Maní and several Peninsulakin repelled by the fratricide, accompanied the Prairiekin as far as Kekionga. Kendawa, bent on making his one-time ally Wabskeni answer for his abominations, went on—directly into Wabskeni's trap. None had foreseen how far Wabskeni would carry his deception.

Young Mota had set out with the scouts of Wabskeni's ambushing party. When the front line of painted Prairiekin passed Mota's hiding place, Mota stayed where he was, terrified by what he took to be Serpents, the world's fiercest warriors. But when the dog travois and the women and children approached him, Mota immediately recognized Ozagi and Mangashko.

The boy let out a cry to drown thunder. The Serpents are aunts and cousins returning to Bison Prairie, Mota cried. But fifty of the Prairiekin had already been ambushed. Among the dead was Mangashko's one-legged Kendawa. The slayers as well as the slain were led by carriers, Nangisi's grandchildren, Wiske's nephews.

Sagikwe rejects every word of her son's story. She insists Ozagi was bewitched by Shutaha.

The first to be repelled by Sagikwe's blindness is her closest friend, my daughter. Mangashko furiously says the dead

Ahsepona and the slaughtered Redearth kin were the only ones who fought Sagikwe's battle. While they died, Sagikwe wasted her songs on the mutilator who disembowled her Peninsula, on the conjuring kin-hater who made men take the flesh of their brothers to his dog feast.

Prairiekin from the sunset join with those of Bison Prairie in calling for the instigators of the fratricide. But Wabskeni and his loyal pillagers are already on their way to the Northern Straits. Angry voices demand a council. Winámek is called to answer for Wabskeni's slaughter and deception.

While the council is being prepared, Nangisi and his carriers return from the Strait bearing gifts. Mangashko rages against her ancient grandfather. She says he sat in Tiosa Rondion drinking poisoned water with Scabeating hoarders while his grandson was perpetrating his horrors. Nangisi thought the poisoned water absolved him of all responsibility because it turned him into a foolish child who saw nothing, heard nothing and knew nothing.

Nangisi hears his granddaughter's anger. He learned of her Eagle's death the moment he arrived in Bison Prairie. He speaks before the council. He confronts Kukamigokwe's Winámek for the first time. During one of the rare moments when he hasn't been drinking, Nangisi names himself and Winámek the real instigators of the fratricide. He says he helped Winámek lead Rootkin to war when the Serpent enemies were eastern Turtlefolk. He helped Winámek when the Serpents were Redearth kin of the other shore. But now that the Serpents are his own nephews, Nangisi sees that he had fallen into the jaws of the only real viper on the Peninsula.

Winámek answers Nangisi. He says he has used all his strength to gather Peninsulakin around the three fires. If he fought against Serpents, it was only to clear the ground where a strong, healthy tree could grow. He brought gifts to help reconstitute the lost fourth age, to eliminate hunger and misery from the Peninsula. His weapons provided meat, his pots meals, his clothes and blankets warmth. Without his gifts, Peninsulakin would be powerless, cold and miserable.

Winámek has learned much from my father and sister. He has added a great deal of his own. His words wake even Sagikwe. She sees, for the first time, that Winámek's soul wears a long beard. Sagikwe pours a bowlful of water on Winámek and then, to make herself perfectly clear, spits in his face.

While we deliberate, word reaches us of yet another massacre perpetrated by Winámek's son. The homebound remnant of Lamina's Redearth kin was ambushed near Greenbay by Wabskeni's northbound pillagers. But this time Wabskeni erred in his choice of battleground. He was near the center of Lamina's homeland. Redearth kin saved Lamina's band from being completely exterminated. They arrived from every direction and routed Wabskeni's pillagers. They proceeded to disarm all Scabeaters on the other shore of Mishigami. They now maintain scouting parties on every trail and stream between Mishigami and the Long River. They're even dispatching armed bands eastward to raid caravans of Scabeaters on the Strait's periphery.

Hearing this news, the already humiliated Winámek slinks to his lodge. But I fear his member is still inhumanly long.

Some speak of staying armed, others of attacking. I resolve to abandon Winámek and his gifts. That's Shutaha's way. Mangashko agrees to go with me and with most of the remaining Prairiekin to Kekionga.

Mangashko thinks we're going to join Kendawa's and Lamina's allies, the real enemies of the Scabeaters.

Sagikwe, ashamed, stays in her lodge. She wouldn't share Mangashko's enthusiasm. She knows that Pyerwá and Ubankiko are in Kekionga and are not enemies of the Scabeaters.

Ozagi and his friend Mota see us off.

Chapter 4.

Miogwewe continues

Ubankiko

The leaves have fallen forty-two times since the day Shutaha ran up the embankment of Bison Prairie convinced that we had reached the place her father had sought. I didn't know what Shutaha saw. When Nopshinga and I left Bison Prairie and reached Chacapwe's lodge on the Strait, I knew Shutaha had found her center, but I didn't feel it as mine. When I returned to Bison Prairie with Sagikwe, I felt even further from my center. Yet now, as we bank our canoes on Kekionga's tree-lined shore, I see as Shutaha must have seen. I recognize Kekionga as the place I'm seeking. The carryingplace between the eastern Lakes and the sunset, between the Strait and the valleys of the Wabash is the center where I want to remain.

As soon as we arrive, my Nopshinga's niece, fatherless Ubankiko, asks me to arrange a founding ceremony and guides me to the lodges of her village. Pyerwá beams to me. Their Maní, already turning into a woman, immediately adopts my granddaughter Menoko. Ubankiko takes me to lodges of Prairiekin from every valley between the Peninsula's wrist and the Long River. And she takes me to lodges of guests from east and south, men who dress like Invaders and speak like Winámek. They're Rootkin of the ancient Eastbranch and Southbranch.

I immediately ask the question Wedasi asked Winámek: do they remember themselves as Rootkin? And they do! A man of the Southbranch remembers the embroilments and the wanderings. And a man of the Eastbranch, Lenapi, enters his lodge and reemerges with a scroll. I beg him to untie the scroll. My heart misses a beat. It's like the fragment in Ozagi's bundle, but it's complete. It's what Wedasi spent his life seeking, a scroll from the old times. I recognize the edge of the first water, the path followed by the first Neshnabek, the land of ice, the arrival in Kichigami, the first meeting with Tellegwi and Talamatun. There I stop. Lenapi tells me the rest. I see his ancestors after Wiske's great embroilment, moving eastward with Talamatun. At the scroll's end I see Lenapi's Eastbranch ancestors reaching their center on the Oceanshore.

I dance with abandon at the founding ceremony. Kukamigokwe's ghost has not followed me to Ubankiko's village. Every omen is good.

I want to share my joy with my Mangashko, to dry the tears she still sheds for her dead Eagle. But Mangashko continues to see with Sagikwe's eyes. She sees only the scars. To her, the guests are Rootkin only in speech. Mangashko sees that what draws Ubankiko to the guests is not the scroll or the memory of ancient days.

Ubankiko, like Pyerwá, is drawn to the objects the guests bring from the Eastern River. She stretches to the world of objects Shutaha's dream of transplanting healthy shoots. Ubankiko has adopted not only Pyerwá but also beads, pots, hatchets, knives, kettles, awls, blankets, clothing, and poisons made from grapes and grains.

Mangashko knows that these are not earth's gifts but the Invaders'. She knows that the Invaders do not give lovingly, as earth does. She sees our hunters depopulating forests of their living beings to satisfy the Invaders' insatiable hunger for dead animals. She sees that Ubankiko and Lenapi, like the Scabeaters, no longer know the use of stone, bark, bones or quills. Mangashko, like Yahatase, keeps the disabling objects out of our lodge. She longs to repeat Shutaha's feat of feeding all the unearthly gifts to a great fire.

Ubankiko regards the Invaders' gifts as the very ground on which her village can grow. She doesn't regret losing the ancient knowledge and ways. Her main fear is that she'll lose access to the new things.

Word comes that the Strait's headman intends to plunder those who gather furs without his permission. Ubankiko and Pyerwá hurry to the Strait to seek that permission. Maní goes with them to visit her grandmothers.

I seem to have moved beyond Winámek's reach, but not beyond that of his allies. The Strait's long-membered Scabeaters can't bear to leave Kekionga alone. They want their enemies to be ours. They want Pyerwá not only to seek permission. They want Pyerwá to carry all his furs to the Strait and give none to Southbranch or Eastbranch or Redearth kin who carry them to Serpents and Oceanshore Invaders.

Pyerwá returns from Tiosa Rondion shackled with a friend, a young Scabeater called Shen. Permission is granted to the friends, but only so long as they remain friends. The Scabeaters know what strengthens their ways. The friends are to act on each other like the armed men in their enclosures. They are to keep each other inside.

It's Maní who gives me an account of the visit to Tiosa Rondion. She comes to me with Shen's sister Manyan, a child halfway between Maní and Menoko in age. While Maní speaks, I hear things my Mangashko seems deaf to. Maní, barely a woman, speaks not as a Scabeater's daughter nor even as Chacapwe's granddaughter. She speaks as Shutaha's child and Yahatase's grandchild. She scattered seeds alongside Shutaha as I once did alongside Yahatase. She learned Shutaha's songs and dreamt in Shutaha's fasting lodge. She looks back to Yahatase the way I look back to the Neshnabek of the fourth age. She has no more use for her mother's objects than Wedasi or Yahatase did. To Maní the objects are scabs that form on wounds. She's unhappy about the changes brought to her Tiosa Rondion by the Scabeaters. She tells me the coast of the Strait is lined with square lodges. The vines and fruit trees are destroyed. The fields behind the lodges are divided by ugly pickets. Deer and bear can no longer be seen. Cows and horses eat all the grass. On beautiful Rattlesnake Isle, pigs eat everything. Fish Isle is full of Scabeaters' refuse. Only the Isle of Fruit Trees and the Isle of White Trees remain as she remembers them.

When Maní's young friend Manyan speaks, I hear things that make Shutaha dream. Manyan wants me to build her a fasting lodge. She's as much a Neshnabek child as Mangashko's daughter Menoko. Yet Manyan and her older brother Shen were born to Scabeaters of Hochelaga. Her mother died soon after Manyan's birth. Her traveler father took the youth and the girlchild to Tiosa Rondion. One day she heard an owl's screech and a dog's howl and saw a canoe with twelve men in the northern sky. She knew her father would not return. While her brother, as fluent as she in Rootspeech, mingled with Scabeaters, Manyan grew up in Chacapwe's lodge. She speaks of Blackrobes as clowns. She wears a cross but considers it nothing more than an ornament. She describes the armed men of the enclosure as dogs who pull Stadacona's travois, and she tells me her view is shared by most of the Strait's Scabeaters. Tears come to my eyes when I listen to this child. I realize that Shutaha was not demented when she dreamt of Scabeaters turning into Turtles. While Ubankiko reaches for the Invaders' things and ways, the children of Scabeaters are recovering the dreams and ways of Turtlefolk and Rootkin.

Sagikwe's son arrives in Kekionga with his friend Mota and a band of young carriers. Ozagi, a fat and cheerful youth who continues to act and look like Chebansi, tells us Bison Prairie has become insupportable even to Nangisi. Wabskeni returned from Mishilimakina with a crosswearing wife and a son who bears a Scabeater's name, something like Nagmo. Wabskeni arrived with numerous Scabeaters, some of them manhunters, others Winámek's allies from the Hochelaga fur gang. The manhunters were invited by Wabskeni to protect him from reprisals by Lamina. Wabskeni and his Scabeater army are bent on eliminating the Redearth kin from the western Lakes. The manhunters are fed by Winámek and the fur gang Scabeaters. Winámek expects all hunters and carriers to give him all the furs they gather. He even expects Kekionga hunters to take their furs to him, out of loyalty toward the three fires and enmity toward the Serpents of the other shore.

Winámek expects as much as he ever did. But his newly enlarged league consists only of the enlargements; it has no core. When Sagikwe spat in his face five springs ago, Winámek's admirer became his foe. Sagikwe, never a lover of the Scabeaters' gifts, went among the wives of carriers and shamed them for abandoning earthen bowls, stone knives, quills and roots. She shared her secrets of herb-gathering, quilling and canoe-shaping with girls whose mothers had forgotten them. She showed that earth was ornamented by flowers, leaves and quills, not by glass beads and metal crosses. The Rootwomen of Bison Prairie heard Sagikwe, and they avoided Winámek and rejected his gifts. Bison Prairie's Rootkin soon had so little to do with Winámek, one would have thought the two camps lay on opposite ends of the Peninsula.

When Rootkin abandoned Winámek, Nangisi and his carriers had no choice but to abandon him. Nangisi was given little for his furs. The fur gang even skimped on its poisoned water. And thanks to Sagikwe, Nangisi found few who were grateful for the little he could give. So he finally decided to let Kukamigokwe's big man and her son play their games with each other. Nangisi and his carriers went to Tiosa Rondion, whose Scabeaters treat manhunters and the fur gang as obstacles to circumvent. There Nangisi found free-flowing poison water as well as beads, knives, hatchets and firesticks. He intended to take these gifts toward the sunset, to bison hunters who roast a bear in its skin, singe the fur off animal skins and use pelts only for winter clothes. He wanted to carry his and his uncle's ways to people who still remember his grandmother's.

Mota and Ozagi accompanied Nangisi to the Strait. But they stayed only long enough to learn that Tiosa Rondion's armed Scabeaters had plundered a band of carriers returning with gifts from the Eastern River. Mota remembered that Kendawa had been similarly plundered. Mota vowed to return to the Strait only with war paint. Like his idol Kendawa, Mota thinks free men carry their furs wherever they please. He brought his friend to Kekionga to seek the Redearth kin who make paths toward the sunrise. He and Ozagi are enchanted to sweat and smoke with Kekionga's Eastbranch and Southbranch Rootkin, and eager to join their caravan to the Eastern River.

Ozagi moved from his aunt's adoption to his mother's rejection of Scabeaters during his childhood in Tiosa Rondion. As a boy in Bison Prairie, he was exposed to Sagikwe's admiration and my antipathy toward Wiske and Nangisi and Winámek. Although nearly killed by Winámek's son, Ozagi did not turn his back on carriers when his mother set out to shame them. He moved between Sagikwe and Nangisi, impersonating each to the other, as Chebansi had done so well. Quicker than Chebansi and more independent, he has a trait his father lacked, a trait he shares with Nangisi. Ozagi is ever ready to absolve himself of responsibility. Like his grandfather Wedasi, he refuses to use firesticks. But he's willing to carry them to those who use them. How else could he gather furs, he asks with a self-justifying twinkle. Maní notices her young uncle's twinkle. The two children of Tiosa Rondion are drawn to each other. But their view of each other is brief. The eastbound caravan leaves Kekionga accompanied by the two youths and their band.

The Scabeaters have long, restless members which they seem unable to keep from prowling into every tree hollow. A band of uniformed manhunters arrives in Kekionga, headed by a Scabeater called Lekomandá Shak, a member of the Hochelaga fur gang. They raise a large square lodge and surround it with a picketed enclosure. Lekomandá Shak spreads the word that he's come to protect us from invasion by eastern Serpents.

Maní and Manyan tell me the armed men are here to stop Kekiongans from carrying furs to the Eastern River. Maní tells me the Scabeaters' headman called her father dissipated and revoked his permission to gather furs. Pyerwá drinks eastern poisons. Pyerwá shares his gifts with his kin, unlike Manyan's brother Shen, who hoards gifts. The armed men are here to attack Shutaha's dream, to make Pyerwá a hoarder like the other Scabeaters. Their enclosure exists to protect the hoards from angry kin.

Manyan says the Scabeaters are recruiting Rootkin for a war against Lamina and the Redearth kin who still keep Scabeaters from landing on the sunset shore of Mishigami.

Pyerwá's former friend Shen rushes to ingratiate himself with the uniformed fur league member.

I judge that it's best to do like Sagikwe: ignore them, isolate them, if possible starve them out of Kekionga. I show my quiet granddaughter the secrets of pelt dressing. I build her a fasting lodge. In the midst of all the alarms and apprehensions, Menoko dreams of deer, beaver and muskrats calling her to enjoy the clear water of a stream, the peaceful sunset, the rustle of leaves in the wind. The child of Mangashko and Kendawa has none of their rage. She's like a butterfly who sees only flowers. I can think of no one like her. Perhaps my mother or Yahatase's sister Maní were such peaceful spirits.

Outside of Menoko there is no peace. Lekomandá Shak's armed men ambush and plunder the caravan returning from the Eastern River. The Eastbranch and Southbranch kin are forced to move elsewhere. Mota and Ozagi are maltreated and taken to the enclosure.

Mangashko rages against the murderers of Ahsepona and the Redearth kin. She calls Prairiekin to a council. There's talk of sending warbelts to Lamina and to Prairiekin of the western valleys.

Ubankiko urges Pyerwá to talk to his friend Shen. But Shen is deaf to Pyerwá; he has a new friend now. Ubankiko turns to Manyan, but the girl refuses to talk to her brother. Manyan says she'll welcome the Redearth warrior Lamina into Kekionga, and she'll take him to her mat if he'll have her.

Menoko, who has been crying since she learned of the maltreatment of Mota and Ozagi, takes her tears to Manyan. She begs. She abhors the thought of war. Fratricidal war in Kekionga is inconceivable to her.

Manyan cannot but bend to her young friend's entreaties. She speaks to her brother. Shen goes to Lekomandá Shak. The two Scabeaters council for a whole afternoon.

Suddenly there's a flurry of activity. Shen rushes to Pyerwá's lodge. Ubankiko emerges with him and says their friendship will resume. Pyerwá doesn't emerge.

Mota and Ozagi are released from the enclosure. Their plundered gifts are returned.

Ozagi invites all Kekionga to a feast. He shares poisoned water with everyone, even the armed Scabeaters who enclosed him. He says the Oceanshore Invaders call their drink Wiske. It waters dry fields and reconciles enemies. And it seems to do just that. Kekionga fills with laughter. Mangashko drinks alongside Ubankiko.

Mota carries blankets, cloth and beads to his deliverer, Menoko. The girl wears her emotions like outer garments. Before the release she was all gloom. Now she's all rapture. Menoko accepts the gifts with such radiant joy that she makes all the rage and apprehension seem like no more than a preparation for this moment of bliss. Mota had not noticed Menoko before he had learned of her tears. Now he notices nothing else.

Ozagi gives an amulet to his niece Maní and a packet of cloth to Manyan. Maní is ready to welcome Ozagi to her lodge. But Ozagi is eager for more adventure. He wants to carry his gifts into the monster's very jaws, into Winámek's Bison Prairie. No Mota will save him from the murderous Wabskeni this time. But Ozagi insists there's nothing to fear. He says he wants to express his gratitude to Winámek and Wabskeni, just as he's thanking Lekomandá Shak. He says the Oceanshore Invaders on the Eastern River do not give much to their allies. But when they learned that Mota and Ozagi were enemies, they couldn't give them enough. It was their fear of Lekomandá's and Wabskeni's manhunters that made them so generous.

Shutaha's nephew thinks he can slip the eastern gifts into Bison Prairie under the very noses of Winámek and Wabskeni. He says all the carriers will welcome the gifts. The enclosed Scabeaters, who hate Winámek's stinginess, will beg the carriers for poisoned water. If Wabskeni tries to pounce, no one will join him. His own manhunters will beg Ozagi to go east and return with more.

We hear no word from Ozagi. We begin to fear he wasn't able to keep the jaws from closing. Maní is often in tears.

Mota leaves Kekionga to seek Lenapi, hoping to find Ozagi with him.

Menoko makes a cloth and bead animal, a beaver or a bear, with Mota's gift to her. Just as Shutaha left me her pendant when she left Bison Prairie, Menoko intends to give the animal to Maní when the friends separate.

Pyerwá and Ubankiko avoid me. Ubankiko behaves strangely. She seems to be hiding something. The Scabeater Shen visits her lodge frequently, but not to visit Pyerwá. It seems almost as if Shen resumed his friendship, not with Pyerwá, but with Ubankiko.

Mota returns from the east with Lenapi and with more gifts, but without Ozagi. Mota thinks Wabskeni may have killed Ozagi for his audacity. Maní despairs.

Mota tells us Ozagi underestimated the ferocity of the monster he wanted to play with. With Lenapi's help, Mota counciled with Oceanshore Invaders. He found them to know more than he about the Scabeaters' movements and strengths, and much more than Ozagi knew. The Invaders moved their post from the Eastern River to a Turtlefolk village called

MIOGWEWE CONTINUES 1725

Shuagan on the shore of the Easternmost Lake. From this new post they have a clear view of the Scabeaters' movements on the Lakes. They knew how many Scabeaters came to Kekionga with Lekomandá Shak three springs ago. They told Mota the same number of armed men had been placed at the Great Falls to keep our carriers from reaching the Eastern River. Four times that number had been placed in Bison Prairie, which the Scabeaters regard as their power center on the Lakes. Mota cannot believe that Ozagi safely carried his eastern gifts into the very center of this grasping power. Apparently the Scabeaters did not send more armed men to Tiosa Rondion. They must fear dissipation in Shutaha's village.

Manyan says she dreamt that Lamina and his warriors were on their way to Kekionga. She has ceased to be close to Menoko and Maní. She's contemptuous of their dread of war. She says that if Ozagi has any sense, then he's not dead in Bison Prairie, but sharpening his arrows alongside Lamina.

Menoko is too taken up with Mota to notice Manyan's distance. She accepts Mota's gift. Her love is so great, it fills the body of everyone who looks at her. Life itself, when it first emerged from the water, couldn't have been more exuberant. Mangashko tells me she feels her whole life has been moving toward this happy climax, the linking of her daughter with Mota.

Suddenly Ubankiko bursts through the happiness like a thunderstorm on a cloudless day. She announces she will make arrangements for the celebration to be a double one. She says Maní has consented to share her mat with the Scabeater Shen.

Manyan must have known this was coming. I begin to see why Ubankiko behaved so strangely.

Maní doesn't come to consult me, so I go seek her.

My grandniece tells me she's decided to do what Shutaha would have done. She's sacrificing herself for Ubankiko's village. She'll make a Turtle out of Shen and out of all the Scabeaters who dare to come to Kekionga. She'll transplant healthy shoots from their poisonous surroundings and place them in fertile soil. She wants Kekionga to be a gatheringplace of peoples from the four directions, like Shutaha's Tiosa Rondion. She says she loves Ozagi but is convinced he's dead.

I have nothing to say to Maní. I don't believe Ozagi is dead. But I cannot insist, as Manyan does, that he's with Lamina's warriors. If he's as much like Chebansi as I think him, he'll go to battle only to avenge his mother's death. He doesn't even like to hunt.

Ubankiko makes her celebration coincide with the spring planting. It is not a happy event. The only joy comes from Mota and Menoko, and from the spring air. Ubankiko beams, but Pyerwá and Maní look miserable. Maní obviously dislikes Shen, and she misses Manyan. Shen misses Lekomandá Shak. I'm told the uniformed Scabeater thinks a linking ceremony can be held only in the idol-lodge of Tiosa Rondion's Blackrobes. Mangashko's absence is felt by everyone. She already celebrated Menoko's linking, and she refuses to celebrate Maní's. She regards Shen a member of the clan who murdered Ubankiko's father, Maní's grandfather, Ahsepona.

While Mota prepares to accompany another caravan to the eastern post called Shuagan, several of Lenapi's kinsmen from the Oceanshore arrive in Kekionga. Lekomandá Shak is now as generous to the men from the east as the other Invaders were to Mota and Ozagi. The Scabeater welcomes them and showers them with gifts.

The Eastbranch kin are fleeing from the Invaders to whom Mota carries furs. The Invaders strangled a peacemaker by hanging him from a tree with a rope around his neck. The peacemaker's kin abandoned their ancestral home on the coastal river and fled to the Sunrise Mountains. Some of them continued westward in search of the Southbranch Rootkin in the Beautiful River's valleys. There they learned of Lenapi's presence among us.

Lenapi says Ozagi underestimated the ferocity of the Scabeaters. But Mota underestimates the Oceanshore Invaders, whom Lenapi considers still fiercer. Menoko joins me in listening to Lenapi's every word.

Lenapi tells us his kinsmen keep the scrolls that remind them of the first Neshnabek and the journey to the Oceanshore. But they don't need scrolls like those of our medicine lodges to remind them of the coming of the Invaders and their diseases. The invasion is inscribed on all their memories. He says the Invaders do not grow big by swallowing things they bring with them across the Ocean. They grow big by swallowing the world of the Rootkin.

Lenapi's words remind me of those I heard Winámek deliver in the same quaint tongue when I was a girl. Lenapi tells that the Invaders were small and weak when they first disembarked on our Oceanshore. They begged for gifts. They begged to be taken by the hand as brothers. Rootkin gave the Invaders corn and squashes for their feasts, wood for their lodges, furs for warmth. The Invaders grew big from the Rootkin's gifts. And the bigger they grew, the more they were able to swallow. Like their own cows and pigs, they take from earth every berry, shrub and blade. They take corn, animals, trees, and they leave their excrement—but only a small portion of that. The Invaders themselves swallow the biggest portion. Lenapi says their gifts are the excrement that they form out of all they swallow. He smiles when I tell him the gifts are scabs that form on earth's wounds, and that the Invaders become voracious from eating the scabs. He says the Invaders' gifts affect Rootkin the same way. After their world becomes depleted, Rootkin become small and weak. Now it's the Rootkin who go to the Invaders to beg. But now the Invaders, surrounded by their excrement, have none to spare. The fleshless Rootkin are depleted to their bones. The Invaders give presents for the scalps of powerful people and the skins of lively animals, but not for bones. They remove the bones from view.

Lenapi says the Invaders in Shuagan are generous because we're strong. He forecasts that they'll turn mean when they swallow and deplete the world of the Great Lakes Rootkin.

Lenapi's kinsmen think the Kekionga Scabeaters are altogether different birds. They seek to council with Lekomandá Shak and to give him a belt from their kin.

While the Eastbranch Rootkin smoke with the head Scabeater, Manyan announces she intends to take him to her mat. The girl hasn't spoken to me and I assume she's playing a prank. I cannot imagine her accepting the Scabeater merely to spite Maní.

I still haven't learned Manyan's secret when Ozagi turns up in Kekionga. No one expects him. The joy of seeing him is dampened by sadness for Maní. He brings numerous gifts. Mota sweats, smokes, drinks and councils with him to keep him from seeking out his niece.

Ozagi comes with horses from the Plains beyond the Long River, with barrels of liquid poison and with various ornaments and cloth. He tells us he returned to Bison Prairie and, as he had expected, the carriers welcomed his gifts. Wabskeni's armed men drank most of his liquid poison and urged him to seek more.

Ozagi intended to return to the Eastern River by way of Kekionga. He intended to bring eastern gifts to Maní. But Nangisi was in Bison Prairie guiding a blackrobed traveler through the lakes and valleys. Nangisi invited his grandnephew and the two accompanied the Blackrobe as far as Cahokia, where the Great River of the Plains flows into the Long River. They were welcomed by Prairiekin and by Invaders who hail neither from the north nor the east but from the south. These are the Invaders who were ousted by the Stonelodge people at the time Nopshina and I celebrated our love. They've apparently returned. Nangisi, laden with gifts, returned to Tiosa Rondion.

Ozagi carried his gifts to Bison Prairie and once again walked proudly past Wabskeni. It was Sagikwe who stepped into her son's path. Sagikwe said Rootkin grew strong by depending on earth's gifts, not on the contrivances of distant sorcerers. Ozagi heard only her words. In his understanding, all gifts are earth's gifts, and Rootkin always gathered all that earth generously offered them. He thinks earth is particularly generous now, when three clans of Invaders war against each other from three corners of the world. Each Invader gives more to his enemy's allies than to his own. Ozagi has Chebansi's ability to appear to each as the other's ally. He's riding on waves from crest to crest, just as his father did until Wabskeni murdered Shutaha's son.

His gifts depleted, Ozagi intended for the second time to greet Maní in Kekionga. But my father once again turned up in Bison Prairie and invited Ozagi to join his caravan. They again went to Cahokia, but this time they separated.

Nangisi and his small band crossed the Long River with steel knives, firesticks, cloth, beads and poisoned water. They set out to cross the endless Plains in search of people who have not seen Invaders or their gifts. The ancient carrier still hasn't heard his brother's words. Of the earlier days he knows only Wiske. For Nangisi, the Beginning was not when life emerged from the sunrise, but when death emerged in disease-laden ships. His fourth age began when he started carrying the Invaders' gifts to the people gathered around three fires. I imagine him lighting three fires at the foot of the Sunset Mountains. Nangisi is the host. Around the fires sit men who appear to be Stonelodge people, Turtlefolk of Earthlodges, bison-hunting

Tellegwi. But none of them are what they appear. They're all carriers. Ozagi thinks Nangisi set out on his last journey. Ozagi came directly to Kekionga.

Ozagi

Maní listens to Ozagi. She stands behind him, leaning on Menoko, visibly pregnant. In her eyes I see the sorrow of a broken heart mingling with rage at the ease with which her beloved excuses himself for not returning sooner.
Menoko cries. She sheds tears for her trapped friend. She also sheds tears for Ozagi. Earth is so generous, so ready to reciprocate love with love, she cannot understand Ozagi's fondness for enmity.
Ozagi hears Menoko's sob. He turns and sees pregnant Maní. His humor leaves him for an instant, only long enough to let him tell himself he's not the one who failed her. She failed him. He's absolved. He turns back toward the fire and acts as if he hadn't seen her. He says he would lose his powers if he allied himself with one or the other enemy. To the Invaders, he's hostile Winámek's kinsman. To Winámek, he's hostile Sagikwe's son.
Ozagi's words hurt Maní. If he had returned in time, Maní would not be allied to one of the enemies. But Ozagi isn't remembering this. He's seeking reasons that will rub away the pain of broken love. He ends his visit quickly and sets out toward Sagikwe.
I cannot bring myself to say anything to heartbroken Maní. I feel partly responsible. I said nothing before it was too late. Now I long to learn if Manyan intends something equally foolish.
Suddenly both are out of reach. Ubankiko announces they're leaving to celebrate the double linking ceremony in the

Blackrobes' idol-lodge in Tiosa Rondion. I'm left with Mangashko, Menoko and Mota.

Maní returns from the Strait with a boychild, but without the joy that comes from new life. She seems miserable. Shen beams with pride, but he's alone in his joy. Pyerwá smiles only to return his new grandson's smile. Ubankiko's face seems longer and older than it did when she left. Lekomandá Shak and his uniformed Scabeaters return a moon later. Manyan confines herself to the picketed enclosure.

I notice Maní heading toward the enclosure. She doesn't return to Ubankiko's lodge until dark. That very night she comes to my lodge with her son, her blanket, and the amulet Ozagi gave her. There's a frightening look in her eyes, something like Yahatase's.

Menoko is all love. She embraces her older cousin as she would embrace her own child. My mother must have been such a sister to Yahatase. Unlike Menoko, it was Binesikwe who left her carrier's lodge and took me to Yahatase's. Menoko installs Maní on the spot where the bead and cloth animal perches on a shelf, Menoko's own spot. She and Mota move to my corner. I don't know if Menoko acts from the simple generosity of her own loving soul, or if my young granddaughter actually grasps all that tears Maní. Mangashko's hostility toward our guest for sharing the Scabeater's mat is softened by Menoko's love, and by Maní's condition.

At sunrise there's a great commotion on the village councilground. Shen threatens Lekomandá Shak with a firestick. All the enclosure's Scabeaters surround the two men and shout to them in their tongue. Lekomandá and his men retreat into their enclosure and close the enraged Shen out.

Soon there's word that Lekomandá Shak will go to the Strait to seek placement at a different post.

Vexed by my ignorance, I beg solicitious Menoko to grant Maní to me for a day.

Maní sobs uncontrollably. Between sobs she tells me she's too ashamed to talk to me, ashamed of herself, of Ubankiko, of Ozagi.

Pretending to be angry, I tell her the time for shame is long past.

I learn from Maní that the embroilments began at the time when the armed Scabeaters plundered Mota and Ozagi. Shen counciled with Lekomandá Shak for an afternoon. The two reached an agreement. Then the uniformed Scabeater released Mota and Ozagi from the enclosure.

Maní knew nothing of the Scabeaters' agreement. She assumed, as I did, that Shen had urged Lekomandá Shak to release our two youths instead of trying his strength against the angry Prairiekin counciling around Mangashko's fire.

For Maní the troubles began with her mother's strange behavior. Ubankiko repeatedly invited Shen to their lodge. She insisted Ozagi was dead and urged Maní to forget him. She said Rootkin would survive only by taking Invaders' gifts to their lodges.

Ubankiko knew of the two Scabeaters' agreement. Pyerwá knew nothing. He liked Ozagi, and he resented his former friend Shen's frequent presence in his lodge.

When Mota returned from Shuagan and echoed Ubankiko's guess of Ozagi's fate, Maní gave in to her mother. She felt only bitter rage toward Ozagi when at last she saw him, six moons too late. Her young friend's cold distance further embittered Maní. Manyan's sudden resolve to accept the aging Scabeater was incomprehensible to Maní.

Having accepted the linking, Maní also accepted Shen's invitation to a second ceremony in the idol-lodge on the Strait. A Blackrobe poured water and chanted, pretending to join Maní to Shen and Manyan to Lekomandá Shak. After the ceremony, Maní and Manyan separated, saying nothing to each other. Manyan accompanied Lekomandá Shak to the Scabeaters' council of big men and their women, a council Maní calls Lemond.

Maní carried her weight to Chacapwe's lodge. She was left with Chacapwe and Shutaha when Pyerwá and Ubankiko accompanied Shen to seek admission to Lemond.

Maní was giving early birth to her child when Pyerwá and Ubankiko returned from Lemond. Maní named her tiny son Miní. But the birth did not dispell the gloom. Pyerwá was like a beaten dog. Ubankiko was in tears. Lemond accepted Shen and Pyerwá and Manyan. It did not accept Ubankiko.

Chacapwe tried to console Ubankiko. Shutaha responded to Ubankiko's tears with anger. Shutaha said many of the Scabeaters adopted by her and Chacapwe's kin had changed their ways. They had learned the songs, dances and games of the original people. They could see the earth, sun, moon and sky, and enjoy what they saw. Their enjoyment was so great that they shed former skins which had kept them from seeing, feeling and moving freely. Young Invaders were turning into Turtlefolk and Rootkin. Shutaha said the Scabeaters' headman in Stadacona and across the Ocean were alarmed by this transformation. Tiosa Rondion was the largest camp of Scabeaters on the western Lakes. Yet their armed men could not raise war parties as large as Bison Prairie's, and their Blackrobes could not feed their idols as amply as the Blackrobes who had returned to Mishilimakina. Shutaha said Lemond was the Invaders' arm for stopping this transformation. Lemond's Scabeaters cultivated ignorance of our languages and songs. They did not exist to enjoy earth but to bind and break her, to make a cow of her, to make her yield milk and meat. They saw only what they could turn into food and loot. They saw trees as wood-bearers, animals as meat- and fur-bearers, earth herself as a grain-bearer, and other people as loot-bearers.

Shutaha said Ubankiko did not need to hover like a moth around Lemond's fire. Ubankiko was Kekionga's Lemond. She was turning Turtles and Roots into Scabeaters. Maní heard Shutaha's words with intense shame. She insisted on returning to Kekionga immediately, with or without Shen.

As soon as Manyan returned to Kekionga, Maní threw Shutaha's words at her friend. She asked why Manyan, who had been devoted to the Rootkin's warrior, had accepted a warrior bent on destroying Rootkin.

Manyan was enraged. She said Maní and Ubankiko had done all the accepting, and the children of the linkings would all be theirs. In her rage, Manyan told everything. She said Ubankiko was a Scabeater, Menoko a frail flower who feared every breeze. She had thought her older guide Maní a human being. She couldn't swallow her disappointment. When Ubankiko had entreated her to beg for Mota's and Ozagi's release, Manyan had refused. She had bent to Menoko's entreaties. Her brother went to Lekomandá Shak and the two came to an agreement. The armed man released our youths because he liked the agreement, not because he heard the songs being sung at Mangashko's fire. Lekomandá Shak had not known a woman during his forty and some winters. He had learned that Shen's sister had not known a man during her seventeen springs. The Scabeater offered himself. Shen agreed to arrange a union between them, provided Lekomandá Shak restored Pyerwá's permission to gather furs. Shen was not interested in Pyerwá's permission, but in his daughter. And he knew he could not dangle the permission before Pyerwá's eyes. He would dangle it before Ubankiko's.

When Shen told his sister the conditions of the release, Manyan spat in his face and laughed. She said Maní would die before sharing her mat with Shen. She said Shen and Lekomandá Shak would encounter Lamina's arrows. She wagered that if Maní ever gave Shen as much as a kind word, Manyan would turn against all she loved and accept the Scabeater as her companion.

Maní cried that she hadn't pushed Manyan to entreat her brother. She didn't share Menoko's fear of war. She would never have accepted Shen if Manyan had told her of the agreement.

Manyan said she wasn't a cheat. She had made a wager and she would hold by it. She had always been guided by Maní. She would be guided by her one more time. Maní's resolve arrived too late.

Maní was driven to distraction by her friend's words. She said she would never stop loving Ozagi. She had agreed to sacrifice her love only when she thought Ozagi was dead, and then only because she thought Shutaha would have made such a sacrifice. But capitulation to the Scabeaters' agreement wasn't sacrifice. It was worse than cowardice. Maní rushed out of the enclosure determined to undo what she had done.

She abandoned her Scabeater's lodge.

Shen thought Maní was enraged by Lemond's treatment of her kin. He accused Lekomandá Shak of breaking the agreement, and challenged him. The headman of the enclosure had to choose between confronting his wife's brother or leaving Kekionga.

The day she left, Manyan told Maní she had laughed in her brother's face for the second time. She had told Shen that Maní hadn't left him because of Lemond's insults, but because she wasn't linked to him. Maní was and would always be Ozagi's bride. Manyan had won the wager.

Another armed man arrives in Kekionga to replace Manyan's Lekomandá Shak, a Lekomandá Darnó. The Scabeater promptly invites Pyerwá to the enclosure and presents himself as Pyerwá's new friend. Pyerwá tells me the friendship means that Lekomandá wants half the gifts Pyerwá receives for his furs. While demanding such generosity toward himself, Lekomandá urged Pyerwá to be less generous with his kin and to keep a hoard, like other Scabeaters.

Pyerwá acquires a friend, but Shen loses his permission to gather furs. The enraged Shen struts out of Pyerwá's and Ubankiko's lodge. Shen shouts into my lodge, vowing to prove himself a greater warrior than all the Laminas and Ozagis. Mangashko and Mota rush out to meet his challenge. But Shen has already set out to join a band of uniformed manhunters. There's a moment of peace, of undisturbed joy. Menoko gives birth to my great-grandson. She names him Oashi. Menoko gleams like the midsummer sun in a forest clearing. Even Maní's eyes recover some of their lost mirth. Her Miní has acquired a cousin even smaller than himself. While the infant cousins reach for each other's tiny hands, Menoko takes her cousin's hand and guides her toward the sugar in the trees and the honey and corn in the fields. Maní knew where she could find shelter. Menoko sees the color of flowers and hears the humming of bees. She's blind to all the struttings and deaf to all the noise.

More armed Scabeaters arrive in Kekionga's enclosure. Neither Mangashko nor I can keep ourselves from seeing them. And Menoko's Mota watches every move like an eagle. The eyes and claws of Menoko's father seem to have gone to her child's father.

Then Shen returns, uniformed like the rest of his band. He gathers listeners to boast of his feats. The only person he wants at his council stays beyond his voice's reach. He does well to hold his council near the enclosure's gate. All his listeners are hostile to what he tells.

When Shen reached the Strait, he learned that the armed Scabeaters had suffered their first major defeat. In the sunset land beyond the Long River, Redearth kin allied with horse-riding Tellegwi had routed a camp of armed Scabeaters and demolished their enclosure. The Scabeaters' Sun, sitting in his lodge across the Ocean, declared war against the western Serpents. Three armies set out. The first was guided by Wabskeni, the second by Winámek. The third, headed by Lekomandá Shak, included Scabeaters from Hochelaga and descendants of Prairiekin who had hunted for Panis with Falsetongue.

Shen rushed to the third army to seek reconciliation with his former friend. He tells us the Redearth kin blocked every path between Mishigami and the Long River. Their strongest warriors were camped with Lamina at the Lakebottom, in the very village where Nopshinga and I stayed when Wedasi and

Shutaha went on their peace mission. Shen says the Scabeater armies besieged the Redearth kin until their arms were depleted and then proceeded to massacre them.

This time I do fear for Ozagi's fate, and for that of many others.

Mota asks Shen what part he played in the massacre.

Shen, suddenly aware of the hostility surrounding him, admits that Lekomandá Shak's army arrived in time to celebrate the victory. The listeners laugh. Shen is strong only in cunning. He's weak in courage.

Mota is enraged by the news. He breaks loose from pleading Menoko and accompanies Prairiekin to Shuagan, for arms.

Mangashko councils with angry Prairiekin. She thinks the Scabeaters' war against the Redearth kin of the other shore is the beginning of their war against Rootkin of this shore. Today they say the Redearth kin block their path to the Long River. Tomorrow they'll say we block their path to Mishigami. Yesterday they excluded Ubankiko from Lemond. Tomorrow they'll exclude Ubankiko's kin from Tiosa Rondion.

When Mota and the carriers return with firesticks from Shuagan, Kekionga's youth are ready to remove the Scabeaters and their enclosure. But Mota intends to relieve those who still survive at the Lakebottom. He takes gifts to Menoko, but doesn't remain in the lodge long enough to hear her pleas.

Mota gives Maní a blanket. She cares only for news of Ozagi. Mota has none to give her. He doesn't repeat his earlier guess, but Maní knows he thinks it. After distributing gifts and poisoned water to the villagers, Mota and the carriers and many youths set out toward the sunset.

There's something frightfully familiar to me in Kekionga. It doesn't take me long to recognize the swellings. Twenty-seven winters have passed since Chebansi and Nopshinga died of smallpox on the Strait.

I rush to my lodge. Maní has the terrible swellings. Yet she looks almost happy. She tells me she can now join Ozagi in the ghost lodge.

Menoko, holding her cousin's hand, sits as still as a rock. Either she cannot grasp what is happening, or she grasps it more profoundly than the rest of us. Her eyes, fixed on something visible only to her, express neither sorrow nor pain. They're like a dead person's.

Maní weakly removes Ozagi's gift from around her neck and places it around Menoko's. She tells Menoko to give the amulet to their childhood friend Manyan.
I begin to ask Mangashko to help me arrange the renewal ceremony we had enacted for her father and Chebansi. But Menoko's eyes stop me. Menoko has never seen the plague. Yet she seems to know it is beyond the reach of our four ages.
Instead of trying to heal, I go seek Ubankiko and Pyerwá. I'm terrified when I cross the village. People are dying everywhere.
Ubankiko is hysterical. She pleads and begs to the daughter she so cruelly misled. Pyerwá fetches the headman of the enclosure. Lekomandá Darnó places his bundle of medicine beside Maní. He's angry about the crowd in the lodge. Pyerwá carries the children, Miní and Oashi, to his lodge. Mangashko and I separate Menoko from her dying cousin. Menoko begs us to help Maní find Ozagi.
I follow Ubankiko when she carries a caged bird to the top of a mound. When the bird sings, she caresses and then frees it. The bird flies toward the sunset, carrying the soul of Ubankiko's daughter.

Pyerwá comes to tell me Ubankiko and Lekomandá Darnó are nursing my Mangashko. He says the uniformed man urges the rest of us to leave Kekionga. The headman told him the smallpox is a children's disease and is spread by afflicted people, not by sorcerers. He didn't know why the children's disease attacked Pyerwá's Maní and my Mangashko. He told Pyerwá it could be carried in gifts, like blankets from Shuagan.
With my granddaughter, great-grandson and Maní's son, I accompany Kekiongans fleeing toward their kin in Bison Prairie. The dead look has left Menoko's eyes. She's frightened. She's thinking of her Mota. She cries like a child.
Mota's scouts told him we were approaching Bison Prairie. Mota intercepts us and guides us to a lodge on the other side of the river. He says one out of every four people has swellings. Many are already dead. Sagikwe is ill. Ozagi is alive. Menoko doesn't know whether to greet the news with relief or sorrow. Maní will not meet her beloved in the ghost lodge.
Leaving Menoko and the children with Mota, I make my way to Sagikwe's lodge.

A young Redearth woman from the other shore greets me with the hostility of a trapped animal. She has kindness only toward Ozagi's ailing mother.

Ozagi tells me the woman shares his mat. He says his new life began the day he returned to Bison Prairie with the horses from the Plains and the other gifts from Cahokia. He found Sagikwe counciling with angry Firekeepers and Prairiekin. The Scabeaters had just suffered the defeat Shen had told us of. Ozagi says the Scabeaters used to be guided by Nangisi, but are now guided by Wabskeni. They sent to the Plains, not Blackrobes or a Falsetongue, who knew how to make allies before they made enemies. They sent a band of Hochelaga armed men, who knew only how to make enemies. They were so thoroughly routed by Redearth kin allied with Plains Tellegwi that not a trace of their enclosure or camp remained. Instead of admitting that their old ways had served them better, they let themselves be guided further along their foolish path. Wabskeni named the attackers Serpents, and the Scabeaters declared war on the western Serpents. Winámek revived his ancient league and dispatched runners with the story that Serpents were bent on exterminating the Rootkin of the Peninsula. Winámek then went to Greenbay to recruit youths whose grandfathers had raided with Falsetongue. Wabskeni gathered pillagers and manhunters in Bison Prairie. Youths who didn't know sunrise from sunset enlarged both armies, but not adequately. Armed Scabeaters set out from Hochelaga to reinforce both armies, and also a third, which was to attack from the valleys.

Sagikwe was not only enraged. She was as convinced as Mangashko that the three armies intended to exterminate the Peninsula's Rootkin. She said people who let themselves be turned into ants could not bear to let free human beings exist. She urged Ozagi to go to the other shore and warn Redearth kin of the Scabeaters' preparations.

Ozagi could not find the western warriors as quickly as he could find poisoned water. He started out toward Greenbay. By the time he found Lamina's warriors at the Lakebottom, they already knew what he had to tell them. Wabskeni's army was moving toward them from the east. Lamina's warriors, armed with firesticks from Shuagan, beat back Wabskeni's army. But they were out of powder when Winámek's army approached from the north.

Ozagi realized he didn't have a warrior's stomach. He kept his eye on the only direction from which no army approached. He joined warriors who were retreating very rapidly westward toward the Long River. They were followed by Wabskeni's scouts. Ozagi was spotted by a scout he recognized as Wabskeni's son Nagmo. But Ozagi escaped unharmed. He and the other survivors reached Cahokia and sought more arms for the resisting Redearth warriors.

Ozagi did not return to the battleground as quickly as he had left it. He found time to drink with Prairiekin and bearded men, and time to learn that a Scabeater enclosure near the mouth of the Long River had been devastated by the Naché moundpeople of the south. He thought the news would please Lamina's warriors. But by the time he reached the Lakebottom with his arms and news, Lamina and most of his warriors had been massacred by Winámek's and Wabskeni's armies.

Sagikwe's strength returns as she tells me that the news of Lamina's death traveled in every direction. While Wabskeni and Winámek celebrated their victory in Bison Prairie, Redearth kin and their allies on both shores of Mishigami converged at the Lakebottom. They were not numerous, but they were determined to fight in a way Rootkin had never fought before. They built a picketed enclosure. All but those too young or too old vowed to fight until they fell.

Sagikwe says earth herself was rising up against the Invaders. The lakes, woodlands and prairies were defending themselves in the warriors on the Lakebottom.

Winámek was annoyed by the news that his three armies had not exterminated all western Serpents. He was annoyed by the interruption of his victory celebration. Refusing to believe his own scouts' report of the warriors' strength, he set out against them with part of his own army. His followers were routed. Winámek was killed, perhaps on the very spot where Wedasi had been murdered. Ahsepona and Kendawa were avenged. The great embroiler had stuck his long member into his last tree-hollow.

Wabskeni did not make his father's mistake. He waited until his and the head Scabeater's men recovered from the celebration. Then he waited until yet more men and arms arrived from Hochelaga. At last he pitted his entire force against the last stronghold of the Redearth kin. The warriors he confronted were no longer the people who had asked Scabeaters what they wanted on the Strait. They were no longer Rootkin who had not shed a drop of Scabeaters' blood. They had been warring for a generation. Reduced to bows and arrows against firesticks, they fought until the last of four hundred warriors fell.

Wabskeni, enraged by his father's death, turned all his force against grandmothers, mothers with children, girls. His army hunted them as if they were beaver.

Wabskeni's own pillagers stopped the carnage. They rounded up the five hundred survivors. A hundred were taken to Hochelaga by uniformed Scabeaters. The rest were brought to Bison Prairie. Wabskeni wanted them all killed. The head Scabeater wanted them sent to Hochelaga to be reduced to Panis.

Sagikwe and the Firekeepers and Prairiekin stepped between the captors and the captives. Even carriers rose to their feet. They knew it was Lamina's intransigence that had made the Scabeaters generous with gifts.

That was when Ozagi returned to Bison Prairie with arms from the southern Invaders.

Firekeepers and Prairiekin promptly took charge of the captives.

Ozagi, no longer on the battlefield, regained all his humor. Chebansi's son took a gift to the fiercest captive he could find. Shutaha's nephew would make the captives inviolable by adopting them. If his aunt could turn Scabeaters into Turtles, Ozagi would turn a fierce Serpent into a Firekeeper.

The girl greeted Ozagi's gift by spitting in his face.

The mutilator of Shutaha's son moved to stop her nephew, but not before Mota arrived with carriers and firesticks from Shuagan. Wabskeni strutted and raged. But his allies, the Scabeaters, were not ready to unleash a war in their own stronghold. The uniformed men retreated to Greenbay and the Northern Straits. Wabskeni, surrounded by armed hostility after his two victories, accompanied Blackrobes and crosswearers to Mishilimakina.

The fierce girl, whom Sagikwe named Wagoshkwe, accepted Ozagi's gift when she was told Ozagi's cousin had been murdered by Wabskeni. Wagoshkwe wanted the Firekeepers and Prairiekin to pursue retreating Wabskeni as he had pursued her kin.

Ozagi's mother was among the few who heard Wagoshkwe. Sagikwe was trying to shame Mota's carriers for their readiness to be Lamina's allies in distant Shuagan but not in the face of Lamina's enemies.

But the carriers were fit neither to fight nor to travel. Many of them were swelled with the smallpox. Soon Sagikwe herself was confined to her mat.

Mota learned of our approach and hurried to stop his Menoko and Oashi from entering Bison Prairie.

Sagikwe says the mere presence of the ant-men is the plague. She says Rootkin will regain their strength only by chasing the Invaders and their diseases back to the salt sea. Like Yahatase, she accepts fratricide, perpetual war, sacrifice.

Young Wagoshkwe is of the same mind. Sagikwe gives the girl Wedasi's arrowhead. The girl must assume it came from someone like Lamina. With her last breath, Sagikwe urges the young bride to fight the plague with plague.

Wagoshkwe begs her kin to help her arrange the burial ceremony for Ozagi's mother. They raise an earthen mound. The girl seems to retain a dim memory of a Tellegwi festival of bones, but not of its meaning. Her mother's kin are bison hunters in the Plains, perhaps descendants of the Tellegwi who once raised great mounds in the Beautiful River's valleys.

Ozagi senses himself an outsider at his mother's death ceremony. He too has dim memories of things whose meaning he never learned. His dreams have given him little guidance. Wedasi's grandson empties his bundle before me and asks me to sing to him of the objects in it. I take up the fishbones and sing of ancestors who came from the Ocean. Sagikwe thought only Invaders and their diseases came from the salt sea. I take up the feather. My mother Binesikwe could fly like a bird before she was weighed down by a cross. The shell, like the otterskin bundle itself, comes from a distant grandmother who dreamt of new life coming from the salt sea. The scroll fragment sings of the four ages of our ancestors. The herbs were gathered by Ozagi's great-grandmother. Their songs are lost.

The villagers of Bison Prairie are still mourning their dead when Menoko entreats me to return to Kekionga.

Wagoshkwe

We return to a half depopulated Kekionga. Pyerwá and Shen have just returned from Tiosa Rondion. Pyerwá is distraught. He lost his daughter, wife and mother. He gives Menoko the bead and cloth animal that had rested above Maní's mat in our former lodge. Menoko gives it to Maní's and Shen's son. Pyerwá gives Mangashko's pendant, the one Shutaha made for me, to Menoko's Oashi. Mangashko had wanted her grandson to wear it.

Pyerwá tells us Ubankiko as well as Lekomandá Darnó died nursing my Mangashko.

Pyerwá accompanied Shen and other survivors to the Strait. But Tiosa Rondion was not a refuge from the plague. Chacapwe, like her dead kin, like Lekomandá Darnó, died of what he had called a children's disease. Chacapwe died nursing half her village.

I cannot accept, any more than Menoko, that earth is not replacing the fallen, that she's blind, even hostile.

Manyan and Lekomandá Shak return to Kekionga from Uiatanon on the Wabash. Their two small children, Magda and Jozes, are quickly adopted by Oashi and Miní.

Manyan tells us that her plague was the news of the massacre of Lamina and his warriors. The smallpox did not visit Uiatanon.

Pyerwá and Shen insist that the plague didn't reach the Wabash because Mota failed to reach it. Pyerwá was convinced by Lekomandá Darnó that the smallpox came in the blankets from Shuagan. Shen encourages Pyerwá in this view.

The two men are friends again. Shen wants Pyerwá to restrict his gift-giving to his grandson, Shen's son Miní, and not to share gifts with Mota's kin. Shen pretends that earth's creatures exist for people acceptable to Lemond.

Menoko's pleading eyes keep Mota in fields and forest, away from caravans of furs and gifts. Menoko and Manyan help me arrange ceremonies of planting, of peace, of renewal.

When Kekionga's meager renewal is disrupted again, so soon after its depopulation, I dream Yahatase's dreams.

Wabskeni struts in, followed by his pillagers and manhunters and with new Scabeaters to people Kekionga's enclosure.

Wabskeni is recruiting yet another army to hunt down Redearth fugitives in plains and prairies beyond the Long River.

With Shen's aid, Wabskeni recognizes Mota as an ally of eastern Serpents. Then he remembers Mota as the man who gave strength to Ozagi's adoption of a Redearth captive. Looking closely, he recognizes in Mota the boy who exposed Wabskeni's murder of Kendawa. Wabskeni's men take Mota into the enclosure.

Menoko, who persists in believing earth is as generous as she is, cannot grasp the hostility.

I realize how incomplete Kekionga is without my Mangashko.

I remember Nopshinga's angry dance after the murder of Shutaha's son. I gather Kekionga's Prairiekin and carriers to a council. I encourage youths to paint themselves and sing loudly.

Menoko begs me to stop. She says she'll give herself if that gift will end the hostility. I see that I'm not Sagikwe or Yahatase. I'm Wedasi's adopted daughter, a Firekeeper, a peacemaker. I can accept fratricide, war and sacrifice no more than Menoko.

I beg Manyan to repeat the errand that embittered her life. Lekomandá Shak promptly releases Mota and comes with propitiatory gifts. The capture has been carried out without his knowledge.

When peace comes, it's flawed. Wabskeni's army leaves. Pyerwá leaves with it. To me, this is news of something as bad as plague. I hope Shutaha never hears of it. Manyan tells me the Scabeaters pressured Pyerwá to prove himself their kinsman and not Mota's. She says her brother urged Pyerwá to avenge the death of all his beloved by striking the plague-bringers. She thinks Shen inflamed Pyerwá against Mota and then sent him to confront Mota in the shape of distant warriors of the Plains.

I think Pyerwá sensed himself a stranger in dead Ubankiko's half-populated village. He had never felt close to me, and he had no close kin left except his grandson. Miní rejected Pyerwá's and Shen's gifts and spent his days with Menoko's Oashi. Pyerwá returned to the vessel that brought him, a Scabeater army.

The release of Mota and the departure of Wabskeni does not disband the council I called into being. Its flames are fed by news of more Scabeater victories, and by Mota's hostility to his two-time captors.

Shen, after Pyerwá's departure, openly expresses his hostility toward Mota's kin.
Yet the children are at peace. They enjoy each other as their mothers did a generation earlier. Shen's Miní and Mota's Oashi are not only cousins but each other's closest friends, and they are gentle guides to Lekomandá Shak's Jozes and Magda. All four consider themselves Firekeepers. Magda wears the amulet Ozagi once gave to her aunt Maní.
The arrival of Ozagi and several Firekeepers drives Shen completely out of sight. Manyan probably told her brother that Ozagi had come to avenge the massacre of Lamina. Ozagi's Wagoshkwe might give Shen reasons to hide behind the enclosure's pickets. But Wedasi's grandson set out from Bison Prairie to try to calm Wagoshkwe.
Ozagi proudly tells us his son Nanikibi was born shortly before Wabskeni's army returned to Bison Prairie. As soon as Wabskeni's pillagers joined forces with the Scabeaters who had returned to Bison Prairie's enclosure, Wagoshkwe and other adopted Redearth kin sent runners with warnings to the other shore. The enclosure's headman led his army toward Greenbay with the intention of converging with Wabskeni's beyond the Long River. Pyerwá joined this army.
Ozagi asks me what Pyerwá had against the Redearth kin. Nothing, I tell him; no more than he had against us when he first came with Boatmaker's army. Perhaps he seeks another new start.
Ozagi says neither the headman nor Pyerwá got beyond Greenbay. Warned by the runners, the few remaining Redearth kin on the other shore resisted the Scabeaters fiercely. Pyerwá was among the first to fall.
Wabskeni's army turned toward Greenbay on hearing the news. His massacre of the last Redearth kin on the other shore was horrifying even to his own followers. Then Wabskeni continued toward the sunset.
Bison Prairie's Redearth kin formed a council. Wagoshkwe called for the elimination of the Scabeaters' enclosure. Ozagi advised holding off until Peninsulakin had the strength to eliminate the enclosures in Mishilimakina, on the Strait and in Kekionga as well. He said he would set out in search of such strength. Most agreed with Ozagi. Wagoshkwe saw through him. She knew he was setting out, not to prepare war parties, but to prepare a peace council. Ozagi and other Firekeepers left Bison Prairie quickly and headed in the four directions.

Ozagi's lifelong friend Mota is hostile to the peace mission. But Ozagi knows that Mota wants to eliminate, not the Invaders, but their enclosures. Mota wants to take his furs where he pleases. Ozagi says that if we force the Scabeaters to make peace with the Redearth kin, we'll force them to empty the enclosures. They'll no longer need them.

Mota says no number of peace councils will force the Scabeaters to close their enclosures. Warring against Serpents is part of the Scabeaters' character. They'll find new Serpents in all four directions.

Kekionga's Scabeaters echo the disagreement among Rootkin. Shen, who is still uniformed, seeks revenge against the killers of Pyerwá and Maní. He struts and rages like a long-membered world-embroiler. Manyan ridicules him. She says Shen, like the Scabeaters' headman in Hochelaga and their Sun in his great lodge across the Ocean, is eager to celebrate victories over enemies who are distant.

Lekomandá Shak seeks peace. It's a mystery to me how the Scabeaters choose the men who head their war parties. Lekomandá Shak is no more of a warrior than Ozagi. His sole concern is to gather furs and hoard gifts. He would accompany the caravans to Shuagan if he could do so without losing his post and his permission to gather furs.

I stop dressing pelts. Few of my skins remain on the backs of Rootkin. They enlarge the hoards of Lekomandá Shak and his likes in Shuagan.

Menoko and Manyan and their children, as well as Shen's Miní, look forward to the council. I initiate my granddaughter and Manyan into the rituals of the ceremony of the three fires.

When we set out for Tiosa Rondion, Mota says Ozagi has prepared a council of women. Mota nevertheless accompanies the hundred or more Prairiekin from Kekionga.

We are not the first to reach the Strait's shore. Shutaha and more than two hundred Turtlefolk welcome us. Rootkin from Greenbay and the Lakebottom, Peninsulakin from Mishilimakina and Bison Prairie, are already counciling.

Even Ozagi's fierce Wagoshkwe is in Tiosa Rondion with her two sons and a daughter named Tinami, and she's pregnant with a fourth. Perhaps her children are turning her into a Firekeeper. Mota seeks a place near Wagoshkwe and her adopted Redearth kin.

All are gathered on a spot where, it is said, a split tree and a round rock once stood, the spot of the first Wiske's village.

Seventeen armed and uniformed Scabeaters stand like a grove of unnatural trees. Behind them, Blackrobes, the enclosure's headman, his scrollkeepers, Lekomandá Shak and the Strait's Lemond view the councilground from a distance. Manyan and Miní translate their pronouncements for Rootkin. Other Scabeaters, the hoarders, haulers and runners, mingle with Rootkin and Turtlefolk in Shutaha's village.

After many mutual welcomes and several harangues, Shutaha shows the belts which speak of Lekomandá Kadyak's binding himself in kinship with the people of the Strait. Shutaha says to the Scabeaters that all the original people on the Lakes are Redearth kin. She reminds the Scabeaters that kin do not war against kin, either here or in the world across the salt sea.

The Scabeaters' headman, Lekomandá Boarnoá, announces his agreement with the council's demands. He says the Scabeaters are ready to send peace belts to the Redearth kin on the other shore and even to those beyond the Long River.

But before the rejoicing, before the ceremony of the three fires and the expulsion of Wiske, before any belts are sent, Kukamigokwe's ghost arrives in Tiosa Rondion. The council is disrupted.

Wabskeni's son Nagmo comes from Mishilimakina with Blackrobes and uniformed Scabeaters. He seeks reinforcements for his father's army. Nagmo is told of the council and the agreement. He laughs. He says Wabskeni doesn't need reinforcements to fight Redearth kin. There are too few of them left. He says Wabskeni is fighting people of a different tongue who ride horses and attack with iron hatchets.

I wonder if it's Nangisi who carries the iron hatchets from southern Invaders of a different tongue to the horse-riders. My father would now be seeing his hundredth winter. He couldn't live without carrying. His grandson can't live without warring. Wabskeni matters to the Scabeaters only so long as there are enemies. Menoko shudders.

Shutaha and I remind Ozagi that the Scabeaters bound themselves to all of Tiosa Rondion's kin. The people Nagmo describes are not strangers but cousins. They're descendants of Beautiful River moundbuilders who once counciled at Tiosa Rondion's second fire.

Ozagi tells the Scabeaters that the horse-riders are embraced by the agreement.

Nagmo sarcastically asks if Tiosa Rondion's council embraces all of the Scabeaters' enemies, even the Naché and Chicasa people of the south. Lekomandá Boarnoá says the Turtle council does not have hegemony over all the tribes, as he calls them, of the west and south.

I tell Nagmo that the southerners are also distant kin of Beautiful River Tellegwi. The Scabeaters laugh. My grandnephew Nagmo is as much a Scabeater as Boatmaker or Falsetongue or this Lekomandá Boarnoá. I learned in Lekomandá Kadyak's day that Scabeaters make agreements only so as to put people to sleep.

Wabskeni will pursue this war. Few from Tiosa Rondion join Nagmo, who returns to Mishilimakina to wait for reinforcements from Hochelaga.

While Nagmo waits, Wagoshkwe and her kin dispatch scouts to warn their western kin. Mota sets out with the scouts.

Wagoshkwe gives birth to her fourth, a girl named Namakwe.

Shen moves in with Lemond. He takes the sister of a Scabeater as companion and becomes the headman's interpreter. He invites Miní to the celebration.

But Miní keeps his distance. He stays with Shutaha and seeks the company of Mota's Oashi and Wagoshkwe's oldest, Nanikibi.

The three boys are the first to learn the news from Mota and the scouts who return from the Plains. The horse-riders destroyed the Scabeater army. The great mutilator, the murderer of Shutaha's son, of Menoko's father, of Manyan's warrior, of so many of Wagoshkwe's kin, is dead. Mota says Wabskeni died slowly and badly. He refused to pass his mantle to his son. He begged to be revived. I remember what Wedasi told me about his uncle. He thought death came only to his singing, dreaming, bow-armed kin. He thought a fire-spitter who gave his life to the Invaders was invulnerable.

Wabskeni's son enters Tiosa Rondion on the heels of Mota. He's in a rage because the Plains warriors had been warned. His father had obviously preferred to attack unsuspecting victims. Nagmo mourns for his father by calling for war against those who betrayed him.

Mota and numerous Prairiekin are armed. Wagoshkwe's kin are ready to strike for their revenge. The Turtle council is destroyed.

In the face of impending fratricide, Shutaha leaves Tiosa Rondion. The unity Shutaha dreamt of is rupturing into fragments, and the fragments are flying apart. She tells me to nurse the great Turtle back to life in Kekionga. She seems to think we will not meet again. Crosswearing Turtlefolk make space for their Tiosa Rondion kin on the Isle of White Trees at the Strait's mouth.

Lekomandá Shak with several armed men accompany the retreating Turtlefolk. Kekionga's headman pretends to be protecting the Turtlefolk from Mota and the hostile warriors. Actually this Scabeater is getting himself out of the tension. He wants the fratricide no more than Shutaha.

Mota and the warriors distance themselves from the Strait's enclosure and wait for Nagmo's attack.

But Nagmo doesn't stir from the Strait's enclosure. The son, it seems, is not like the father. Perhaps he's more like the great-grandfather. Nangisi wanted people from all four directions to gather around his three fires. But he was satisfied with people from his own band of carriers. Nangisi's great-grandson wanted to eliminate all those who had betrayed his father. But he seems satisfied when he can no longer see them on the Strait's shore. He prepares no pursuit.

Menoko and I ready the canoes for our return to Kekionga. Mota and the other warriors tire of waiting, and they don't feel themselves strong enough to storm the enclosure.

When we're about to leave, we hear a message from Lekomandá Boarnoá. He has sent peace belts to the Redearth kin.

Ozagi, lip-biting Wagoshkwe and their four children leave the Strait's shore alongside us.

At the Strait's mouth, we pause at the Isle of White Trees. Oashi takes leave of his closest friend, who remains beside Shutaha. Miní tells me the island's Turtlefolk have resolved to stop sharing their corn with the Strait's armed men. This is undoubtedly the best way to remove the enclosure from Tiosa Rondion. It's the first time in forty winters that the Turtlefolk have moved to starve their Scabeating kin out. Miní tells me Shutaha is drinking poisoned water with crosswearers. I leave her, happy with the thought that the island's Blackrobes are about to lose their followers.

As soon as we reach Kekionga we learn that the Scabeaters' southern army destroyed the village of the Naché. The Scabeaters massacred all the warriors. They bound women and children and shipped them to islands in the Ocean. They left no one. I suppose the Scabeaters will now send peace belts to the Naché people.

I stay close to Ozagi's Wagoshkwe, although I still fear she'll spit in my face. There's something of earth in her, something I lack, something of earth defending herself from brutal assault.

More Eastbranch Rootkin seeking refuge from Oceanshore Invaders arrive in Kekionga. Lenapi's kinsmen come laden with eastern gifts.

Wagoshkwe greets the Eastbranch kin as allies who once guided her Redearth kin to the sources of the Oceanshore Invaders' weapons. But her gratitude isn't warm. She knows that in a world without the Invaders' firesticks or powder, her kin could not have been massacred.

Menoko's gift to me is a great-granddaughter. Mota proudly tells the Eastbranch kin they came in time to celebrate his daughter's naming. Menoko recruits Manyan to help with the arrangements.

Manyan is changed. She lost her fierceness when Lamina was massacred. She worries for her children. She has become a peacemaker. She's committed to reviving Ubankiko's village.

Wagoshkwe considers Manyan an enemy, a uniformed headman's woman and no more.

Menoko and Manyan complain to me of Wagoshkwe's hostility. Manyan asks me how I can be close to Shutaha and also to Wagoshkwe. Shutaha knows anyone can be either a Turtle or a crosswearer. People can wear each other's skins because they are kin, they're all each other's cousins, they're all children of the same great-grandmother. But Wagoshkwe seems to think only Redearth kin are real people. She thinks others are children of a beast.

I tell Manyan that the mother, the first parent, was a beast who ate her children. Some of her children acquired her voracious appetite. I start to tell about those who ate scabs, but I stop. Manyan hears only an old woman's story. But Menoko is in tears. I realize that Menoko, who cannot easily grasp what a beast is, feels my story more profoundly than I do, and her delicate frame has no room for what she feels. I'm afraid for my granddaughter.

I name her child Binesikwe, after the bird who flew out of Wiske's and into the Firekeeper's lodge. Wagoshkwe calls out the name Katabwe, warrior. Menoko's Oashi and Wagoshkwe's Nanikibi smile knowingly to each other. The two boys already know the peacebelts to Redearth kin will not bring peace to Kekionga. Menoko shudders. She carries her Binesikwe to her lodge, away from Wagoshkwe.

The gifts and liquid poison brought by Lenapi's kinsmen pull Mota away from forests and fields. Mota and Ozagi examine the cloth, the iron knives and hatchets, the pots and firesticks, as if they were spirit-powers. They repeatedly express wonder at the quantity given by the Invaders. Ozagi says Bison Prairie's carriers would give their arms to return from Shuagan with so many gifts.

Lenapi tries to dampen their enthusiasm, but Nangisi's heirs are deaf to his warnings. Mota and Ozagi gather the furs of every pelt dresser in Kekionga. They're determined to go east.

Lenapi is not inclined to accompany the carriers' caravan. He places himself alongside Manyan's son when Oashi and Nanikibi initiate Jozes into the mystery of shaping stone. Lenapi is intent on learning to make an arrowhead.

Wagoshkwe sees the Eastbranch man learning from the boys. She doesn't find the situation humorous. She doesn't admire the man for his openness. Wagoshkwe is repelled by what she sees. She finds Ozagi and pulls him to the spot. She asks if Ozagi wants his children to grow to such helplessness. She says Lenapi and his kin are unlike any of the creatures that share the world. The Eastbranch kin are unable to decorate themselves, feed themselves, or keep themselves warm. They depend on distant Invaders for their ornaments, for the weapons to hunt with and the pots to cook in, for the very coverings on their backs. They're incomplete people.

Ozagi hears Wagoshkwe with the same ears with which he heard Sagikwe: a hare's ears. Long-eared Wiske, the world-changer, is in Nangisi's grandnephew when he speaks to his children's mother, so like his own mother. He says the original people grew strong because they accepted earth's gifts. They knew the preparations needed to receive the gifts, and they knew how to use what they received. He says only the preparations have changed. Instead of doing a bone ritual, Rootkin now carry beaver pelts to Invaders. And the beaver brings everything. The beaver brings food, warmth, health and joy.

Wagoshkwe sees through Ozagi as if he were transparent. She says he and the Eastbranch kin are strong only from the smell of poisoned water. She says she can see them at a winter camp when all their gifts wear out. They starve and freeze like no other creatures that make earth their home. They sit on earth but cannot shape her clay into vessels. They're surrounded by stone but cannot shape arrowheads. Wagoshkwe says all living beings depend on earth's gifts. Only dogs depend on men's gifts. She says Ozagi fills himself with poisoned water to forget how weak he is. And then he puts the blame on the poisoned water.

Ozagi hears Wagoshkwe, perhaps more clearly than he ever heard his mother. But he does act like someone filled with poisoned water, someone who can't help himself. He says he's already part of the way to Shuagan, as if that explained why he had to go the rest of the way. And he returns to Mota and the carriers preparing the caravan.

Wagoshkwe readies her four children for the journey to Bison Prairie. She's pregnant with a fifth. She's intent on repopulating Kichigami without adopting Invaders or any of their gifts. Her Ozagi accompanies Mota and the carriers to Shuagan.

My great-grandson is already on the threshold of manhood. After his friends and his father leave, Oashi retreats to the fasting tent Menoko and Lenapi build for him.

While her son dreams, Menoko has me listen to Lenapi. She tells me he helped her hear Wagoshkwe's words to Ozagi. Menoko says Wagoshkwe is the only one among us who is looking up; the rest of us have our eyes turned to the ground.

Lenapi says many of his kin see with Wagoshkwe's eyes. But their hands no longer know how to shape stone, clay or bone. They are no longer able to accept earth's gifts.

Lenapi says the Invaders' gifts are not made by people as we know them. He once saw the makers of cloth in a large village of Oceanshore Invaders. He says the place in which he saw them was more like a hive than a lodge. Inside it, women and children were dwarfed by enormous metal and wood contrivances. They were enmeshed in a web of ropes and threads. They breathed steam. Each stayed fixed to a spot and endlessly repeated the same motions. Their faces expressed neither joy nor will nor pride.

Lenapi says those people were not kept inside the hive by armed men, but by a very powerful sorcery. They had been turned into something other than people. They were limbs of contrivances.

He says the Invaders' villages teem with such mutilated people. They have neither dreams of their own nor a will of their own. They are wielded, the way the Invaders' firesticks and other contrivances are wielded. They are made to burrow into earth's bowels for stones. They are made to stand in ovens wringing liquid metal out of stones. They are made to stay in steamy hives spinning thread and weaving cloth. The will to do these things is not in the people who do them. The entire hive is nothing but a contrivance for the making of cloth. The will is in the wielder of the contrivance.

Those who bring us the cloth and the pots, the Invaders in Shuagan, are no more able to make those things than we are. They are neither the wielders of the contrivances nor the mutilated limbs of the contrivances. They are hunters and carriers like the Rootkin whose pelts they take. Most of them are also hoarders. Each of these hopes to accumulate a hoard which will make him powerful enough to wield a contrivance made up of mutilated human beings.

Lenapi says the wielders of the contrivances, the masters of the hives, are not mere Scabeaters. He says we have no names for such beings because our stories do not encompass them. He names them shitmakers. He says the hives are enormous stomachs. They turn earth's substance into excrement. With each meal, the stomachs grow larger, earth's substance smaller. Once earth's substance is depleted, earth's creatures have nowhere to turn. They go to the shitmakers and beg for their substance. And when they eat this substance, they become addicted, like the Invaders themselves.

Lenapi tells me a great deal more, but it's beyond my grasp. Menoko is frightened. I ask myself if she hears more than I do. I hear Lenapi confirming the story of the Scabeater.

I see that a shadow has fallen across the world, and it's not our shadow. Yahatase thought the shadow was cast by the Blackrobes. Sagikwe thought it was cast by the ant-men. I thought it was cast by Kukamigokwe and Wiske's heirs. Wagoshkwe thinks it's cast by all the Invaders. But Lenapi says not all the Invaders cast shadows. He confirms what I told Manyan. Not all the monster's children acquired the parent's voracious appetite. Many of them are healthy shoots stunted in sunless hives. Shutaha knows how to cultivate a field where they can grow. I wonder if she knows how to make the sun's warm rays reach her field.

Menoko

Mota returns from Shuagan with heavily laden canoes. Ozagi goes on to Bison Prairie without stopping.

Mota tells us the Oceanshore Invaders and their helpers stumble over each other to greet carriers from the western Lakes. More than twenty Invaders keep their gift-laden lodges open day and night. Each tries to outdo the nineteen others in generosity.

Lenapi tells us these givers are not as generous as they seem. They take our furs to the Oceanshore, where they receive many times more gifts for them than they give our carriers.

Mota shows us objects that look like blankets, shirts, needles, kettles, firesticks, thread, cloth, timekeepers and shells for belts.

Menoko keeps away from the gifts. After what I heard from Lenapi, I see that the objects are not what they seem. They have an aura of unreality. Each blanket is identical. Each shirt is the twin of another. These objects were not made by human hands. They are creations of contrivances.

Mota is proud. He thinks he's enhancing Kekionga with things everyone needs. But he tries to hide his pride. He suspects a wasp in the bush. He gives the things away without ceremony. He frowns at any mention of Wiske.

While the strange gifts are being passed from hand to hand, Miní and his father arrive in Kekionga.

Shen prevailed on his son to help him repair his relations with the kin of the youth's mother. But Miní knows that Shen's sudden concern for Maní's kin is only a pretext for his return to Kekionga.

Miní tells me the Invaders are at war on the other side of the Ocean. The war keeps ships from reaching the Northern River.

The Scabeaters have no access to gifts, and they've gathered such a sea of furs that they're drowning in them. Their Sun across the water removed their permission to gather more. Each dreams only of disposing of his furs and getting his hands on gifts, any gifts. The only Scabeater on the Strait who has their Sun's permission is the headman of the enclosure, and he gives less than a trifle for a canoe full of furs. Word of Mota's caravan to Shuagan reached Tiosa Rondion. Shen and his new wife's brother, a Scabeater named Kampó, suddenly remembered Shen's kin in Kekionga.

Shen has never spoken to us with such kindness. He tells us of the hardships the war is causing Shutaha and the Strait's Turtlefolk. He councils with Lekomandá Shak. The two Scabeaters then send Manyan as their emissary to Mota—she who once pleaded for him to them. She's better suited for her present mission than she was for her earlier one. Manyan now dreams of reconstituting Ubankiko's village, of reconciling Mota with her brother and even Wagoshkwe with Lekomandá Shak.

Mota is not happy to let Shen carry his eastern gifts to Tiosa Rondion, even if Shen gives more furs than other gatherers. But he gives in to Manyan's entreaties.

After Shen and Miní leave, Oashi tells me he and his friend made a blood pact never to turn against one another. Oashi tells me that Miní has no sympathy for Shen's hardships. Shutaha urged Miní to accompany his father to Kekionga. Shutaha thinks that when Scabeaters take their furs where they please, they become loosened from their Sun, their headmen and their Blackrobes. While loose, they hear our songs, take part in our ceremonies, and seek adoption in our lodges.

Ozagi is back in Kekionga before the season ends. If he had returned as quickly twenty springs ago, Maní's life would have been happier.

Many of the carriers with Ozagi are nephews of Wabskeni's pillagers. Ozagi says Wabskeni's own son is anxious for more gifts from Shuagan. It seems that Nagmo, who once spared Ozagi's life, is more like his great-grandfather than like his father.

Ozagi tells me that after the peace with the Redearth kin, Nagmo and the remnants of Wabskeni's army moved to the Leaning Tree village near Mishilimakina. Like Nangisi, Nagmo took as companion a crosswearing Rootwoman who remembered the Rootkin's ways better than Nagmo. The war among the Invaders brought Nagmo the same hardships it brought Shen. Like those in Wagoshkwe's vision, the Leaning Tree villagers were no longer able to live without the Scabeaters' firesticks, cloth or food. Nagmo remembered his kin in Bison Prairie. He told his Katwyn about Bison Prairie's three fires and about the fourth age. Nagmo referred, not to the days of the old scrolls, but to the days of his great-grandfather Nangisi's youth.

Nagmo and the other remnants of Wabskeni's army were too much like Scabeaters to endear themselves to Bison Prairie's Firekeepers.

Nagmo's Katwyn was welcomed in most of Bison Prairie's lodges, though not in Wagoshkwe's.

While Ozagi was in Shuagan, Katwyn gave birth to a dead child. Wagoshkwe's eight-spring Tinami adopted herself into Nagmo's lodge to replace the dead child.

When Ozagi returned from Shuagan, he found the Leaning Tree people eager to accompany him in search of yet more eastern gifts. He found Wagoshkwe in a rage. She wanted Ozagi to implement her son's dream. Nanikibi had dreamt he had seen a wounded fox in a field of dead animals. The fox begged Nanikibi to avenge all the dead.

Wagoshkwe said those from the Leaning Tree village had murdered her kin and were now kidnapping her children. She wanted Ozagi to arm against them. Ozagi hastily left Bison Prairie with the former pillagers from the Leaning Tree village.

Mota and his carriers prepare to accompany Ozagi to Shuagan even though they've just returned. This time even Lenapi sets out with the caravan that carries furs and gifts from one Invader to the other.

When Mota is gone, Menoko comes to tell me what her son dreamt. His dream was similar to his friend Nanikibi's. Oashi saw himself on a trail lined with flowers. He was following a procession of animals, large and small, all wearing Shuagan cloth, all of them fat and awkward. They came to where the trail was covered by corpses of emaciated animals. The fat animals walked over the corpses. Oashi stopped. He woke.

Menoko cries when she tells me. She thinks the flowers are earth's ornaments. The fat animals are Shen and Lekomandá Shak who cannot see the ornaments, Manyan and her children Jozes and Magda who no longer comb earth's hair, Ozagi and

MIOGWEWE CONTINUES   1746   167

Menoko's own Mota who cannot see the emaciated corpses on the trail. The corpses are little Binesikwe, Menoko and I. The caravans move between the Peninsula and the Easternmost Lake like migrating birds, only more frequently. Mota stays lean. Ozagi grows fatter. The fattest of all are Lekomandá Shak, Shen, and the brother of Shen's wife, Kampó. It is said these three are becoming the fattest Scabeaters west of Hochelaga.

The war among the Invaders has ended, and the Scabeaters again have access to their own gifts. But the Scabeaters' gifts are made by human beings and are not as plentiful as the eastern gifts. The Strait's Scabeaters look with greedy eyes at the size of their three cousins' hoards. Their greed moves them to treat Lekomandá Shak as their grandfathers treated Lekomandá Kadyak. Their headman summons Lekomandá Shak to Tiosa Rondion.

Manyan takes leave of me with tears of rage. She tells me she dreamt of a new Lamina leading his warriors eastward from the other shore. Magda sadly embraces her five-spring cousin Binesikwe. Jozes promises to carry Oashi's greeting to Miní.

A Lekomandá Sentanj arrives. It is said he's a kinsman of Tiosa Rondion's and Bison Prairie's headman. This Scabeater's first act is to mutilate the forest behind the enclosure. Armed men turn the living trees into pickets and a scouting box. The Scabeater's second act is to pillage Mota's and Lenapi's returning caravan. He sends part of the loot to kindred headmen who stayed lean while Shen and Kampó grew fat. The rest of the loot turns up among the gifts Lekomandá Sentanj offers Kekionga's hunters for their furs.

Mota and the other carriers paint themselves and sing.

Mota seeks allies intent on destroying the Peninsula's enclosures. He finds a band, the warriors of Manyan's dream. Only the warriors he finds are not from the other shore. They're from the village of the Leaning Tree. They're former allies of the Scabeaters, nephews of Wabskeni's pillagers, crosswearing cousins of Nagmo's Katwyn. Kekionga's councilground is alive with war dances.

Lenapi leaves us. He tells us he'll spend his last days in Pickawillany in the valley of the Beautiful River, a village of Southbranch Rootkin beyond the reach of the Scabeaters' grasping arms.

Menoko despairs. There's a look in her eyes that hasn't been there since the smallpox killed Maní. It's the look I often saw in

Yahatase's eyes. I try to draw her eyes away from the councilground. Her children help me arrange the old ceremonies. Menoko's youthful Oashi, always in thought, always peaceful, helps me imagine Wedasi as a youth. Oashi's little sister helps me see myself when I had six springs. Perhaps she'll take my name instead of my mother's when I pass. Menoko's love for the two makes the terror leave her eyes. But I cannot keep it away. Its cause is beyond my reach.

The fat Scabeaters have lean spirits. The pettiest dreams guide them. They're cutting down Shutaha's tall tree, a tree that weathered forty-five harsh winters. They're not content with the tree, which most of them despised. The greed of a few is leading the Scabeaters to put out the three fires Nangisi lit in Greenbay ninety winters ago, fires which had burnt for them.

Ozagi arrives in Kekionga with his oldest son Nanikibi, not to join another Shuagan-bound caravan, but to seek peace. Bison Prairie too has divided into armed camps.

Ozagi tells us the enclosure's headman behaved the same way as the Invaders in Shuagan. When Nagmo started to accept Ozagi's eastern gifts, the headman suddenly became generous. He showered Nagmo with firesticks, powder, knives, red paint and much else. He gave nothing to carriers from the Leaning Tree village who refused to accept Ozagi's gifts.

The headman was generous only to those turning toward the enemy. He filled Nagmo, not only with gifts, but also with stories of raids and massacres perpetrated by eastern Serpents. He reminded Nagmo of his grandfather's league. And Winámek's grandson responded to all this sudden attention like an erection. He and many of the former pillagers were renewed. Rootkin used to be renewed by plantings, harvests, births. Nagmo's men are renewed by war, plunder, death. Nagmo entered the enclosure, reemerged wearing a uniform, and led an army to the eastern Woodlands.

As soon as the army left Bison Prairie, the headman's generosity ended. Nagmo's Katwyn and her kin from the Leaning Tree village grumbled. Katwyn grew so angry that when Wagoshkwe and her Redearth kin arranged a war council, Katwyn joined them. Wagoshkwe considered Katwyn a Scabeater and did not welcome her. Yet two of Wagoshkwe's children, Tinami and Kittihawa, were more at home in their aunt Katwyn's lodge than in their own. Wagoshkwe's Sigenak and her Namakwe saw with their mother's eyes. Nanikibi, the oldest, who had dreamt himself an avenger, tried to make peace.

Ozagi feared that the war dances would blind the dancers. He feared that, like Lamina in Tiosa Rondion, the enraged would strike at kin as well as enemies. He feared his children would face each other across a battlefield. He and Nanikibi set out to arrange another peace council on the Strait, to let the Scabeaters know that their tightness and haughtiness was poisoning their kinship with all the Peninsula's peoples.

Mota listens to his friend without sympathy. He's angry at Ozagi for arriving with talk of peace while Kekionga's warriors prepare for war. He's angry at Ozagi for still thinking he can council with the Scabeaters. He says Ozagi's wavering walk between the two Invaders is not the stride of an independent man but the gait of one who has drunk too much poisoned water. Such drunken peacemaking is not a sign of strength but of weakness. Mota says everyone who is awake has abandoned the Scabeaters. Only Nagmo and Ozagi remain asleep.

I urge Ozagi to seek Shutaha's help on the Strait. Ozagi expects help from Shen and Lekomandá Shak and other Scabeaters who have lost favor with Lemond. Oashi urges his friend Nanikibi to seek Miní.

Mota has not revealed his intentions to Ozagi. He accompanies Kekionga's painted men to the shore of the Lake of the Ehryes. They are to council with Turtlefolk from the eastern Woodlands, crosswearers from the Leaning Tree village, and some Turtlefolk who abandoned Shutaha's Tiosa Rondion. There's talk of removing all the hoarding cousins from the Peninsula, of destroying the enclosures, of burning the kinship belts that withstood forty-six winters.

Runners come to warn us. We leave our lodges and set up a camp in the forest.

Mota and carriers from the Ehrye shore surround Kekionga's enclosure. There's no resistance. The warriors enter the enclosure, seize eight uniformed Scabeaters, take the remaining gifts, and burn down the pickets and scouting box. They disarm Lekomandá Sentanj and his friends and send them scavenging.

Mota tells me a larger number of warriors set out to perform the same deed in Tiosa Rondion.

It's the first war between Scabeaters and Peninsulakin. Yahatase had wanted to cut off the first Scabeaters who reached the western Lakes. Sagikwe had known this war would come. But both would look with disbelief at the Peninsulakin engaged against the Scabeaters. They're mainly crosswearers, carriers, pillagers, those most like the Scabeaters, once their most loyal allies.

Menoko's Binesikwe, unlike her brother or her terrified mother, dances with joy, proud of her victorious father. She's not like the peaceful soul I named her after, and she's not a Firekeeper.

We return from our forest camp to Kekionga, only to find ourselves surrounded by the largest Scabeater army I've seen. The Strait's headman, flanked by Lekomandá Sentanj and a Hochelaga headman, lead all their uniformed men to Kekionga's councilground.

The attack on Tiosa Rondion failed to take place. The Strait was not embroiled in fratricide. Shutaha's tree did not fall. Only Menoko's terror-stricken expression keeps me from laughing.

Mota thinks Ozagi betrayed the Ehrye warriors' intentions to the Strait's Scabeaters.

Lekomandá Sentanj wants to retake Mota's gifts once again, but Mota no longer has them; they are in the bundles of Prairiekin who are leaving Kekionga. The Scabeaters want to disarm Mota and the warriors. But the warriors hold firm, and the Scabeaters, with all their armed men, are not ready to do to Mota what they did to Lamina. The headman boasts that his is the only army between the Sunrise Mountains and the Long River. Mota promises to return with an army that will disabuse the Scabeater of his illusion.

We leave Kekionga to the armed men. They can feed themselves, hunt and dress their own pelts, give their gifts to each other. That's Shutaha's way.

We make our way toward Lenapi's refuge among the South-branch kin of Pickawillany. Kekionga was my center for thirty-four springs. But Kekionga has stopped being a refuge to people from the four corners.

Oashi supports his mother, who shakes from sorrow. Menoko's heart is broken. Earth is not returning Menoko's love. Her village is dead.

Even Winámek's league of Scabeaters with Rootkin is finally dead. Carrion birds are eating its remains.

Mota hopes to find in Pickawillany another league, with the other Invaders. Oashi tries to make his father hear Lenapi's warning. The Invaders will aid us until we're depleted. Then they'll remove our bones and swallow our world.

Menoko's children have no sympathy for Mota's alliance. Oashi is a peacemaker. Binesikwe likes the Invaders of one tongue no more than those of the other. Our Southbranch hosts are of the same mind. They asked no one's permission to camp by the Beautiful River. Their council fire is independent of Scabeaters, Oceanshore Invaders, southern Invaders, eastern Turtlefolk. They welcome Eastbranch Rootkin from the Oceanshore, Firekeepers from every corner of the Peninsula, Prairiekin from Kekionga and from every valley. They remember the ancient Riverpeople's festival of bones. They know the mounds of this valley hold bones of ancestors of all the cousins gathering at Pickawillany.

Oashi and I stay close to Menoko. I feel my strength leaving me. I can no longer support my granddaughter. Menoko's joy is gone. She remembers the fields and forests of Kekionga, not the Riverpeople or their festival of bones. She's like a picked flower.

Lenapi builds a dream lodge for our lively Binesikwe. The girl brings her dream to me. Menoko listens to distant sounds and cannot hear her daughter.

My great-grandchildren have been dreaming of battlefields, corpses, wars. Binesikwe dreamt of an eagle swooping down on a serpent. The serpent offered to guide the girl, if she could ward off the eagle.

I am unable to interpret the entire dream for the child. I tell her the serpent is Yahatase and Shutaha. The serpent is the child's ancient Talamatun grandmother and her Tellegwi grandmother. The serpent is earth, who holds the grandmothers' bones in the valley's mounds. But I cannot speak of her dream's eagle. This eagle is not the child's namesake, my winged mother, whom only Yahatase thought capable of swooping down. My mother's descendants, Nangisi's heirs, swooped down, but as buzzards, not as eagles. Nor is the eagle the child's grandfather, who bore only the name. I urge Binesikwe to consult Lenapi. Her dream's eagle swoops down from the sky above his world.

Ozagi arrives with his five children, Yahatase's great-grandchildren, all beautiful, healthy and unscarred. Their coming completes the circle. Pickawillany is the refuge Kekionga once was, a gatheringplace of kin from the four directions.

But the joy is restrained. Ozagi comes without his fierce Wagoshkwe. And he tells us Shutaha is dead.

Ozagi seeks peace with his friend Mota. Nanikibi tells Oashi and me that neither he nor his father knew of the intentions of the Ehrye shore warriors, and could not have betrayed them. Mota's secret was known to everyone on the Strait. Ozagi and Nanikibi learned it from dying Shutaha.

Carriers of the Leaning Tree village had come from the Ehrye shore to council with the Strait's Turtlefolk. Their voices had reached everyone. They had asked the Turtlefolk to bury grievances that had been alive since Wabskeni's first attack on Tiosa Rondion. They had urged the Turtlefolk to help them destroy Tiosa Rondion's enclosure and remove the Invaders from the Strait.

To Shutaha, Wabskeni's heirs were no more attractive as the Scabeaters' enemies than they had been as the Scabeaters' loyal army. She knew that kin as well as foes would look like enemies from the Ehrye shore, as they had to Lamina.

Many Turtlefolk nursed the same grievances as the Leaning Tree carriers. When some among them joined the warriors on the Ehrye shore, Shutaha fell ill. She didn't want to see the fratricide that tore her village apart.

Ozagi and Nanikibi found Shutaha being nursed by Chacapwe's great-grandson Miní and surrounded by those she'd transplanted, nursed, adopted: Miní's aunt Manyan with Lekomandá Shak and her Jozes and Magda, Miní's father Shen and his wife and her brother Kampó, and the many whose names are strange to me. Manyan's fourteen-spring Magda regretted that Oashi had not come with a gift; Lekomandá Shak wanted her to take Kampó as her companion.

Nagmo and the Scabeaters' western army arrived in Tiosa Rondion from their eastern raids. They were immediately recruited to help defend the Strait's enclosure.

A few days later the Ehrye shore warriors camped on the Strait's other shore.

Shutaha was already dead. She had seen eighty-four winters. She did not live to see her tree stand through another storm.

The attackers sent emissaries to Turtlefolk and Rootkin. They were joined by no one in Tiosa Rondion. The emissaries re-crossed the Strait with the news that the armed men in the enclosure were not those the attackers had expected, they were not the few untried uniformed men who had been sitting on their firesticks drinking poisoned water with Shutaha's kin.

The attackers dispersed. Some returned to the Leaning Tree village, others to their camp on the Ehrye shore. The Scabeaters didn't follow them. They learned of Mota's victory and headed toward Kekionga to undo it. The uniformed men were not strengthened by Shutaha's kin. Even Nagmo didn't accompany them against near kin. He promptly set out to Bison Prairie.

When Ozagi and Nanikibi returned to Bison Prairie, they found only Sigenak and Namakwe in their lodge. Wagoshkwe's oldest and youngest daughters, Tinami and Kittihawa, had moved their mats to Nagmo's lodge, and both wore Katwyn's crosses. Wagoshkwe was gone. She had hoped the murderers of her kin would be removed from the western Lakes. She had danced with that hope until Nagmo returned from the Strait with the news that the attack on the Strait's enclosure had failed.

Wagoshkwe gave Sigenak her arrowhead and begged him to protect her children from traitors. She was convinced Ozagi had gone to the Strait to warn the Scabeaters. She and other Redearth kin of Bison Prairie set out toward the Long River and the Plains beyond, in search of survivors from the other shore who had learned to hunt bison on horseback. She went to live with kin who were not poisoned by the Invaders' gifts nor surrounded by picketed enclosures. It pained Ozagi to know that Wagoshkwe had left thinking he had betrayed her battle.

Ozagi was not in Bison Prairie long before the enclosure's Scabeaters again spoke of depradations committed by Serpents. They said Kekionga's Prairiekin had stepped into the Serpent's jaws. They described Pickawillany as a trap planted by Oceanshore Invaders. They said Pickawillany blocked their paths to the Long and Beautiful Rivers' valleys. Nagmo once again grew rigid.

Ozagi knew that the Scabeaters were already preparing another war, and he suspected they would send Nagmo against the kin in Pickawillany. Ozagi told Nagmo he would go to Pickawillany to warn his kin of the trap and urge them to return to Kekionga.

Sigenak and Namakwe were eager to join those they considered Wagoshkwe's allies, but Sigenak refused to leave Bison Prairie unless all of Wagoshkwe's children left. Nanikibi convinced Tinami and Kittihawa to leave Katwyn by telling them the Scabeaters were preparing to war against their father.

Nagmo, with the enclosure's headman and a Blackrobe and scouts, left Bison Prairie shortly before Ozagi. Nagmo and his band are said to be planting metal plaques in the Beautiful River's valleys, from the Sunrise Mountains to the other side of Pickawillany. Mangashko had known that the Scabeaters' war on Redearth kin was only the beginning of their war on all Rootkin.

Ozagi no longer wavers between Invaders like a drunken man. His last departure from Bison Prairie transforms him, as it transformed his father. Ozagi now understands Wagoshkwe—too late, as always. He scoffs at Mota for wanting to use the arms of one Invader against the other. He says the Oceanshore Invaders are waiting for Mota, eager to make of him what the others made of Nagmo. He says every metal button, every beaverhat, every ornamented coat they give so generously is a plea for murder, a scalping, a maiming of a kinsman.

I keep away from the strangers who come and go, bearing gifts from the Oceanshore. Menoko's children help me arrange my last ceremony. Ozagi agrees to impersonate the hare. Oashi lights the fires. I place a bear's head over mine. The dancers of the outer circle form themselves into the shape of a hand surrounding those around the fires. The chanting, dancing and whirling grow ever more frenzied. All at once the circles become a shapeless multitude. A hare chases the group at the first fire, then moves to extinguish the other fires. I block his path. He tries to chase me with a stick. But bears from every circle—my great-grandchildren, Wagoshkwe's children, Eastbranch and Southbranch kin—encircle the hare. We follow the fleeing hare to the fringe of the forest, poking him with our sticks.

I've given all my songs and stories to Oashi and Binesikwe. I'm as frightened for them as Menoko. I sense that another guest has arrived in Pickawillany. It's the guest I saw in Greenbay as a child, in Tiosa Rondion as a mother, in Kekionga and Bison Prairie as a great-grandmother. I do not want to see this guest a fourth time.

I have seen many beautiful things. I concentrate on them. Maybe this is what Menoko does when she looks so distant.

I want to lie down by my Tellegwi ancestors in the valley of the mounds. I long to be re-adopted by Yahatase and Wedasi. I long to rejoin Shutaha.

I remove the mask of the ancient woman with the long white hair.

Chapter 5.

Katabwe

Lenapi

Again I find myself by the Strait's edge, vaguely aware of a self separate from the mask, but not of a body. It's dawn, the eighth moonless night is ending. The same shadowy figure approaches, a mask in one hand, a bundle in the other. Putting on the mask, I remember myself as Katabwe; I recognize the figure as lean Sigenak and the bundle as his brother Nanikibi's. Eagles darken the sky, dead serpents cover the ground. This is the day I dreamt of, the day I dreaded.

My dream's eagle had swooped down on the serpents and killed them. I was a child when I dreamt; I thought the eagle was my father Mota, who had swooped down on Kekionga's Scabeaters. When I told my dream, brother Oashi frowned, great-grandmother Miogwewe told me I was a daughter of Serpents, grandfather Lenapi said the rumcarriers from the east were eagles, weird eagles that looked like gift-bringing men but hid their beaks and claws behind the cloth, meat and bread they brought. He said they were worldeaters, they ate land and animals and people, but my father Mota couldn't see their beaks or claws, his hatred of Scabeaters blinded him. I didn't believe grandfather Lenapi, I was proud of my father's hatred, I wanted him to chase the Scabeaters from Kekionga, I hated Pickawillany and wanted to return to my birthplace.

When granduncle Ozagi and his five joined us, I found allies in Sigenak and Namakwe, who saw as I did, who admired my father for hating the Scabeaters, who said their mother Wagoshkwe had tried to oust the Scabeaters from the Lakes and had joined Redearth kin beyond the sunset with whom she would try again. I hated fat Tinami and little Kittihawa for wearing crosses and seeing with the eyes of Scabeaters, and I hated Nanikibi for straddling the two camps, unable to decide.

My father smoked and drank with the rumcarriers and asked them to bring their weapons to Pickawillany. That made everyone frown, except me and Sigenak and Namakwe. Sigenak defended my father; he said his mother's Redearth kin had fought the Scabeaters for twenty winters with weapons from the Oceanshore Invaders.

If those Invaders were my dream's eagle, then it was with them I wanted to ally myself, alongside Sigenak and Namakwe and their mother Wagoshkwe and the Redearth kin. If I was a daughter of Serpents, as great-grandmother Miogwewe insisted, I was anxious to coil my body and spring, I had no patience for her dances and songs. She herself had told me that my Serpent ancestor Yahatase and my grandaunt Wagoshkwe hadn't used up their bodies in dances nor their tongues in song.

I helped prepare the masks for great-grandmother's ceremony only because Oashi begged me to. I had never seen a Firekeeper's ceremony, but I knew that dancing bears would chase a hare through the woods to make the hand in the Lakes whole and strong, and I was sure great-grandmother's dances wouldn't succeed where father's arrows had failed.

My father didn't help with the preparations; he brought rum after the dances began. The rum, or mere contact with the rumcarriers, spread disease among the dancers.

Great-grandmother recognized the presence of the disease before anyone was afflicted; she broke off the celebration and pulled my brother and me to our lodge; she sang to us of manybodied Digowin who had risen from the Ocean to reclaim her children, who had swallowed the Rootkin of the Oceanshore and the bison-hunting Tellegwi of the Beautiful River's valleys. And then she closed her eyes.

I went with Oashi to look for our mother. We found only our father, drunk and ill. He spoke of leading an army against the Scabeaters with the rumcarriers' weapons, and he showed us the belt they'd given him.

Oashi's face was wet with tears; his eyes told me he knew where our mother was: she'd sensed the presence of the smallpox as soon as great-grandmother had, she'd known greatgrandmother was going to her lodge to die, she'd heard our father boast of his new alliance while he broke out in blisters, and she'd left Pickawillany at night to walk alone toward Kekionga.

Wagoshkwe's five hovered in front of their father's lodge. Granduncle Ozagi was blistered; he had given his otterskin bundle to undecided Nanikibi, the oldest.

The last council in Pickawillany was a gathering of the plague's survivors. Wagoshkwe's five were motherless and fatherless. Of all my near kin, only my brother was alive.

I was confused. When grandfather Lenapi spoke, I listened carefully to every word. His words were meant for me and Namakwe and Sigenak and my father's companions. He said we thought the plaguebringers existed to help Rootkin oust Scabeaters from the Lakes, we wanted to pit one Invader's strength against the other, because we were young and had young memories. He said all the Invaders were deadly as enemies and deadly as friends, they existed to oust Rootkin from the world, they treated forest allies the same way they treated the forest's trees and animals, as things to be enclosed, tamed and eaten. After every clash when Rootkin had allied with one or the other Invader, both Invaders had remained, but the Rootkin had vanished.

Grandfather Lenapi said the Peninsulakin, meaning my father's companions and Namakwe and Sigenak and I, knew something of the Invaders my great-grandmother had called Scabeaters, but we knew nothing of those we embraced as allies, who were meaner and more numerous.

He said there were thirteen different gangs of Invaders along the Oceanshore, and we knew only one such gang, those he called Witchburners because they set fire to their medicine women, those who had burnt the villages of my ancestor Winámek's Oceanshore kin, those called heretics by the Northern River's Blackrobes. Winámek had allied with the Scabeaters against the Witchburners, my uncle Nagmo was still entangled in that alliance, and after six generations of war, there were no Rootkin on Winámek's Oceanshore or on the Northern River, the Witchburners were as numerous as sands, the Scabeaters remained strong, and the only original people between them were Turtlefolk of the Eastern River bound together in a league that treated all others as enemies.

Harassed by Nagmo's northern allies, my father's companions sought to ally with the generous strangers who brought rum to Pickawillany. To grandfather Lenapi the rumcarriers were neither generous nor strangers, they were emissaries from two gangs who occupied the Oceanshore to the south of the Witchburners.

The rumcarrier with the wagons, a man called Kraw-on, came from among the Cheaters who had invaded the shore of Grandfather Lenapi's Eastbranch Rootkin. Less murderous than the Witchburners north of them or the Slavers south of them, the Cheaters used their rifles only to kill animals; against people they used rum, gifts and tricks. When they'd first arrived, they'd formed a chain of friendship with the Eastbranch Rootkin, and had accepted gifts with gratitude. When they grew stronger they brought gifts, and when they gave, they wanted more than gratitude. First they wanted corn, then animal furs, then the fields where the corn grew and the forests where the animals roamed. Exasperated Eastbranch kin told the Cheaters to take what they wanted once and for all, and then stop nibbling. The Cheaters said they wanted only so much land as they could cross on a day's walk. When the Rootkin agreed to grant them so much and no more, the Cheaters dispatched their fastest runners along a prepared course in relays. The Eastbranch kin, who had given their word, abandoned their ancestral shore, rivermouth, bay, fields, forests and villages, and retreated to the Sunrise Mountains. And now the Cheaters' emissary Kraw-on crossed the mountains to the Beautiful Valley looking for other Rootkin with whom to form a chain of friendship, but not because he was friendly.

The other rumcarriers in Pickawillany were emissaries from Invaders grandfather Lenapi called Slavers, Invaders as land-hungry as the Cheaters north of them, but without the Cheaters' scruples about murdering people. The Slavers had first landed among Oceanshore Rootkin of the outer banks just south of the Eastbranch shore. After being fed and warmed and then guided from outer to inner banks, after being feasted and caressed by the eloquent Powhatan's kin, they had murdered their hosts, they had hunted Powhatan's Rootkin as if they were game, and they had enslaved all those they hadn't killed. All their ingenuity went into measuring and dividing the earth, granting patches of earth to landsuckers and empowering each to kill everything on his patch so as to repopulate it with enslaved human beings. Having exterminated Powhatan's kin and divided Powhatan's shore into slave patches, their emissaries now crossed the mountains into the Beautiful Valley looking for more patches. Those who had promised my father weapons and given him a belt were emissaries for a landgang familiar to grandfather Lenapi, and soon enough to me, the landgang of Ua-shn-tn and Kre-sop.

Grandfather Lenapi said he intended to leave Pickawillany: the village was no longer a refuge; there was too much disease, too much rum, there were too many Cheaters and Slavers. None spoke against him, not Sigenak nor Namakwe nor my father's companions. Grandfather Lenapi invited his friend Shawano and other Southbranch kin of Pickawillany to join the Eastbranch kin in the Sunrise Mountains. He said the Cheatérs and Slavers who were crossing the mountains were avoiding the Eastbranch villages because the Eastbranch kin had nothing left that the Invaders could take away. He took it for granted that Oashi and I would go with him.

Oashi loved the valley of the mounds and the Southbranch kin in it, but he agreed to leave it, saying the Sunrise Mountains were the gateway to the Valley, a place for councils and ceremonies, for peacemaking. To me, a mountain gateway was a place for ambushes.

We invited Wagoshkwe's five to go with us, but Sigenak and Namakwe hadn't heard Lenapi; they still burned to revive my father's alliance and resume Wagoshkwe's war; their sisters Tinami and Kittihawa couldn't wait to rejoin their crosswearing cousin Katwyn in Nagmo's lodge of the opposite camp; while Nanikibi, still undecided, as convinced as greatgrandmother Miogwewe that songs and dances would make clawed eagles kind, wanted to unite the two camps by lighting three fires. Oashi and I accompanied Lenapi and Shawano toward the rising sun, past the fork that makes the Beautiful River, to the pair of Eastbranch villages cradled in a wooded valley of the Sunrise Mountains. The mountain village of Lenapi's Eastbranch kin reminded me of my childhood's Kekionga: I was happy; I seemed to be living closer to the first times, when there were no Invaders. While I learned to hunt with a bow, Oashi learned the songs of Eastbranch Rootkin, immersed himself in ceremonies, memorized each detail on grandfather Lenapi's scroll. He told me the irruption of Invaders in our world was temporary, the rhythms lived by the generations described on the scrolls were bound to resume.

But I had dreamt of clawed eagles swooping down on the world, and my dream told me more than the ancient scrolls did. Our happiness didn't weather four seasons.

The Cheaters who occupied the Eastbranch shore, having scruples about fighting their own wars, showered rum and gifts on an Eastbranch man named Shingis and named him headman of all Eastbranch Rootkin, hoping he would do for them what my father no longer could: defend their rum caravans from attacks by Scabeaters and their western allies. Meanwhile, a landgang among the Witchburners on Winámek's shore began granting patches of the Sunrise Mountains to rifle-armed landsuckers, claiming that the Sunrise Mountains had been given to the Witchburners by the Turtleleague of the eastern Woodlands. Landsuckers arrived; they aimed their rifles against everything that stirred on the patches they'd been granted.

Lenapi's kin grew alarmed; they counciled; they urged Shingis to speak to those who'd named him headman. Shingis visited the chief Cheaters and he was assured the Sunrise Mountains were inviolable and would belong to Rootkin until the sun no longer rose; that assurance was all the Cheaters would offer Shingis, since they were averse to armed clashes. Shingis went to the others, the Slavers who occupied Powhatan's shore, offered to scout for the army they were preparing for a clash with Scabeaters and western Rootkin, and asked if this army, after its victory, would help oust the destructive landsuckers from the Sunrise Mountains. The army's headman, called Bra-duck, told Shingis neither wolves nor wild men would inherit the land his army conquered. Stung by this response, Shingis and his warriors resolved not to help this army to victory; they joined the western army and helped see to it that Bra-duck inherited no land. Bra-duck and most of his army were killed; the remnants fled like rabbits from wolves; it was said that no Oceanshore Invaders had ever suffered a greater defeat.

As soon as they learned of Bra-duck's defeat, the Cheaters who occupied the Eastbranch shore lost their scruples about killing people. Betrayed by their man Shingis, they turned their wrath on Shingis's kin, proclaimed that the sun would no longer rise over the inviolable Eastbranch villages, and offered bounties for the scalps of Eastbranch men, women and children. They had swallowed the Oceanshore by cheating; they turned to their neighbors' ways to swallow the Mountains. They sent ammunition to the landsuckers and urged them to postpone the killings on their patches and join the roving bands of bountyseekers.

Peace and happiness were now part of a brief past. Alarms and rifle shots made up the rhythm of days. Eastbranch and Southbranch men took turns as hunters, scouts and warriors; women took up hatchets and bows.

The end came on a day when Oashi had left with hunters. I was in grandfather Lenapi's lodge; Shawano was visiting. Scouts told us a gang of bountyseekers was guiding three hundred redfrocked soldiers toward our village.

I heard shots, the village was surrounded, the forest was infested with scalphunters, the Redcoats and their guides began to set fire to the lodges, foodstocks, even the fields.

Grandfather Lenapi said we were too few to fight, but when our lodge filled with smoke he said we were too many to die. Handing me his bark scroll, he grabbed the old rifle he hadn't used since his first days in Kekionga and rushed out of the burning lodge. I rushed after him. Shots deafened me and I fell. Shawano had pulled the bow from my hand and tripped me; he held me to the ground, motionless; more shots rang out. Then the Invaders moved away from the ashes of our village.

Shawano and I weren't scalped. But grandfather Lenapi was dead. He hadn't killed any Invaders; his old rifle was jammed.

Flames burnt the Eastbranch Rootkin out of the last corner of their original home.

The flames that burnt the village burnt in my heart. I left the scroll with Shawano, picked up my bow and ran toward a circle of dancing Southbranch warriors. I covered my body with the charred remains of lodges. The dance filled my head with thoughts of plagues, rumcarriers and scalp-hunting landsuckers.

I accompanied the warriors to the nearest patch of downed trees and furrowed earth. We didn't ask if the landsuckers we encircled had been among the killers of our kin; they hadn't asked if their victims had been among those who'd routed Braduck. My arrows hit a rifle-armed man and an unarmed woman. When the woman fell, I lost my rage.

I was relieved when at last the warriors returned to the camp by our burnt village. I was expected to keep track of two of our captives, yellowhaired children of the Invaders I had killed, the older of whom stared at me with hate-filled blue eyes. Shaking from exhaustion, hunger and disgust, I spat in her face.

The camp was full of strangers. I found Oashi lying in Shawano's tent, with a bullet in his leg. He clutched grandfather Lenapi's scroll, said nothing about his wound, and told me we were alive only thanks to the strangers, who were our western Rootkin; our uncle Nanikibi was ill among them.

Our western kin, after routing Bra-duck, had defeated every army the Oceanshore Invaders had sent against them, and had stalked the Redcoats sent by the Cheaters against the Eastbranch villages. Their arrival had kept the bountyseekers from gathering all the scalps in our burnt village, and had tied up the defenders of the patches I had raided.

The westerners urged the Southbranch and surviving Eastbranch kin to move toward the setting sun and join the Rootkin of the Lakes and Prairies.

I yearned to return to the places where my grandmothers had lived, but I didn't want to go encumbered by captives; I wanted to kill the yellowhaired sisters.

Oashi took my hand and placed it on the pendant that hung from his neck, binding me to it; he said the pendant's maker, our great-grandmother Shutaha, had taken the children of clawed eagles into her lodge as her own kin. Shawano and other Southbranch kin who thought as Oashi did adopted the girls.

When we separated from Shawano's kin near the fork where two mountain rivers merge to flow toward the sunset as the Beautiful River, the younger girl stayed with the Southbranch kin, but the older clung to the Eastbranch survivors who accompanied the western warriors to Bison Prairie on the Peninsula. During the long journey, Yellowhair cared for the wound on Oashi's leg and began to call me Nitis, friend, although she had cause to want me dead.

I was miserable during my first spring in Bison Prairie, and not only because of the hunger, the injuries, the disease. I felt closer to Yellowhair, who nursed Oashi until he began to limp, than to the villagers who lodged and caressed us. To me the villagers weren't only strangers, they were hated Scabeaters, and I was dismayed to learn they were cousins or aunts or uncles, all my kin.

Uncle Nanikibi recovered slowly in the lodge of the crosswearers Nagmo and Katwyn, nursed by his crosswearing sister Kittihawa.

Nanikibi remembered the name his mother Wagoshkwe had thrown against my great-grandmother's at my naming; he called me Katabwe, warrior, half admiring and half teasing me for having thrown myself into raids without knowing that an army protected me from behind.

Oashi plied Nanikibi and also Miní with questions, eager to learn how our uncle and cousin, both peacemakers, had arrived in the Sunrise Mountains as warriors in uncle Nagmo's army.

Many springs earlier, before I was born, Oashi, Nanikibi and Miní had sworn never to become embroiled in the wars of the Invaders; they considered themselves heirs and keepers of the fires ancient Wedasi had lit on the Peninsula. Oashi stayed away from our father's warriors in Kekionga, Nanikibi from his cousin Nagmo's army in Bison Prairie, and Miní from the enclosure's armed men on the Strait.

Miní included others in the pact, among them Batí, the son of the enclosure's haircutter, Aleshi, the nephew of the enclosure's headman Belést, and Miní's own cousins Jozes and Magda when they moved from Kekionga to the Strait. A growing number of the Strait's youth counciled and danced with Miní in Karontaen, the village of Shutaha and the Strait's Turtlefolk. The old men of Lemond, the Scabeaters' council, including Jozes's and Magda's father Lekomandá Shak, disliked their children's ever freer ways. Lekomandá Shak pulled Jozes into the store he shared with Miní's father Shen and their partner Kampó, and he pushed Magda into a marriage with Kampó. Miní, Shutaha and Magda's mother Manyan opposed this marriage; ever since she'd left Kekionga, Magda had dreamt of Oashi. But Magda would never be reunited with my brother. Lemond's army set out to Kekionga to retaliate against my father's capture of their enclosure; Shutaha died, Miní became the keeper of the Strait's belts, Lemond's army returned to the Strait and boasted of having eaten my father and all his allies. Fearing Oashi dead, Magda walked into the arranged marriage like a person asleep. Nine moons later she gave birth to a son and left the world to look for Oashi among the ghosts, not knowing that my brother and I were dancing in Pickawillany. The day Magda died, uncle Nagmo, with Bison Prairie's headman Jumon and an army of warriors from the Leaning Tree village, arrived on the Strait to recruit warriors against the Oceanshore Invaders in the Beautiful Valley. Few of the Strait's youth joined Nagmo. Miní's friends had in the meantime become kin by marriage; Batí's brother Antó had married Kampó's sister; Aleshi's older sister had taken Magda's place in Kampó's lodge. The friends refused to be embroiled in a war between the Invaders.

Mini

Lekomandá Shak was among the few from the Strait who joined Nagmo's war party; he had been removed from the Kekionga enclosure for letting furs reach the Oceanshore Invaders, and he wanted to redeem himself in Lemond's eyes.

But when Nagmo led the party toward Pickawillany his small force disintegrated: the Leaning Tree warriors refused to attack my father, Lekomandá Shak refused to attack Ozagi. Nagmo retained a remnant of an army only by diverting it against a distant enemy; instead of attacking Pickawillany, he went to Cahokia on the Long River, plundered two caravans of rumcarriers, and then went to the eastern end of the Beautiful

Valley and planted metal plates on sacred spots. These plates, it was said, shouted insults to the Oceanshore Invaders, and provoked the Slavers on Powhatan's Oceanshore to dispatch against Nagmo an army led by the brother of the landgang headman Ua-shn-tn. The two armies met and called each other intruders; each demanded that the other leave the Beautiful Valley. Nagmo's was the smaller and called a truce. Lekomandá Shak and Bison Prairie's headman Jumon carried a truce flag to Ua-shn-tn's tent, and never again emerged. Ua-shn-tn and his cohorts suddenly rode off on their horses. The bodies of Lekomandá Shak and Jumon were inside the tent, their scalps removed.

While the Scalper Ua-shn-tn rode eastward to boast of his victory against a western army, Nagmo and his reduced band became the nucleus of a western army larger than the legendary army gathered by his grandfather Winámek. News of the scalping under a truce flag was carried to councils in every corner of the Peninsula; when Oashi's friends learned of the scalping, they broke their oath and became embroiled in the Invaders' war. On the Strait, Miní, the scalped man's nephew, as well as Batí and Aleshi, prepared to go to war.

Nanikibi, Sigenak and their three sisters had just returned to Kekionga from Pickawillany; their father was dead; Oashi and I were on our way to the Sunrise Mountains. When Nagmo passed through Kekionga to recruit more warriors against the scalper, Wagoshkwe's five separated in three directions. Sigenak and Namakwe remembered that Nagmo's grandfather had hunted their mother's kin from their first appearance at the Strait to their final demise on the Lakebottom, and Sigenak wanted to attack, not distant Ua-shn-tn, but Nagmo, as well as Jozes, Kampó and Shen, who had reopened their Kekionga fur-gathering post. Nanikibi hesitantly joined Nagmo. Little Kittihawa set out for Bison Prairie to rejoin her crosswearing cousin Katwyn. Tinami stayed in Kekionga to do what her father Ozagi would have done, to make peace between Sigenak and Jozes, who remained in his fur post when the warriors set out to avenge his father's death.

The western warriors found Scalper Ua-shn-tn barricaded in a small enclosure near the fork that makes the Beautiful River. This time Ua-shn-tn and the outnumbered Redcoats advanced with truce flags. They weren't scalped; they were marched out of the Beautiful Valley to the beat of drums, their tails drooping between their legs. Scalper Ua-shn-tn looked closely at the drummer Batí and at Miní, Aleshi and Nanikibi; he would remember them.

Nanikibi, Miní and their companions set out again when it was learned that another army of Redcoats was moving into the Beautiful Valley, Bra-duck's army of thousands, guided by Shingis and Eastbranch Rootkin. This army hadn't yet reached the mountain pass when Shingis and his kin turned up in the westerners' camp; they said the Redcoats treated the Eastbranch guides as slaves, rejected all advice, expected the guides to be in the front line, and boasted that only Slavers would inherit the fruits of victory.

Smug Bra-duck moved toward the mountain pass without guidance, even Ua-shn-tn's, having relegated the drummed-out scalper to the baggage train in the rear. Bra-duck and his thousands advanced directly into the ambush of waiting Rootkin. The headman and most of his Redcoats would inherit no more: they shot and stabbed each other in their mad rush to escape from the mountains, led in their flight by the rear, by Ua-shn-tn, who abandoned weapons, powder, cattle, horses, baggage wagons, and ran at the head of the fleeing remnant.

The victorious westerners, strengthened by Southbranch and Eastbranch kin and by Hochelaga crosswearers, went on to drive Invaders from Shuagan on the Easternmost Lake and from enclosures along the Northern River, pushing them toward the strip of Oceanshore where Rootkin no longer roamed. At one of these enclosures, the treacherous Redcoats, pretending to want a truce, gave the westerners blankets taken from men afflicted with smallpox. The disease spread more suffering and death than all the Oceanshore Invaders' armies had been able to do. Nanikibi was one of the many who broke out in blisters but survived.

It was this disease-afflicted but still undefeated army that routed the villageburners who had killed Lenapi and destroyed his village; these were the victorious warriors Oashi and I and my yellowhaired captive accompanied to Bison Prairie on the Peninsula.

The three of us, Oashi and I as well as Yellowhair, were made uneasy by the kindness of aunt Katwyn and Nanikibi's youngest sister Kittihawa. We were repelled by the crosses and pictures, by the iron kettles and needles, by the clothes and the alien ways. We didn't have tears to shed for the privations suffered by uncle Nagmo's kin, privations they said came from Redearth hunters abandoning Bison Prairie for the Plains and Firekeeping planters for Pickawillany.

We were relieved when kin from the Strait arrived to celebrate the victories, when Nanikibi's sister Namakwe, who wore no cross, and Batí's sister Nizokwe, Miní's bride who filled the air with song, helped us raise a lodge at a comfortable distance from Nagmo's.

Oashi was together with his childhood friends for the first time in ten springs. Yellowhair and Nizokwe took to each other as if they had spent their childhood together. I felt among my own kin, the ways of Miní and Batí and Nizokwe being no more alien to me than my great-grandmother's. Yet Batí and Nizokwe were no more Rootkin than Yellowhair, being two of four children of Lemond's haircutter and his Hochelaga woman. All four loved to make songs with their voices, with flutes, with strings, even with reeds and sticks. Three of them, Batí, Nizokwe and their brother Antó, had grown up in aunt Manyan's lodge close to Magda, Jozes and their cousin Miní, close to the bowlmaker Shutaha.

Nizokwe had stopped singing only three times in her life: when great-grandmother Shutaha died, when Nizokwe's closest friend Magda died giving birth to Tisha, and when her brother and Miní left the Strait with the western army; she had become Miní's bride on the eve of the army's departure. She had remained silent all through the warriors' absence. Aunt Manyan had tried to revive Nizokwe's voice by giving her a bead and cloth animal that my mother Menoko had once made for Miní's mother, and by saying that Menoko's spirit lived in Nizokwe. But Nizokwe kept silent; she learned from refugees fleeing from a distant eastern island that armed Witchburners had chased people from their lodges and fields; she saw Lemond's Navár and Decuánd chase villagers from the Isle of Rattlesnakes which all had shared in common; she thought the world was ending.

Nizokwe's voice returned only when she reached Bison Prairie and threw her arms around Miní and Batí. She kept on singing while helping us raise our lodge, while showing Yellowhair the secrets of bowlmaking.

Before long, Yellowhair sang songs of Rootkin and Turtlefolk alongside Nizokwe, spoke with increasing fluency and danced. Oashi, whose eyes were ever on his healer, called my yellowhaired captive Lókaskwe, Bowlmaker.

Lókaskwe told us the people my arrows killed, her kin, were innocents. Their name was Ba-yer, they spoke a tongue different from that of the Oceanshore Invaders, they'd had little to give and gave it all to the landgang that sent them to the Sunrise Mountains. They had left their world so as to flee from landgangs, had crossed the Ocean to find people who shared and gave as freely as their own kin had used to do. But rifle-armed bountyseekers intimidated Lókaskwe's father into joining a raid against those he'd come seeking. He'd wanted to be accepted by the unfamiliar people he raided, but he was familiar with oppression and desolation and he knew only to oppress and desolate, until he was stopped by people who defended themselves as his never had.

Oashi begged Lókaskwe to repeat her story over and over; he couldn't believe that the Invaders overrunning our world had themselves been overrun; he couldn't believe that those who had experienced desolation could be so inhuman as to carry desolation to others.

Oashi drew Lókaskwe away from singing Nizokwe and sang his songs to her, great-grandmother's songs. Sitting by Lenapi's unrolled scroll, he sang to her of the Tellegwi, Neshnabek and Talamatun who had inhabited the lakes, valleys, woodlands and oceanshores before desolation arrived in great ships. Lókaskwe said her father had told her of the world Oashi described: its name was Paradise.

Oashi, who wore the pendant Shutaha had made for Miogwewe, begged me and Nanikibi and Miní to help him arrange an adoption and renewal ceremony as our great-grandmother would have arranged it.

On the eve of the ceremony, Nanikibi brought me a gift, which I accepted. The adoption and renewal was a double linking.

Lókaskwe and Oashi would share songs as well as lodge and mat and food.

Nanikibi and I, descendants of ancient Wedasi and the first Nangisi, of ancient Yahatase and the first Binesikwe, reunited all the peoples of the Lakes and Prairies: on Nanikibi's side Wagoshkwe's Redearth kin, Sagikwe's Peninsulakin of Sagi Bay, Yahatase's Turtlefolk of Morningland; on my side Menoko's peaceful dreamers, Mangashko's Prairie warriors, Miogwewe's Firekeepers, Binesikwe's Rootkin of Kichigami.

But the life Oashi described to Lókaskwe did not resume in Bison Prairie.

Those of the Strait left us, and when Miní again came to Bison Prairie, it was to bring us terrifying news. After all the defeats inflicted on them by Nanikibi, Miní, Batí, Aleshi and the other western warriors, the Oceanshore Invaders had returned to the Sunrise Mountains with Redcoats more numerous than Bra-duck's. The western scouts at the fork that makes the Beautiful River, on the lookout for caravans of rumcarriers, receiving no aid from nearby Southbranch kin, abandoned their small enclosure and fled to the Strait. The headman of the Strait's enclosure, Aleshi's uncle Belést, led a force against the redfrocked Invaders, but retreated after half his force was destroyed; Miní's father Shen was among the dead. And then news reached the Strait that yet larger armies of Redcoats had surprised the enclosures at the Great Falls, on the Eastern River and on the Northern River itself: Stadacona and Hochelaga had both fallen to the Oceanshore Invaders. The strongholds had been poorly defended; in its hour of need, Winámek's alliance of western Rootkin with Northern River Invaders had been a cracked bow. While the Rootkin defeated the Redcoats' armies, Lemond's headmen, including Aleshi's uncle Belést and my cousin Jozes, had greedily enlarged their pelt hoards; then, while the Rootkin rested, Lemond's warriors couldn't hold their ground because the weapons and provisions of the enclosures had been given away by headmen for pelts. Two bands of Invaders no longer confronted each other across the world; the Oceanshore Invaders' armies now confronted none but the world's original people.

The Strait's enclosure was the only Scabeater stronghold that had not yet fallen to the redfrocked armies; its headman, Aleshi's uncle Belést, was bent on keeping it from falling: at the gate he placed a pole with a crow pecking at the head of an Oceanshore Invader.

The Strait's Turtleyouth and Rootkin, among them Miní, Nizokwe's brothers Batí and Antó and their cousin Aleshi, were ready to pounce on any Redcoats who approached, and eager to carry belts to every corner of the Peninsula.

But no redfrocked army came. Instead, a band of bountyseekers like those who had burned Lenapi's village, a motley band who called themselves Rah-jerks Rain-jerks, came to deliver a message, a talking leaf, to the enclosure's headman.

The Strait's warriors couldn't wait to annihilate the message-carriers, but headman Belést and the rest of Lemond were demented by the talking leaf. Belést and his armed men evacuated the enclosure as if defeated by an invincible army, abandoning weapons and provisions to the Rain-jerks. Lemond's scroll-keeper Navár and Scabeater Decuánd took Slaver Rah-jerks into their lodges, even into scalped Lekomandá Shak's house, where aunt Manyan fell ill from rage. And then headman Belést and all his armed men left the Strait altogether and headed toward the Long River, leaving the Strait's warriors trapped between enemies ahead and enemies behind, enemies lodged without a battle in the stronghold of former allies. The talking leaf that had demented Belést said that one overman across the Ocean had ceded to another overman across the Ocean all the valleys, forests, prairies and lakes between the Long River and the Oceanshore; had the overman ceded earth, moon and sun, demented Belést would have had to seek a path to the stars.

This capitulation to a talking leaf was the last of Lemond's many betrayals since the day, sixty winters earlier, when great-grandmother Shutaha and the Strait's Turtlefolk and Rootkin had invited Lekomandá Kadyak and his hundred Scabeaters to a council. The Scabeaters would betray no more; Shutaha's council was dead.

The Invaders from the Oceanshore installed themselves in Lemond's lodges; they posted armed sentinels by the lodges of other villagers, greedy for the objects in them, particularly the furs. Headman Rah-jerks, as well as his companion, Cheater Kraw-on, whom Oashi and I had seen in Pickawillany, resumed where Belést and Lemond had left off; they grabbed all the furs they could reach. Unlike the previous furgatherers, these gave only rum, and even watered this single gift. Told by the headman of all the Redcoat armies, a man called Am-first, to give hunters neither weapons nor bullets, they gave watered rum for the furs taken from women's and children's backs.

Oashi and I remembered Lenapi's warning: the Invaders were generous only when Rootkin were strong; they turned mean when they thought the Rootkin depleted.

All that remained of Shutaha's village were the belts of the first council, in Miní's keeping. Lemond's fat men shamelessly prostrated themselves to the scalpers of their cousin Lekomandá Shak. Aunt Manyan's last word to Miní was a plea to carry red belts and flaming rage to all descendants of the Redearth warrior Lamina.

Miní stayed the winter in Bison Prairie, hunting with Oashi and Nanikibi, counciling continuously, in and out of the village, with Firekeepers and Prairiekin and everyone disposed to listen.

A son was born to Nanikibi and me; I named him Topinbi, bear that sits quietly and waits for the ice to thaw. When the ice did thaw, fifteen armed Redcoats and a rumcarrier were spotted on the trail toward Bison Prairie. Uncle Nagmo and several warriors, fur carriers all, rushed out to intercept the Invaders. But Nagmo without orders from Scabeater allies was like a village dog in the forest; he couldn't cope, he couldn't decide between killing the Redcoats and ingratiating himself as the Strait's Lemond had done. Given strouds, blankets and rum, Nagmo escorted the Redcoats into the village, where angry warriors surrounded them. Even aunt Katwyn, repelled by Nagmo's slavishness, urged that the Invaders be killed.

Bison Prairie's Firekeepers, among them Nanikibi, Oashi and their friend Miní, already had another plan. They urged restraint; the killing of these fifteen would only provoke the arrival of many times their number, whereas the elimination of the Invaders' strongholds would stop the arrival of any. The gatheringplace of all those committed to the larger goal was Karontaen, as the Turtlefolk called their village on the Strait's shore, the place where Shutaha and her kin had counciled with the previous Invaders, who had come as guests.

The fifteen Redcoats and their rumcarrier were left to exert their powers over each other as virtually everyone else set out toward the Strait.

On the eve of our departure, Lókaskwe learned that the rumcarrier, a man called Shap-man, spoke her father's tongue, came from her father's part of the world across the Ocean, and had no love for the Invaders he had been intimidated into joining.

We went by way of my birthplace, Kekionga, where we found Nanikibi's sister Tinami, who had stayed in Kekionga to make peace between her cousin Jozes and her brother Sigenak. Tinami was sharing her mat with Jozes and heavy with child. Magda's son Tisha, already old enough to scout and hunt, had been with his father Jozes since Manyan had died. The peace between Jozes and Sigenak had not been made by Tinami but by the arrival of a detachment of Rah-jerks Rain-jerks, one of whom had entered Jozes's store with armed companions and simply taken it over, another of whom had demanded Sigenak's horse and, on being refused, shot and killed the beautiful animal. It took the loss of his store to rouse Jozes, who hadn't been so roused by his mother's frustrated end or his father's scalping under a truce flag. It took the death of his horse to sour Sigenak on the allies he'd been waiting to embrace since he'd learned of my father's raid.

On the Strait, Nanikibi and I, Oashi and Lókaskwe, Jozes and Tinami and Sigenak were made much of by Nanikibi's sister Namakwe, who had recently become Batí's companion, and by Mini's birdlike Nizokwe, who together with her three brothers surrounded the gathering warriors with music so gorgeous that it almost made me forget my rage and my reason for being on the Strait.

I had heard of many great councils on the Strait, but couldn't imagine one greater than this. Into this place called Tiosa Rondion by ancient Turtlefolk and Karontaen by Shutaha's heirs, this center of the first Firekeepers, ancient Wedasi's village before the wanderings began, there came warriors from every corner of the world: Rootkin came from Boweting, Mishilimakina and Greenbay; carriers came from the Leaning Tree village and from Sandusky Bay in the Lake of the vanished Ehryes; Southbranch kin and even a few Eastbranch kin came from the Muskingum, Tuscarawas and Kanawha in the Beautiful Valley (Lókaskwe unsuccessfully sought her sister among them); there were even two emissaries from the eastern Turtleleague, the people considered Serpents by ancient Winámek and his Scabeating allies; the only places from which no warriors came were Lemond's former strongholds Hochelaga and Stadacona.

Firekeepers were anxious to reveal their plan to the counciling warriors, but the time wasn't right, the lines weren't clear, there were many at the council who had already gone over to the Invader. Near the council's center sat Lemond's Navár and Decuánd with other fat men and two lean Blackrobes; these were present as spies for their new master, dogs who licked the new hand that rewarded them. The rest of the center was taken up by uncle Nagmo and his fellow fur carriers from Greenbay, Leaning Tree and Mishilimakina. These two groups yelled at each other. Navár shouted that rifles and bullets and other gifts would be given only to the deserving: he spoke from his own experience. Nagmo shouted that rifles and bullets were not gifts, but the very condition for the hunt; withholding these was a fool's decision, since none could reach furs without them, deserving or undeserving. Nanikibi reminded Nagmo of Ozagi's prophesy: when one Invader eliminated the other, his generosity would end, for he would no longer need Rootkin as allies.

Sigenak said the Invader withheld weapons and powder because he intended to attack the Peninsulakin as the former Invader had attacked the Redearth kin, and for the same reason: the kin of the Peninsula blocked his path. Sigenak was loudly approved by many carriers, formerly my father's allies, formerly enemies of Shutaha's village and friends of the Oceanshore Invaders but now their loudest enemies.

Miní raised his voice against the carriers' approval; he said the carriers as well as Nagmo were ready to come to terms with the new Invaders if only the terms were the same as those granted by the earlier Invaders. He displayed the belts of the agreement made two generations earlier by the Strait's villagers and guests, promising mutual enhancement, and he said no such agreement had been made with the Slavers, who promised not to enhance but to oppress, break and remove, because they regarded kinship as a burden, because they applied horse-breeding and -breaking tricks to human beings, because they saw horses, people and earth herself as nothing but obstacles to be enslaved and put to use. Miní said Slavers were not wanted on the Strait no matter what terms they granted; their mere presence was a provocation.

After the silence that followed Miní's words, the two Turtleleague emissaries rose. Many eyes had been fixed on these two redoubtable warriors whose mere presence on the Strait was a surprise, who were viewed as long-lost cousins by some and as mortal enemies by others. It was the first time Turtleleague warriors had ventured into a council of western Rootkin since the days when Blackrobes had named them Serpents and tried to reduce Rootkin to tools for the extermination of Serpents. The Turtleleague had grown strong by allying with one Invader and then with the other, playing with both and trusting neither, as Nanikibi's father Ozagi had done, until the last war between the Invaders, when they lost their sense and gave all their strength to the Invaders of the Oceanshore, even to the point of advising their allies to strengthen themselves by uniting their thirteen bickering gangs into a single league like their own. The victory of their allies brought the Turtleleague defeat, which was something Lenapi could have and the Turtlefolk should have foreseen. After helping defeat those who called them Serpents, the Turtleleague warriors returned to their eastern woodland homes to find their kin hungry and their allies camped in hunting grounds, destroying plants and game, their allies' headman Am-first granting lands to redfrocked underlings and insisting that Turtlefolk be given rifles and gifts only for slavish services performed for Redcoats. Western members of the league rose up against their redfrocked allies, but their eastern cousins didn't rise, and the great Turtleleague tore.

The two men who rose at the Strait's council were not emissaries for the whole league, but only for its angry western half. They presented two red belts to the council and called for the simultaneous annihilation of every enclosure west of the Sunrise Mountains. This was exactly the plan that Firekeepers were waiting to reveal. But the Turtle emissaries, unfamiliar with western Rootkin, had no sense for the time or the place to reveal the plan, and they addressed their war cry and gave their belts to Nagmo, in their eyes the heir of Winámek's great league of western Rootkin with northern Invaders.

Nagmo gave the belts to Lemond's Navár. This predictable betrayal was the last act of Winámek's great league. Navár promptly carried the belts to Mad-win, the redfrocked headman in the Strait's enclosure. Their task accomplished, Lemond's fat men as well as Nagmo and his companions left the council.

Now at last the lines were clear. The time was ripe for a second council, this one among those who had always been hostile to Winámek's league, among those who had allied with Redearth kin against Winámek and his heirs, among those to whom Mini's great-grandfather Ahsepona had sent belts. Now Firekeepers and Turtlefolk without crosses and Prairiekin who had fought alongside Redearth kin and carriers who had turned against the remains of Winámek's league began to elaborate the details of the plan prematurely announced by the Turtleleague emissaries, a plan that in any case wasn't new: ancient Yahatase had tried to kill the first Invaders in the western Lakes, my grandmother Mangashko had rejected all the Invaders' ways, Nanikibi's mother Wagoshkwe had fought to push the Invaders toward the salt sea.

Lókaskwe

It was during the interlude between the first and second council that yellowhaired Lókaskwe began to have her dreams. She dreamt of the landgang who had given her father a talking leaf, of the armed men who had forced her father to join them in raids against the people he had come to join, of the Redcoats who had arrived in Bison Prairie, of the rumcarrier who had arrived with them, and after each dream she woke up screaming, terrified, afraid of sleep. Her friend Nizokwe and Nanikibi's sisters tried to soothe her by exorcizing the spirit responsible for her bad dreams, Nizokwe with songs, Namakwe with herbal potions, Tinami with gibberish learned from Blackrobes.

Oashi and I, and also Nanikibi, sensed that we were in the presence, not of dreams to be exorcized, but of visions to be shared, and we urged Lókaskwe to tell all she saw and to fathom its meaning. Oashi saw quickly and I very slowly that the meaning of Lókaskwe's dreams was very close to the deepest meaning of our own.

Before leaving Bison Prairie, Lókaskwe had spoken to Shap-man, the rumcarrier who spoke her first language; she had asked him who the Redcoats were and what they wanted in Bison Prairie.

Shap-man's answer was at the root of Lókaskwe's visions. He told her two things: the Redcoats considered themselves heirs to ancient people chosen at the beginning of time by a power outside the world to be the world's improvers, and the improvement consisted of enclosing people, animals and earth herself in a net so strong that none of those caught in it could ever emerge.

Nanikibi and Oashi immediately recognized the great entangler Wiske, but Lókaskwe insisted the Invader was something larger, something not encompassed by our stories. The Invader considered himself one of the chosen, and his very contempt toward all that wasn't chosen confirmed his self-image as chosen. He considered himself chosen because he put last things first, because he felt contempt for earth's body as well as his own. Public display of his contempt for women, Rootkin, unpenned animals and uncultivated plants, ostentatious display of his shame of his own body, desires, natural acts and even nakedness, made him great among his likes and gave him a license to cheat, plunder and kill without qualms. These acts, when done by the chosen, were not called cheating or plunder or murder but always improvements, and they were never inflicted on kin, since the chosen called none kin, neither earth's plants nor animals nor people but only the outside power that chose them. The affirmation of that outside power led to the denial of everything else.

Lókaskwe said the outside power was Death, and the improvements performed by Death's chosen consisted of enclosing, enmeshing and swallowing everything that had emerged as Life. She was terrified because she felt enmeshed, not by her birth and childhood among the Invaders, but by the net of objects that lay over our villages, by the cloth and metals and rum and flint which mangled us by making us dependent on the world-improvers, which entangled us in a net so strong that none caught in it ever emerged.

Oashi and Nanikibi shared Lókaskwe's vision with their counciling kin. But the vision was too demanding, even for warriors preparing to destroy every enclosure this side of the Mountains.

Many heard Oashi and Nanikibi, even the renowned Mashekewis of the Northern Straits, and were eager to begin life anew, adopting from the Invaders only their children so as to let them grow into human beings.

But many were impatient of words and visions and eager to begin to push the Invaders toward the Oceanshore and even back to the salt sea they came from. Sigenak and my dead father's allies were among the most eager.

Hasty preparations to seize the Strait's enclosure were made. Lókaskwe and I followed Namakwe and other women to replace the village men in the fields, for among the Strait's inhabitants the men did the seeding.

Five hundred warriors then surrounded the enclosure; sixty entered on the pretext of wanting to confer with headman Mad-win, knives and hatchets (as I then thought) hidden under their cloaks, ready to open the gate to the five hundred outside. But once inside, the sixty found themselves surrounded by all the hundreds of Redcoats inside the enclosure, and they could only retreat, ashamed and frustrated.

Then the hunt for those guilty of betraying the plan began. From the enclosure itself came the story, devised by Lemond's

Navár, that a Rootwoman called Katwyn had warned Mad-win from affection; this story was devised to turn Rootkin against each other, but it convinced no one: it was known that Mad-win, who treated Rootwomen as if they were goats, could not inspire affection. According to another story that came from the enclosure, Aleshi's younger sister Anjelík had revealed the plan to the man she loved, a cheating rumcarrier named Star-ling, who then warned Mad-win. This may have happened, since Anjelík later married Star-ling, and the story turned many warriors against the carriers in their midst, for the carriers, as was known by Navár inside the enclosure, wanted to install Anjelík's father Kuyeryé into the post of Lekomandá and the carriers also sent talking leaves to Anjelík's uncle Belést composed by Anjelík's brother Aleshi. Whether true or not, this story, like the first, was sent out of the enclosure to create dissension among the attackers.

It was the attackers themselves who warned the Redcoats. Several days before the planned entry, carriers had visited every gunsmith on the Strait to have their rifles shortened, and these visits were known by Anjelík as well as all the other villagers, including those serving the Invaders. When the carriers entered the enclosure, not with knives and hatchets but with shortened rifles under their cloaks, the bulges couldn't have been a mystery to Invaders familiar with sawed-off rifles.

The carriers hadn't heard Lókaskwe's vision, they couldn't live without the Invaders' weapons, they no longer knew how to use stone and wood, they couldn't imagine how their ancestors had warred and hunted.

There was no time to be disgusted with the carriers; the failed attack did not impair the rest of the plan; the destruction of the other strongholds would cut the supply lines to the Invaders on the Strait, and in the east, Turtleleague warriors were ready; their belts were accepted by the second council.

Sigenak set out toward Sandusky Bay in the Lake of the vanished Ehryes with my father's one-time allies and also with my father's one-time enemies Jozes and Miní and their cousins Batí and Aleshi.

Lókaskwe and Oashi, Nanikibi and I set out toward Bison Prairie with Firekeepers and Prairiekin, unencumbered by the Invaders' weapons or alliance, Nagmo and Bison Prairie's carriers having retired to the Leaning Tree village in the north.

The Redcoats stopped us on the path into Bison Prairie, almost on the very spot where Nagmo had stopped them. After aunt Katwyn and Nanikibi's sister Kittihawa made it clear to the Redcoats that we were kin returning to our own village, the Invaders let us pass, and we immediately surrounded every Redcoat. Those who raised their rifles were downed by arrows; the rest were disarmed. Bison Prairie was freed of its Invaders without rifles, without metal, in a battle that lasted a few moments.

The captives were prepared for their journey toward the rising sun. They were hostile and contemptuous; no one wanted to adopt any of them except the rumcarrier Shap-man. Katwyn had welcomed the rumcarrier into her lodge, her younger son had befriended him. Katwyn wanted Bison Prairie's Firekeepers to adopt the rumcarrier; she couldn't live without his gifts. Lókaskwe too urged his adoption, not for his gifts but for his insights and his sense of humor.

Oashi arranged great-grandmother Miogwewe's ceremony of three fires, not only to adopt the rumcarrier, but to celebrate the rebirth of Bison Prairie. During the chaos that accompanied the ritual expulsion of the hare, in which even crosswearing Katwyn and Kittihawa took part, the unfortunate rumcarrier almost lost his wits: he didn't understand he was being adopted and apparently thought the fires had been lit to roast him! When a party of warriors, Nanikibi among them, escorted the captive Redcoats out of Bison Prairie, adopted Shap-man accompanied them, evidently afraid to be left among his new kin.

Nanikibi returned before the moon had completed two phases with news that sweetened the very air. The Firekeepers' plan was being carried through; all Invaders had been ousted from the valleys and prairies.

After escorting the captives to the Strait's enclosure, Nanikibi had joined Sigenak in Kekionga. Sigenak and the other warriors had just ambushed and captured the headman of the Sandusky enclosure, downed the Redcoats who tried to shoot, and burned the enclosure. In Kekionga, the warriors captured three Redcoats and a hostile rumcarrier outside the enclosure; the headman, demented by fear, shot at shadows, and then foolishly ran out after a girl who promised him love and safety; surrounded, he shot in every direction until he was killed; all the Redcoats in the enclosure promptly surrendered. Leaving Kekionga, the warriors were joined by carriers who had surprised a caravan of Redcoats moving from the Great Falls to reinforce Mad-win at the Strait. The force that went from Kekionga to the Wabash to attack the Uiatanon enclosure consisted of Wagoshkwe's sons as well as sons of warriors who had once fought alongside Wabskeni and Lekomandá Shak against Wagoshkwe's Redearth kin. The Redcoats in Uiatanon, surrounded by peoples all of whom were hostile to their presence, were easily captured and disarmed; none were killed. All the Invaders west of the Strait were now ousted. Miní, Aleshi and Batí escorted the captives to the Strait. Sigenak, Jozes and Magda's son Tisha, who had gone as a scout, stopped at Kekionga.

Nanikibi learned of yet more captures before he returned to Bison Prairie. At the second council on the Strait, the northerners with the renowned Mashekewis had listened carefully to Oashi's impersonation of Lókaskwe's visions. Mashekewis and the northern Rootkin set out toward the Northern Straits unencumbered by crosswearers or carriers, who had retired with Nagmo to the Leaning Tree village. Mashekewis' warriors camped in front of the enclosure at Mishilimakina, the Blackrobes' long-time stronghold and the greatest fur post on the Lakes. The warriors played bagataway with visiting kin from Sagi Bay while Redcoats watched the game and Rootwomen entered the enclosure with concealed knives and hatchets. The ball, as if by chance, bounded into the enclosure; the players bounded after it, grabbed weapons, surrounded the Redcoats and disarmed them before any could shoot; a rumcarrier called Soli-man, a cousin of our Shap-man, was among the captives. News of the capture traveled quickly to the nearby Leaning Tree village and to Greenbay. Carriers and crosswearers in the Leaning Tree village were insulted because they and their rifles had not been invited to help capture the great enclosure on the Northern Strait. Mashekewis conciliated Nagmo by letting the carriers escort the captives eastward. Before Nagmo's party left Mishilimakina, the Redcoats who had occupied the Greenbay enclosure arrived on their own and voluntarily added themselves to the captives, terrified by their isolation: they already knew of the fall of the western enclosures and of the capture of enclosures on the Easternmost Lake and in the eastern Woodlands by warriors of the Turtleleague.

From the first planting until the leaves fell, Bison Prairie was alive with dance and song. Wagoshkwe's dream was coming true, and in the way she would have wanted, Lókaskwe's way.

Even Katwyn and Kittihawa were beginning to enjoy life unencumbered by alien contrivances. But our joy fell with the leaves. Aleshi brought the bad news. All warriors who had followed Lókaskwe's way had succeeded; those on the Strait had failed, and there was no word from those at the fork that makes the Beautiful River.

Miní, Batí and Aleshi returned to the Strait celebrating their victories in Sandusky, Kekionga and Uiatanon. They soon learned that the Strait's enclosure was the only stronghold on the Lakes still in the Invaders' hands. Carriers wanted to storm the enclosure with rifles and fire. Miní and the Strait's Turtlefolk remembered the Redearth kin's siege and warned that such an assault would mean a loss of life human beings could not sustain. Aleshi warned that such an assault would not even frighten the enclosure's headman; Aleshi had learned from a renegade Redcoat named Hop-kin that headman Mad-win was a block of stone who served his distant power with the rigidity of a contrivance, something like the monster that took the shape of an eagle in my dream; no dog could be broken to such extreme loyalty; Mad-win was determined to hold fast until every one of his Redcoats was killed, and he was convinced of the wisdom of such idiocy. There were no blocks of stone among the besieging warriors to lead such an assault.

The warriors prepared another ruse, for they knew that the enclosure's Redcoats were running out of provisions: Jozes and Tisha were summoned from Kekionga; together with other sons and grandsons of Lemond whose involvement with the warriors was unknown by those inside, they were to open the enclosure's gates and let the warriors flood in.

Carriers who had been capturing every supply caravan approaching the Strait from above and below precipitously abandoned their ambushing posts and camped outside the enclosure with all their weapons, letting several hundred Rahjerks Rain-jerks, led by a hothead called Dah-sell with twenty dugout canoes of provisions, slip into the enclosure unobserved.

The plan was put off. Inside the enclosure, hothead Dah-sell, enraged by the warriors encircling the enclosure in plain view, led his hundreds out to exterminate the encirclers, but not before those inside the enclosure had sent out warnings. Dah-sell and his entire force rushed in blackest night directly into the ambush that awaited them; almost half were killed, the rest ran bleeding and screaming toward the enclosure, saved only by the fog.

The carriers celebrated the victory; this was a battle they could understand: rifles against rifles. But Jozes and Tisha had been spotted warning their companions; the plan was ruined. The carriers went back to capturing caravans of provisions heading toward the Strait.

Suddenly Lemond's Decuánd turned up in one of the carrier camps, Navár in another, with word that Redcoat headman Mad-win as well as overman Am-first were willing to come to terms with the Strait's besiegers; they were willing to resume the fur trade, to provide weapons to hunters, and to block incursions of landsuckers beyond the Sunrise Mountains. These were the terms ancient Nangisi's heirs had fought for; they agreed to return captives and dispersed to their villages to prepare for their winter hunt.

Headman Mad-win promptly captured Miní, Aleshi, Jozes and Tisha. Miní and Jozes were placed into a wooden trap. Kampó's son Tisha and Anjelik Star-ling's brother Aleshi were released and banished from the Strait.

Aleshi's bad news was only the beginning. The arrival in Bison Prairie of Eastbranch and Southbranch refugees from the Beautiful Valley, most of them pockmarked, confirmed Lókaskwe's vision of the Invaders as nothing like eagles, even contrived ones, but as Death's agents. Shawano came with the emaciated refugees, his face marked by the dread disease, as well as Lókaskwe's younger sister, named Magidins by those who'd adopted her, fluent in Rootspeech, a young Southbranch woman with yellow hair.

After fleeing from the ruined Eastbranch village in the Sunrise Mountains, Shawano and his kin had camped near the fork that makes the Beautiful River. They were followed by rumcarrier Kraw-on and by a Blackcollar called Brother Post-err, who spoke Magidins' first tongue and used her as translator. This Post-err spoke of himself as one of several black-collared Brethren who carried no weapons, and to whom the ways of the original people were dearer than the Invaders' ways. After Brother Post-err won the confidence of the Southbranch kin, Kraw-on delivered the message that an army of Redcoats would return to the Sunrise Mountains solely in order to keep landsuckers from invading the Beautiful Valley on the pretext that the valley had been granted to them by the Turtleleague.

Impressed by Brother Post-err's evident sincerity and not eager to paint themselves for war, Shawano's kin looked on while Redcoats under a headman called Bow-kay, Bra-duck's successor, built, fortified, and entrenched themselves on the fork itself, in an enclosure they called Pit-strength. Southbranch women were hardly done placing their first cornseeds into the ground when a steady stream of landsuckers began to pour through the mountain passes, each armed with a rifle and a talking leaf that conferred what the Invaders called a title. Shawano's kin had been taken in by Post-err's sincerity; apparently Brother Post-err himself had been taken in; he had been sent to impress the Southbranch kin with his sincerity; it was Kraw-on who had delivered the false promises. The Redcoats had promised to oust landsuckers who invaded on the pretext that the land had been granted by the Turtleleague; but the Redcoats protected those who invaded on the pretext that the overman of Invaders of one tongue had granted the land to the overman of Invaders of another tongue. The Invaders proceeded by sheer force, but they apparently needed to believe they proceeded by right—otherwise, as Lókaskwe observed, they couldn't feel chosen. This need was easily met: any pretext, any illusion, seemed to satisfy it.

Southbranch kin were alarmed. Shawano, accompanied by Magidins, led an embassy to the Blackcollar Post-err. They learned that Brother Post-err had spoken for headman Bow-kay only when he had believed Bow-kay's words; disabused of his belief, Post-err spoke for no one. Cheater Kraw-on greeted the embassy with a greedy grin; he still spoke for the headman; he now said that possession of the mountains and valley resided in an overman and a permanent army, and that wandering tribes, as he called the Southbranch kin, could not possess land. This language of armed hatred was as incomprehensible to Magidins as to Shawano, and while they wasted themselves on this pointless mission, Invaders continued to pour past the Southbranch villages, killing all life in their path: plants and plant-eating animals and meat-eating animals and people.

The Southbranch kin heard rumors of the capture of the Sandusky and Kekionga enclosures. When Turtleleague warriors arrived with warbelts, Shawano's kin accepted the belts. Southbranch warriors, and even a few warriors from among the remaining Eastbranch kin, joined with Turtlewarriors for the first time since the days described on the ancient scrolls; they emptied two enclosures in the Sunrise Mountains, pushed a rum caravan over a precipice, ambushed two red armies, and prepared to remove the Invaders from the Pit-strength at the fork. Unlike the warriors on the Strait, those who gathered against the Pit-strength were desperate and ready to storm the enclosure.

As soon as the attack began, headman Bow-kay himself emerged from the enclosure, with gifts, mainly blankets, and a message. After the gifts were distributed, Bow-kay delivered the same arrogant message Kraw-on had already delivered: wandering tribes could possess no land. It was the gifts he had come to deliver.

Death stalked the Beautiful Valley. The smallpox ravaged every Southbranch village, wherever messengers carried Bow-kay's words and gifts.

The Invaders wielded the smallpox as a weapon because they knew its effect on Rootkin. Am-first, the overman of all the redfrocked armies, had ordered headman Bow-kay to take no prisoners, to spread smallpox-infested blankets among the valley's Rootkin, to empty the valley of its inhabitants, to extirpate the entire execrable race, as he called original people, by every stratagem in his power. Magidins learned of this order from blackcollared Brethren who visited the afflicted villages; it was common knowledge among the Redcoats in the Pit-strength.

Fear spread in the villages of survivors throughout the Beautiful Valley. Kinless Eastbranch survivors sought protection by hovering around the blackcollared Brethren the same way broken Rootkin had hovered around Blackrobes in the first Nangisi's times. Only in Nangisi's times, the Blackrobes' converts had actually found some protection; the converts of the Brethren found none. Magidins learned of a band of Rootkin who had been converted earlier by the Brethren. When the war between the Invaders broke out, these converts who had renounced war sought refuge in a crowded town of Cheaters, fellow crosswearers, presumably kin. Enclosed and weaponless, they were beset by a mob of landsuckers who called themselves the Pox-tn Boys; they were hacked to pieces, their scalps were taken for bounties. Among the Cheaters, scalps, like furs and metal pieces, were exchanged for coveted gifts.

While Southbranch kin learned of this massacre by Pox-tn Boys, they saw landsuckers rushing over the Sunrise Mountains into forests, groves, burial grounds and abandoned fields as far as the mouth of the great Kanawha. The flood was kept from the northern banks of the Beautiful River only by the successful war of western Rootkin against the Invaders' enclosures and then by the agreement between the Invaders and the Strait's carriers.

Pit-strength headman Bow-kay was not pleased by the agreement, and he twisted its meaning to continue his war of extermination. When overman Am-first had promised to block further incursions of Invaders, carriers had agreed to end their siege and return their prisoners. Bow-kay now moved his army against plague-desolated villages and threatened to raze them unless they returned not only war-captives but all people like Magidins and our Lókaskwe who had been adopted, who spoke the language and followed the paths of Eastbranch and Southbranch Rootkin, who were daughters, sisters, uncles and cousins, who thought themselves free human beings and regarded the Invaders' towns as prisons, who would become prisoners only after they were returned.

Bow-kay knew what Shutaha had known, what was becoming common knowledge: the smallpox decimated those who had not been exposed to it, it decimated original people, it spared the Invaders who had been exposed to it for countless generations, and the villages of original people were being repopulated and reconstituted by people Bow-kay chose to call prisoners, by adopted kin, who now made up a large proportion of the surviving Eastbranch and Southbranch Rootkin.

Villagers who feared total annihilation dragged themselves to the Pit-strength and gave up to Bow-kay's captivity the brothers, sisters and cousins with whom they had shared lives. When the returned prisoners shed their Invaders' clothes and tried to return to their forest kin, they were murdered.

Magidins and her kin came to Bison Prairie to be out of Bow-kay's reach; she dreaded the thought of living without meaning and dying without dignity among penned-in Pox-tn Boys.

All my insides flowed out as tears when I heard of the desolation of the Beautiful Valley's Southbranch Rootkin. Oashi was sad beyond description; he said the desire for revenge was drowned by deeds so gross, so vicious, so unthinkable. My sadness drew me yet further from Bison Prairie's carriers and Firekeepers, yet closer to Lókaskwe and Oashi, to Magidins, Shawano and the Southbranch kin.

I was heavy with my second child, Lókaskwe was carrying her first. We rarely parted. I barely noticed that Aleshi had

KATABWE 1765

returned to the Strait because news had come that Miní and Jozes had been released from their trap. Lókaskwe and I told each other our dreams. Mine were vague, like memories I could no longer reach. I dreamt myself something suspended above the ground, never able to reach the ground, never able to embrace earth or touch earth with my entire body like a serpent, and I woke with a vague sense of loss, a sense of incompleteness; I felt that the plagues, persecutions and wars had separated me from earth and from kin, had invaded my mind and my very blood, had turned me into a contrivance that floated because it could no longer stand with feet on the ground, had made me unable to put first things first and forced me to plant leaves and destroy seeds.

The birth of Lókaskwe's Aptegizhek and my Cakima, a moon apart, coincided with the return of Nagmo and the birth to Katwyn of their second son, whom they named Winámek to honor the memory of the great embroiler. Nagmo sought to reconcile enmities and restore peace to Bison Prairie with a mound of gifts—pots, cloth, blankets—things Katwyn and Kittihawa embraced with joy, and with a lot of rum.

While Southbranch kin had been perishing, Nagmo had been reestablishing his lost position, emerging with an importance enjoyed by no one since his great-grandfather Nangisi. Nagmo had turned the capture of the Mishilimakina Redcoats to his own use. Mashekewis and the northern warriors had given up their captives to Nagmo and other carriers who had done nothing except to fume after the capture. On the way to occupied Hochelaga with the captives, Nagmo learned that the rumcarrier Soli-man, our Shap-man's cousin, was eager to reestablish the fur trade network first established by Nangisi and the Scabeater Falsetongue. Nagmo, who trusted the Oceanshore Invaders no more than the rest of us did, learned that Soli-man didn't trust them either, for they treated him as an outsider whom they tolerated in their midst. The two came to an agreement: Nagmo was to gather the furs of all Mishigami from the Lakebottom to Greenbay, and to return with gifts acquired in Hochelaga by Soli-man and distributed in Mishilimakina by Batí's brother Antó. It was the wealth of gifts from this net that Nagmo brought to the celebration of the three namings.

Unfortunately for Nagmo, Sigenak and Magda's Tisha arrived during the celebration and destroyed Nagmo's hopes for reconciliation and peace. In Sigenak's eyes, the war against the

Invaders' enclosures wasn't over, couldn't be over, since none of the western warriors engaged in it had been defeated, and the agreement between the Invaders and the carriers bound no one; the agreement was nothing but an insult.

Oashi

Sigenak and Tisha came with a stranger who originated neither among Rootkin nor among any Invaders familiar to me; he was called Sandypoint after a place on a distant Ocean island where he was born, and he came with gift bundles. Katwyn welcomed the stranger to Nagmo's lodge.

Sigenak had been in Kekionga when Tisha had brought him news of the carriers' agreement and of the imprisonment of Tisha's uncles Miní and Jozes. Sigenak had been livid with rage when the cheating rumcarrier Kraw-on turned up in Kekionga, guided there by Jozes, who had been released on condition that he guide the wily emissary to the gatheringplaces of Prairiekin. Kraw-on carried horse-loads of gifts as well as the message that the Invaders would take no lands by force, not even the land for their fortified enclosures, but would beg Rootkin for the right to take any land. This forked-tongue who had recently told Southbranch kin they had no right to land because they lacked an overman and a permanent army did not go to Kekionga accompanied by a Blackcollar who actually believed his words, and none were taken in. Sigenak, and also Tisha, nevertheless decided to accompany Jozes and the rumcarrier to Uiatanon; Sigenak intended to translate Kraw-on's intentions while Jozes translated his words.

Once on the Wabash, Sigenak found that western Prairiekin did not need his translations. They accepted Krawon's gifts by plundering and capturing him. The western Prairiekin were as fond as Sigenak of the carriers' peace, and had been plundering and capturing every rumcarrier who had reached the Wabash.

Jozes fled to the village of Kithepekanu on the Wabash. Tinami and her two sons soon joined him.

Tisha guided Kraw-on to nearby Uiatanon so that the rum-carrier's very life wouldn't be taken as well.

Sigenak was enchanted by what he found west of the Wabash: the Prairiekin with whom he had captured the Uiatanon enclosure were allied with Redearth survivors from the other shore of Mishigami and with Tellegwi from across the Long River, and all had rifles and horses from southwestern Invaders called Senyores who had once been ousted by Stonelodge people of the Sunset Mountains, Invaders considered too distant and weak to threaten the invasion of the Plains or Prairies. To Sigenak, this was the alliance his mother Wagoshkwe had dreamt of, and he accompanied Prairiekin to Cahokia on the Long River, the great mound that held the remains of the last Riverpeople of the Beautiful Valley. There Sigenak was given warbelts with which to remind Rootkin of Bison Prairie, Kekionga and the Strait that the war against the Oceanshore Invaders had not been completed.

In Cahokia Tisha had met Sandypoint, a gift-carrier and fur-gatherer with the ways, language and clothing of Lemond, a man whose ancestors hailed from a world distinct from that of the other three Invaders, a man who had come up the Long River looking for crosswearing Rootkin converted by Blackrobes to the Invaders' language and ways like his own ancestors, a man who feared the Oceanshore Invaders because, he said, they were too stupid to recognize his kin as human beings. Tisha brought the stranger to Bison Prairie when Sigenak came to deliver his belts.

Bison Prairie's Firekeepers counciled with Sigenak and welcomed the belts; many of them were, like Sigenak and Nanikibi, children of Redearth kin.

Nagmo avoided the councils; perhaps he already knew he would war alongside Oceanshore Invaders against Sigenak's allies as his father and grandfather had warred alongside northern Invaders against Wagoshkwe's kin. He and Katwyn and their children moved to the Lakebottom, where the brave Redearth kin were said to have been annihilated.

Kittihawa once again chose her crosswearing cousin Katwyn over her brothers, and she too moved to the Lakebottom. My son Topinbi, already old enough to dream and decide, accompanied Kittihawa to be with his friends, Nagmo's sons.

Those of us who were not taking part in Sigenak's councils were soon invited to celebrate Kittihawa's marriage. Oashi and

I and Lókaskwe heavy with her second child went to the Lakebottom. Kittihawa and Sandypoint had found each other; both were crosswearing converts who had made the ways, language and clothes of Lemond their own. Oashi and I, although fond of neither, helped them raise a lodge near Nagmo's on the midpoint between Cahokia and Mishilimakina, between the fur-gatherers at the mouth of the Long River and those of the Northern River.

A daughter was born to Lókaskwe on the Lakebottom; Oashi named her Shecogosikwe.

Oashi and Lókaskwe, as well as Shawano, Magidins and the Southbranch kin, were eager to be gone from Bison Prairie and the Lakebottom. Rumor reached us that the Pit-strength army had stopped hunting for prisoners and that headman Bow-kay had been replaced. Magidins was repelled by the idol-worshipping Katwyn, Lókaskwe by Nagmo's fur-gathering network, Oashi by the embroiling alliances.

My brother, Miogwewe's great-grandson, was disappointed by his friend Nanikibi's involvement with Sigenak's belts and councils. Oashi saw that Sigenak's and Nagmo's alliances were the same, they were both revivals of embroiler Winámek's League between Rootkin and Invaders, alliances between jaws and meat, in which Rootkin were the meat. But Oashi said nothing; he didn't dream of trying to turn Nanikibi against his brother, or of trying to turn both brothers against their mother. He delayed our departure until Sigenak and Nanikibi were ready to set out toward Kekionga and the Strait with the belts of the Cahokians.

In Kekionga I separated from Nanikibi, sadly, for I too was attracted to Sigenak's league; I had been attracted to Sigenak's league many years earlier, in Pickawillany. I remembered that I had been too young to see, and Lenapi had helped me. Now I was old enough to see with my own eyes.

I accompanied my brother and Shawano's kin to the valley of vanished Riverpeople, the Beautiful Valley of mounds and memories. Oashi carried Lenapi's bark scroll to a village of Southbranch and Eastbranch survivors camped on the Muskingum; he wore a pendant shaped by Shutaha as he carried the two children born by Mishigami's shore to a visionary mother adopted from the Invaders' world.

Our return to Southbranch and Eastbranch kin must have been like legendary Yahatase's return to plague-devastated

Morningland after a childhood of imprisonment in the Blackrobes' mission in Stadacona. Shawano and Magidins were embraced by celebrating kin who had thought them dead. The familiar faces, language and songs, the corn-filled fields, gave an impression of life renewed, vibrant and strong, until memory intervened with its reminder that the people on the Muskingum were no longer whole, that they were mere fragments of what they had once been. The Eastbranch kin were not guests from among numerous people who inhabited the Oceanshore, but mere remnants. The Muskingum village was not one of the countless and teeming Southbranch villages that dotted the Beautiful Valley, but one of the few depopulated villages that remained. The councils were not occasions for dance and song but for rum drinking; they were not sessions of remembering the Beginning described by the scrolls, but sessions of forgetting the plagues and wars, the humiliation and devastation.

Oashi was dismayed to learn that even the lifegiving spirit of adoptions was waning. Southbranch kin had adopted a lone landsucker who had come from among Oceanshore Cheaters, and had then pushed him to take up his discarded skin and put it on again, to become a rumcarrier, to bring cloth and beads, rifles and metal hatchets and rum from the Pit-strength, the Invaders' camp at the fork.

This rumcarrier, called Con-err, had wanted land, but not badly enough to kill for it; he had responded with gratitude to the offered kinship, for he had never before experienced kinship; he took up his role as go-between hesitantly and with shame, the shame I remembered on my father's face whenever he returned with the Invaders' gifts.

Oashi was more dismayed by the dependence of the Southbranch kin than by Nagmo's or Katwyn's, because the Southbranch kin knew what Lenapi had known; they knew the men who pushed the rum, the men who scalped for bounties, the men who aimed rifles at every living thing that stirred, the men who murdered for the sake of a patch of land which they then denuded and ravaged, the men who considered earth and all its creatures to be nothing but weapons for dominating, disabling and killing. The Southbranch kin knew that the Invaders' gifts disabled Rootkin and made them dependent on the very net that held the Invaders themselves inside their enclosures.

The Eastbranch survivors in the Muskingum villages, hardly a thousand, the last remnants of Lenapi's once numerous kin, were driven by a great fear: they who for ages had celebrated and sung and recorded their event-filled trajectory feared that soon none would remember it, soon no living person would have ancestors who had followed that path, soon there would be no memory of Eastbranch Rootkin ever having existed. Some hundred of the Eastbranch kin, largely survivors from Lenapi's Sunrise Mountain village, had adopted several blackcollared Brethren who originated from Lókaskwe's and Magidins' part of the world, and had formed a village on the Tuscarawas, a village of neat wooden lodges surrounded by fenced-in gardens.

Lókaskwe was hostile to the Blackcollars in the Tuscarawas village. She remembered that Brother Post-err, himself sincere enough, had been used by the Pit-strength headman to deceive Shawano's kin. Lókaskwe questioned one of the Blackcollars, a Brother Kanish, who was less tight-lipped about things that mattered than the other Brethren.

Lókaskwe learned that Blackrobes, who for ages had crossed ocean and mountains to convince people broken by plagues and wars that their misery came from their own failings, had been suppressed by their overmen across the Ocean. Now only blackcollared Brethren crossed ocean and mountains with a message, and their message was altogether different from the Blackrobes'. Kanish told that his and Lókaskwe's ancestors had once been as free and healthy as Rootkin before the invasion. Devastated by plagues and wars and driven by a great fear, the ancestors had allowed protectors and Blackrobes to come among them. The protectors exacted ever-heavier burdens for ever-less protection; the Blackrobes said people had fallen, were vicious and depraved, and would be at each other's throats if the protectors didn't keep peace among them. Shortly before the first Invaders crossed the Ocean, Kanish's ancestors rebelled against protectors and Blackrobes; they still remembered the time before the protectors, they knew that their only fall had been to let themselves fall to protectors. At a mountain called Tabor they disencumbered themselves of protectors and Blackrobes and celebrated the return of their original condition. The rebellion spread until it threatened to dislodge all the world's protectors, who sent their combined armies to suppress it; the rebels defended themselves by forming an army, and quickly found themselves again beset by protectors, this time their own; those who weren't killed by the combined armies were reduced to underlings by their own. Kanish and the other Brethren considered themselves these rebels' heirs. They had drawn the lessons of the great rebellion and they carried its memory to all the world's corners, secretly, because they were persecuted; they considered themselves teachers of the rebellion's lessons. But many, to avoid persecution, had corrupted their message and come to terms with the world's powers.

Lókaskwe saw that Brother Post-err was one of the corrupted, since he'd let his sincere and peaceful self be used by liars and killers as the front line of the invading army. And she lashed out against Kanish himself: she asked if the people of the mountain called Tabor had disencumbered themselves of protectors only to enclose their own gardens with protective fences, if they didn't know that earth, sun and clouds grew corn and greens as well as berries and fruits for all to enjoy. She asked why people who were not depraved, fallen creatures needed teachers, since free people learned from each other and only the fallen needed to be raised up; she said the Brethren had come to complete what the Blackrobes had begun, to get the lame to walk, not on their own, but leaning on crutches.

Oashi and Shawano grew increasingly alarmed by the landhungry Invaders who continued to flow over the mountain passes into the valley, and they took their alarm to a council with the Redcoats at the Pit-strength. They were told that no Invaders were to cross the mountain divide, that they had bound themselves to stay on the side where the rivers flow into the Ocean.

After promising to stay away from war parties if the Redcoats agreed to remove Invaders who nevertheless crossed the divide, Oashi and Shawano learned that the Redcoats were helpless: their overman across the Ocean had given the task of removing the landsuckers to the very landgangs that sent the landsuckers over the mountains.

Oashi heard what he was told, but Menoko's son couldn't take in the duplicity of it, and he couldn't learn to act in the face of such duplicity. He saw, with Lókaskwe's eyes, that the Invaders who came ever closer to the Muskingum were more pathetic than vicious. Like the adopted Con-err, like Lókaskwe's own father, they were men who'd had little on the Oceanshore and who had given most of that to a Ua-shn-tn or a Kre-sop in exchange for a title to land in the Beautiful Valley granted to the landgang by the Turtleleague of the eastern Woodlands or by an overman across the Ocean or by someone else who didn't live in the Beautiful Valley. Such a man came to the valley with a pot in one hand and a rifle in the other, grew lonesome on the patch where he had no human contact, feared the forest and nursed resentments; he resented the landgang that had skinned him of all he'd had; he resented the rumcarriers to whom he became increasingly indebted because he needed more bullets, more pots, nails for the cabin in which he imprisoned the mother of his children, and rum; he resented rocks and trees and the land itself because of the joyless sweat and labor he had to expend before his seeds would grow; above all he resented Rootkin whose joyous songs he sometimes heard, because they neither sweated nor labored, and if any dared to venture onto his planted field, he killed without remorse. This man whose sweat and labor all went to fatten landgangs and rumcarriers was sustained by the illusion that the land and the plants that grew on it were his; he thought it was not earth or sun or rain that made seeds grow but his sweat and labor, and he eliminated everything in his reach that didn't confirm his illusion; he destroyed whatever thrived without his sweat and labor: trees and bushes, deer, beaver and wolves.

Neither Oashi nor Shawano nor any on the Muskingum took up arms against the encroaching Invaders, but Southbranch kin west of us, in villages near the Serpent Mound, did take up arms. They raided the Invaders' patches and lodges; they were joined by allies and their raids became more numerous. Thanks to these raids, the invasion slowed down and in some places even receded. The Redcoats' overman across the Ocean, unwilling to provoke another war against the Invaders' enclosures, unwilling to send forces to protect the landsuckers, decided to give back to the Redcoats the task of keeping landsuckers east of the mountains.

Oashi thought the Redcoats were keeping their promises for the first time; Redcoats were turning against landgangs.

Oashi and Shawano, both peaceful men, actually believed the Redcoats were going to remove the intruders from the Beautiful Valley. They went hunting near the Kanawha expecting to find the hunting grounds undisturbed.

Neither Lókaskwe nor Magidins were as trusting as Oashi and Shawano. Lókaskwe, heavy with her third child, learned that angry bountyseekers attacked by the Serpent Mound warriors had returned to the east to rouse their likes to a frenzy of hatred against Rootkin, and she knew that landgangs among the Cheaters and the Slavers were waiting for the slightest excuse to send armed men to every rivermouth and every intersection of paths. Both sisters remembered the killers who had intimidated their father into taking up a rifle against Rootkin, both remembered the bloodlust that spread like a disease through a mob of aroused killers.

When rumors reached us of armed bands moving from the east, Magidins became nearly demented with fear. She sought refuge in the Tuscarawas village of Brethren and their Eastbranch converts who drank no rum and carried no rifles. But once there, she feared attack from both sides; she thought the Serpent Mound warriors would take the village, with its orchard, its gardens fenced by rails, its square lodges and large common lodge, for a settlement of Invaders; and she was sure the Invaders would destroy it as a village of Rootkin, envious of its neat lodges surrounded by oaks, hickory, maple and ash, its nearby game and berries and herbs by a river teeming with fish; she remembered how the Pox-tn Boys had viewed earlier converts of the Brethren. She abruptly left the village and accepted the invitation of the adopted Con-err; she felt safe in the fur and gift post, since to Southbranch warriors she would be a kinswoman lodged in a carrier's lodge, and to the Invaders she would be the wife of one of them, the Pit-strength rumcarrier Con-err.

Lókaskwe's and Magidins' fears were confirmed by an unimaginable horror. Shawano and the hunters returned to the Muskingum village with my brother's body, bloody and scalped.

The hunters had been aware they were not alone in their hunting ground near the Kanawha; armed members of Kre-sop's landgang were measuring patches which, they said, had been given to them by the Turtleleague. I later learned Kre-sop had gotten some Turtlefolk to admit the Beautiful Valley wasn't theirs, and Kre-sop had given many gifts for this admission. Oashi and Shawano disregarded the measurers and they separated in their quest for deer; they told themselves Kre-sop's men were armed against the Pit-strength Redcoats who had promised to keep landgangs out, and were relieved that the two bands of Invaders were intent on wiping each other out. Kre-sop's men lost a horse, and these men who boasted of their agility in taking the horses of Rootkin set out on a manhunt; they pounced on the nearest camp of isolated hunters; they shot, cut and scalped Oashi and his companions, Shawano's cousin and nephew, in a frenzy of bloodletting.

Uncontrollable fury welled up inside me, restrained only by Lókaskwe's hysterical state. Lókaskwe gave premature birth. With trembling hands she gave the bark scroll, Lenapi's scroll, to Oashi's firstborn, tear-covered Aptegizhek; she gave the pendant to Shecogosikwe; she named her newborn girl Wagoshkwe. Lókaskwe's eyes burned with the desire to push the manhunters, not only beyond the Mountains, but beyond the Oceanshore and into the salt sea.

We still hadn't buried Oashi when word came that a band of Invaders had approached the hunting camp of Shawano's only surviving brother, had offered cloth and rum for the hunters' furs, and when the hunters were ill from the rum, had murdered and scalped every one of them.

After these two massacres, there were no more peacemakers among the Southbranch kin of the Muskingum. I joined the dancing warriors, Shawano joined them, even Lókaskwe would have joined them if her sister hadn't fallen ill while giving birth to her first, to Con-err's child.

Without Lókaskwe or Oashi beside me, I suppressed all I knew of dependence on the Invaders' weapons and I took up a rifle; my single thought was to kill Oashi's murderers. We sent belts to near and distant kin, and were soon joined by the Southbranch warriors from the villages near the Serpent Mound, by cousin Miní and his friends Aleshi and Batí together with Turtlewarriors from the Strait, finally by Nanikibi with Firekeepers from Bison Prairie. The friends who had made a pact as children remained loyal to their pact-brother Oashi after his death. Shawano led a hundred of us toward the spot where Kre-sop had attacked. We found and surprised the front of the Invaders' force near the mouth of the Kanawha; our charge routed the men in the front line, who stabbed and shot each other fleeing from us, until suddenly the rout ended, and the Invaders stood their ground. We saw that we were face to face with myriads of rifle-armed Invaders, we were outnumbered ten to one. Shawano, satisfied that our rout of their front line had already inflicted more damage than all of Kre-sop's bands had, signaled a retreat. Like the storming of the Strait's enclosure, this was a battle only demented killers would have fought, it would have led to the death and maiming of many of the remaining Southbranch Rootkin in the Beautiful Valley. A handful of warriors diverted the monstrous army away from the river; the rest of us were in our hidden canoes and across the river before the Invaders knew the war was over; our retreat was as unnoticed as our approach.

I returned to Lókaskwe. Magidins had given painful birth and was still ailing. I had already decided to leave the Muskingum and I begged Lókaskwe to come with me. I had learned from Miní and Aleshi that the force we had faced on the Kanawha was not Kre-sop's landgang; it was the combined force of all the Oceanshore Invaders. Those of the Strait already knew what they would be facing when they decided to respond to our belts.

Nanikibi and Miní urged Shawano and the Southbranch warriors to go to the Peninsula and join warriors more numerous than those we faced on the Kanawha; they said even the Redcoats on the Strait were ready to take up arms against the Invaders of the Beautiful Valley.

But Shawano and Lókaskwe chose to remain with the Southbranch and remaining Eastbranch kin, heeding dead Lenapi's warning against entanglement with allies who swallowed Rootkin in victory and defeat. Shawano chose to depend on no powers other than his own. Lókaskwe would have gone for my sake or for Miní's Nizokwe, but she felt no love for Nagmo or his kin; she preferred to live alongside her sister's compromises, beset by daily threats, yet clean and whole; she didn't want to live alongside Katwyn and Kittihawa who no longer knew how to give without taking, or alongside the Strait's perpetually armed warriors who were ever more similar to the armed men they hunted.

I took my Cakima and accompanied Nanikibi to Bison Prairie.

Miní and the Strait's warriors already knew that Kre-sop's murder of Shawano's kin and Oashi was the first incident of the Invaders' new war against the Beautiful Valley's Rootkin.

The war was unleashed by the Slavers who occupied Powhatan's shore. While one of them, the landgang leader Kre-sop, went to the Kanawha to measure land, a slaver called Done-more, leader of another landgang, went to the Pit-strength to oust the headman who had committed himself to ousting the landgangs from the Valley. Slaver Done-more turned the force of the Redcoats, not against Oashi's murderers, but against Oashi's kin, and he enlarged this force tenfold by recruiting the victims of the landgangs, the lonely landsuckers who condemned themselves to war against trees, bushes, roots and rocks in order to make room for tame plants which, when harvested, were swallowed by landgangs and rumcarriers.

This alliance of spiders with flies was not laughable. The flies, the landsuckers who called themselves pioneers, did not vent their pent-up resentment against those who victimized them, but against those who stayed clear of the victimization, against free people. Some of these landsuckers had, like Lókaskwe's father, crossed the Ocean in order to find paradise; they had been cheated by landgangs on the Oceanshore and sent west to remove all the varied inhabitants from a patch of land. Trapped in a net of debts and obligations that demanded ceaseless labor, they found paradise at last by eating it, by swallowing Rootkin and their world, by becoming manhunters, and once they experienced the murderer's joy, they sought no other paradise.

These manhunters were what Bra-duck's army had lacked. Nowhere could the landgangs have found better front lines than among their own victims.

This alliance of landgangs with their victims had proclaimed itself independent of the Redcoats and their overman across the Ocean. Thirteen different bands of Oceanshore Invaders, among them the Witchburners, Cheaters and Slavers, had united themselves in a league that was a loose parody of the Turtleleague, a league in which neither the villagers nor the longhouse grandmothers made any decisions. The victims chose their overmen from among the landgang headmen who oppressed them, and these overmen made all the decisions. The central overman of the entire alliance was Slaver Ua-shn-tn, the man well-remembered by Nagmo and Nanikibi in Bison Prairie, by Jozes in Kekionga, by Miní on the Strait, as the scalper of Jumon and Lekomandá Shak. The purpose of the alliance was to invade the Beautiful Valley, a venture begun twenty winters earlier by Ua-shn-tn. The Redcoats had lately been hampering this venture; that's why the landgangs had proclaimed themselves independent of the Redcoats.

The landgangs had acquired their right to the Valley by having Turtleleague warriors disclaim such a right, and when they failed to convince even the Redcoats of their right thus acquired, they expressed their resentment against the one and their gratitude to the other by having young Scalpers dump the Redcoats' tea into the Ocean dressed as Turtleleague warriors.

Chapter 6.

Katabwe continues

Namakwe

In Kekionga, and at last in Bison Prairie, I was made much of, as were the other warriors who had fought on the Kanawha. We were lauded, not for our artful retreat, but for our victory; we had dared to attack the league of Witchburners, Slavers and Cheaters, we had routed scalper Ua-shn-tn's front lines, a feat as yet unequalled by all the Redcoat armies.

The league was on everyone's lips; its frightful coherence was the subject of every council. Unfortunately, the army that would confront the monster was slow in forming; the Peninsula's kin lacked coherence, not because they were all guided by different visions, but because, like the Invaders, they were guided by none.

Nanikibi's sister Namakwe came to Bison Prairie with her Batí and the others who had stopped off on the Strait, including Miní and Aleshi, and with two warriors from the Turtleleague who came on a mission, but not their own, and brought belts, but not warbelts.

The Turtleleague warriors were sad figures. Their league was broken; it had split precisely at the moment when thirteen gangs of Oceanshore Invaders formed a league. I already knew that the Turtleleague had allied with one Invader against the other once too often; after helping the Redcoats defeat the Blackrobes and Lemond, the Turtleleague warriors had found their allies helping themselves to Turtleleague lands and fields, destroying warriors with rum and treating them as underlings. I now learned that some Turtleleague warriors turned to the landgangs for protection against the Redcoats while the rest turned to their red allies for protection against the landgangs. Warriors who had once boasted that free human beings went wherever they pleased were no longer free.

The two in Bison Prairie came on an embassy for the Redcoats; they urged the warriors in Bison Prairie to accept the Redcoats' peacebelts now that the Redcoats were beset by new enemies.

I wondered, and surely Nanikibi wondered, if these broken warriors were heirs of Yahatase's kin, if these sad messengers were the fierce Serpents against whom Blackrobes had fumed, against whom Winámek had formed a league of western Rootkin. The saddest and strangest thing of all was that the one person who would have accepted their belts was Winámek's grandson Nagmo, but Nagmo was in Mishilimakina with his younger son Winámek and with my Topinbi, delivering furs to the Redcoats.

Nanikibi and other Firekeepers turned their backs to the emissaries. Bison Prairie's warriors had defeated every army the Redcoats had sent against them, and had no reason to submit to a peace offered by them.

I felt closer to Nanikibi than I ever had before. He knew something Lókaskwe knew, something Oashi had known: our strength was in what we gave, not in what we took; it was in our ceremonies and our songs, in the powers given to us by earth, in the guidance given by our dream animals. Tears came to my eyes when he brought out the contents of his bundle and begged me for the songs and stories more familiar to me, thanks to

KATABWE CONTINUES 1778

Miogwewe, than to Ozagi's son: the feather of the first Binesikwe, whose namesake I was to be; the disintegrating piece of bark scroll with marks as vanished as the world it had described; the shell and the fishbones and the otterskin itself, with their promise of giving, of renewal to come from the inaccessible, invaded Oceanshore.

Namakwe was enraged by Nanikibi's and my absence from the council with the Turtleleague warriors, by our indifference to their mission. Batí and Aleshi supported her, and even Miní, though not wholeheartedly. Namakwe's rage was hysterical; she exaggerated and she gesticulated, just like those of Lemond, whose close neighbor she was. Namakwe divided the world into two halves: one half consisted of her kin of Karontaen allied with the Strait's Redcoats; the other half consisted of Scalper Ua-shn-tn and his league of landgangs. She said her brother couldn't turn his back to both halves because there was nowhere else to turn.

I heard Namakwe with dismay; I would have been like her if I hadn't grown alongside Lenapi, Oashi and Lókaskwe.

She spoke of her three children, of her nieces, twin daughters of Batí's brother Piér, of Miní's and Nizokwe's Isadór and Isabél. She said most of the Strait's children looked up to fathers and uncles who had made a blood pact and never broken it until now.

She said all these warriors had responded to Shawano's call after the murder of Oashi and had bravely faced a monster on the Kanawha. They had returned from the Kanawha intent on forming an army that could confront the monster and had sat in a council with all those who had fought in the war against the enclosures: Turtlefolk of the Strait, Rootkin of Kichigami, Kekionga Prairiekin, carriers from Sandusky below the Strait and from the Leaning Tree village above it, as well as Turtleleague warriors from the eastern Woodlands. The former enemy, the new headman of the Strait's Redcoats, named Hamtin, had come to this council with words, belts, deeds.

With words, Ham-tin had committed himself to keeping all Invaders out of the Beautiful Valley. Miní added that this was a commitment to continuing the fur trade with the Valley's Rootkin, for this trade fattened the fur gangs behind the Redcoats, gangs which had already reduced the former northern Invaders to gatherers and haulers of pelts hunted by Rootkin.

With belts, Ham-tin committed himself to war against Scalper Ua-shn-tn's league.

And with deeds, Ham-tin had already curbed the greed of some of his own Redcoats, who had tried to take Rattlesnake Isle and other common grounds away from the Strait's inhabitants. Miní told us that the Redcoats had denuded Rattlesnake Isle after the war against the enclosures, on the pretext that its trees offered hiding places to hostile warriors, and had then granted the entire island to Lemond's Decuánd, to reward him for his collaboration. The indignant villagers persuaded Tisha's father, Kampó, to fight for the return of the island to the inhabitants. Kampó was threatened with the loss of all he had, and the island was taken from Decuánd and given to a Redcoat. Ham-tin returned the island to the Strait's inhabitants only when he needed an army to confront Scalper Ua-shn-tn.

Miní was less enthusiastic than Namakwe about the good intentions of headman Ham-tin, but he too divided the world into the same two halves. He saw no alternative to an alliance with the Redcoats; he too was upset by the absence from the Strait's council of Shawano and the Southbranch kin, Nanikibi and the Bison Prairie Firekeepers, Sigenak, Jozes, Tisha and the Wabash Prairiekin.

Failing in their mission, dismayed by the indifference, even hostility, of their own kin, Namakwe and the Strait's warriors drew closer to the redfrocked headman of the Strait's enclosure, whom they considered a doubtful but necessary ally, a source of weapons and provisions somewhat less reliable than Lemond's Lekomandá had been earlier.

When I saw Miní again, he said the Strait's warriors could no longer envision fighting with wood and stone. They learned that the Scalpers at the Pit-strength were moving toward the Strait and they set out toward the Fork armed with the Redcoats' weapons, expecting to be strengthened along the way by warriors from among the Southbranch kin and the Eastbranch survivors. Again they were disappointed. Shawano and his kin persisted in viewing both Scalpers and Redcoats as enemies, even if the two were momentarily at each other's throats, and of the two, Shawano feared the long-unified Redcoats more than he feared the thirteen recently-unified Oceanshore gangs. The Strait's warriors were even more dismayed by the false neutrality of the Eastbranch survivors gathered around blackcollared Brethren on the Tuscarawas: they were used as spies and messengers, as Brother Post-err had been used earlier by Redcoats; villagers told Brethren of the doings of their kin, Brethren seeking provisions at the Pit-strength told Scalpers what they'd heard, and returned to the Tuscarawas with the Scalpers' good words. The western warriors were isolated in this sea of indifference and outnumbered by their enemies; they returned to the Strait without attempting to seize the enclosure at the Fork, their only consolation being that the Pit-strength Scalpers had been similarly unable to gather forces for an assault on the Strait. But a surprise awaited the Strait's warriors. They learned that another Scalper army, one led by a landsucker known as Rah-jerks-lark, had reached the western part of the Beautiful Valley, had not been stopped by Sigenak and Prairie warriors, and had been allowed to establish a stronghold on the Wabash.

Seen through Namakwe's eyes, Sigenak had turned his back on past and kin and had thrown himself into an adventure that could only engulf Wagoshkwe's children in fratricidal war. But I knew that Sigenak was doing what he had always done, he was trying to revive my father's alliance, Wagoshkwe's alliance, with those near at hand. Namakwe was doing the same thing, only with those near to her.

Sigenak lodged near the great mound at Cahokia on the Long River with Manato and their six sons; he maintained close contact with Magda's son Tisha, already married and with a daughter in Uiatanon on the Wabash, his mother's birthplace, and engaged in the fur trade between Kittihawa's Sandypoint and the southwestern Invaders on the other side of the Long River, called Senyores. Sigenak was also in contact with Tisha's uncle Jozes, who maintained a fur post in the Prairie village Kithepekanu near Uiatanon.

For Sigenak, the war against the enclosures had never ended, and he took part in the frequent raids of Prairiekin against Redcoats, rumcarriers and landsuckers who ventured into the valley of the Wabash. In one of these raids, Sigenak captured a youth named Will-well, the age of his oldest son, and adopted him. The raiders, Prairiekin allied with Plains warriors and armed by the shadowy Senyores, were in Sigenak's eyes the heirs of Wagoshkwe's Redearth warriors.

When the Scalpers under Rah-jerks-lark reached the Wabash, Sigenak and other Prairie warriors who had known of the Invaders' approach placed themselves in their path as Nagmo had once placed himself in the path of the Redcoats who came to Bison Prairie. But then Sigenak and the Prairie warriors fell into a trap. This Rah-jerks-lark was a consummate liar; he styled himself a renegade from the Oceanshore Invaders, an ally of the shadowy Senyores, and a friend of all who opposed Redcoats. Knowing nothing of the Scalpers' invasion of the Sunrise Mountains or of the massacres on the Kanawha, Sigenak and the Prairie warriors let the self-styled renegades install themselves in the Uiatanon enclosure whose redfrocked occupants Sigenak had helped oust a generation earlier.

As soon as this news reached the Strait, Redcoat Ham-tin decided to set out against Rah-jerks-lark, but very few of the Strait's warriors agreed to accompany him. Enraged by what they considered Sigenak's betrayal, Miní, Aleshi, Batí and others nevertheless refused to shed the blood of kin alongside whom they had fought. Headman Ham-tin's undisguised contempt for Rootkin, something he shared with his forerunner Bra-duck as well as his enemy Ua-shn-tn, drove away many of the warriors who did start out with him, so that Ham-tin walked to Uiatanon all but alone, as intrepid as his predecessor on the Strait, muleheaded Mad-win. Redcoat Ham-tin tried to enlighten Sigenak and the Prairiekin about the Scalpers' intentions, but he met only hostility. Completely isolated in every quarter, the pathetic Ham-tin let himself be captured by the Scalpers, whereupon Rah-jerks-lark sent out runners with the message that he had captured an army of Redcoats allied with western Rootkin.

The force that finally moved to dislodge the Scalpers from the Prairies did not originate on the Strait but in the north, in Mishilimakina and the Leaning Tree village, and it was led by my uncle Nagmo. The northern carriers, many, like Nagmo himself, in red coats, would not shy away from fratricidal war; they were heirs of warriors who had fought without qualms against kin alongside Winámek and alongside Wabskeni, and they viewed the Cahokians as their traditional enemies, Redearth kin, western Serpents.

Nagmo's armed carriers arrived in Bison Prairie accompanied by an unarmed gift caravan which included his two sons and their women, my Topinbi and his newly-named daughter Mimikwe, as well as a Cheater from the Oceanshore named Burr-net. Nagmo began his fratricidal war by capturing Kittihawa's Sandypoint on the Lakebottom during the naming ceremony for Sandypoint's first son. This capture of Katwyn's friend, of a man who, like Nagmo himself, was a crosswearer and a gift carrier, was incomprehensible to me and Nanikibi and Bison Prairie's Firekeepers, until we remembered the connection between the armed carriers and the unarmed gift caravan.

Sandypoint had been gathering furs on the Lakebottom and sending them, with Tisha's and Sigenak's help, not to Mishilimakina and thence to Hochelaga, but to Cahokia on the Long River and thence to Senyores in the southwest and to Lemond's kin at the Long River's mouth. Nagmo and his sons, as well as my Topinbi and Nizokwe's brother Antó and his friend Soli-man, were all embroiled with Hochelaga fur gangs who insisted that all furs gathered in Mishigami follow the traditional route established by the first Nangisi.

The Hochelaga fur gang had been waiting for a pretext to stop Sandypoint from sending pelts to other fur gangs; the war between Redcoats and Scalpers and news of Rah-jerks-lark's success on the Wabash gave them that pretext. Sandypoint was captured as an enemy and escorted by Nagmo's younger son Winámek to Mishilimakina's headman Star-ling, the rum-carrier who had married Aleshi's sister Anjelík.

The Cheater Burr-net was to replace Sandypoint as the region's fur-gatherer; he would send pelts to Mishilimakina, with the help of Topinbi and Nagmo's sons, and he would distribute gifts more generously than Sandypoint, for his gifts, made not by free people but by contrivances operated by people enclosed in hives, were more plentiful. The capture was carried out as a ritual, almost tenderly: my multi-lingual Cakima translated for Burr-net as he begged for Sandypoint's permission to store furs at the Lakebottom post, permission which Sandypoint granted as he welcomed Burr-net and told him there was room enough in Mishigami for both of them. Burr-net even prepared talking leaves for the brothers Antó in Mishilimakina and Piér on the Strait assuring them of Sandypoint's harmlessness to the northern fur gang.

Nagmo didn't do as well in Cahokia. Although his well-supplied force didn't disintegrate, it was outnumbered, not by the noisy Rah-jerks-lark, whose force vanished as completely as Ham-tin's, but by Sigenak's allies: Prairiekin allied with mounted Plains warriors, armed by Senyores, and aided by a surprise that neither Nagmo nor anyone else had anticipated. A

Lekomandá Labám had come up from the mouth of the Long River with an army of Scabeaters, precisely the army Lemond had waited and longed for twenty winters earlier, when the Redcoats had first approached the Strait, only Labám's army came as allies of the Scalpers because their overman across the Ocean, like Sigenak, was still warring against the Redcoats. This unlikely alliance destroyed Nagmo's army, killed Nagmo, and promptly disintegrated. Nagmo, the last heir of Winámek's league, had been the only person in Cahokia with whom Labám had anything in common. A crosswearer accompanied by Blackrobes, loyal to his overseas overman, hostile to renegades, Lekomandá Labám shared no more than a common enemy with Rah-jerks-lark, who spat on crosses, despised Blackrobes and recognized no overman other than the landgangs; Labám shared even less with Sigenak and Prairiekin who had loved the Scabeaters no more than they loved the Scalpers.

Flushed with the victory over Nagmo, and so contemptuous of his allies that he attributed the victory to himself, Labám set out to complete his mission and defeat the remaining Redcoats on the western Lakes, but he set out alone, with no more men than he arrived with except a few scouts, among them Tisha.

Tisha told his uncle Jozes of his engagement. Jozes sent a warning to the Strait. Aleshi and other warriors met Labám's army in Kekionga, but not in time to save Kekionga's lodges from destruction. Aleshi and the Strait's warriors killed Labám and destroyed the force they would have embraced with unqualified joy a generation earlier.

Tisha guided a remnant of Labám's army to Bison Prairie. He found refuge in my and Nanikibi's lodge and promptly sent word to Sigenak of Sandypoint's capture and Labám's defeat.

The Cahokians' revenge against Aleshi was not long in coming, but it was a cowardly revenge, unworthy of Sigenak and Prairie warriors. The Cahokians set out, not toward Aleshi and the Strait's warriors responsible for Labám's defeat, but toward dead Nagmo's kin in Bison Prairie, where Sigenak knew they would find no opposition; even Nagmo's sons were away when the Cahokians arrived. It was clear that Sigenak was no more anxious than the Strait's warriors to shed the blood of kin. And it wasn't clear whose blood Sigenak's allies wanted to shed. As soon as they entered Bison Prairie they turned on each other.

The survivors of Labam's army and the few Cahokians who with pride traced their parentage to Lemond were eager to avenge Labám; they wanted to raze Bison Prairie to the ground, as Labám had razed Kekionga. They were supported by Plains Redearth kin who remembered Bison Prairie as the stronghold from which Wabskeni's armies annihilated the brave Redearth warriors, but were opposed by carriers and fur-gatherers who wanted nothing destroyed, who wanted to install themselves in Burr-net's and Sandypoint's fur posts, who wanted the furs that Sandypoint no longer brought to their posts.

The few Senyores who came with Sigenak were eager to leave as soon as they arrived; they wanted only to plant their flag and run off with booty; their eyes grew large with greed for the contrivance-made cloth and metal objects in Burr-net's store.

Sigenak's adopted son Will-well, fluent in the language of Rootkin, was the only defender of Rah-jerks-lark among the allies; his sole desire was to convince us that Oashi's murderers were liberators from the oppression of Redcoats. Sigenak's oldest son, Meteya, had stayed in Cahokia, refusing to take part in an expedition against the village of his father's brother. The three sons who came with Sigenak—Gizes, Wapmimi and Wakaya—wanted to please and impress their Bison Prairie kin, and exerted all their efforts trying to keep their father's allies from each other's throats and from doing harm to any of us.

At the Firekeepers' council, Sigenak tried to excuse and even praise his allies, but his words described an altogether different entity than the army he brought. He spoke of an alliance powerful enough to push all Invaders into the Ocean, of the alliance he'd been seeking since the day my father attacked the Kekionga enclosure, of Wagoshkwe's alliance. He told us the Senyores in his army were not Invaders but descendants of the Stonelodge people who in Yahatase's day ousted all Invaders from their valleys and mountains. He said the Blackrobe with the Senyores was not kin to the Blackrobes who had imprisoned Yahatase. This man, a follower of an ancient Blackrobe who had urged the invaded to rise up against the Invaders, raged against all the justifications with which Invaders covered their deeds, insisted that no pretext, no reason whatever could justify the oppression and slaughter of some people by others, and praised all those who had risen, among them the Stonelodge people, the Redearth kin, people called Tupakamaru who had just risen against Senyores at the opposite end of the world, as well as Rah-jerks-lark's half among the Oceanshore Invaders.

Sigenak was strong with words, but his armed allies were visibly unfit to face the Strait's warriors and Redcoats, or even Bison Prairie's Firekeepers; those who weren't prostrated from bouts with rum were bickering with each other. Sigenak's immediate task was not to push Invaders to the salt sea, but to satisfy the greed of his allies while keeping them from harming his kin, no easy task.

Some of the Senyores wanted to plunder Sandypoint's store at the Lakebottom, which was protected only by little crosswearer Kittihawa; they had to be reminded that they had come to revenge the capture of Sandypoint, not to consummate it. Senyores and carriers wanted to plunder dead Nagmo's lodge, which contained the greatest wealth of objects in Mishigami, but Kittihawa came to her cousin Katwyn's defense, insisting that Katwyn was Sandypoint's most loyal friend.

This left only Burr-net's store, and all of the allies, including Sigenak, converged on this object for plunder, eager to carry off the furs, the gifts, and Burr-net himself, as retaliation for the capture of Sandypoint. Such a deed would not have been a fit monument to Wagoshkwe, nor worthy of Sigenak. But it did not take place. My and Nanikibi's children Topinbi and Cakima prevented the deed before any of Sigenak's allies had acted, and they prevented it with a ruse, like Rootkin; I suspect the ruse originated with Cakima. I was proud of both, in spite of my dislike for the object of their victory, a cheating rumcarrier.

Topinbi and Cakima had heard all the stories and songs about Ozagi's adoption of Wagoshkwe and her Redearth kin in the face of Wabskeni's army. Topinbi invited all in Bison Prairie and on the Lakebottom, including Sigenak and his allies, to celebrate the marriage of Cakima with Burr-net. The enemy, the object for plunder, became Sigenak's nephew, and many of Sigenak's allies, those who weren't drunk, left Bison Prairie.

Seventeen-spring Cakima made up in energy what she lacked in beauty. She asked her crosswearing aunts to help with the arrangements, but Kittihawa was all taken up with Sandypoint's post and Katwyn was mourning the death of Nagmo, so Cakima took on all the arrangements herself. She was everywhere at once, fluently speaking every language except that of the Senyores; she was Burr-net's window to the world of Rootkin; she had learned his language from the rumcarrier Con-err on the Muskingum.

In great-grandmother Miogwewe's day, the adopted Pyerwá, Minî's grandfather, had felt obliged to learn the language of his hosts. But this Burr-net seemed to feel no such obligation; he was mute; Topinbi and Cakima were obliged to speak to him in the Invaders' tongue. If the spirit of Shutaha was present at this adoption, it could only have been dismayed. Cakima arranged the ceremony of three fires, the only part of which Burr-net seemed to understand was the part to which he contributed: the rum-drinking. It wasn't a ceremony in which Bison Prairie's Firekeepers adopted Burr-net, but rather one in which Burr-net adopted the Firekeepers as well as the hostile remaining Cahokians. He was the host. Cakima knew this. It was this that she had arranged. My daughter was a descendant of the first Nangisi, the carrier who used the ways of Rootkin as things with which to enhance his power among Rootkin.

Neither Nanikibi nor I could understand why both of our children were fascinated by a cheating rumcarrier who seemed to have no praiseworthy qualities. Lenapi's insights didn't help me: he had spoken of people who were debilitated and trapped; my Topinbi and Cakima were strong and free. The closest I could come to understanding them was to imagine that in their eyes they were becoming important in a league that was larger and more powerful than the first Winámek's, a league whose warriors carried invisible weapons (well-hidden members, Miogwewe would have said). That was why my Topinbi as well as Katwyn's two sons Nangisi and Winámek, so well-named, felt no need to prove their prowess as warriors with visible weapons; they were peacemakers, innocents all, yet more powerful than armed warriors, and they knew their own powers while no one else knew them. Privation, misery and death were near the root of their powers. The death of Nagmo, their own beloved uncle Nagmo from whom they'd learned so much, was not a loss for Topinbi and Cakima but a gain. Topinbi and Cakima inherited the position first occupied by ancient Nangisi; they became the intermediaries between the animals in the forest and the gifts of the Invaders. With Sandypoint gone, Topinbi and Cakima, together with Katwyn's sons, reached over the entire length of Mishigami from Greenbay to the Lakebottom along both shores. The rumcarrier Burr-net connected them with the part of the gift-giving league that lodged in the Invaders' world, for Burr-net was linked to Nizokwe's brother Antó and to Soli-man in Mishilimakina and to Nizokwe's musical brothers on the Strait, Piér and Batí, Namakwe's Batí; they in turn carried their bundles to fur gangs on both sides of the Ocean. Soli-man, married to a crosswearing Turtlewoman from the Bay of Rolling White Sands, had connections with fur gangs in Hochelaga and with fur gangs of three different tongues across the Ocean. Piér, a father of twin girls, had connections with a fur gang headman on the Strait who came from among the Witchburners, a man called Jaymay who had raised his trading post on land given to him by Soli-man's cousin Shap-man, the rumcarrier unsuccessfully adopted by Bison Prairie's Firekeepers. It was said Shap-man had acquired land on the Strait by feeding rum to one of the Bison Prairie warriors who had escorted him to the Strait, and by having the drunken warrior put a mark on a talking leaf.

Miogwewe had been wary of Winámek's noisy and very visible league. I wondered who among my kin was as wary of this silent, invisible and insidious league: perhaps Mashekewis in Boweting, perhaps Miní on the Strait, certainly Lókaskwe in the Valley—and who else?

Cakima's marriage celebration ended abruptly. The smallpox broke out in Bison Prairie, among the children. Topinbi's baby Mimikwe was stricken, as well as Nangisi's Manilú and Winámek's Miaga. Siegnak's drunken allies were ignored, all enmities were forgotten; Katwyn and I nursed grandchildren alongside each other. The children began to recover; I started to think we were at last gaining the immunity that was the strength of the Invaders. But then Katwyn succumbed to the swellings, and she failed to recover.

Aptegizhek

Sigenak and his sons, as well as Tisha, were still in Bison Prairie when a tall and proud warrior arrived from the Strait, cousin Miní's son Isadór, with the news that the smallpox had not attacked only our village. Nanikibi and I took Isadór into our lodge, to share a corner with his enemy Tisha; Pyerwá's great-grandson and Manyan's grandson were, after all, cousins. Tisha was upset by the arrangement; Isadór was too preoccupied to notice Tisha's presence.

Isadór said Labám's army had carried the smallpox in its train, perhaps unintentionally. After defeating Labám's army, Aleshi and the Strait's warriors, Miní and Isadór among them, had gathered up the weapons and provisions abandoned by the defeated, and had distributed them among the Kekiongans who had taken refuge on the Strait. The smallpox had immediately broken out on the Strait.

Tisha vehemently denied that Labám's army was to blame; Labám had earlier distributed gifts and provisions in Cahokia, and no one had fallen to the pox.

Isadór didn't insist; he had yet more news. His face as rigid as a mask, suppressing tears with all his inner strength, Isadór told us there were numerous refugees from the Turtleleague on the Strait. Shutaha's eastern kin, ancient Yahatase's people, the once fierce Serpents of the eastern Woodlands, had been all but exterminated by the landgang alliance under Scalper Ua-shn-tn. I felt as if I'd heard that a corner of the world had fallen through a hole; it was inconceivable. Thirteen mutually hostile bands of Scalpers had united in the fashion of the Turtleleague at the moment when the Turtleleague had split into mutually hostile bands, some allied with one, few with the other, most allied with none and neutral at last.

On the pretext that some Turtlewarriors were allied with Redcoats, Scalper Ua-shn-tn declared war against the entire Turtleleague, and he charged an unscrupulous killer, a headman Sullied-van, with the task of extermination. At the head of a vast army of thirsty landsuckers and greedy bountyseekers, headman Sullied-van set out, not against the Turtlewarriors allied with Redcoats, but against the unprepared, against the neutrals, against those who were planting, hunting, dancing, and not seeking any more allies or enemies. After filling their bags with the scalps of the unarmed, the Scalpers became demented with murderous frenzy; they set fire to forests with all their living beings, burned fields and villages. Next they turned, not against the Redcoats' allies but against their own, against Turtlefolk who had helped Scalpers against Redcoats, and they murdered all, the old, the women, the children, and then they set fires, intent on leaving no life in the eastern Woodlands, on denuding that part of the world. The only

Turtlefolk the Scalpers didn't confront were those they had declared war against, those actually allied with the Redcoats, those who were armed and ready, but the devastation had destroyed these warriors as well, leaving the Turtlewarriors isolated among their redfrocked allies, without villages or kin to defend. Never before could a great people have vanished so suddenly.

Isadór was still narrating the horrors when all three of Oashi's and Lókaskwe's children arrived in Bison Prairie: Aptegizhek with a bandaged head and clutching Lenapi's scroll, Shecogosikwe wearing Miogwewe's pendant, her eyes filled with terror, and young Wagoshkwe shaking with fear. Lókaskwe, my dearest friend and only sister, was dead; Shawano was dead; Aptegizhek's head was bandaged because he'd been scalped.

The tears Isadór had suppressed now burst from his eyes. He had never met his cousin, but he embraced Aptegizhek with all his strength; the pact their fathers had made was renewed with the two youths' tears. Isadór already knew some of what Aptegizhek told us; he no longer made the effort to hide his sadness.

The Scalpers under Ua-shn-tn proceeded as if unerring seers guided their every step. After headman Sullied-van's devastating attack, surviving Turtlewarriors, those who had been ready to meet the Scalpers, set out with a fury equalled only by Sullied-van's. These few hundred homeless and kinless men demented by sorrow, destroyed and burned every lodge, field and tame animal between the Eastern River and the Sunrise Mountains, from the Northern River to the Pit-strength. Ua-shn-tn and his landgang council, as if they had been waiting for this retaliation, roused their own people to raging hatred by spreading lurid stories of the Turtlewarriors' brutality amplified with details from Sullied-van's atrocities, and promptly declared war, not against the raging Turtlewarriors, but against the Rootkin of the Beautiful Valley.

The landgangs justified the scalping of captives by convincing themselves Rootkin ate their captives. Their council now tried to discourage its armed men from taking the scalps of women and children, not because of a sudden outburst of humanity but because of unwillingness to cover the bounties; the council was interested in the killing, not the scalping or eating.

But the armed men depended on the bounties. They poured across the Sunrise Mountains into the valley's Southland all the way to the Beautiful River's falls near its mouth at the Long River, drawn that far by all they had heard of Rah-jerks-lark's single-handed victory over Ham-tin's Redcoats. Wherever they went they avoided armed warriors, pounced on villages with absent hunters, gathered the scalps of women and children, burned fields, lodges and stores of corn. On the Muskingum, Shawano, still believing the unity of the thirteen Oceanshore bands was temporary, still convinced he could council with some among the Scalpers, even after the loss of all his near kin, led an embassy to the Pit-strength to hold the Invaders to their promises. He was told the headman was willing to council. Once inside the enclosure, Shawano and all his companions were murdered.

Aptegizhek was interrupted by the arrival of news of yet another tragedy. Sigenak's oldest, Meteya, came to tell his father and brothers and Tisha that the smallpox had broken out in Cahokia. Manato and Sigenak's youngest sons, Kulswa and Pilawa, had gone to the Prairie village Kithepekanu on the Wabash, where a Blackrobe had taken Tisha's two children, Likét and baby Jozes, their mother being dead. In nearby Uiatanon, Rah-jerks-lark and his band were terrorizing the inhabitants, threatening and plundering. Meteya said the smallpox had been brought by Rah-jerks-lark from the east, or by Senyores from the west, or by Labám from the south. Tisha didn't protest; he and Sigenak and their remaining allies rushed out of Bison Prairie.

The rest of what Aptegizhek told wasn't known to Isadór. The news of Shawano's death, murdered while seeking peace despite the loss of all his kin, had spread like fire to every village of Southbranch and Eastbranch kin. Everywhere neutrality ended; everyone was exasperated with peacemakers; all who could walk painted themselves and joined war councils. One such council, held at Sandusky Bay, included Isadór, Maní, Batí, Aleshi and others from the Strait. Only three or four villages remained neutral, and these had in them largely Eastbranch survivors who were afraid of vanishing altogether.

Dead Shawano's village on the Muskingum, where Lókaskwe and her children lived with Southbranch kin and with many of the survivors from Lenapi's Sunrise Mountain village, was away from the main paths followed by warriors, furs, rum and rifles, was defended and protected by earth, trees, animals and ceremonies, was rich in meaning and self-respect but poor in corn and meat.

The camp that had grown up around Magidins' and Conerr's fur and gift post on the Tuscarawas did not thrive. Hunters took few furs to Con-err, who traveled to the Pit-strength rarely, with little to give and less to tell, and he returned with few gifts for Rootkin.

The village, or rather group of villages of Eastbranch converts and blackcollared Brethren on the Tuscarawas, was on one of the main paths through the Beautiful Valley toward the mountain passes, and these villagers maintained their neutrality by giving help to both sides: villagers fed neighboring Southbranch warriors with their corn and vegetables, for they had much to give, while Brethren carried news of the warriors to the Scalpers at the Fork.

Informed by the Brethren, a band of Scalpers attacked a village whose men had left to join the warriors at Sandusky, scalped women and children, burned lodges and food stocks, and then moved to the Beautiful River to join Rah-jerks-lark, who intended to make a swath of destruction in the Beautiful Valley on his way to the Strait.

Isadór and the Sandusky warriors knew of this plan, and they met and surprised the Scalper band before it reached the Beautiful River, but they failed to surprise Rah-jerks-lark, who had been warned by messages originating with the Brethren.

Exasperated by the odd neutrality of the Brethren, the Strait's warriors sent a party to the Tuscarawas to capture the blackcollared men and escort them peacefully to the Strait.

And then a rumor came that Rah-jerks-lark intended to make his swath, modeled on Sullied-van's, along the Tuscarawas. The Eastbranch converts were terrified; they all knew of the slaughter of Brethren's converts by the Pox-tn Boys a generation earlier. They hurriedly abandoned their neat lodges, gardens and unharvested fields and fled to the neutral kin of Lókaskwe's village, away from all main paths. Lókaskwe's kin welcomed and lodged the refugees, but had barely enough food for themselves in the war-surrounded village, and little to spare for the hundred guests. Ninety or so of the converts, accompanied by Lókaskwe, Aptegizhek and other Eastbranch kin, resolved to return to the Tuscarawas, with their talking leaves and their children, to harvest the corn in the fields and hide it at some distance from their village.

KATABWE CONTINUES 1782

Before leaving her village, Lókaskwe told Aptegizhek to care for his father's scroll, as if she already knew she was going to die at the hand of those she might have grown among. The unarmed converts had barely reached the baskets with which to gather their corn when a group of armed men entered the village: pioneers, Kre-sops, Ua-shn-tns, murderers of Oashi. Aptegizhek had never before seen them on a manhunt. The armed men herded the Eastbranch kin like tame animals into several lodges. Aptegizhek was separated from his mother. Only one voice among the armed men spoke of the helplessness and innocence of the converts; the others greedily eyed the harnesses, clothing, tools and other objects made by the converts. One man stroked Aptegizhek's head and spoke of the large bounties given for such plentiful scalps. Another took a metal mallet and lowered it on the head of an old woman with a prayer on her lips and a bundle of talking leaves in her hand. Aptegizhek lost consciousness. When he opened his eyes, his head pained; he saw a sight too horrible to describe; he saw a scalped head rise from among the mangled dead, their eyes met but neither recognized the other. An armed man rushed in, saw the moving head, beat it down and continued beating with demented frenzy, as if he were the cornered victim. Aptegizhek pretended to be dead; when the voices moved away, he loosened a board and slipped out the rear of the lodge, toward bushes. He heard loud talk and laughter. He saw the killers gather their plunder, set fire to the lodges filled with the bloody scalped bodies, and ride away on their victims' horses.

    The youth made his way to the Muskingum village; his very appearance spread the news of the massacre to every remaining village on the Muskingum and the Tuscarawas, and all the villages dispersed. Terrified Southbranch and Eastbranch kin fled westward, hundreds of them toward the Strait, including Lókaskwe's sister Magidins and the rumcarrier Con-err and their children. Young Shecogosikwe and Wagoshkwe pulled their scalped brother as far from the place of the massacre as they could reach, toward their aunt Katabwe and their father's pact-brother Nanikibi.

    I was too shaken to comfort Lókaskwe's children. I kept seeing my dream's eagle, that contrivance with a metal beak and steel claws, hovering above Rootkin disarmed, enclosed and disabled like the Brethren's converts, exposed on bare earth denuded of all shelter, shade and refuge. I saw the contrivance swoop down on its helpless victims and cut them to pieces with its metal beak and claws before flying off, its beak filled with scalps.

Lókaskwe's daughters fled yet further, toward the outermost edge of the world known to Shecogosikwe, toward her birthplace, the Lakebottom, and into Kittihawa's lodge. Aptegizhek stayed with Isadór, Nanikibi and me. We didn't need to council with our Bison Prairie kin. All who heard the youth headed toward the war councils on the Strait, all except Cakima, who stayed with the kinsman of Lókaskwe's murderers. Even Topinbi came with us, but only to deliver Burr-net's horses and furs to the Strait.

I no longer cared who my allies were; I was determined to answer for Oashi and Lókaskwe; they now lived only in me.

The Strait had more people on it than any place I've ever seen; there was no room for plants or animals. At least a thousand human beings were crowded into the adjacent villages; there were refugees and warriors from every part of the embattled Beautiful Valley, from the Sunrise Mountains, from the eastern Woodlands, from the Wabash, from every corner of the world. Namakwe and Batí barely had room for Nanikibi and me. Aptegizhek was welcomed by Nizokwe and Miní. Nizokwe's daughter Isabél embraced Lókaskwe's maimed son as warmly as Nizokwe's son had in Bison Prairie.

I was burning to set out against the Scalpers in the Beautiful Valley and had no sympathy for the problems of the refugees; every delay increased my impatience.

The surviving converts, their Brethren, Magidins and many of Lenapi's remaining kin were as terror-stricken as Lókaskwe's daughters, and they too wanted to go far from the place of the massacre. Rootkin from Sagi Bay guided them to a marsh covered by dense brush along the shore of the Clear Lake north of the Strait, a place the landgangs were not likely to invade. The adopted rumcarrier Con-err was supplied with food, weapons and clothing by Batí and Piér; the Witchburner Jaymay sent with Con-err provisions destined for Sandypoint, who was cutting trees in Sagi Bay for headman Star-ling. Forty or fifty people, most of them heirs of Rootkin who had once roamed freely on the Oceanshore, made their way to the brush-covered marsh by the Clear Lake.

Namakwe's and Miní's kin, all but Sigenak and Jozes, had at long last come to terms with the alliance on the Strait.

Namakwe was all energy and hope. Namakwe's son Nawak was as anxious as I to leave with the warriors.

Before we finally did leave, Miní warned the Wabash refugees that the alliance on the Strait was not all that Namakwe would have it be. The Strait's villages were no longer Shutaha's or his great-grandmother Chacapwe's village. Kinship was much talked about, but only because it was vanishing. The Redcoats recognized no one as kin, and those who had formerly been Lemond were increasingly like the Redcoats. Tisha's father Kampó knew that his son was on the Strait, but he pretended not to have a son. Kampó had been chosen by the Strait's inhabitants to fight against their exclusion from the commons on Rattlesnake Isle. He had won only because the Redcoats' headman had needed a loyal army, but during the fight he had become entangled with the landgrabbers to the point of agreeing to arrange a marriage between his niece Ceciĺ and a land-measurer named Will-yams. This union had not made Will-yams Tisha's cousin; it had merely strengthened a link in the land and fur nets which were the only circles of kinship recognized by the Invaders.

The delays abruptly ended. The problems of the refugees were forgotten, for word had come that one of Rah-jerks-lark's bands was heading toward the Sandusky Bay village, undoubtedly because they knew that the Sandusky warriors were on the Strait. The band was led by a headman named Kraw-fur, one of the men who had taken part in the massacre of Lókaskwe and the Eastbranch converts on the Tuscarawas.

No council was needed, nor belts nor the recruitment of allies. Warriors emerged from their lodges fully painted and armed and ready to dance, the bandaged Aptegizhek foremost among them. Nizokwe and Isabél gazed at Lókaskwe's angry son, their admiration mixed with pity.

I took part in the dance; what boiled inside me seemed to come from the bowels of the earth, as if earth herself were rising up against what was tearing her. I felt Yahatase, Sagikwe, Mangashko and Wagoshkwe in the strength of my limbs.

All of Oashi's pact brothers danced: Nanikibi and Miní, Aleshi and Batí. Batí's son Nawak was setting out on his first scouting mission. Tisha took the place of absent Jozes. Oashi's own son Aptegizhek wielded a weapon for the first time.

But Oashi was missing, as was Lókaskwe's wariness toward the redfrocked ally and his weapons, and I was too eager for revenge to fill the void. Only Miní raised his voice, but even he didn't question the need for the ally against whom these warriors had fought during the best part of their lives, nor the need for the weapons which maimed their users by making them dependent. Miní only complained; he was angered by the ally's stinginess with provisions and weapons that were plentiful inside the enclosure because they were made by contrivances; he was angered by the ally's open contempt toward warriors ready to give their lives for everyone on the Strait including the Redcoats. Miní knew that the redfrocked allies were all too similar to the Scalper enemies; the unending sweat and labor of both gangs of Invaders made them stingy and contemptuous toward free people for whom hunting was a sacred ritual and harvesting the occasion for a feast.

We went with the Redcoats' weapons, but no actual Redcoats accompanied us. We found the band of Scalpers camped by the river that flows into Sandusky Bay. Headman Kraw-fur and his men, aware of our presence only after our attack began, ran like hares from wolves; it was probably the first time they had faced warriors and not women and children. We followed the fleeing Scalpers and captured most of them, including Kraw-fur. No one spoke for adopting a single one of them. Those known to have taken part in the Tuscarawas massacre with Kraw-fur were tortured.

A Southbranch messenger brought news that another band of Rah-jerks-lark's men were camped on the Blue Licks across the Beautiful River, as if waiting to be ambushed. This band was led by a Scalper named Dam-doom, who was said to tell his men that killers of Rootkin were pioneers of independence and revolution. We learned that he didn't refer to the killers of enemies in war, but to the murderers of women and children; as soon as we attacked, Dam-doom and his men fled like Kraw-fur's; we downed most of them as they fled. We returned to Sandusky.

Tisha, whom Rah-jerks-lark would still take for an ally, went to the Scalpers' councilground to learn what other armies the landgang agent intended to send against the Beautiful Valley's inhabitants.

Miní and Aleshi went directly from the Blue Licks to the Strait to describe our two victories and to replenish the warriors' provisions. They returned with the news that our redfrocked allies had capitulated to the Scalpers! All were indignant, but not all were surprised. This was not the first time Invaders had betrayed forest allies. Nanikibi, Miní, Batí and many others remembered that over twenty springs earlier they had defeated Ua-shn-tn and Bra-duck and several other Invading armies, and after all their victories, their Scabeating allies across the Ocean had capitulated to the enemy.

Aleshi said that, already before we had set out against the Scalpers on the Sandusky, talking leaves had arrived on the Strait, leaves which said the Redcoats' overman across the Ocean had granted the Beautiful Valley to the Scalpers' league. This explained the Strait headman's wavering, his delays, his stinginess. Our peace with the Redcoats, the peace Namakwe and Miní and even Turtleleague warriors had beseeched us to make, had served only to give the Redcoats the illusion that they had the power to give our world away.

Aleshi's message was greeted by all the derision it deserved. Aptegizhek said the Invaders could grant each other the moon on their talking leaves; this was a game the Invaders played with each other and wouldn't deprive the rest of us of moonlight unless we let them exterminate us. Miní said even the redfrocked headman on the Strait recognized that his overman exceeded his powers when he granted the Beautiful Valley, and promised to give Rootkin all the aid needed to pursue the war.

The headman's mind, Miní said, was on the furs gathered in the Beautiful Valley. Miní, keeper of the peacebelts of Shutaha's village, had been treated as a nuisance by the headman, while redfrocked loyalists seeking refuge from the renegade landgang league were given all the headman's attention and care. Miní lost all his qualified enthusiasm for the alliance with the Redcoats, having also learned that the headman, no longer needing to recruit villagers to his army, had allowed the Isle of Rattlesnakes, the villagers' commons, to be seized by a Redcoat.

Tisha returned to Sandusky from the Scalpers' council on the Beautiful River and told us Rah-jerks-lark kept his camp surrounded by people Tisha called rumsacks, broken and homeless Rootkin who clung to the Scalper for his rum. Rah-jerks-lark addressed these rumsacks as if they heard and spoke for all the Rootkin of the Valley, although they no longer heard or spoke for any. When Tisha reached the camp, Rah-jerks-lark, pursued by defeats—his sole victory had been the one over

Ham-tin—told the rumsacks that his sole concern was to keep Invaders out of the Beautiful Valley. Then news of the Redcoats' capitulation arrived from the Pit-strength. Once again boastful of a victory that wasn't his, Rah-jerks-lark told the rumsacks that the Beautiful Valley's Rootkin were defeated people, and that defeated people had no right to any land. Rah-jerks-lark apparently thought that Kre-sop and those who started this war by murdering Oashi had won the war. Rah-jerks-lark fumed and threatened, declaring war on the Valley's inhabitants because he thought they had buried their weapons.

The rumsacks laughed at him; they knew that none of the valley's armed Rootkin had been defeated, and they also knew that the Scalpers' threats were as empty as their promises. The Scalpers' threats and promises were not expressions intended to convey meanings to listeners, but ejaculations intended to impress other Scalpers with the prowess of their utterer. The headmen these people chose for their councils, invariably the greediest and most vicious victimizers of their fellows, were chosen for their ability to utter ejaculations that gave their listeners the illusion of prowess.

Neither the Scalpers' threats nor the Redcoats' capitulation worsened the situation of the Beautiful Valley, but they didn't improve it either. Aptegizhek set out with Southbranch warriors against Invaders crossing the Beautiful River. He hoped the mere presence of warriors on the river would send the cowardly pioneers running, so that he could return with good news for Isadór and his beautiful sister Isabél.

Isadór and Tisha returned to the Strait with Miní, Aleshi and Batí, uneasy about their dependence on the treacherous Redcoats.

Nanikibi and I and most of the Firekeepers and Prairiekin did not accompany those of the Strait. We went to Kekionga on the edge of the embattled valley, my birthplace at the intersection of paths from Bison Prairie, the Strait, the Beautiful River and the Wabash.

For the first time since our capture of the Redcoats in Bison Prairie, I was with warriors who did not seek the Invaders' help or their weapons. I understood, as I never had before, my great-grandmother's ceremony of three fires, ancient Wedasi's ceremony, in which the Peninsula's Firekeepers, their Turtlekin of the Strait and Rootkin and Prairiekin from the eastern and western parts of the Beautiful Valley come together to expel

Wiske from their midst, Wiske the Invader, the contrived eagle of my dream. But I also understood, during flashes which made my head spin, that the Kekionga to which I returned was no longer a village in which a beautiful soul like my mother Menoko could grow; it was not a place where even a child could live immersed in the antics of gulls, in the dance of bees, in the look of a deer or the petals of a flower. A day didn't pass without news of a murder, an atrocity, a massacre, and all those who heard the news were impoverished and narrowed. All their acts and thoughts concentrated on not being victimized, not being murdered. Kekionga was no longer on ancient Wedasi's peaceful Peninsula but in the war-embattled Valley, on its edge; it was no longer a village but a war camp; its three fires lit the faces of warriors from the four quarters; it was a gatheringplace of warriors who had no other home, who had no surviving kin, whose villages and fields had been destroyed. The cowardly Scalpers who declared war against armed enemies but warred only against unarmed men, women and children, knew what they were doing.

Nanikibi understood this too as he fumbled through his otterskin bundle and perused its contents, trying to grasp what his grandfather Chebansi had been like, and his great-grandfather Wedasi, the peacemaker, and those who had come before Wedasi, who lived before the coming of the Invaders.

Aptegizhek was gone for barely two seasons. He arrived in Kekionga before the snows melted to tell us that several bands of armed landsuckers had crossed to the Beautiful River's northern shore and were moving to converge at the mound village of Southbranch kin at the mouth of the Muskingum. Besides their rifles they carried talking leaves which, they said, gave the mound village and all the fields around it to a band that called itself the Beautiful Landgang, newest heir to the gangs of Uashn-tn, Kre-sop and Done-more. This landgang had forced a group of broken Turtlewarriors to admit, at gunpoint, that the Turtleleague did not claim any part of the Beautiful Valley, and had then gotten a group of rumsacks who had once been Southbranch kin to put their marks on a talking leaf. This was a game the Scalpers played to entertain each other, but the converging landsuckers were too numerous for the warriors on the Muskingum, and the titles fired their holders with righteous bloodlust.

Sigenak

The Strait's warriors returned with Aptegizhek to council and dance in Kekionga, unencumbered by their redfrocked allies. All of them came: Isadór as well as his father Miní and uncle Aleshi; Nawak as well as his father Batí. But Aptegizhek was crestfallen and seemed self-conscious about his maimed head. Isabél had welcomed him as a close cousin; Isadór had told him she had been accepting gifts from a meek rumcarrier named Lion.

Too few to remove the Invaders from the Southland below the Beautiful River, the counciling warriors, I among them, resolved to stop any Invaders from establishing a foothold on any part of the northern shore. Tisha was to carry our resolve to the Cheaters' headman at the Pit-strength. Aleshi helped Tisha formulate the message: the Scalpers' game of having rumsacks place marks on talking leaves was nothing but an insult to Rootkin; the armed men at the Pit-strength were going to be tolerated only if they hurried to remove their own landsuckers before our hatchets removed them; if the Pit-strength headman wanted to address western warriors, he should send messages to their councils, not to rumsacks who heard and spoke for no one.

Many, including Nanikibi and I, were dissatisfied with Aleshi's formulations, but Miní said it was necessary to speak to the Invaders in a language they could understand, and Aptegizhek and his companions from the Muskingum urged haste.

I wasn't as strong as I had been on my first raids in the Sunrise Mountains, and the horse ride alone exhausted me. I thought of Lókaskwe, of her final resolve to live surrounded by earth's unstinting beauty, away from the battlegrounds, and I felt myself a cornered serpent lashing out in self-defense, the defended beauty receding ever further from my reach.

I was repelled by the enemy when we sighted him exactly where we expected him; he seemed unaware that the Valley was full of vibrant life, all of it hostile to his presence. Two bands of Scalpers were camped outside the mound village, one on each side, each waiting for the other to attack first because both knew there were not only women and children in the village but warriors as well. We retreated to the forest to dance before we split up to ambush both bands simultaneously. During the dance I thought of the bountyseekers who had surrounded Lenapi's mountain village, of Kre-sop and the land measurers who had murdered Oashi on the Kanawha, of Kraw-fur and the monsters who massacred Lókaskwe and the unarmed converts. Both Scalper bands panicked as soon as they saw us; as many of them were killed by each others' rifles as by our arrows. We let survivors flee across the Beautiful River, hoping they and their likes would keep on swimming until they reached the other side of the Ocean. A few enraged warriors scalped corpses. Aptegizhek and Nanikibi tried to stop this repulsive act; we were denatured enough by the Invaders' ways. Aptegizhek and then others, I among them, stuffed earth into the mouths of corpses, letting them satisfy their landlust now, when they weren't merely taking but also giving, at last acknowledging Earth's generosity by offering her their bodies.

Isadór stayed at the mound village with his friend Aptegizhek when the rest of us returned to Kekionga.

We found Tisha waiting for us, together with my Topinbi and Nagmo's son Nangisi and a horse-drawn gift caravan. News of our defeat of the Scalpers at the mound village had reached the Pit-strength shortly before Tisha had, and the Pit-strength headman had treated Tisha with excessive obsequiousness, speaking endlessly of the Scalpers' disposition to be generous to the people of the Valley. Rah-jerks-lark was no longer headman; the landgangs had learned more about his long and noisily boasted victory over Ham-tin, and they were incensed by his practice of cheating not only his underlings but also his fellow headmen. His successor was a headman Harr-marr, a less boastful man who was directly answerable for his words and deeds to overman Ua-shn-tn. This Harr-marr admitted to Tisha that the Beautiful Valley's Rootkin were not defeated people who had lost the valley, since they hadn't been defeated, and said that overman Ua-shn-tn was pulling all his landsuckers, with or without titles, away from the valley's northern shore, and was disbanding all his armed bands except Harr-marr's. After hearing Tisha's message, Harr-marr said he and his armed men would stay at the Pit-strength only long enough to remove all landsuckers from the north of the valley. Harr-marr then confronted Tisha with a talking leaf and urged Tisha to accept gifts and put a mark on the leaf, thereby acknowledging Harr-marr's presence and role in the Valley. Tisha refused to mark anything, and was dismayed to learn that the armed man had already gathered marks, not only from rumsacks who pretended to speak for Southbranch kin, but from Nagmo's Nangisi pretending to speak for Bison Prairie's Firekeepers, and from my Topinbi pretending to speak for Kekionga's Prairiekin, as Nanikibi's son, and for the Strait's Turtlefolk, as Namakwe's nephew. They and all others who marked the Scalpers' leaves were named chiefs of tribes by Harr-marr.

Let the Invaders play their games, some said, but many others, myself included, didn't like their games.

Nangisi and Topinbi were full of self-justification; Topinbi was the more eloquent of the two; he reminded me of his grandfather Ozagi. He said the war was damaging the Bison Prairie fur trade, and the gifts he and Nangisi had received were anxiously awaited, not only by those eager to drink rum, but above all by the children—his own, Cakima's, Nangisi's and Winámek's. He told us Sandypoint had returned to the Lakebottom, only to find the source of his gifts so blocked up that he had begged for gifts from the Strait's Jay-may, to whom he had given paintings instead of furs; the other, Cakima's Burr-net, had been captured and taken to Mishilimakina by Hochelaga Redcoats who wanted Burr-net to take his furs to their posts and not to Soli-man and Antó.

Topinbi insisted that his mark on a leaf gave the Invaders nothing and bound no one, since no council of Rootkin had empowered him to speak for them. By refusing to mark the leaf he wouldn't keep Invaders out of the Valley, he would merely let the Invaders' gifts be dissipated by rumsacks who drank all they were given.

I was disturbed by my son's inability to live without the Invaders' gifts, but I was more upset by the message Tisha had taken to the headman at the Pit-strength, a message formulated by Aleshi which even Miní had justified in terms of the need to speak to the Invaders in their language. My ancestors had not spoken to Miní's grandfather in his language; Pyerwá had learned the language of Rootkin. The Invaders' language was incomprehensible to us not because its sounds differed from ours, but because its meanings did. Their language put last things first. Tisha had gone to the Pit-strength to tell the Invaders to stay east of the mountains and south of the river, he had gone to speak about borders. But borders were not first things, they were last things. Earth hadn't put such constraints in the way of the creatures enjoying her fruits. Borders came with the

Invaders. Tisha had told the headman to remove Invaders who crossed the borders, as if it could be up to him or any man to give or withhold permission, as if he or any man could have the power to determine who was to live in the Beautiful Valley, as if we had suddenly forgotten that it was this very power we were warring against.

Tisha's, or rather Aleshi's message did not go unheard by the Scalpers' headman. Isadór was soon back from the Muskingum mound village confirming my worst fears. Headman Harr-marr had sped from the Pit-strength to the mound village with Aleshi's words, surmising that formulations acceptable to counciling warriors of Kekionga would not be rejected by a council of peaceful villagers on the Muskingum. Using Tisha's words, Harr-marr spoke of the inviolability of the mountains and the river as borders separating Invaders from Rootkin, and of his commitment to remove Invaders who crossed those borders. He even promised to leave near the mound village a detachment of armed men to carry out this task, and agreed that the Valley's warriors would retain the power to remove all Invaders he failed to reach. Regaling his hosts with gifts, Harr-marr then asked them to mark his talking leaf, a mark which committed them to nothing but acceptance of Harr-marr in his promised role, and only so long as he continued to carry it out.

Southbranch kin tired of continual war marked the leaf; Aptegizhek, son and heir of peacemakers Oashi, Lenapi and Shawano, marked the leaf; Eastbranch survivors who feared extinction marked the leaf; Isadór, son of the Strait's beltholder, enchanted to be part of an agreement with mutual benefits and obligations, like Shutaha's with Lekomandá Kadyak, signed the leaf.

Isadór was still enchanted when he reached Kekionga on his way to the Strait with the message that peace had at last come to the Beautiful Valley.

The illusion lasted for a season, during which two sons of Magidins and Con-err the rumcarrier, grown youths, came to Kekionga from the marsh by the Clear Lake. Their village had dispersed. The Strait's rum and fur gangs had been using Con-err to reduce the Brethren's converts to the gangs' appendages, and the converts had moved their village to the Morningland. The youths, fond neither of the converts nor of the gangs, had left their father and Magidins at the marsh with their younger children.

Aptegizhek, together with fear-driven Eastbranch kin, was back in Kekionga soon enough; he came shortly after Sigenak arrived with terror-stricken refugees from the Wabash. Aptegizhek and the people from the mound village weren't injured; no armed gangs had attacked them. Yet they looked and spoke as if, like the ancient Riverpeople, they had seen mountain-sized white serpents moving across the Beautiful Valley swallowing all life, as if they had seen the flying contrivances of my childhood's dream.

After Aptegizhek and the others marked Harr-marr's leaf, the headman left the promised detachment near the mound village and moved on; Sigenak would tell us where Harr-marr went next.

The detachment, headed by a fat man called Sun-clear, removed all landsuckers who crossed the river to squat on the northern shore; it seemed intent on carrying out its obligation. It was even reinforced by more armed men so that no squatters would be missed.

Lulled by Sun-clear's conscientiousness, the mound village kin were slow to notice that headman Sun-clear's own camp, the army that kept Invaders out of the Valley, was itself swallowing all the life surrounding it. Forests were falling; dead animals lay where they had been shot, rotting; tame animals bellowed in picketed enclosures of bare earth. Rootkin looked on with fascination, incredulous of what they saw, as if entranced.

Headman Sun-clear was misnamed; he was murky; none could fathom his real intentions. Only after questioning Sun-clear's armed men and reflecting on what they heard did it begin to dawn on Aptegizhek and others that the detachment Harr-marr had left behind was a landgang and that Sun-clear was its headman. It was a landgang consisting of armed men who had served overman Ua-shn-tn since the days of his scalping of Jumon and Lekomandá Shak and his retreat with Bra-duck's baggage. It fulfilled its obligation to Rootkin by removing from the Valley all Invaders who had not been Ua-shn-tn's associates, all who squatted without its permission.

The detachment quickly became a village that encroached on the Riverpeople's mounds. The forest surrounding it became a vast clearing. Devastation such as Eastbranch kin had seen on their Oceanshore during a generation was seen during less than a season at the mouth of the Muskingum. The Southbranch village by the mounds was soon surrounded by armed men who were indistinguishable from the lonely pioneers, the landsuckers sweating and laboring over their enclosed tame animals and tame plants destined to fatten landgang headmen and their agents, landsuckers answerable for their every act to headman Sun-clear; those who exhibited any independence were enclosed in a wooden trap.

Eastbranch kin then learned that the metamorphosis of the detachment didn't just happen, but had been intended; headman Sun-clear possessed a talking leaf, called an ordinance, in which his father Ua-shn-tn empowered him to remove unauthorized squatters, to destroy the trees and animals which were the shelter, the food, the companions of Rootkin, and at last to kidnap the children of starved-out Rootkin and turn them into land-scratching pioneers.

Aptegizhek and the Eastbranch kin, whose thoughts were never far from the massacre on the Tuscarawas, envisioned themselves as unarmed converts herded like cows into square lodges, prayers on their lips and talking leaves in hand, beset by grinning Pox-tn Boys, Kre-sops and Kraw-furs, their bodies cut to pieces, their scalps removed by bountyseekers, the lodges with their scraps at last burned.

Terrified by this vision, many Eastbranch kin fled westward, intending not to stop until they reached the Stonelodge people of the Sunset Mountains. Others accompanied Aptegizhek to their kinsman Lenapi's one-time home, to kin who had made no agreements with Scalper Ua-shn-tn or his headmen.

Tisha's uncle Jozes was in Kekionga, as was Sigenak with five of his seven sons, but without Manato. Sigenak was together with his kin of the Lakes for the first time since the war against the enclosures. He had been slow in seeing through the masks of the Scalpers.

Sigenak had carried Wagoshkwe's arrowhead pendant into the Scalpers' net. When Tisha left the Wabash to seek refuge on the Strait, Sigenak remained in Kithepekanu and proudly proclaimed himself neutral; he refused to break his alliance with the Senyores, but he wanted nothing to do with the Senyores' ally Rah-jerks-lark.

Sigenak helped Jozes establish a fur post in nearby Uiatanon, and when Sandypoint returned to the Lakebottom, Sigenak accompanied Nagmo's youngest son Winámek on the caravan route from Sandypoint's post on the Lakebottom to Cahokia.

When they learned that overman Ua-shn-tn had granted the lower Wabash Valley to Rah-jerks-lark, Sigenak and his son Meteya made a game out of granting each other the Oceanshore and the Sunset Mountains, amusing their kin, all of whom would have laughed if one had told them of the Scalpers' singleness of purpose; they had seen Rah-jerks-lark plundering his own men, Senyores plundering Rah-jerks-lark, finally Rah-jerks-lark heading east to plunder other headmen.

Jozes, who only moved between Uiatanon and Kithepekanu, nevertheless knew better than Sigenak that the Scalpers' games had lasting consequences. Rah-jerks-lark's successor arrived in Uiatanon with the message that only people loyal to Ua-shn-tn would be allowed to live in the village. When the villagers laughed, the Scalpers plundered various lodges, including Jozes's post. Lemond's kin united with Prairiekin and chased the Scalpers out of Uiatanon, and were then subjected to daily ambushes and atrocities. Jozes and others begged Sigenak and the Prairiewarriors to intervene, but Sigenak persisted in thinking himself neutral.

Among Sigenak's sons, only Wapmimi attached himself to warriors who raided the Scalpers. Adopted Will-well wanted only to keep peace between Sigenak and the Scalpers. Meteya was neutral by inclination. Pensive Wakaya stood apart, and Kulswa and Pilawa were not yet old enough to scout.

It was learned that a new headman with an army was camped at the falls of the Beautiful River—this was Harr-marr, who had just left his detachment at the Muskingum mound village. Sigenak, his older sons, and a sizable number of warriors left Kithepekanu to council with the new headman and to make him answer for the Scalpers' atrocities.

Headman Harr-marr, with Will-well translating, promised to remove from the Wabash, not only the troublemakers, but all other unauthorized Invaders.

When Sigenak told of this, I couldn't believe that Will-well didn't grasp Harr-marr's intention to remove some while authorizing others.

The warriors happily put marks on Harr-marr's leaf and returned toward Kithepekanu.

As they approached their village, they saw burnt fields, burnt cornstacks, burnt lodges. Manato and her two youngest sons were among the ashes.

The warriors of that village had been neutral or even friends of those who burned it. None of the warriors were dead.

The dead were all old people and women and children.
Jozes, who had now lost his post in Kithepekanu as well, was returning from Uiatanon when the massacre occurred. Armed men encircled the village, a few entered. There were twenty horses in the village and the armed men wanted them. Tinami and other village women resisted. The armed men broke out in a frenzy of shooting, stabbing and scalping, letting none escape, at last burning the remains. Tinami was among the burnt remains.
Jozes had never seen anything like it; neither had Sigenak. The warriors, Jozes, Sigenak and his remaining sons, all headed directly to Kekionga, where they knew they would find warriors who were allied with no Invaders.
Jozes shook with fear. Sigenak and Wakaya narrated. When they were done, Aptegizhek embraced Wakaya as he had been embraced by Isadór after Lókaskwe's death. Sigenak's rage compensated for all his years of neutrality; his rage made every warrior's heart blaze.
We sent a belt to the Strait's warriors. Virtually everyone came to the Kekionga council.
On the councilground, I helped Nanikibi light three fires. There was no rum, there were no gifts, there were none of the accretions that had dimmed our fires since my ancestor Nangisi's days. I felt that something almost lost became reconstituted during that angry council and ceremony. We were all together: Yahatase's, Binesikwe's and Chacapwe's heirs with kin from the Oceanshore, the mountains, the valleys and the prairies. Wagoshkwe's Namakwe was with her two brothers at last. Oashi's pact brothers were with each other again and Oashi's son was with their sons. Even a Redcoat from Hochelaga took part in the council; Namakwe's daughter Mikenokwe had made him my and Nanikibi's nephew. Called Shandoné, this talkative man was better informed about the Scalpers' forces than any of the Strait's warriors.
Sigenak and his hotheaded son Gizes, as well as Namakwe's and Batí's youthful Nawak, wanted to set out immediately and pounce on the nearest Invaders.
Miní and Aleshi, as well as Nanikibi, wanted to wait until one of the Scalpers' armies moved. Sigenak's Meteya and Wakaya, as well as Aptegizhek, urged Sigenak to wait and prepare for an encounter more significant than a raid.
Both Meteya and Wakaya listened in rapt attention to my and Nanikibi's songs and stories; Sigenak had told them of

nothing other than the war of the Redearth kin. Wakaya was wide-eyed as he gazed on the bark scroll Aptegizhek unrolled for him. The youth made Aptegizhek or Nanikibi or me repeat every detail about the world's extent, the names of the ancient people, the names of the vanished and the nearly vanished. Slowly the thoughts sank in: Wagoshkwe's thoughts, Sagikwe's, Yahatase's; the youth's eyes burned with a desire to push the murderous Invaders away.

Wakaya generously offered his thoughts to his older brother Will-well, but the adopted youth was no Lókaskwe. Will-well shook with fear, like Jozes, like Shecogosikwe had shaken when she had pulled Aptegizhek to Bison Prairie, like Magidins must have shaken when she had left her Eastbranch kin to seek refuge in rumcarrier Con-err's post.

I didn't trust the nervous Will-well, who clung to Sigenak and said nothing to anyone; but I didn't trust many closer kin, among them Nagmo's sons, Magidins' sons, my own Topinbi and Cakima.

We knew the Scalpers would not come to seek us in Kekionga. We would have to seek them. They attacked women and children, and turned on warriors only when the warriors were unarmed and begging to council, like Shawano. They excluded chance and fairness at the very outset; they faced warriors only if they were certain of overwhelming superiority. The murderers of Lókaskwe had no need for wit, skill or daring; they were people who hunted wolves, deer and beaver with rifles, in a hunt where there's no danger of retaliation, even the rabbit's against the wolf. They didn't hunt, they penned their chickens in and then simply wrung the necks of tame animals who couldn't flee.

We thought there were two large armies in the Beautiful Valley. The Redcoat Shandoné insisted there was only one, Harr-marr's. The concentration around the fat Sun-clear at the Muskingum was anything but clear. No one knew if it was a budding army, or the brain of the entire invasion, or simply a gathering of landgangs fattening themselves with gifts from those to whom they granted portions of the Beautiful Valley.

We did know that Harr-marr's was an army, far from its Pit-strength stronghold, camped by the Beautiful River's falls at the western end of the Valley, implementing Harr-marr's only concrete promise: to remove unauthorized squatters from unmeasured lands.

Aleshi jokingly explained that Harr-marr's promise was not a lie but a half-truth, since it was not Harr-marr's army but a different gang, Kre-sop's heirs, who did the measuring, and still another gang, Ua-shn-tn's and Done-more's agents, who did the authorizing. We knew that Scalper Ua-shn-tn, overman of the league of Slavers, Cheaters and Witchburners, was still committed to invading the Beautiful Valley; he had been trying to do it for nearly forty years, and his league had been formed for that purpose. But Shandoné told us overman Ua-shn-tn wanted to conquer the Valley without a battle, to defeat the enemy without ever facing him. He sent reinforcements to Harr-marr, but his intercepted messages all urged Harr-marr to punish the enemy, to flog the enemy, yet to avoid battles. The Scalper saw us as recalcitrant horses or children; he saw himself as the horse-breaker or bullying father. He would treat us as he treated his children. Democracy was his name for the world of children, infantilized men and imprisoned women crowded like tame animals into his landgangs' enclosures.

Harr-marr was unable to flog horses who weren't enclosed, so for the time being he contented himself with illusory flogging. He surrounded himself with rumsacks and with gift-seekers like my son Topinbi, and got them to place marks on leaves that spoke of Ua-shn-tn as their Great Father.

But Harr-marr wasn't witless. It soon dawned on him that gift-seekers like Topinbi and his cousins Nangisi and Winámek laughed at him when he turned his back; they were willing to mark anything to compensate for their poor fur hunts. Harr-marr grew restive, and our bored scouts had to watch for his next move. The Kekionga council was ready when scouts reported three movements of the Scalpers' armies.

Sun-clear gave the name Marr-yet to his stronghold by the mound village on the Muskingum and then moved westward to the Serpent Mound, the place where the legendary Wiske and his Rootkin first met the Valley's Riverpeople. Sun-clear's intentions were still unclear.

Harr-marr's force left the falls and split into two groups, one heading toward Kekionga, the other toward the Wabash destroying every field and undefended village on its path.

Sigenak burned to meet the force moving toward the Wabash, to avenge the massacre of Manato, Kulswa and Pilawa, to realize Wagoshkwe's dream of removing the Invaders. His sons Meteya, Wapmimi and Will-well accompanied his force of Prairiekin, as did Nanikibi and I. His son Wakaya stayed with Aptegizhek and the Strait's warriors to defend Kekionga.

As we approached the Wabash, we learned that the Scalpers had destroyed re-risen Kithepekanu for the second time, and scalped the people of several other villages whose warriors were in Kekionga. But we never met the army. As soon as they learned that warriors were heading toward the Wabash, the Scalpers' force dispersed, all six hundred of them, in as many directions, without knowing how many warriors were heading toward them. We were enraged that so many of us had gone to meet them; Sigenak and Meteya and a few scouts could have dispersed them.

If most of us had stayed in Kekionga, we might have prevented the death of Miní. The army we went to meet was a diversion, and it accomplished its purpose by tying us up.

The army that moved toward Kekionga was Harr-marr's main force, an army three times as numerous as the warriors in Kekionga. This army, like the other, attacked villages on its path, but the villages were empty as their Rootkin had been warned. Even so, Harr-marr attacked thousands of bushels of corn, enough to feed the Valley, and he attacked squash and beans, as if earth's gifts were his enemy. Many of the Southbranch villages near the Beautiful River were destroyed for the fourth time since Kre-sop's and Done-more's war.

Kekionga was empty when Harr-marr reached it; even food had been taken to the forest, as much of it as horses could pull. Three hundred of Harr-marr's men entered Kekionga to burn it, but a hundred warriors with Wakaya, Aptegizhek and Miní were waiting in the forest, ambushed the Invaders and drove the remnants back to Harr-marr's force. Thinking he had discovered the position of the main body of warriors, Harr-marr moved his entire army toward the spot from which Wakaya had sprung—and was trapped on three sides by the warriors with Isadór, Batí and Tisha. Nearly a fourth of Harr-marr's numerous army fell. Most of the packhorses were captured. Harr-marr and his surviving men fled in a rout, but not before having gunned down nearly a hundred of the bravest and most beautiful human beings of the western Lakes, among them Miní, keeper of the belts of Shutaha's village, Chacapwe's and Ahsepona's great-grandson, my cousin.

Miní's son Isadór, his nephew Tisha, his Nizokwe's brother Batí were unable to hide their tears. Nizokwe arrived as soon as the news reached the Strait—silent, like my mother Menoko before her end, all her music gone.

Nanikibi

Many in Kekionga rejoiced after the victory, among them Meteya and Wapmimi, who didn't know the landgangs well, and Aptegizhek, who longed for peace and thought the invasion had been stopped, its cudgel broken.

Runners went in all directions, not only to villages of victorious and of fallen warriors, but also to the Scalpers' strongholds at the Serpent Mound and the Pit-strength. The messages were brief and clear: the Invaders' army had been decisively defeated; they were now asked to pull all their squatters, measurers, landgang agents and enclosures out of the Beautiful Valley. Those who helped formulate the messages—Sigenak and Wakaya with help from Isadór, Aptegizhek and Aleshi—still believed, as Miní had believed, that the Invaders understood their own language and abided by their own rules. The Scalpers had told undefeated Rootkin that conquerors inherited the land, that the defeated had no right to land. Ua-shn-tn himself had been defeated, not once but every time he had sent an army against western warriors. By his own terms and rules he was obliged to retreat, not only from the Beautiful Valley, but from the Oceanshore as well.

But the Scalpers grasped their own terms no better than ours; they observed no rules, respected no limits, not even their own; fairness was as strange to them as kinship and giving.

Their answer came at the end of a short winter, during the time of games and dances celebrating earth's renewal, when it was least expected; previous attacks had come after the furs were dressed and the corn and vegetables harvested, so the

Invaders could plunder all they could carry before destroying the rest.

The Scalpers learned only one thing from our messages and from their headman's defeat: to avoid Kekionga, to confront only those they could overwhelm, to war only against those they could butcher like their enclosed cattle. The answer crossed the Beautiful River in the form of a thousand bountyseekers from the Southland.

The men on Ua-shn-tn's council did not boast of their overman's youthful scalping expeditions. They now scalped only by deputy. Their deputies from the Southland were led by a headman named The Terror by his own men. Their model was the swath of desolation cut through the Turtleleague's woodlands by Sullied-van. They moved from their landingplace, across the prairies, all the way to the Wabash, murdering and scalping all villagers they could reach, killing all animals, looting and burning all villages. Almost all their victims were villagers who had never warred against Scalpers, some of whom had been the Scalpers' allies. They destroyed Sigenak's Kithepekanu for the third time, and on their return, when survivors were raising new lodges and Jozes was among them gathering the remains of his post, The Terror destroyed Kithepekanu for the fourth time; Jozes was among the scalped victims.

I had never been close to Lekomandá Shak's son, no one had; but the news of his death was painful. Manyan's son was Miní's cousin and Tisha's uncle; he had been Oashi's and Miní's childhood friend and pact brother, and had in the end rejoined them.

Jozes's three sons, Nanikibi's and my nephews, were among the warriors. Marikwe, Jozes's daughter, had no desire to remain in Kithepekanu. I accompanied her and her brother Tisha's children Likét and José to the Strait.

Fear of the Scalpers' atrocities also led my Cakima with her three young sons to seek safety on the Strait. Nogewi, mother of my son's children Mimikwe and Nesoki, had been among the victims massacred at Kithepekanu.

If The Terror's atrocities were intended to intimidate Kekionga's warriors and not merely satisfy the bloodlust of frustrated men too denatured to confront the power that stunted them, they failed to achieve their aim. The ground of Kekionga trembled from unending war dances, the air was thick with war cries. Red belts were sent to the furthest corners runners could reach, from the Turtleleague's woodlands to the Plains of mounted Redearth kin and their western cousins. War parties set out daily with Sigenak's sons, with Isadór or Batí. Aptegizhek, Isadór and others still tried to stop the scalping of victims, but many, including Sigenak and his son Will-well, couldn't be restrained from reciprocating the Scalpers' repulsive deed.

It wasn't long before news came that the fat headman camped by the Serpent Mount, Sun-clear, had started to move. His intentions were finally clear, even to Mikenokwe's Redcoat Shandoné. Sun-clear placed himself at the head of Harr-marr's remaining army, and overman Ua-shn-tn sent him three thousand more seasoned killers, a thousand on horses, to give him absolute superiority over any war party he might meet. His destination was also clear; he moved at a snail's pace toward Kekionga, felling trees to build enclosures at every crossing, afraid of every bush and grove.

I joined Nanikibi and Sigenak and the warriors who set out to meet Sun-clear's force before it reached Kekionga.

Sigenak was nearing sixty winters, but he remained fast and agile; he had a sense for the timing and an eye for the ambush. Wakaya and Will-well were learning quickly.

As soon as Sigenak uttered the war cry, before the hidden warriors had leapt from the forest, Sun-clear's entire huge army collapsed like some beast with feet too thin for the weight of its body. Fat Sun-clear's response to the war cry was to turn his horse and try to flee through his own lines, away from the enemy he'd come to meet. Sun-clear fell off his horse and had himself carried away by runners. He retained his life only because the warriors who saw him burst out laughing.

Sun-clear's army, arrayed in neat rows like the contrivance of a square brain, its men broken, like their horses, to act only on the headman's instructions, panicked when it lost its head. The neat rows were like consecutive walls, each blocking the previous row's retreat; the hysterical men shot their way through the walls, killing far more of their fellows than our arrows reached, leaving a thousand corpses in the field.

Western warriors had never seen such carnage. Aleshi was killed because he planted himself in the way of a retreating madman.

Aleshi and Miní had both been among the warriors who had humiliated Scalper Ua-shn-tn forty summers earlier, near the fork that makes the Beautiful River. Aleshi had only been a boy then; he had gone as a scout.

There was no victory celebration in Kekionga. Sun-clear's losses were as great as Bra-duck's had been; Oceanshore Invaders had never suffered a greater defeat. We lost few, but couldn't bear a single loss; many warriors had no surviving kin, neither elders nor women nor children; they had neither fields nor lodges to return to. A word the landgangs were said to be using stuck in our throats; the word was Empty; it was being used to describe various parts of the Beautiful Valley.

After our defeat of Sun-clear, the Strait's Redcoats were much friendlier to us than they had been to Miní when he had begged for their help. Mikenokwe's redfrocked Shandoné and Jozes's son Gabinya brought the Strait's headman to Kekionga, ostensibly to join us in celebrating our victory and in mourning Aleshi's death. Aleshi, banished by the Redcoats after the war against the enclosures, had been their loyal ally since the split of the Oceanshore Invaders into two hostile gangs.

The headman's real reason for coming was to place himself at the head of the victorious party. He wanted to renew the alliance. He thought we had fought for the wellbeing of the Redcoats' fur gangs. He was pleased to have won a victory with such ease, with neither men nor provisions nor bloody clashes. He wanted us to continue to keep the Valley open to his fur gangs. His advice to us was to agree to grant the Scalpers the empty portions of the Valley, with clearly defined boundaries, like the Muskingum and the Beautiful River, in order to keep the rest of the Valley. He would even help us by building an enclosure near Kekionga.

The counciling warriors were all repelled by the Redcoat's advice, Aptegizhek, Sigenak and Will-well foremost among them. Aptegizhek said such advice would have us accept the murder of our kin, the destruction of our ceremonies, villages and fields; such advice would have us accept that massacres and atrocities gave the Invaders their coveted title.

Sigenak angrily said he would recognize no Invaders in any part of the Valley, he would accept no boundaries, and he would make no agreements. He spoke for most of the warriors in Kekionga.

The Redcoat then told us there were rumors that the Scalpers were preparing a yet larger army at the Pit-strength, this one led by a headman Vain, called Mad-ant for his demented killing sprees during the Scalpers' war against the Redcoats.

Fearful Will-well greeted this news with seeming courage; he boasted he would carry Sigenak's angry message to the new Pit-strength headman.

Sigenak saw through his adopted son's display of courageous defiance. He sadly told the youth he had not esteemed his other sons above his adopted son; he had accepted what Will-well gave and he had given what he could; he had no reproaches; Will-well had a father in Kekionga, as well as four brothers, a young bride, a son, and numerous cousins; Will-well was a Rootperson, he was free to choose his own path, to go where he pleased.

Will-well had slept with bad dreams since he had returned to burnt Kithepekanu and seen the ashes of his young brothers and their mother; his fear of such an end was greater than his kinship.

Sigenak knew he was losing another son, and he knew that the Scalpers' army would not turn away a warrior who still remembered their language, who had scouted, surprised and ambushed alongside Sigenak's son Wakaya; they were in sore need of such scouts. Sigenak remembered that Will-well had often spoken of Redcoats as conspirators who had instigated the war between Rootkin and landgangs, and of Scalpers as freedom-loving natural allies of Rootkin against the repressive Redcoats.

Sigenak wasn't prepared for the defector's first deed, which was perverse. The adopted son seemed intent on rubbing his father's face in dirt. Will-well guided a landgang agent, a Blackcollar and several captive Prairiekin to a council in Cahokia at the Valley's westernmost extremity. Will-well was welcomed by the Redearth and Prairiekin in Cahokia as a kinsman, as Sigenak's son. The Blackcollar, a successor to Brother Post-err named Brother Hack-a-well, presented the captives as a gift from people who, he said, sought only peace. This Blackcollar who pretended that the murderers of his converts on the Tuscarawas were all Brethren was obviously not as sincere a man as Brother Post-err. The landgang agent then got Redearth and Prairiekin to agree not to oust his peaceloving people from their homes on the Muskingum (precisely the boundary suggested by the Redcoats so hated by Will-well). The Cahokians marked the agent's leaf; those among them who had heard of the Muskingum weren't sure if it was on the Oceanshore or across the Ocean. The landgangs couldn't have gone further from the Muskingum in search of their marks.

All the tricks in the bag were familiar, but Sigenak was angered by the very existence of a leaf which spoke of Wagoshkwe's kin granting the eastern portion of the Valley to the Scalpers. The war council that prepared to confront the Scalpers' newest army was smaller than the previous two. Most warriors whose villages had not been destroyed left Kekionga, not because they feared Mad-ant Vain's army, but because they feared the Emptiness that would be the lot of villages without warriors in them. There remained in Kekionga only those who had nowhere else to go, who were numerous enough, together with their cousins from the nearby Strait.

Sigenak's sons, Wakaya and Wapmimi in the circle of Southbranch kin, Meteya with Nanikibi in the circle of Firekeepers, Sigenak himself in the circle of Prairiekin, danced with the resolve to confront whatever came against them. Those of the Strait, Namakwe's son Nawak with Isadór and the Turtlefolk, Tisha with Batí and the Rootkin, danced with less resolve, and Mikenokwe's redfrocked Shandoné as well as Tinami's son Gabinya were already seeking refuge in the enclosure the Strait's Redcoats raised near Kekionga.

I didn't join any of the four circles. I didn't paint myself, even though many dreams and signs told me this would be the last council in Kekionga and I would never again dance with the warriors. I felt myself turning into a wrinkled old woman, too slow and weak to accompany youthful warriors. I regretted not having followed the path Lókaskwe had sought, not having lived, loved, sung, planted and died with a joyful song on my lips among waving cornstalks and spreading vines. I regretted having followed the twisted path, Wabskeni's path, a killer's path.

Heavy with such thoughts, I wasn't hostile to Topinbi when he came to Kekionga with his gifts. He was following some kind of straight path, a carrier's path, ancient Nangisi's, not Wabskeni's. He spoke radiantly of my and Nanikibi's grandchildren, as if they all were well. My Cakima already had four, and all of them preserved the old names, if not the old ways. Instead of facing the blood and gore, I could have been a grandmother to these children; Nanikibi and I could have sung to them of Yahatase, Miogwewe, Shutaha, even Wagoshkwe; we could die with the thought that these children would realize our dreams better than we had.

Nanikibi's thoughts were far from mine. He danced; he seemed as youthful and agile as Sigenak had appeared before the confrontation with Sun-clear. Nanikibi knew the eyes of the youths were on him, particularly Wakaya's, Meteya's, Aptegizhek's, Tisha's. He had sung to them of the objects in his bundle, of the world described on Aptegizhek's scroll, of the regions sinking beyond the reach of memory, and he was as resolved as they to keep yet another village, field or even single tree from sinking.

Scouts told us Mad-ant Vain's army was leaving the Pit-strength with eagles on its standards, crossing the valley of mounds so loved by Southbranch kin, so briefly a refuge to the remaining Eastbranch kin. The army was moving toward Sun-clear's former stronghold by the Serpent Mound, with each step wiping out beauty its denatured landsuckers couldn't grasp, with each step destroying the living and their food, plundering earth's cover, razing even the great mounds, the traces, the memory—with each step making an infinite world uninhabitable, turning it into the Emptiness they lusted to possess.

The final atrocity was the renaming: the fork that makes the Beautiful River became the Pit-strength, the Muskingum mound village became Marr-yet, the Serpent Mound was becoming Ua-shn-tn's Strength, the Southland was becoming Slaveland and a huge army was preparing to turn the most beautiful part of the world into Scalpers' Valley.

Overman Ua-shn-tn's newest deputy in the valley was apparently resolved to put an end to the old Scalper's forty summers of defeats, retreats and humiliations, to erase the very memory of those defeats by annihilating every last one of the warriors who inflicted them, and to spread the overman's member over the length and breadth of a once-beautiful valley at last uncovered and ravaged.

Will-well, Sigenak's former son, wearing a Scalper's uniform, came to Kekionga as Mad-ant Vain's messenger. Wakaya turned his back on his former brother and left the council to rejoin angry Southbranch kin. Wapmimi, who had a bride and child among the Southbranch kin, prepared to kill the defector, but was stopped by Sigenak.

Despite Will-well's unforgivable stunt of having Redearth kin give the Valley to the Scalpers, Sigenak did not want his former son killed. He asked for a description of Will-well's new brothers.

The defector obliged unstintingly. He said Mad-ant Vain had not recruited among the survivors of Harr-marr's or Sun-clear's defeats; he had recruited among the killers who had accompanied The Terror on the swath of gore from the Southland to the Wabash; his council included a young heir to a landgang named Will-hen-garrison who would stop at no obstacle. His scouts and spies, besides Will-well, included young Navár, son of Lemond's former scrollkeeper, as well as Southern people who descended from mound builders and remembered the people of the Strait as Wabskeni's murderous allies who destroyed the Naché and other kin. Mad-ant Vain's men wouldn't walk in neat rows, like Sun-clear's, but loosely, like Rootkin—but not in order to escape freely, for there would be no escape; they were being broken, drilled, to kill any of their own who turned away from the enemy. Overman Ua-shn-tn was tired of feeding and provisioning armies who ran away. This army would go on killing until its last man fell.

The message Will-well brought, which was also his own, was that overman Ua-shn-tn did not want to war against Rootkin, but only against Redcoats; that Ua-shn-tn did not claim a single tree in the Beautiful Valley; that he recognized the Valley belonged to the people who lived in it. Will-well spoke as if he had forgotten whose victories had prompted Ua-shn-tn to drop his claims. He said Ua-shn-tn wanted only to help Rootkin keep the Redcoats from invading the Valley, as they'd begun to do with their new enclosure near Kekionga. And the Great Father Ua-shn-tn sent gifts: blankets, cloth and peace medals, to encourage his children to respond to his generous offer to help them.

Sigenak picked up one of the offered peace medals and showed it to those of us who were still at the gathering. At first glance the picture on the medal showed a Rootperson and an Invader extending their hands toward each other, a leafless tree behind the one, an ox-drawn tool scratching treeless earth behind the other. The man on the left was naked but the earth behind him was covered, the man on the right was covered but the earth behind him was naked. A second glance revealed that the naked man on the left had his right arm hanging at his side, his hand empty, holding neither bow nor hatchet; his left arm extended, not toward the other, but toward the bowl of a calumet the length of his arm; he stood unsteadily, as if he were full of rum or the Slavers' drink Wiske; he was a rumsack who didn't know where he was or why he was smoking. The man on the right, covered from his false hair to his boots, was the Slavers' overman himself, Scalper Ua-shn-tn; his left hand rested on a sword handle, ready to kill; he hadn't buried either his rifle or his scalping knife; he stood solidly; the seeming outreach of his right arm toward the other's calumet-supporting arm was actually a threatening gesture blocking the calumet smoker from stepping onto the scratched treeless field. The rumsack had nowhere to go but up the tree behind him. Sigenak threw the medal to the ground and buried it with his foot. Kicking other gifts toward Will-well, he said he understood headman Vain's message perfectly and would give his answer to it on the battlefield.

Aptegizhek, trying to reason with the defector, formulated a return message. He said most of the Invaders were desperate because they had nothing, like Aptegizhek's own grandfather and Will-well's father. The landgangs and Slaver Ua-shn-tn had much, and they used much of it on gifts for Rootkin and on armies sent against Rootkin. If they really wanted peace, they would call their desperate men back to the east and give them all the gifts and provisions. This way they would relieve their miserable men, allow denuded earth to recover, and leave us in peace.

But Will-well, despite all his winters and summers among Rootkin, was guided by fear, not by reason. He couldn't grasp the unreason of a world where the fat feed on the lean, where the lean plunder for the fat instead of turning on them, where the fat protect themselves from the wrath of the lean by making the lean face the wrath of the plundered. Aptegizhek knew they didn't really want peace, but Will-well seemed not to know that without wars of plunder the landgangs wouldn't need armies to protect them from the plundered, and without armies they couldn't have made their desperate men give either their harvests or their lives to overmen.

I accompanied the noncombatants who abandoned Kekionga before the battle. I found refuge in dead Mini's, now Nizokwe's silent lodge, on a spot on the Strait's shore where, it was said, a two-branched tree and a roundish rock had once stood, monuments to the gift-bringer Wiske. Cakima was in the neighboring lodge, Namakwe's, with her four children and heavy with a fifth. I played with Namakwe's, Tinami's, Nizokwe's, Magda's and my own grandchildren. I learned of the battle from messengers' fragments.

Sigenak set out with Wakaya and a small party of warriors to meet Mad-ant Vain's army as it moved past the desolate villages and burnt fields of Aptegizhek's Southbranch and Eastbranch kin. Sigenak wanted to find out if Will-well's description was accurate, or if this huge army, like the two before it, would double back on itself when Sigenak cried out and disintegrate when Sigenak's small force leapt from the forest. The warriors returned to Kekionga unharmed, but with the news that the enormous force hadn't budged.

The expedition made Sigenak cautious; the desolation of the Southbranch villages made Wakaya enraged.

Sigenak told the counciling warriors that Mad-ant Vain's huge army was an inhuman thing, a thing that never slept. It was worse than the Redcoat army he had opposed forty summers earlier, Mad-win's army on the Strait, determined to hold the enclosure until every man fell. Vain was certain his army would hold until every man fell. The threat that all who fled would be murdered by their own companions was no empty boast: men who had tried to flee from Vain's camp were already dead. Those men feared the enemy less than they feared their headman; they would kill Rootkin for fear of being killed by their own men; they had been reduced to members of a being which existed not to protect and preserve them but to kill and keep on killing; they were parts of a monstrous worm which went on murdering no matter how many pieces it was cut into. The life of that army's human constituents was neither its goal nor its limit. Such a monstrosity couldn't be opposed by people who loved life. Human beings could not vie with it as death-dealers. No one among the people of the Lakes and Valleys could take on himself the responsibility for all the warriors who would fall before the monstrosity was stilled.

Wakaya expressed himself as willing to take on that awesome responsibility. He said earth would be shamed, the dead betrayed, if none among the living rose up against the Invaders' unnatural deeds; the desolation cried for revenge.

Sigenak removed the pendant from his neck, the arrowhead given to him by Wagoshkwe, said to have come from the Redearth warrior Lamina, and placed it on Wakaya's neck.

Sigenak knew and Nanikibi knew that the only alternative to Wakaya's reckless willingness to confront the monster was to flee toward the sunset, toward the Plains where Wagoshkwe had fled. All Rootkin were now Redearth kin.

After the battle, Sigenak told the mourners gathered on the shore of the Strait that the warrior fought bravely and wisely.

Wakaya chose a position between the advancing army and the Redcoats' enclosure on the fringe of Kekionga, and he chose well: the battleground was a field of trees blown over by the wind, with hiding-places for warriors ten times as numerous. The dead trees kept The Terror's mounted force from getting anywhere near the battle. The attack was well timed, the ambush well prepared. The war cry followed by the volley from the fallen trees would have sent any earlier Scalper army scampering. But Vain's men weren't human, they had been remade into contrivances, they didn't panic when surprised, they didn't turn when ambushed, they didn't run when their companions' bodies littered the ground; they stood and shot, as soulless as their rifles, docile and unnatural, whip-trained like dogs or horses, broken humans without hearts or minds, their freedom flogged out of them. And then they came after the retrenching warriors with their steel knives. Sigenak was beside Nanikibi when a bullet hit Nanikibi's leg. Nanikibi kept on aiming at the advancing Invaders like a young warrior on his first proving ground. Nanikibi told Sigenak of his childhood dream: a wounded fox in a field of dead animals had begged Nanikibi to avenge the dead. He was doing it.

Wakaya shouted the retreat. His ancestor Lamina was said to have learned from the Invaders to hold his ground until the last warrior fell; Lamina's brave deed had a sad sequel. Wakaya had no taste for such bravery; only a murderer would invite his kin to remain in a death trap. Wakaya didn't want to answer for all the deaths which would follow from such a decision. Sigenak approved, but his thoughtful brother Nanikibi, the peacemaker, did not approve; lame and bleeding, he stayed behind, downing another and still another Invader. Sigenak shouted to him that a single warrior couldn't stop a moving wall. Nanikibi turned, not to seek safety, but to urge his brother to seek it, and while he was turned a bullet pierced his back.

Nanikibi wasn't scalped. Sigenak hid his brother's body in a hollow tree; he and Aptegizhek and Isadór returned at night and buried Nanikibi in a grave near the source of Kekionga's river.

Namakwe's songmaker Batí, sad Nizokwe's brother, was among the fallen. He too had been with the warriors who had inflicted two humiliating defeats on Scalper Ua-shn-tn forty summers earlier. Now they were all dead. Isadór shed tears but said nothing.

Sigenak assured silent Nizokwe there would be no more battles. He urged his sister Namakwe to rejoice at the safe return of her brave son Nawak, of Pamoko's hunter Dupré, of Mikenokwe's redfrocked Shandoné, who had stayed in the Redcoats' enclosure next to the battlefield, not opening its gate even to retreating warriors seeking refuge there, and had fled with the other Redcoats to the Strait while Vain and his army were occupied hacking down trees, burning corn-rich fields, razing villages, turning the entire vast beautiful expanse that was Kekionga into a field of fallen trees.

Lean Sigenak gives me all that remains of his brother, the peacemaker's bundle Nanikibi carried to so many battles. I see eagles darkening the sky, dead serpents covering the ground.

A cry comes from Namakwe's lodge where my daughter lies, the cry of a newborn child. I turn to it.

Chapter 7.

Obenabi

Birth and journey

    The baby's cry pulled me out of my grandmother's mask as if I were marrow that was sucked out of a bone. On the night when Sigenak, Wakaya, Isadór and Aptegizhek gathered at Nizokwe's lodge and told of the death of Nanikibi on the field of fallen trees, I was no longer in Nizokwe's lodge, and I was no longer Katabwe. I was a tiny beginning in Namakwe's lodge next door, shrieking alongside Cakima, kicking tiny feet and waving tiny arms. I knew nothing of what had happened, nothing of the people in Namakwe's lodge nor of those next door. My memories would all be given to me later, when I was ready to accept the gifts. On that night I knew nothing of the spot where I lay, nothing of Tiosa Rondion on the strait between the Clear Lake and the Lake of the vanished Ehryes, nothing of the burial mounds behind Namakwe's lodge outlined against the moonless sky by rising dawn, nothing of the bubbling springs that sent their waters past the mounds toward the strait. And of course I knew nothing of the otterskin bundle Sigenak was giving to his dead brother's widow Katabwe, my grandmother.

I would go on knowing nothing of my birthplace because I was carried away from it across the width of the Peninsula toward my mother's and my uncle's birthplace, Bison Prairie.

Fed by Cakima in trader Burr-net's great lodge, I wasn't aware of the falling leaves, of the snows that covered all of Bison Prairie, of the numerous visitors who gathered on the council-ground after the snows melted. I may have heard some songs, seen some commotion, but I didn't know the visitors were angry warriors, nor that my grandmother had burned her son Topinbi's gifts, nor that one of the visitors, my grandfather's nephew Meteya had stayed in Bison Prairie after his companions left, married Bindizeosekwe of the Lakebottom village, and raised a lodge near Topinbi's. More snows had to fall and melt before I could distinguish Topinbi from Meteya; and by then I, like my brother Nashkowatak and my sister Wabnokwe was no longer in the trader's lodge but in Topinbi's, my mother's brother's lodge, with his daughter Mimikwe and her mother and our grandmother Katabwe. By then I thought Meteya and Bindizeosekwe had always been in Bison Prairie and that my brother Wedasi had always lived in their lodge, just as I thought our other brother, Chebansi, as well as Topinbi's son Nesoki, had always lived with Cakima in trader Burr-net's lodge. Brown leaves fell and new buds grew before I was aware of the bad air that flowed between grandmother Katabwe and trader Burr-net. By then the carrier Shabeni had raised his lodge near Meteya's.

The bad air between my father and grandmother became a stench on the day when my brother Nashkowatak returned from the fasting lodge grandmother had raised for him. Nashkowatak didn't return on his own; our father pulled him into the village by the ear, shouted mean names at him, and called our grandmother a witch. Katabwe shouted back. She said the trader was destroying trees, killing animals and eating earth without giving, that he was the witch—but she spoke in our Rootlanguage and trader Burr-net didn't understand. But that night, trader Burr-net came with Cakima to pull Wabnokwe and me out of Topinbi's lodge, and they fetched Wedasi out of Meteya's. We were Burr-nets, he said, and we were to grow in our father's lodge. Nashkowatak and Chebansi were to be sent to the Strait, Wabnokwe to the Lakebottom. Wedasi and I were to remain with cousin Nesoki in the trader's lodge.

Although I didn't understand why, I knew that Cakima and Burr-net wanted to pull all the young people away from Katabwe—not only their own children, but Topinbi's daughter Mimikwe as well. Since Topinbi was often away with the caravans, the old woman would be left completely alone. Cakima waited until Topinbi returned with the summer gift caravan. Then she got Topinbi to help her arrange a lavish marriage ceremony uniting Mimikwe to the carrier Shabeni. But Nashkowatak kept running to Katabwe to tell her what was being prepared and she made arrangements of her own.

The ceremony was grand. Three fires were lighted, and kin from the four quarters gathered on Bison Prairie's councilground. But the events weren't the ones Cakima and Topinbi had arranged, and the outcome wasn't the one Nashkowatak had hoped for. When all were gathered around the fires, grandmother Katabwe carried Bindizeosekwe's and Meteya's firstborn to the center, laid the baby girl on the ground while singing to her, and named the child Koyoshkwe. And then Katabwe began to sing of renewal and regeneration, songs I'd often heard in her lodge; and as she sang, the gathered hosts and guests formed themselves into circles around the fires and began to dance. I was in one of the circles, intent on imitating the motions. Only when those nearest me stopped did I become aware of a disruption: a figure with the mask of a long-eared hare and the clothes of trader Burr-net was putting out the fires. I saw Cakima angrily pulling Burr-net away from the councilground while Katabwe and other women armed themselves with sticks, turned on the masked disrupter and chased him away from the fires, into the forest. From the way the hare ran, I could tell it was Nashkowatak. He had expected Mimikwe to join the chasing women, run to the forest after him, and put an abrupt end to the marriage ceremony. But during the entire chase, Mimikwe didn't budge, and when the chase of the hare was over, she accepted a gift of deer meat from Shabeni.

My brothers Nashkowatak and Chebansi accompanied the following spring's fur caravan to the Strait. Our sister Wabnokwe was taken to the Lakebottom, to the lodge of trader Sandypoint and grandfather's crosswearing sister Kittihawa.

But Wedasi and I didn't remain in trader Burr-net's lodge. Nor did Mimikwe move to Shabeni's lodge. After the ceremony, Wedasi returned to Meteya's, I returned to Katabwe's, and Shabeni abandoned his own lodge and joined Mimikwe in ours. Unlike Topinbi, a Firekeeper who had become a carrier, Shabeni was a carrier who wanted to become a Firekeeper.

The trees had shed and renewed themselves five times when a second daughter was born to Bindizeosekwe and Meteya, and then a son to Mimikwe and Shabeni. I wanted to take an active part in the naming ceremony, and I begged Katabwe to sing me the songs and show me the movements. Shabeni was always at my side when the old woman sang and danced. He said his people had all but forgotten the old ceremonies. Sometimes Wedasi also listened and watched.

I hummed the melodies and repeated the words when I accompanied Meteya or Shabeni to the forest, when I went with Bindizeosekwe and Mimikwe to the cornfields. When the ceremony began I was ready. Katabwe named the baby girl Wamoshekeshekwe, the boy Komenoteya. And I started one of the dances.

My grandmother was pleased with me, but my mother was not. Cakima let it be known that trader Burr-net wanted Wedasi and me, and also our sister Wabnokwe, to leave Bison Prairie with the following spring's fur caravan. I was eager to see the hand-shaped Peninsula, and especially eager to see my birthplace at the opposite corner of the wrist. But Katabwe spoke of the Strait as a gatheringplace of Scabeaters who were kin to us and of others—she called them villageburners, shitmakers and manhunters—who didn't mean us well. She spoke often of Nashkowatak's losing himself in their midst because he had no dream spirit to guide him. By now she knew—the whole village knew, thanks to Nesoki's spying and telling—that Nashkowatak hadn't waited for a dream-spirit in his fasting lodge, but for Mimikwe.

I begged Katabwe to build me a fasting lodge so that I wouldn't be lost. She said I was too little; the spirits wouldn't see me. I kept begging, and at last she asked Shabeni to raise a lodge for me. It was midwinter. Shabeni and I huddled around the lodge fire while Katabwe prepared him for the lodge-raising and me for the dream-spirit. I was already fasting. Late one night, when the fire was nearly burnt out, she unpacked the contents of grandfather Nanikibi's bundle. It was so dark I could barely make out the tiny bones of the water dweller, the feather of the air dweller, the shell that gave life to earth dwellers, the bark that depicted the dwellingplace. She sang of crawlers, walkers and fliers, of great sufferings and deaths, and of earth's renewal.

The following morning, wrapped in blankets and hides, Shabeni and I set out on snowshoes. We didn't go far. Shabeni dug through the snow until he exposed an opening between two rocks, a cave just big enough for a person his size, more than enough for me. We dug up brush and fallen leaves with which he lined the floor, and with the snow itself he raised a wind barrier at the entrance. Then he left me.

Wrapped in my blankets, my head leaning on the rock, I sat and waited. I heard a sound and thought Shabeni was still outside the cave. I also thought it whould have been night, but it was brightest day. Peering through the brush past the wind wall, I saw, not Shabeni, but an enormous bird, an eagle. Its wing was spread on the ground, the tip touching the cave entrance, like a matted path toward its back. I followed the path, sank into the offered seat, and rose toward the clouds. Looking down, I saw that the forest I'd traversed with Shabeni was snowless. I thought I recognized the riverbank and the village when suddenly the bird swooped down, almost crashing into the top of a lodge. Now I saw that the lodges were hulks, mere skeletons of lodges, without walls or hearths; the village was empty; the trees surrounding the village were tangles of leafless branches and trunks, all fallen, and no life stirred. Feeling tears flooding my eyes, I buried my head in the down, but something pulled my head back up. I felt myself lifted and carried. I knew I was no longer on the bird's back, but I was too exhausted to open my eyes. I must have slept then, because I woke in trader Burr-net's lodge; Cakima was trying to feed me broth.

I later learned that Nesoki had seen Shabeni guide me to the forest, had then seen Shabeni return alone. Nesoki had told Cakima, and when she'd told Burr-net, the trader had raged about the savagery of exposing helpless children to winter's cold. Cakima had then asked Topinbi to learn my whereabouts, break into my fasting lodge and interrupt my dream.

I returned to my grandmother's hearth only once before I left with the caravan. I told Katabwe my incomplete dream. She pondered for a long time. Then she smiled. She said my dream was complete. My spirit had come to me and spoken to me. She told me to call on my spirit when I needed it, and she told me to trust my dream. I resented her smile and her words. I thought she considered me too young to be visited by a real spirit. I thought she was dismissing me with pat phrases. I knew that my dream had been awful, had told me nothing meaningful, and couldn't serve me as a guide. I grew eager to leave Bison Prairie. When the ice thawed I threw myself into the preparations for the journey. I avoided Katabwe. Yet I was relieved to learn that I wouldn't be completely separated from her stories and songs, because Shabeni intended to accompany the caravan, not to carry furs but to visit kin in the north and companions on the Strait. I begged Shabeni to promise to build me another fasting lodge, one where I wouldn't be found and interrupted.

Wedasi and I were in Shabeni's canoe, right behind Topinbi's, when we pushed off. Meteya's and Bindizeosekwe's young daughters Wamoshkeshekwe and Koyoshkwe were ill and Mimikwe was nursing them in an isolated place, but the other villagers gathered on the shore to watch us leave. Grandmother stood behind them. I felt a sudden sadness and wanted to run to Katabwe. But we were already midstream. I turned my eyes downriver and cried. I already knew that she hadn't dismissed me with pat phrases.

We camped at the Rivermouth until we were joined by the canoes from the Lakebottom. My father had gone to fetch furs, messages, as well as my sister Wabnokwe, and he came with the Lakebottom caravan that would join us on the northward part of the journey. Before we set out, Wedasi and I climbed the hill overlooking the Rivermouth, to have a look at the ruins of the wooden enclosure once raised there by the bearded Scabeater called Boatmaker. Topinbi told us it was the only enclosure on the Peninsula that had not expanded into a gatheringplace of Invaders.

Trader Burr-net insisted that Wedasi and I join our mother and sister in his canoe, so that instead of sharing grandmother's songs with Shabeni, I heard Wabnokwe talk of our Lakebottom kin. I was surprised by the disparaging way Wabnokwe spoke of Shecogosikwe and Wagoshkwe, the daughters of the bowlwoman Lókaskwe and grandmother's brother Oashi, our closest kin on the Lakebottom. Shecogosikwe was married to Bindizeosekwe's cousin Topash, and their daughter Menashi had just been named, but Wabnokwe spoke only of Shecogosikwe's addiction to dementing drink. Of Wagoshkwe, our own great-grandmother's namesake, of carrier Lalím and of their son Naganwatek, Wabnokwe said only that they shunned the ways of Lemond. Wedasi and I knew of crosswearers like grandfather's sister Kittihawa, but we knew nothing of Lemond. Wabnokwe told us that Kittihawa's man, trader Sandypoint, and their daughter Suzán, were the center of the Lakebottom's Lemond. She pointed out Suzán's husband Jambatí in one of the canoes as an exemplar of a man from the real Lemond. To me he looked like a man paddling a canoe.

She said Kittihawa's son Kegon had turned his back on Lemond by moving into the lodge of the Firekeeper Meshewokwe, Bindizeosekwe's sister, joining the circle that included Lókaskwe's daughters. After filling our heads with Lemond, she told us there was also a false Lemond, and our uncle Nangisi's daughter Manilú, as well as our uncle Winámek's daughters Miaga, Kitasmo and Nogekwa were its centers. She said they wore Lemond's clothes while knowing nothing of Lemond's ways. She pointed toward the canoes of Nangisi and Winámek, whom I had seen before, and told us the men with them, men named Lashás, Laframboáz, Lemé and Lepetí, were the husbands of the false Lemond. To me they looked no more false than Lemond's Jambatí; they were upright in their canoes, pushed their paddles from front to back. At last my sister boasted that she would soon outshine both of the Lakebottom's Lemonds, the false as well as the real, because our final destination, the Strait, her and my birthplace, was the very heart of Lemond, and she intended to immerse herself in it.

Wedasi listened to our sister with complete indifference. He was as eager to reach the Strait as she, but not to immerse himself in Lemond. Wedasi couldn't wait to see Meteya's brother, the warrior Wakaya. Wedasi had moved to Meteya's lodge so as to be with a warrior, and had been disappointed. Meteya, like our grandmother, had ceased to be a warrior when he moved to Bison Prairie. Wedasi and I had both learned from Meteya to hunt with bows. Wedasi hadn't learned to use a firestick until Shabeni had showed him. But even Shabeni shunned the warrior's ways. Wedasi was sure that Wakaya would not disappoint him.

Wedasi and I were eager to reach our first stoppingplace so as to go back to Shabeni's canoe. My heart throbbed with excitement when Cakima pointed to the Beaver Island and when the

sand hills came into view. We reached the village of the Leaning
Tree. On shore, crowds of dancers waved and shouted toward us.
Wadasi, Wabnokwe and I were all but pulled out of our canoe by
welcoming celebrants. The entire shore seemed to be in motion.
Hot stones were carried to innumerable sweat lodges. Countless
fires were lit, and a circle of dancers formed around each hearth.
I stayed close to Wedasi. The throbbing councilground, the fires,
the cries of the dancers, made my head spin.

Wedasi and I lost track of all our kin. We wandered along
the outskirts of the councilground, past the mounds of pelts
standing before the lodges. Walking behind the lodges, we saw
enormous wooden crosses on the hills; outlined against the
moonlit sky they looked like angry thunderbirds hovering over
the dancers. We returned to the councilground. The dancers had
formed themselves into a vast circle. They were doing a war
dance. They seemed to be propitiating the angry hilltop giants
with imaginary victims. We heard the names of some of the
victims and we shuddered. Wedasi and I had both heard our
grandmother sing of those names. They were the names of our
own kin. We realized that the dancers were reenacting the
exploits of ancient Winámek's league; they were celebrating the
league's victories against ancient Yahatase's Turtlefolk, Sagikwe's Peninsulakin, Wagoshkwe's Redearth kin; they were
glorifying Wiske instead of expelling him. It dawned on us that
Shabeni's kin, the people of the Leaning Tree, identified Wiske
with the wooden giants on their hills, called him the savior, and
offered our great-grandmothers' people to his greed.

Wedasi and I were baffled and angry. I found no rest until
the canoes left the Leaning Tree shore. We set out in Shabeni's
canoe and plied him with questions. Shabeni told us he shared
our anger, he hadn't taken part in the dance. But he reminded
us that our uncles Nangisi and Winámek, who had taken promi-
nent parts in the dance, were not great-grandsons of Yahatase
or Sagikwe or Wagoshkwe. Like Shabeni himself, our Lakebottom uncles did descend from people who had fought against
Turtlefolk, Redearth kin and Peninsulakin. And like Shabeni
before he'd come to Bison Prairie, before he'd heard grandmother's songs, our uncles and the Leaning Tree people knew
nothing of the earlier descendants; they had forgotten those
who'd lived on the Peninsula before the coming of the crosses
and fur posts and leagues. Shabeni told us he was ashamed of
the crosses and the names, but not of the dance itself. He told us

the dance came from the world described on our grandmother's scroll, and that his kin would remain Rootkin so long as they continued to dance, even if they named their own kin enemies and the Invaders saviors. When they forget the dance as well, he said, they'll die.

The canoe caravan reached the top of the hand. Far toward the sunset was the great Greenbay, one-time refuge of Yahatase and ancient Wedasi. I could see only the rippling waters of Mishigami as we started to circle the Peninsula and turned toward the sunrise.

We beached among countless canoes and larger vessels, many of them fur-laden, near the fortified enclosure of Mishilimakina. Kin as well as strangers greeted our arrival, but not with ready sweat lodges or lit hearths. Men rushed to help our Lakebottom kin set their pelt-loads on shore. The pelts had reached their destination.

Wabnokwe hurried to immerse herself in what she called Lemond; she followed Jambatí toward his brothers Lou and Izzy and their sister Angie, and was soon warmed by the embraces of Izzy's wife Sofí and daughter Felice. The rest of us were led to the enormous lodge of the songmaker Antó, where we were to feast. We were embraced by Lesotér and Marikwe and their four children, by Will Soli-man and the medicinewoman Agibicocona. Wedasi clung to Shabeni and both left with Antó's son, Lesotér, grandnephew of the warrior Mashekewis and himself a warrior who, like Shabeni, had stood alongside Wakaya on the field of fallen trees. My father and Sofí's brother Will Soliman filled the air with pelt talk which turned my stomach and I too slipped out of the lodge before the feast.

I drifted back to the landingplace and watched the men who carried pelts from canoes and stacked them in mounds, the rows of men who moved from one pelt mound to the next with measuring implements, the men who shoved each other while gesticulating and shouting. The unrhythmical noise was as unrelenting as the motion. Even when I understood words, their meanings passed me by, and I was sure the shouting men understood each other no better than I understood them. I put my hands to my ears, let my elbows flap rhythmically, and found myself above the roar, hovering over the bundle-carrying men. Fixing my eyes on the bundles, I saw that they were not pelts, but cadavers. I shrieked, my flapping lost its rhythm, and I tumbled to the ground.

I found myself on a mat in a room of the enormous lodge. Agibicocona sat beside me. From the shouting in the feast hall, I knew that the others were done eating and had started to drink. The medicinewoman told me the others thought me sick; Burrnet thought me demented. Agibicocona had tears in her eyes. She said she knew what I had seen, for she had seen it too. She said furry dam-builders were being annihilated, undammed rivers were running dry, earth was being washed away, and the sweet water of Kichigami was turning bitter. Her aunt Bowetinkwe, her granduncle Mashekewis, her companion's mother, the Turtlewoman from the Bay of White Sands, had all seen this. She begged me to go on seeing, to go on dreaming. But she warned me not to see in the company of those who could no longer see, those who chased dreamers from their midst. I thanked Agibicocona for her gift; I didn't then know just how precious her gift would be.

Our departure from the northern fur-gathering place was apparently delayed because of me. Burr-net was not convinced by Agibicocona's assurances that I was well enough to travel. He spoke of me as demented, bewitched by my grandmother, and he seemed ashamed to have me near him. Our Lakebottom kin had already filled their canoes with gifts and headed toward the sunset.

When we finally left Mishilimakina, Shabeni and Topinbi paddled the canoe that carried our mother and father. Wabnokwe was with Jambatí's sister Angie and brother Izzy, with Sofí and Felice. Wedasi and I were crowded into Lesotér's canoe with our aunt Marikwe and her four children, the oldest of whom, Sharlokwe, attached herself to Wedasi. Sharlokwe, like Wedasi, admired warriors, particularly her father Lesotér and her granduncle Mashekewis.

While Lesotér paddled, his sons Zozas and Medár taking turns with Wedasi and me, Sharlokwe spoke without pause. Her younger sister Rina listened wide-eyed but said nothing. Sharlokwe told of the Rootkin who had once inhabited the Peninsula's sunrise shore; I had heard some of her stories from Katabwe. She told of the plagues, cheatings and killings that had driven the original people toward distant places of refuge. When we traversed Sagi Bay, between the Peninsula's finger and thumb, Sharlokwe spoke with anger of her aunt Anjelík Kuyeryé, sister of the warrior Aleshi, who had betrayed the Strait's warriors to her Redcoat called Star-ling, and had then guided the Redcoat to Sagi Bay. While Mashekewis and Aleshi had fought alongside Lesotér's uncle Batí to oust the Redcoats from the Strait, Anjelík's Star-ling attacked the pines of Sagi Bay. Helped by treecutters from the Strait and even by my Lakebottom kinsman Sandypoint, this Star-ling removed the Bay's pines, starved out the deer, moose and beaver, and made the soil itself run into the Bay. The treekiller had defeated our Sagi kin without once facing them in battle; he did it by destroying their forest. The Bay's Rootkin had fled in four directions, some toward the Rootkin on Kichigami's shores, others to the remaining Turtlefolk in Morningland, still others toward the carriers by the Leaning Tree, the rest toward the surviving Redearth kin in the Greenbay on Mishigami's other shore. She said the Cheaters and Scalpers wanted to remove our kin from the Strait as well, but her father Lesotér was ready to confront them with talking leaves which spoke a language they understood, and if the Scalpers failed to understand the talking leaves, Lesotér and his cousin Isadór and Marikwe's cousin Wakaya would resume the battle they had called off when I was born, the battle on the field of fallen trees.

The Strait

At last we landed on the shore of the Strait that separates the Morningland from the Peninsula, Wabnokwe's and my birthplace, Tiosa Rondion, the village of the three fires. Wabnokwe leapt toward the embraces of Lemond, Wedasi ran to seek the warrior Wakaya. I stepped cautiously out of the canoe, filled with apprehension.

Sad faces greeted us. Antó's sister Nizokwe was dead. Her burial was underway. Grandmother Katabwe had spoken fondly of Nizokwe. I had hoped to hear her sing.

Since we were Nanikibi's grandchildren, Lesotér, the dead woman's nephew, led my brother, sister and me to the head of the burial procession. Nizokwe's and Miní's granddaughter

Beth knew who we were and she told us who the others were: Nizokwe's son and daughter Isadór and Isabél; Nizokwe's surviving brother Piér and two of his daughters, Jozét and Monfk; and the son and daughter of Nizokwe's dead brother Batí, Nawak and Pamoko. Beth told us our grandfather's sister Namakwe was elsewhere helping Piér's daughter Margít give birth.

The procession stopped on the hill by the bubbling springs. Isadór and Piér placed the body into the ground, and next to it they placed a musical instrument carved for Nizokwe by her brother Antó. Buckets of earth were carried to the hilltop until a mound of tear-soaked earth rose above the body. In the moonlight, Isadór unfolded and displayed the belts left to him by Nizokwe, belts which spoke of the second founding of Tiosa Rondion. And then another procession moved toward the hilltop, with candles, flags and crosses, with wails and chants. This procession was led by Tisha, son of Minf's cousin Magda, by Tisha's daughter Likét, and by my aunt Mikenokwe, sister of Nawak and Pamoko. These chanting mourners placed a cross on top of the mound.

The sound of musical instruments filled the air and many of the mourners began to dance on the councilground between the hill and the springs. The three of us stayed with Beth, and were soon joined by Jozét and Monfk who said they remembered Wabnokwe's birth in their father's great lodge; they made much of Wabnokwe's yellow hair. Beth's cousin Likét joined us. Likét showed us an amulet left to her by her grandmother Magda. My great-grandfather Ozagi had given that amulet to Beth's great-grandmother Maní, who had passed it to Magda, Manf's niece. The amulet linked us. Beth showed us another link, a bundle made of beads and cloth which, she said, had once been shaped like an animal. Katabwe had told me of this gift. It was made by Katabwe's mother Menoko for Beth's great-grandmother, and its last possessor had been Nizokwe. Beth cried while telling of the recent night when Nizokwe gave her the little animal that had lost its shape. Beth said she knew then that her grandmother was dying; she knew that Nizokwe's village, the village where three hearths had been kept burning since the days of the great-grandmothers Ubankiko and Chacapwe, was dying with Nizokwe.

I didn't grasp the depth of Beth's sorrow because I didn't yet know enough, and also because my concerns were elsewhere.

Wabnokwe was whisked away by Monîk, presumably toward Lemond. Our uncle Topinbi and our father Burr-net were with the Cheaters, disposing of pelts and haggling over gifts. Shabeni counciled with Isadór and Wakaya. I knew that Sofí and Felice were attending the wedding of Izzy's sister Angie. I lost track of Lesotér, Marikwe and their children. Wedasi and I were lodged with our mother at Namakwe's, where I was born. We shared the lodge with crosswearing Mikenokwe and her son Shandó, who wanted to be a fur carrier like Topinbi.

Namakwe, Nanikibi's sister, returned from the birth at Piér's, but soon left again to help her own daughter Pamoko give birth. Namakwe's hands had pulled me out of Cakima's womb. From the little I saw of Namakwe, I knew that she was altogether unlike my grandmother Katabwe. If Namakwe remembered the days when ancient Wedasi lived on the spot occupied by her lodge, if she knew of the days before the Invaders came, she gave no signs of knowing or remembering them, she sang no songs recalling them. I realized that I was among kin who remembered Ubankiko and Chacapwe and the second founding of Tiosa Rondion but who knew nothing of the first, kin for whom the coming of the Scabeaters was the beginning. I knew that the belts displayed by Isadór at his mother's grave were ancient Shutaha's belts, that these belts celebrated the union of Turtlefolk and Rootkin with the Scabeaters whose plagues had destroyed the first Tiosa Rondion's Turtlefolk and Rootkin.

Wedasi often joined Isadór, Shabeni and Wakaya at their councils, and accompanied them on a short hunt. I stayed close to Namakwe's, looking for the spot on the water's edge where a double-trunked tree had once cast a shadow of hare's ears on a roundish painted rock. The uppermost windows of Piér's enormous lodge were visible above the trees behind the lodges of Namakwe's neighbors, and upstream along the shore I could see a corner of the Invaders' forbidding enclosure.

I learned the cause of Beth's grief abruptly, when an argument broke out between my brother and our lodge-mate Shandó. I learned that Beth's Tiosa Rondion, the second, Shutaha's village, was about to break, to split in two. Shandó defended his uncle Dupré, aunt Pamoko's man, who had counciled with the Scalper married to Piér's daughter Jozét, a man called Wit-nags. Shandó praised Dupré for emerging from the council with a leaf on which Wit-nags pledged that if he ever camped near Tiosa Rondion, he would protect the inhabitants of Namakwe's village, as well as the trees, animals and burial grounds. But Wedasi had heard Wakaya and Isadór talk of the leaf and say they would rather be given a poisonous rattlesnake than the Scalper's pledge. I realized that Tiosa Rondion's kin were pulling apart. Wakaya and Isadór remained hostile to the Scalpers against whom they had fought alongside my grandfather. Namakwe's son Nawak had also fought against the Scalpers. But Nawak's hostility had cooled, because he and his sister Mikenokwe had been betrayed by the Scalpers' Redcoat enemies. These differences had not been aired while Nizokwe lived. Now they sundered the village.

I didn't pay much attention to the argument. I was more concerned about Shabeni's departure from the Strait. He was leaving with Topinbi, my mother and father, and Shandó as Topinbi's apprentice. I reminded Shabeni of his promise to build me another fasting lodge. Shabeni smiled. He said I would have a lifetime in which to dream, but only a few seasons to examine my birthplace. He renewed his promise before he left.

Wedasi and I wintered in Tiosa Rondion; Wabnokwe stayed in Piér's lodge. Wedasi accompanied Wakaya and Isadór on their hunts. He already knew how to use a rifle, and he didn't like to hear about the ancestor whose name he bore. I occasionally accompanied them. Once I went with Nawak and Dupré, but I confined myself to my bow and hit nothing with my arrows.

In midwinter Namakwe fell ill, and Pamoko was constantly in our lodge with compresses and herbal potions. When the snows melted, Pamoko went to Piér's lodge to celebrate the marriage of Nizokwe's widowed daughter Isabél, Beth's mother, to a man called Gore-nags, brother of Scalper Wit-nags. When Wedasi learned of this marriage he told me not to be surprised. Isabél was not like her mother, brother or daughter. Wedasi had heard Isadór tell that Isabél had once loved our uncle Aptegizhek, son of Oashi and Lókaskwe; she had loved Aptegizhek until he lived through the massacre on the Tuscarawas in the Beautiful Valley, and had then turned her back to him, repelled by his wound.

When the first leaf buds appeared, it became clear to everyone that the Scalper's pledge to Dupré had been a rock made of ice. It melted in spring. Wit-nags and a crew of treecutters came to the edge of Tiosa Rondion and began to down a part of the forest. When Nawak and Dupré confronted him, Wit-nags explained that his people's lodges were somewhat different from ours, and he pointed to Piér's enormous wooden lodge to illustrate the difference. Nawak and Dupré counciled with Namakwe and decided to keep the peace.

But when Isadór and Wakaya returned from the hunt, they, as well as several youths from the lodges of the Turtlefolk, confronted the treecutters with weapons in hand. Wakaya asked the intruders the question the Redearth warrior Lamina is said to have asked the first Scabeaters on the Strait: What do you want here? Scalper Wit-nags answered Wakaya differently than he had answered Nawak. Wit-nags said he was building a lodge on land that belonged to his wife's father Piér and to her cousin Dupré, and he waved a copy of Dupré's leaf in Wakaya's face.

Nawak, Dupré and the other Firekeepers were as determined to let the Scalper build his lodge as Isadór and Wakaya were to stop him. I was sure Lesotér would have sided with his cousin Isadór, but Lesotér had left Marikwe and his children on the Strait and returned to the north with Izzy and Sofí after the marriage of Izzy's sister to a Scalper named Whip-o. Many of the Turtleyouths painted themselves for war. But Wakaya and Isadór were waiting for the entire village to respond to the incursion; neither of them wanted to take up arms without, or possibly against, the other half of his kin-village.

The Turtlefolk of Tiosa Rondion counciled without Firekeepers, around a single hearth. Wedasi attended their councils. Many of the youths remained painted, ready to put an end to the cutting as well as the cutters. But the lodge mothers and the warriors who stood by them, such as Wakaya and Isadór, at last prevailed. There would be no fratricide. The Turtlefolk resolved to keep Scalpers out of their village by moving their village away from the Scalpers. They dismantled parts of their lodges, abandoned the rest, and moved downstream to a place across from Turkey Isle, a place they called Karontaen. Isadór carried the belts woven by ancient Shutaha, belts which described a village with four peoples around three hearths, to a village where all were Turtlefolk, either born or adopted. Isadór's niece Beth accompanied her uncle to the new village. Wedasi wanted to go there too, but Wakaya told my brother that Namakwe's village would be a sad place if it hadn't a single warrior in it. Wedasi stayed, as I did, in a village that was no longer Tiosa Rondion. Namakwe's kin continued to light the three hearths, but the hearths were no longer meetingplaces. Namakwe's village became a Firekeepers's village, like Bison Prairie.

When the leaves were fully grown, Topinbi and Shandó arrived on the Strait with Bison Prairie's furs. They came by way of Kekionga, having accompanied my uncle Aptegizhek to his village. Shabeni wasn't with them. What came with them instead was the news that my grandmother Katabwe had been buried.

Topinbi told us his mother had died soon after we had left Bison Prairie. I was sure she died when we were in Mishilimakina, when I became a bird and saw that the fur bundles were really corpses. Katabwe the warrior-woman had originally been called birdwoman. I then knew it had been her spirit that had come to me in my first dream and flown me above a Bison Prairie turned barren. When her spirit left her, part of it went to the land beyond the rising sun, the other part lodged itself in me; that was why I could fly on my own. She'd told me my first dream had been complete. Now I believed her. But I still didn't see how it could guide me.

Topinbi said the burial had already ended when the gift caravan from the Strait had returned to Bison Prairie. Oashi's son Aptegizhek had learned of the death and hurried to Bison Prairie from Kekionga; his sisters Shecogosikwe and Wagoshkwe had left the Lakebottom to attend their aunt's burial; Oashi's children remembered that Katabwe had been close to their mother Lókaskwe. Topinbi's daughter Mimikwe had made all the burial arrangements; she had been with Katabwe during the last days.

And then Topinbi showed us a gift—a bundle. Dying Katabwe had told Mimikwe to send the bundle to me, Obenabi. It was grandfather Nanikibi's otterskin bundle, the Firekeepers' medicine bundle. I hadn't cried when Tiosa Rondion, my birthplace, the village of three fires, had broken up. But I couldn't stop my tears when I accepted the bundle Topinbi brought me. Like my brothers and my sister, I had abandoned our grandmother. But she hadn't abandoned me; she had known that her spirit would lodge itself in me.

Topinbi had also carried talking leaves from our father to the Cheater called Jay-may, the gatherer of Bison Prairie's furs.

One of these leaves asked this Jay-may to see to it that Wedasi and I meet more people than our closest kin; Burr-net wanted us to go among those our grandmother had called Witchburners, Cheaters and Shitmakers, those whom Wakaya, and after him, Wedasi, called United Scalpers.
 Cheater Jay-may asked our brother Chebansi to do us this favor. Chebansi, as well as our oldest brother Nashkowatak, had recently returned from a long stay in Hochelaga, the onetime center of Turtlefolk which was now a center of beaver furs. Wedasi and I hadn't seen our older brothers since Mimikwe's marriage to Shabeni in Bison Prairie.
 Chebansi did as he was bid, but not joyfully. He led Wedasi and me out of Namakwe's lodge toward the crowded village shared by Scabeaters and United Scalpers. The fortified enclosure was the largest structure, but it seemed to me the entire village was an enclosure. Large, square houses blocked the view of the forest as well as the strait, and the paths between the houses stank of refuse. The tallest of the houses was the one in which the crosswearers lodged all their spirits, including the one they called Savior, their Wiske. Chebansi led us to a tiny room in a lodge he called the schoolhouse, a room we were to share with him. The room was barely larger than the inside of a sweat lodge, and there were no nearby woods to run to when we were covered with sweat.
 Chebansi confessed to us that he wasn't pleased to drag us into the Invader's world, but that if he hadn't done it, Nashkowatak would have. Wedasi and I were surprised, since in Bison Prairie Chebansi had avoided Katabwe and all the other Firekeepers and had confined himself to trader Burr-net's lodge. We were even more surprised when he told us that our father wanted us not only introduced to the Invaders, but totally transformed by them. He warned us of the Invaders' powers which, he said, were not limited to the instant death that rushed from their firesticks. He told us they knew how to take the meanings out of words, not only the words of their language but those of ours as well. Once we lost the meanings, we would be unable to remember our own ways or to think of our kin.
 Wedasi boasted that he was impervious to the Invaders' powers; he said he was coming among the Invaders as a scout from Wakaya's war camp. I wasn't as sure of myself, especially after Chebansi told us that Nashkowatak and Wabnokwe had already been transformed. The news of Wabnokwe did not sur-

prise me, but the news of Nashkowatak shocked me, for I remembered that our oldest brother had grown at Katabwe's hearth.

Chebansi told us the Scalpers did their transforming in ceremonial gatherings they called schools, but their schools did not always succeed. He said the gathering which he and Nashkowatak attended had been diverted by our cousins Likét, Monīk and Beth, so that Chebansi and Nashkowatak had had to be sent to Hochelaga for more powerful medicine. But he warned us that Scalpers Jay-may and Wit-nags, together with the Scabeater called Jo Kampó, had prepared another school, and that they learned from their failures.

We were not exposed to the Invaders' transforming process until the birds flew southward. By then I was familiar with many of the other children who were to be transformed. Our aunt Marikwe brought her four children, Sharlokwe, Zozas, Medár and little Rina; they stayed close to Wedasi and Chebansi, just as I did. Their cousin Felice, Sofi's daughter, who had been left in Marikwe's lodge by her mother, stayed away from Marikwe's children and also from Wabnokwe, confining herself to a circle that Wabnokwe called the snobs. Felice had a pretty smile; I was sorry she was a snob. My sister was herself a snob and avoided us as much as Felice did, extending her friendship only to Piér's daughter Monīk and to Isadór's niece Beth. Beth came by horse from Karontaen to be included in the school; she stayed with her cousin Likét in the crosswearers' spirit-lodge. The fourth group, six crosswearers, were relatively friendly to us; one of them, a boy named Bert, shared my apprehensions; Bert's sister Teresa shared Wedasi's scorn toward the Scalpers' powers and was soon on joking terms with my brother. Belle-may, the Scalper's daughter, also came, and kept largely to herself, being shut out of all four groups.

The gathering itself took place in the house in which my brothers and I had our room. I prepared myself carefully for the first encounter, remembering the advice I'd received in Mishi-limakina from the medicinewoman Agibicocona. I flattened the otterskin bundle against my chest and covered it completely with my shirt. I formed my eyes and mouth into a mask of amused attentiveness, a mask that told anyone who looked at me that I had seen nothing, heard nothing, and knew nothing.

The agent who was to accomplish our transformation was a woman who called herself Misus Bay-con, a woman younger than Likét, who understood only the Scalpers' language. Except for two or three of the crosswearers, all the children understood her language. I understood her words perfectly and I also understood Chebansi's warning. Misus Bay-con used familiar words and gave them twisted meanings, so that I grasped as little as I would have if she'd spoken a language alien to me. Words can have different meanings, just as trees can be birches or oaks. But a birch that's twisted or stunted is not a third kind of tree; it's a twisted birch. Misus Bay-con's meanings were like the stunted birch; they weren't meanings that merely differed from the ones I was used to; they were twisted, bent out of shape.

I soon thought that Chebansi's warnings had been exaggerated. I didn't know what conjurings had been worked on Nashkowatak in Hochelaga, but I knew that neither Wedasi nor I were likely to swallow Misus Bay-con's twisted meanings. If we had been mere babies we might have succumbed, but as it was, even little Rina, the youngest, was old enough to distinguish a full-grown birch from a twisted one. The only one who paid attention to Misus Bay-con was Belle-məy, daughter of Jay-may's first wife, and she had already learned the twisted meanings from her father. I actually felt sorry for Misus Baycon, who had no idea how alone she was. Most of the children, and obviously those who couldn't understand her language, wore smiling, attentive masks, said nothing, and heard as much as they said. Monîk and Beth confronted her continually, and she must have thought they were the only ones who disliked what she said. She must also have guessed that Chebansi was less than sympathetic to her, because Wedasi as well as Beth consulted Chebansi whenever they prepared to confront Misus Bay-con.

Misus Bay-con spoke a great deal about property and cleanliness. Chebansi told Wedasi and me what she meant. He told us Scalper Jay-may had had some rotten meat in his store. The proper thing to do with that filthy meat would have been to bury it. But Scalper Jay-may had salted the rotten meat and then given it to people one would have thought to be his mortal enemies, but who considered him a friend. In Misus Bay-con's eyes, Jay-may had done what was clean and proper, for he had gained property instead of losing it.

It was Wedasi who actually confronted Misus Bay-con; he asked her if he, Wedasi, could ever become clean and proper, and she set out on a long tirade about owning and saving property.

When she was done, Wedasi advised her not to visit our kin; or even her own. Almost all the children laughed, but Misus Bay-con's face was blank; she really didn't understand what Wedasi meant. So Wedasi explained that a person who hoarded food while others hungered, who hoarded clothing while others were cold, who locked up a lodge while others had no shelter, would not be considered either clean or proper in any village, by anyone's kin. He told her such a person would be considered an enemy, and not only an enemy but an unadoptable one, an enemy who was hostile to any and all human beings, kin and foe alike; such a person would be expelled as a hideous monster.

Everyone else understood Wedasi, but Misus Bay-con's face remained blank; she said she had no idea what he was talking about. He might as well have spoken to her in the language of Rootkin. Beth and Monîk continued to challenge Misus Bay-con, but Wedasi tired of the confrontations. And he ridiculed Chebansi's warnings. If Misus Bay-con illustrated the extent of the Scalpers' sorcery, then we had nothing to fear from the Scalpers except their killing-sticks. As soon as spring came, Wedasi stopped attending the gatherings, preferring to run to the woods outside the crowded village. I too grew tired of the poor woman's pathetic attempts to twist us out of shape. I retained my attentive mask, but I felt as if I'd been holding my breath; I was starved for fresh air.

The dreary sessions with the scalped words and twisted meanings finally ended, not because of Wedasi's boredom or Monîk's challenges, but because Namakwe died and most of us made our way to the Firekeepers' village. There was talk of sorcery exerted by the Scalper Wit-nags and of spells cast by the Turtlefolk of Karontaen, but Wedasi and I knew that our grandfather's sister had been old and ill, and her death gave us reason to escape from the numbing school and rejoin our kin.

It was my third spring on the Strait. Much had changed since my arrival. The lodges of Nawak, Pamoko, Mikenokwe and the other Firekeepers still stood below the hill by the springs, but there were few signs that these lodges had once been part of a larger village, one with three living hearths, Tiosa Rondion. The remains of the long lodges of the Turtlefolk had been dismantled and burned in winter's hearths. To the north the village was bounded, walled-in by Piér's enormous house and by the nearly-finished monstrosity of Scalper Wit-nags.

Shortly after our return to Namakwe's, Topinbi arrived with Namakwe's grandson Shandó and with guests from Kekionga. Shandó stayed with Wedasi and me in his mother Mikenokwe's lodge, while Mikenokwe and Pamoko and their brother Nawak made arrangements for the burial of their mother. Shandó spoke of Bison Prairie's beavers and hunters, but he brought us no news of Meteya, Mimikwe or Shabeni, except the news that Shabeni had not wanted to accompany the fur caravan.

The kin from Kekionga were strangers to me, although I knew who they were. Gabinya was the son of Namakwe's sister Tinami; he was Marikwe's brother. I knew that when his cousins had fought the Scalpers at the time of my birth, Gabinya had fled from the fallen trees and hidden in the Redcoats' fort next to the battlefield. Gabinya came with a distant kinsman of mine who did not live in Kekionga but in Piqua, in the center of the Beautiful Valley, among Southbranch and Eastbranch kin. His name was Bijiki and he was the son of Lókaskwe's sister Magidins. Gabinya was on the Strait to attend his aunt's burial. Bijiki had come to introduce his son Pezhki and his nephew Muns to Misus Bay-con's school.

Although neither Nawak nor Pamoko wore crosses, they let their sister Mikenokwe prepare a crosswearer's burial. I was not invited to help with the arrangements, so I took my otterskin bundle into the forest where, surrounded by none but trees and birds, I unpacked its contents. I saw and touched the gifts passed on to me, gifts from long-vanished ancestors, gifts whose meaning I could not yet grasp. All I saw was a bundle of fishbones, a feather, a shell, and two rolled sheets of bark which I kept rolled from fear they would disintegrate.

Puritan school

I walked alongside Pamoko to the burial place. She had nursed her mother through the winter. At the end Namakwe had given Pamoko her herb bundle and had asked Pamoko to bring Mikenokwe and Nawak to her lodge. Pamoko told me her mother didn't know that Tiosa Rondion had already dispersed; Namakwe's last words to her son and daughter were to keep the hearths of Tiosa Rondion lit, to make sure the three fires never died.

Wakaya as well as Isadór had come up for their aunt's burial, but they kept themselves in the shadows and I didn't see them. I did see Lesotér and Sofí, who arrived during the burial procession. I learned from Lesotér's daughter Sharlokwe that Sofí's man Izzy had died during the journey to Mishilimakina and that Lesotér had lost his father Antó. Sharlokwe also told me that Sofí's daughter Felice was ashamed of her mother for returning to the Strait with Lesotér instead of coming properly with Izzy's brothers. I also saw Tinami's son Gabinya at his aunt's burial, more intent on chasing after Monίk than on Mikenokwe's crosses and candles.

While the crosswearers kneeled to the spirits on their banners, wailed, and planted crosses, Sofí went from Chebansi to Beth to Isadór spreading news of other happenings in Mishilimakina, happenings which concerned me and all the other children attending Misus Bay-con's school. When the burial ended, Beth invited all those involved with the school to council with Sofí at Isadór's hearth in Karontaen. Chebansi led Wedasi and me, and also the boys from the Beautiful Valley, Muns and Pezhki, to the Turtlefolks' shore. Pezhki's father Bijiki had gone to visit his mother and his younger brother on the shore of the Clear Lake north of the Strait, and he'd left his son and nephew at Nawak's, after asking Chebansi to introduce the boys to Misus Bay-con's school.

Instead of returning to Misus Bay-con's school after Namakwe's burial, more than half of Misus Bay-con's scholars were gathered around Sofí at the Karontaen councilground. My sister Wabnokwe was there with Beth. Lesotér's and Marikwe's four children were there. Beth's cousin, the crosswearer Likét, was there. I found a place in the circle between my cousin Sharlokwe and my uncle Wakaya; Wedasi sat on the other side of Wakaya. It was the first time I had seen the renowned warrior up close; he didn't seem at all formidable. In the firelight I saw the silhouette of the arrowhead dangling from his neck.

Most of the gathered kin were Turtlefolk who had left Tiosa Rondion with Isadór soon after his mother's death, when the Scalpers started downing the trees. Their village, consisting only of longhouses surrounded by pickets and watchtowers, seemed as strange to me as the Invaders' village upstream.

After the usual greetings and expressions of gratitude, Sofí spoke to the gathering in the language of the Turtlefolk, so that I understood nothing of what she said. My three brothers, and even my sister Wabnokwe, had heard Tiosa Rondion's Turtlefolk during many seasons, but I had been carried to Bison Prairie before I had learned to speak.

I was entranced by Wakaya's arrowhead pendant; if Sharlokwe hadn't kept nudging me, I would have dreamt. I had to wait until everyone was heard, and the council broke up, before I learned why they had gathered. Sharlokwe generously translated every speech for me and also for Muns and Pezhki, both of whom had fallen asleep during the council.

Sharlokwe told us that Misus Bay-con had a counterpart in the north, a husband by the name of Rev-rend Bay-con. Both Bay-cons had been invited to the Peninsula by the Scabeater Jo Kampó and by the Scalpers Jay-may and Wit-nags. The Rev-rend was to do in Mishilimakina what Misus did to us on the Strait. Sharlokwe spoke the same way Chebansi had when he'd warned us of the school. She spoke of fallen forests and split villages, of kin pushed out of their ancestral homes. She said the sorcery of the Bay-cons was more powerful than the Scalpers' firewater and even their firesticks. She said the Redcoats who had fought against our grandfathers and granduncles Miní, Aleshi, Mashekewis and Nanikibi had not been able to accomplish so much as the Bay-cons. I protested that Misus Bay-con had not done anything to us. Sharlokwe assured me that Misus was either feeble or less experienced, because Rev-rend Bay-con had done much. He had turned Sofí's brother Will Soli-man and her dead Izzy's brothers Lou and Jambatí into Witchburners and Cheaters. He had separated Sofí's brother from Agibicocona, accusing the medicinewoman of being a sorceress and saying that a proper person could not be married to a sorceress. He had separated Jambatí from Sandypoint's daughter Suzán because, he said, Suzán was too dark to be the wife of a proper person. And when Sofí and Lesotér had returned to Mishilimakina, they'd been locked up together in a small room, accused of being Agibicocona's accomplices and even of murdering Izzy. And all this had been done so that Lou and Jambatí and Will Soli-man could take over Sofí's, Lesotér's and Agibicocona's lodges. Antó had died fighting the schemers, and Lesotér and Sofí had escaped to the Strait to seek allies.

I didn't believe everything Sharlokwe told me because I couldn't see how someone with Misus Bay-con's powers could accomplish so much. But the kin gathered at the Karontaen councilground apparently believed Sofí because the longhouse women and the warriors resolved to oust the Bay-cons from the Peninsula if the crosswearers on the Strait failed to do so. Likét, who had spoken in the language of Prairiekin, had assured the angry Turtlefolk that she and her father Tisha and the other crosswearers would see to it that no armed clash became necessary, at least not on the Strait. Likét's assurances had failed to cool the anger, but I didn't understand the various responses.

Wedasi and I returned to Mikenokwe's after the council dispersed. Muns and Pezhki were lodged next door to us, at Nawak's. Muns and I were the same age, and we soon learned we had many other things in common. Muns's father Onimush and his uncle Bijiki, sons of Magidins and trader Con-err, were themselves traders, like my own father. Muns had no desire to be a trader. He had grown among the kin of his mother Mekinges and her sister Chindiskwe, Eastbranch Rootkin whose ancestors had been driven to the Beautiful Valley from the Oceanshore. One of his ancestors was Lenapi, a man my grandmother had respected. He told me about kin whose whereabouts even Katabwe hadn't known. His closest friend in Piqua was Ojejok, son of Wakaya's and Meteya's brother Wapmimi.

Muns begged me to share the contents of the otterskin with him. He was especially excited about the bark scrolls. He told me his uncle Aptegizhek in Kekionga had a similar scroll, a scroll that spoke of Muns's own Eastbranch kin; I was able to tell Muns how the Eastbranch scroll had come to be in Aptegizhek's hands.

Muns didn't share my doubts of Sharlokwe's veracity. He hadn't yet seen Misus Bay-con, but he was as wary as Chebansi of the United Scalpers' transforming powers. He told me the Scalpers had transformed his uncle Bijiki the same way they'd transformed Sofí's kinsmen in the north. Bijiki had grown among the Rootkin of Sagi Bay, at the Clear Lake just north of the Strait. When he'd been ready to hunt on his own, Bijiki and his brother Onimush had moved to Piqua and married Southbranch and Eastbranch women. They had shared meat with the Piqua kin, smoked with them and counciled with them. But at one council, some of the Piqua kin, and also the preaching Brethren who'd joined them, urged Bijiki to travel to the east to complain of incursions and killings perpetrated by the Invaders pouring over the mountains into the valley. Bijiki had gone east, and he'd returned transformed. He began to hoard instead of sharing. He befriended the Kekionga traitor Will-well who'd once been Wakaya's half-brother. He insisted on being called John Con-err instead of Bijiki. And he brought his older son and his nephew to the Strait to have them undergo a similar transformation.

Wabnokwe and Moník came to Mikenokwe's to prepare us for the final confrontation with Misus Bay-con. We were to pretend we were simply returning to school after our kinswoman's burial, and that we knew nothing about Misus or Rev-rend Bay-con. I was already experienced at pretending, but Muns was not very good at it.

I walked with Muns and Pezhki from the Firekeepers' village; we were accompanied by Moník and Wabnokwe. Wedasi told all he knew to Teresa and Bert, who spread the news to the other crosswearers.

There were several confrontations, some of them so funny that Muns and other children burst out laughing, putting Misus Bay-con on her guard. Moník had recruited my uncle Gabinya to be the agent of Misus Bay-con's downfall, not because Gabinya shared the hostility of the others but because he didn't share it. Gabinya lodged with his sister Marikwe. He knew what had happened in Mishilimakina, but he was completely indifferent to his kin as well as their plight. Gabinya's sole interest was in young girls, and Moník knew that the mere sight of Belle-may demented him. So Moník urged him to assist Belle-may, Misus Bay-con's lone defender, and to present himself to Misus Bay-con as someone eager to learn her teachings.

Monik couldn't have found a better person for the role. Monik herself, as well as Beth and a crosswearing cousin of theirs called Lisa, confronted Misus Bay-con by referring to ancient crosswearers' traditions which Misus Bay-con claimed to understand better than the crosswearers; they exposed Misus

Bay-con's ignorance of those traditions. But Gabinya pretended to agree with Misus Bay-con. Gabinya pretended to defend her statements and haltingly repeating her words, he then translated her words into languages all but Belle-may could understand. Thus he translated her statements about saving money into statements about saving male seed, and her statements about spending, or as she said investing, the money, into statements about pumping the seed into a womb. Muns laughed until tears flowed, the crosswearers were mortified, but Misus Bay-con praised Gabinya's understanding and Belle-may thanked him for his clarity.

The last confrontation was not Gabinya's doing, but Likét's. Outside the schoolhouse, before the session even began, Likét stopped Misus Bay-con the moment she arrived. With her cousin translating, Likét asked in Lemond's language if Misus Bay-con knew where she was leading the children. Misus Bay-con answered that she was lifting the children from below the ground. Likét then asked how Misus Bay-con could lift children who hadn't yet fallen, and if she didn't have to trip the children first.

I didn't fully understand Likét's questions in either language, but Misus Bay-con apparently did, because she burst into tears and ran from the schoolhouse instead of entering it. Belle-may, also upset, ran after Misus Bay-con to console her, and Gabinya ran after Belle-may. Muns and I left the gathering and ran back to the Firekeepers' village; we both knew there would be no more school. But we mistakenly thought Likét had brought the end by humiliating Misus Bay-con; we soon learned that the end wasn't Likét's doing; it was Gabinya's.

The day after the confrontation in front of the schoolhouse, Monîk came to gather us all at Piér's; she didn't say why. I saw, for the first time, the inside of the great lodge that stood beyond the northern edge of the Firekeepers' village, the lodge my sister called Lemond, the center of her world. I remembered she was born in that lodge. It was also the first time I met Monîk's sister Margît, although, like everyone else, I thought I'd met her before, because I had seen her sister Jozét at Namakwe's burial.

Margît led me to a place in the councilroom, the room my sister called the salon. Margît's face expressed a combination of amusement and apprehension; she already knew the purpose of the gathering. Margît was Belle-may's foster-mother, second wife of Scalper Jay-may.

The room filled up. Everyone I knew on the Strait was there except the Firekeepers and the Turtlefolk. Piér himself sat in a corner, said nothing, and seemed more like a guest than a host. Margít's twin Jozét was there as well as her husband, Scalper Wit-nags. Likét and all her cousins were there. Sofí was there with Felice and Marikwe's four, but Marikwe and Lesotér were not there. Almost all of the other schoolchildren were there, as well as Misus Bay-con herself.

Without any preliminaries, Jay-may announced why he had gathered us all there. He said Belle-may, the daughter of his first marriage, couldn't be found. He'd spent the entire night looking for her. Another person who couldn't be found was Gabinya.

Muns burst out laughing and I couldn't keep myself from joining him. Everything became clear to me. Gabinya had run after Belle-may to console her, and he must have gone on consoling her until she agreed to run off with him. Monik must have known something like this would happen when she recruited Gabinya to be Belle-may's helper. Everyone in the room was laughing, except the Scalpers. Jay-may was red with rage. He said his daughter had eloped with a man twice her age, and he blamed Misus Bay-con for allowing such a thing to happen.

Misus Bay-con pointed her finger at Chebansi, but she was so distraught she couldn't speak. Scalper Wit-nags accused Chebansi of leading the schoolchildren to what he called a witches' sabbath in Karontaen, and of instigating a conspiracy to destroy Misus Bay-con's school. Jay-may shouted at Chebansi, calling him a vicious character and threatening him with punishments.

Almost everyone in the room knew that Chebansi had done none of the instigating, that he'd merely guided a few of us to Isadór's hearth. But Chebansi didn't defend himself. He just sat and sweated; soon he started trembling. I could see that he was getting sick.

Sofí leapt from her seat, lunged at Misus Bay-con, called her a liar, and said the only conspiracy was the one hatched by Misus Bay-con and her Rev-rend together with the Strait's Scalpers. It took the combined strength of Jay-may and Wit-nags to keep Sofí from scratching the frightened Misus Bay-con. One of the Scalpers advised Piér to make his salon more selective. The old man didn't acknowledge hearing the advice, but Sofí stormed out of the room. Felice ran out after Sofí; I could tell she was ashamed, not of the Scalper's insult, but of her mother's behavior.

Chebansi left next, bent over and shaking; Likét helped, and almost carried him out of the room. All laughter had long since died. Only Jay-may's voice cut through the stony silence. He spoke of orgies and perversions; he threatened punishments. He continued to blame Chebansi for Belle-may's disappearance, but after Likét left the room he put some of the blame on her. He said the crosswearers wanted to destroy Misus Bay-con's school so as to replace it with a school of their own. At last he threatened to break the nest of conspirators, as he called us, into splinters.

Wedasi and I wanted to join our sick brother, but Jay-may and Wit-nags kept us from him. We returned, with Muns and Pezhki, to the Firekeepers' village. I couldn't believe what had happened. The Scalpers surely knew what Rev-rend Bay-con had done to Lesotér and Sofí and their kin in Mishilimakina. They surely also knew that Sofí and Lesotér were the ones who had conspired and instigated, and with good reasons. Yet the Scalpers had put all the blame on our brother. Wedasi thought he knew why Chebansi had been singled out. Lesotér, Antó's son, was the host's nephew. Sofí had been regarded as a niece by Antó, and undoubtedly was by Piér. On the other hand Chebansi was the son of distant trader Burr-net, and the Strait's Scalpers surely knew that Burr-net would not stand by his son. They singled out Chebansi, not because he was the instigator, but because he was a convenient victim.

Topinbi and Shandó were still on the Strait, ready to carry their load of gifts to Bison Prairie. They were asked to delay their departure until Jay-may implemented his threat and broke up the nest of conspirators. When the gift-caravan finally left, our brother and sister as well as our friends left with it. Chebansi remained ill, and Jay-may insisted he return to Bison Prairie for medicine. Wabnokwe was yanked out of her beloved Lemond and told to nurse her brother during the journey. Bijiki was going to accompany the caravan as far as Kekionga, and he took Muns and Pezhki with him. Wedasi and I were left at Mikenokwe's.

Wedasi was again able to join his Karontaen uncles, especially Wakaya, in their councils and on their hunts; he went with Pamoko's canoe, sometimes with Nawak's horse. The animosity between Turtlefolk and Firekeepers died down, although Nawak himself did not join his downstream cousins. Wedasi spent his days in Karontaen but didn't want to be adopted into one of the longhouses, as Wakaya had been. He was disappointed. When we'd first arrived on the Strait, Wedasi had expected the Strait's warriors to be preparing for their next encounter with the Invaders. His first disappointment had been Nawak's capitulation to Scalper Wit-nags' invasion of Tiosa Rondion. He'd thought the Turtlefolk had moved downstream in order to rally their forces. Now he knew that their councils were not war councils; they too had capitulated. Wedasi still preferred to hunt with Wakaya and Isadór, but on two or three occasions that winter he joined the Firekeepers Nawak and Dupré. On those occasions I went along with my bow. I went for the stillness of the frozen forest and for the glimpses of deer bounding over the snow. And I went to hear Nawak repeat his stories about his uncles Aleshi and Miní and his father Batí, about their wars against the Redcoats who invaded the Strait, about their alliance with those very Redcoats against the United Scalpers, and about their allies' betrayal at the field of fallen trees.

Nawak told how he shielded his injured father Batí while the bullets whistled over them, how he guided his father past the fallen trees to the gate of the Redcoats' fort, how his father expired in his arms while the Redcoats refused to open the gate to the injured warrior. That betrayal permanently cooled Nawak's rage against the Scalpers who had killed so many of his kin.

During these hunts I stayed close to Nawak, away from Dupré, whenever they separated. Nawak would follow tracks, and when he sighted an animal he would pause, listen, watch, drop some tobacco and whisper to the animal's spirit, and only then set out after the prey. And as soon as he had enough to feed his village kin, he'd stop, build a fire, and talk.

Dupré's ways repelled me. As soon as he saw tracks, his face lit up with greed and he ran. If he spotted several animals, he killed and went on killing, with no offerings to their spirits and with no thought to the needs of the village, as if his killing-stick were out of his control; I knew that the Scalpers hunted like that. Nawak and the others helped Dupré lug all the dead animals to the village. Pamoko and the other women dried the meat and dressed the furs, which Dupré then carried to the Strait's traders. He returned with more powder, cloth, food and whiskey than anyone in the village could use.

Toward the end of that winter, Mikenokwe told us that Misus Bay-con and her Rev-rend had left the Strait, and that Likét and her crosswearing friends were preparing to launch a school of their own. Mikenokwe beamed as she told of Likét's intentions, and I saw that my aunt differed in yet another way from her Karontaen cousins. I remembered that Isadór and the Turtlefolk who'd heard Sofí had expressed revulsion not only toward Misus Bay-con, but also toward the daily gatherings of children in a school.

My sister returned to the Strait with Topinbi, Shandó and the Bison Prairie furs soon after the birds returned from the south. Wabnokwe promptly reinstalled herself in Piér's lodge, but she was friendlier toward her co-conspirators than she had been earlier. She told us Chebansi was well, that his departure from the Strait was the medicine that cured him. She told us of an unpleasant encounter she and Chebansi had had with a Scalper who had lodged himself on the Lakebottom. And she told us the content of the talking leaves Topinbi delivered to Jay-may.

On one of these leaves, Burr-net said he hadn't known his son Chebansi was such a vicious character, and he thanked Jay-may for letting him know. Burr-net then said he did not want his third son, Wedasi, to become another idler, shirker and poet, and he begged Jay-may to bind Wedasi. Wabnokwe had no idea what the binding entailed, but she was sure our father did not want his third son cut up and eaten. The leaf didn't as much as mention me, and I supposed my father considered me unredeemable; by the time Agibicocona taught me to hide, Burr-net had already seen me.

Wedasi alternated between wanting to flee to Wakaya's and wanting to prove himself strong enough to withstand the mysterious binding, which didn't long remain a mystery. It wasn't Cheater Jay-may who revealed the nature of the binding, but our oldest brother Nashkowatak. During all our sessions on the Strait, we had merely glimpsed Nashkowatak going in or out of Piér's lodge, or near the fort in the company of armed Scalpers. Chebansi had told us Nashkowatak had been transformed into a Scalper who didn't know his own brothers, and Nashkowatak's long avoidance of us confirmed the description. But I saw right away that Chebansi had exaggerated.

Nashkowatak may have been trying hard to be a Scalper, but he had avoided us because he'd been ashamed to face us in his blue uniform and cropped hair. My oldest brother was the same person I remembered from the days when our grandmother Katabwe still lived. He hadn't then given the impression of being sure of himself, and he seemed even less sure of himself now. When Chebansi had first led us to the schoolhouse, he'd been reluctant and self-justifying. Nashkowatak was even more so. He told Wedasi that the binding simply meant that Wedasi was to assist Jay-may in the Cheater's store. Nashkowatak would accompany Wedasi to the store if Wedasi wanted to go there, but he told us he would neither convince nor coerce. Wedasi left Mikenokwe's, and when Shandó and Topinbi returned to Bison Prairie, I was alone. I played with Pamoko's little son, accompanied Mikenokwe to the cornfield, watched Pamoko dress furs or went with her to gather herbs. Wabnokwe and Beth and their cousins, as well as Sharlokwe, Rina and Felice, went to Likét's school. Only girls went there. Most of the boys I'd met at Misus Bay-con's gatherings now went daily to listen to the Strait's Blackrobe, a cadaverous man who looked like a hungry vulture; I felt sorry for them.

Fire and departure

I didn't exist for Burr-net, but Cheater Jay-may remembered that I was still in the Firekeepers' village, and when the leaves began to fall, Nashkowatak visited again. He told me I could either join the boys who attended the Blackrobe's gatherings, or I could join Wedasi in the Cheater's store, but I couldn't go on watching Pamoko gather herbs. Both of my aunts agreed, so I didn't ask Nashkowatak why. I had started to miss Wedasi and decided to share his binding.
    Jay-may seemed pleased; he beamed when I entered the store. He assured me that he had once been a boy himself, and that he understood what he called my restless love of wilderness and my heedless freedom. But, he said, I was now old enough to

close up those sources of corruption. Order would regenerate me, he said. And since I hadn't acquired order from Misus Bay-con, I would surely acquire it from work. He warned me that I would not like the work any better than Wedasi did, but he promised that as soon as I reaped the reward, I would acquire the habit, then the taste, and finally the need for work.

I saw right away that Wedasi had not yet acquired either the habit or the taste, but Wedasi hadn't yet reaped any rewards. When the Cheater stepped out, Wedasi showed me the types of rewards Jay-may and other Cheaters liked to reap. Wedasi showed me a chest full of decorated shell-belts and paper leaves and round stones, whole or cut up into halves, quarters and eighths. The round stones were so-called coins that came from the Invaders called Senyores, the people among whom Likét and her brother had grown on the sunset shore of the Long River. These objects were the things Misus Bay-con had urged us to reach out for and save. We were amused by the thought that Jay-may carried a Misus Bay-con inside him; he was certainly big enough.

Wedasi had already learned to keep track of the beaver furs and coins that were brought in, and of the blankets, decorated plates and other things that were carried out. He told me Jay-may was greedy about the gifts that were brought in, but stingy about those that went out, and that his stinginess had a reason, Misus Bay-con's reason. The gifts Jay-may held back from every visitor to the store were Jay-may's savings. He hoarded them. And the hoard itself was a power. The hoard could transform itself into houses or boats or even portions of earth. Jay-may was as fond of his hoard as I was of my medicine bundle. But unlike my bundle, Jay-may's hoard wasn't freely given to him by his kin, but was wrenched from people he treated as enemies, and instead of linking him to the people he lived among, it severed him from them. Every gift-exchange in the store was a hostile act, and neither Jay-may's frozen grin nor his day-long repetition of the same joke disguised his relation to his visitors: he was at war with them.

Jay-may's war was not the type of war Wedasi had dreamt of. This was no heroic affair; it was sordid. Wedasi and I began to understand how our own father had related to Bison Prairie's villagers before Cakima had taken charge of the gift-giving and transformed Burr-net from a stingy enemy to a generous kinsman. Wedasi and I decided to do for Jay-may what Cakima had done for Burr-net. Cheater or no, Jay-may was, after all, our kinsman, however distantly related.

We had our chance when Jay-may, Wit-nags and other Scalpers left the Strait to visit a fur-gatherers' center called Pit-strength. Wedasi was left in charge of the store, with me as assistant and errand-runner. Wedasi and I promptly rearranged the gifts, prominently displaying things that Jay-may generally kept hidden. And we urged all visitors to take whatever they needed not only to pursue the hunt, but also to satisfy their kin. Most of the Strait's inhabitants who visited the store glanced at us suspiciously and took no more than Jay-may would have given them. But the hunters from Karontaen, Morningland, Sagi Bay and further north were highly pleased. Their esteem for Jay-may rose immensely. Some of the hunters knew who we were, and they told us such generosity had not existed on the Strait since the days of our great-grandfathers Mota and Ozagi. These hunters spread the word to their kinsmen, and they too were pleased to leave us their furs and to accept our gifts. And Wedasi conscientiously kept track of all that was brought and all that was taken, as he'd been taught.

When Jay-may returned, the store was full of beaver furs, tobacco pouches, shell belts and decorated sashes, but things like blankets, powder, beads, cloth and plates were all depleted. Jay-may beamed when he saw the fur piles; he shook our hands; he called Wedasi a sharp businessman. But when he looked at the ledger his face changed color. He looked at the ledger a second time, and his face became green. He leered at Wedasi. I wanted to tell him that his esteem had risen, but before I could formulate a word, a stream of abuse began to pour from Jay-may's mouth, most of it unintelligible, but all of it loud. I caught words like thief and criminal and bad stock; I understood that Jay-may was saying Wedasi and I were evil characters, just like Chebansi, and that our brother Nashkowatak was well placed in the Invaders' fort where he could do no harm to Jay-may's store.

Jay-may's shouting attracted others to the store, and soon Wedasi and I were surrounded by Scalper Wit-nags and his brother, by the Scabeater Jo Kampó, by several uniformed men, and all of them were shouting at us. All at once we were grabbed and pulled toward a room at the back of the store, a room that had always been locked. Jay-may opened the lock, had two chests removed, and had us thrown in. The last thing I heard him say was that a lengthy lock-up would give us salutary ideas and would break our attachment to savage customs.

The room was barely large enough for us to stretch out on its floor; it had obviously been built to hold the two chests, which must have contained things Jay-may wanted no one to see. The room had one small window, which was high as well as barred; we had to stand on each other's shoulders to see out, and then we only saw the wall of the next-door lodge. Someone sawed off a small piece of the heavy door at the lower corner, and we were able to push our excrement out through the hole. We were given bread and water through the same hole.

Wedasi was in a continual rage; he couldn't sleep. He had tried to do the man a favor; he would never try that again. He talked continually of confronting the Scalpers on a battlefield; Wedasi and his armed companions would surround Jay-may and Wit-nags as they had surrounded us. Wedasi was so agitated he became feverish. I urged him to do as I did. I leaned against the wall, looked up toward the window and imagined myself in a cave or fasting lodge. And I slept.

I tried to help Wedasi dream by showing him the objects in the bundle that had once been Nanikibi's. But these objects only further agitated him. He saw the bound fishbones as ourselves, and he was sure this was what Burr-net had intended when he'd asked Jay-may to bind his third son. He examined the shell, listened to it, and said that it begged him to stop the Jay-mays from turning the world into beach-sand. Wedasi fondled the feather; he placed it in his hair knot and said it was part of the headdress of a western warrior. And he pushed the two scrolls aside resentfully, saying that they couldn't speak to us but only to people who had long been dead, people as unlike to us as we were to Jay-may.

I slept, and I was still on the threshold of a dream when I felt Wedasi furiously shaking me. Smoke poured into the room through the edges of the door and even through the crevices of the walls. My nose filled with the smell of burnt wood and burnt leather. Soon I was choking. Wedasi and I looked at each other with fear in our eyes: we were going to be burnt alive. Only now did Wedasi's restlessness leave him. He became calm for the first time since our lock-up. He stood up, folded his arms, and stared ahead of him, ready to face whatever tortures his enemies devised. I didn't share either his determination or his courage; I coughed, cried, shouted, banged on the walls and door.

Wedasi's bravery went untested. Suddenly the heavy door opened. Outside it stood Margít's father Piér, Lemond's Piér, our sister's host, dead Nizokwe's brother. I almost flew out toward the old man. He rushed us out to the street where he and a cousin of his, an old woman called Cecíl, pulled and pushed us toward the Strait's shore. The old woman was choked from the smoke and from crying; she kept saying the Barbarian, as she called Jay-may, would have Wedasi and me roast. As we rushed toward the water, the lodge next to the store caught on fire. From the canoe it looked like the entire west was on fire.

All of the Strait's inhabitants hurried to the safety of the water, listening to the crackle of the flames, watching walls fall, seeing their village burn to the ground. Wedasi and I, and the two old people who saved us, had been among the last to push off from shore. When the flames died down, canoes headed northward or across the Strait, toward the cornfields of the inhabitants. Piér paddled us toward the Firekeepers' village, to the landingplace by his lodge.

By the time we landed, both Piér and Cecíl were so overwrought they had to be helped out of the canoe and into the great lodge. Wedasi and I were surrounded by Wabnokwe, Moník and all the other young women in Likét's school. They had just returned from a journey to the Beautiful Valley. They plied us with questions about the fire's origin and cause, questions Wedasi and I couldn't answer. And soon Wedasi and I were forgotten; the homeless refugees all had problems of their own. The gatherings in front of Piér's lodge and Wit-nags' lodge overflowed onto the Firekeepers' councilground.

That night Wedasi and I slept outside of Mikenokwe's lodge, which was crowded to bursting with Likét and her father as well as her brother and his wife. Lesotér and Marikwe and their daughters as well as Sofí and Felice all crowded into Pamoko's; Marikwe's sons shared Nawak's small lodge. I learned that Beth had gone to Karontaen while her mother Isabél and her Gore-nags and their son moved in with Wit-nags and Jozét. I also learned that Jay-may was safe at Piér's, and had been at Piér's during the entire conflagration, because Margít had been giving birth to a son. I didn't know how Piér had come to possess a key to the trader's back room, but I knew that Jay-may's joy from the birth of his new son would have been greater if Piér had returned with two chests and a barrel of coins, and not with Wedasi and me.

Wedasi and I prepared a gift for the two old people who saved us, but while we pondered how we would get past Jay-may into the great lodge, we learned that Piér was dead. Cecíl had died a few days earlier. We wondered if the effect of pulling us out of the burning village took their last strength. Wedasi and I were forgotten during the burial ceremonies. We were both determined to join Topinbi's caravan to Bison Prairie. When our uncle finally arrived with the furs and talking leaves, Jay-may made a show of carrying through with his punishment of Wedasi. He assigned Wedasi to the militia of Kekionga. He obviously knew that Kekionga would be the first stop of Topinbi's homeward-bound caravan. Wedasi smiled, as did most others, including Jay-may's wife. Margít and her kin were not ready to tolerate further punishment of us, and they were relieved by Jay-may's pretense that our departure was further punishment. On the day we left, Margít brought me a food bundle and a kiss. She had caught me off my guard on the night of her father's and aunt's burial, when all the mourners had gathered in the great lodge; I had stood by her music box enraptured by the sound, transported out of myself. I realized that Margít was not one of the people I needed to hide from, and I wondered how she had come to be the Cheater's wife.

I had tears in my eyes when our canoe pulled away from the Firekeepers' shore. At first I thought my tears were for Wabnokwe, Sharlokwe, Lesotér and Marikwe, for Sofí and Margít, for Pamoko and her son Jon Dupré. But tears kept flowing, and as the figures blurred and vanished, I realized I was crying because my birthplace had become a prison. The prison had burnt down, and sensible people would have taken the fire as an omen. But I knew, from numerous overheard words, from the very expressions on faces, that those on the Strait were determined to rebuild their prison, and neither the kindly Piér nor his cousin Cecíl would be there to pull me out of it.

We followed the same route I had traveled once before, soon after my birth, when I hadn't known the name of the lake nor that of the river, when I hadn't known that my great-grandfathers Ozagi and Mota had once hunted in the Kekionga forests where few animals now stirred. This time I knew what I was seeing. Shores that had once been gatheringplaces of Firekeepers and Prairiekin were desolate. The innumerable villages my grandmother had described were mounds of refuse, their charred remains still showing through greening plants growing out of them. The lone living village we finally reached was no Kekionga, for to me the name still signified a place too vast to see or shout across. This village was bounded on one side by the visible Scalpers' fort, on another by traders' stores, on the third by square lodges of Invaders, and on the fourth by cornfields one didn't need to shout across in order to be heard. Neither Wedasi nor I were surprised that our welcoming party included our uncle Gabinya and the vanished Belle-may, who had already given birth to a daughter named Anabel. But we were surprised to learn that Belle-may shared a lodge with Gabinya's first wife Nebeshkwe and his first daughter Sukwe. Wedasi couldn't keep himself from asking Belle-may if she'd considered what Misus Bay-con would have thought of her new lodge.

My attentions were drawn elsewhere, for my friend Muns was also in Kekionga, and he quickly pulled Wedasi and me next door, through the store of Gabinya's brother Atsimet and into the lodge of Muns's aunt Chindiskwe. A few doors from Atsimet's lodged my uncle Aptegizhek, son of Lókaskwe and Oashi, whom I had never met.

I had thought Muns was further south in distant Piqua, but I saw that he, his mother Mekinges and his father Onimush were not in Kekionga on a visit; they were there to stay, as were the other Eastbranch refugees I noticed in Kekionga, all newly-arrived and in temporary lodges. Muns's father and uncle had already raised a store on the edge of the village, next to the lodge and store of the traitor Will-well, Wakaya's and Meteya's false brother, Sigenak's false son. I was anxious to ask Muns why he and his kin had abandoned Piqua. But Topinbi and Shandó had spread the story of our near-burning on the Strait, and we were surrounded by the attentions of the Eastbranch women, all of whom descended from kin who'd died by burning.

Wedasi and I had seen strangely-clad men moving in the Kekionga cornfields, and Wedasi asked the Eastbranch women if they shared Kekionga with the strangers whose square lodges bounded the fields. Chindiskwe told us the strangers were not permanent settlers, and they were not Scalpers. She said they called themselves Friends and were as peaceful as the Brethren who hovered around villages of Eastbranch survivors.

These Friends had come to Kekionga at the time Gabinya had brought Belle-may from the Strait. Topinbi was in Kekionga when they arrived, and he smoked with the Friends and accepted their gifts. Atsimet also accepted their gifts; Willwell and Belle-may embraced them as kinsmen. The Friends said they had come to show the Kekiongans how to plant corn. Chindiskwe was wary and Aptegizhek was openly hostile. Aptegizhek told the strange men they would be wiser to take their peaceful ways to their own people, who were destroying more corn than the Friends could help grow in Kekionga. But the Friends were as stubborn as raccoons, and they stayed.

The first spring after the Friends' arrival, Chindiskwe was taken up with her and Atsimet's newborn daughter Mabuzkwe, and she watched the strangers from her lodge. She could see that the Friends were hurting the land, that they understood nothing about cornplanting. She could also see that they treated the land as a hated enemy; they fought with the land until sweat poured from their bodies, as if they were torturing themselves to show their endurance, day after day from sunrise to nightfall. The corn that grew on their stunted plants was unpalatable, there wasn't enough of it to store, and that winter the women almost starved while they waited for their hunters to return. The sly Will-well was happy with the arrangement, because the hunters took their furs to him in exchange for his eastern corn and flour.

The following spring Chindiskwe and the other women reclaimed their fields, but the Friends wouldn't budge, wouldn't listen to the women. The Friends said women should only spin and weave, men should learn to grow corn. Of course not a single man joined the Friends in the fields. The men, hunters, carriers or traders, knew that the Friends hated the land, did not regard the land as the corn's mother, did not see themselves as midwives, and had no love for the child. The men knew that the Friends, like all other Scalpers, considered cornplanting a chore and a punishment and that among the Invaders, the planting was done by penitents, prisoners and slaves. The men had no desire to be turned into slaves; they avoided the fields as they would have avoided a plague.

That spring, Will-well and the armed Scalpers of the fort had kept the women from their own fields. But now that her sister Mekinges and the other Piqua refugees were in Kekionga, Chindiskwe and the women were determined to reclaim their fields and force the Friends to heed Aptegizhek's advice.

When at last we were alone with Muns, Wedasi and I plied him with questions, anxious to learn what had driven his kin to their Kekionga refuge. Muns reminded us of things he'd told us on the Strait. The rift in his mother's village began before his uncle Bijiki took Muns to the Strait. It began when Bijiki returned from the east, transformed by eastern sorcery or flattery. Bijiki had no allies in Piqua; even his brother Onimush, Muns's father, was at best a faltering ally; Bijiki's nearest ally was Will-well in distant Kekionga. It was Will-well who let Bijiki know of Misus Bay-con's school on the Strait. Bijiki hoped to make allies of his son and nephew by having them be transformed as he had been. Bijiki was disappointed. The experiences on the Strait made both Muns and Pezhki more hostile to the Scalpers than they'd been before. As soon as he returned to Piqua, Muns renewed his friendship with Wapmimi's and Shawanokwe's children Ojejok and Omemekwe, both of whom dreamt of the day when the war to oust the Invaders would resume.

Bijiki's wife Shabomekwe had joined her sister in Wapmimi's lodge when Bijiki had taken her older son away, and Bijiki's two sons, Pezhki and Kezhek, stayed close to their mother and befriended Ojejok despite Bijiki's attempts to confine them to his store. Bijiki remained as isolated as he'd been before, and when Will-well invited him to attend a council on the Wabash, Bijiki went accompanied only by his brother Onimush and two Eastbranch men whose sole interest was to drink; Mekinges called these men rumsacks.

Bijiki and his small caravan returned to Piqua laden with gifts and soon after the gifts were distributed, the plague broke out in Piqua. One of every four villagers died of it, among them Pezhki's mother Shabomekwe. Numerous Southbranch kin, including Shawanokwe and Wapmimi, said the plague arrived with Bijiki's gifts. Confrontations began.

Muns was relieved when several of his schoolmates from the Strait, including my sister, passed through Piqua with Likét in search of the Beautiful Valley's burial mounds. Muns escaped from the tension by guiding the young women to the mounds. When he returned to Piqua, Muns found yet greater tension.

Guests had arrived from the Wabash. One of these guests was Wapmimi's brother Gizes, Sigenak's oldest son; another, Shawanokwe's and dead Shabomokwe's cousin, a man considered a prophet on the Wabash. These men came with two aims: to warn their kin of the Invaders' gifts, and to confront the sorcerers who had accepted gifts for ceding Wabash lands to the

Scalpers. Everyone in Piqua except Bijiki and Onimush was bitter about the Invaders' gifts, and all joined the guests in a dance of renewal. The dancers became frenzied; Ojejok and other youths painted themselves; gifts were burned; and finally the two rumsacks who had accompanied Bijiki to the Wabash were carried to the center, both dead.

Piqua ceased to be a village and became a battlefield. Ojejok and other Southbranch youths, Wapmimi and his brother as well as Shawanokwe and Omemekwe, confronted Bijiki and Onimush with weapons in hand. Mekinges and other Eastbranch women stepped between the enraged hunters and their cowed prey. Muns joined the women. His mother railed against her Southbranch cousins for adding the murder of kin to the plague's ravages. The hostile parties moved apart, far apart. Half the villagers moved toward Mekinges's sister's lodge in Kekionga, the other half toward Sigenak's on the Wabash. Bijiki forced Pezhki and Kezhek to accompany him to Kekionga; both of his sons had wanted to accompany their dead mother's people to Kithepekanu on the Wabash.

Wedasi was spellbound. The war he'd dreamt of all his life was about to begin; I could already see its first armed clashes in his eyes. He wanted to know more about his uncle Gizes and about Shawanokwe's prophetic cousin. Muns was surprised. He'd thought Wedasi was as peaceful as I. He told us no one in Kekionga knew more about the Wabash gathering than our uncle Aptegizhek, and he promptly led us into the next door lodge.

Katabwe had told me so much about her brother's son that I felt like no stranger in Aptegizhek's lodge. I felt as if I'd always known the man who'd traveled to Bison Prairie to be at her burial. His face was as she'd described it, sad and pensive, and he wore a bandana to hide his head wound. He knew me as soon as I entered, not from my face, but from the bundle I carried; my grandfather had shared its contents with him before the battle by the fallen trees; I felt the bundle should be his, not mine. As if he'd guessed my thought, he told me to guard the bundle well, and he showed me a scroll similar to the crumbling one in my bundle; he told me his scroll spoke of the wanderings of the eastern kin who had adopted his mother Lókaskwe.

Aptegizhek answered Wedasi's questions, but not in ways that pleased Wedasi. Aptegizhek went back to the days that followed the battle by the fallen trees, the days when the

Kekionga warriors gathered in Piqua to make peace with the Scalpers. The peace was a sham, a humiliation ceremony, and all knew it. When the ceremony ended, the traitor Well-well added insult to injury by inviting Sigenak to travel to the east to meet the so-called Father of the United Scalpers. To everyone's surprise, Sigenak accepted the invitation. Will-well and others took Sigenak to the major centers of Witchburners, Cheaters and Slavers. They showed Sigenak immense lodges made of stone and wide paths teeming with wheeled carriages, and they showed him man-made caves where human beings devoted the waking part of their lives to making firesticks.

Sigenak was taken east to be intimidated; he was to return to his people with the message that the Scalpers were rocks and we were mere dust. Sigenak may have been surprised by the extent of the enslavement of human beings to mindless tasks, but he wasn't intimidated. He began to speak out.

He told the Invaders that human beings weren't made to languish in prisons of their own making. He told them no animals crippled and stunted its own kind, and no animal embarked on a war against any and all creatures that were unlike itself. He warned them that any who embarked on such a war would turn the very elements against them and would gag on the air, be poisoned by the water and be swallowed up by earth. Crowds gathered whenever Sigenak spoke.

Sigenak saw them listen, but he soon realized they didn't hear, couldn't hear, because something inside them was twisted. Many introduced themselves to him, offered themselves to him. Some wanted to teach Sigenak's people the ways of peace, others wanted to teach cornplanting, yet others wanted to teach clothmaking or lodgebuilding. Themselves without a center or a direction, they all offered to guide others. And when Sigenak returned to his village on the Wabash, all these well-meaning people followed him, passing through Kekionga on their way.

Aptegizhek delayed all of them long enough to urge them to turn around and to spread their teaching among people who needed to be taught. But they heard Aptegizhek the same way they'd heard Sigenak: not at all. First came the Brethren, descendants of the well-meaning preachers among whom Aptegizhek spent his childhood. The Brethren joined the descendants of their earlier converts in Piqua. Then came the Friends, with their ears even further clogged and their vision yet more narrow than their predecessors. The Friends stayed in Kekionga and deprived the women of their fields.

After the Friends came people who called themselves Dancers. These people saw and heard more than their predecessors; they knew Earth as the mother of all life, and not as an object that could be fenced off for a bottle of rum; they also knew that living was enjoyment, that all living beings danced, and that those who ceased to dance no longer lived. But although their ears were less stopped up than those of the Friends and Brethren, the Dancers did not hear Aptegizhek tell them that the lifeless ones, the ones who needed the Dancers, were in the east. The Dancers insisted on going west, to Kithepekanu on the Wabash.

Sigenak's son Gizes danced with them, and Shawanokwe's cousin danced with them. It was during one of their dances that Shawanokwe's cousin had his vision: he saw his own Southbranch kin and all their cousins and uncles and nephews reconstitute themselves and regain their strength, with no further need for the Invaders' rum or cloth or firesticks. He became a prophet. His hearing unclogged and his vision broadened, but like the Dancers who inspired him, he heard only a little more and saw only a little further than before.

Before his vision he had placed his mark on innumerable leaves so as to drown himself in the Invaders' whiskey; after his vision he cast his eyes on the nearest kinsman who marked leaves for the sake of whiskey, he squinted and called his kinsman a sorcerer, and his followers promptly sent the sorcerer to the land of the dead.

Wedasi insisted that it was necessary to dispatch the sorcerers who gave away our lands, and that our uncles Gizes and Wapmimi had done well to join the prophet on the Wabash.

Aptegizhek reminded Wedasi that our uncle Topinbi was the first among the treaty signers, that we descended from treaty signers Mota and Ozagi; he warned Wedasi not to leap from Wiske to Digowin; he asked if Wedasi dreamt of helping reconstitute villages, or of depopulating them.

Chapter 8.

Obenabi's guides

Obenabi's dream

Wedasi was on edge during the rest of our journey to Bison Prairie. He wanted to think well of our uncles on the Wabash, he wanted reasons to join them. If I had spoken he wouldn't have listened, but I didn't speak. I reached back to Katabwe's songs and stories. I touched the objects in my bundle, I mused on my first dreams, but I found no guidance; I didn't know who I was or where to go. I had nothing to tell Wedasi.
 I stopped pondering Aptegizhek's words as soon as I saw the familiar riverbanks, the fruit trees I had run among with Nashkowatak and Mimikwe, at last the lodges of the Firekeepers' village. But our welcome was disappointing. Wedasi and I were not expected. Only the gifts from the Strait were expected, and only Burr-net and Cakima, Chebansi and Nesoki

were on the landingplace. Our father thought we had returned so as to join Chebansi in the store. We were surprised that Chebansi had reinstalled himself in the store.

Chebansi was well, and he was unchanged. He greeted us with self-justifications. After hearing the story of our binding and our escape, he told us the Bison Prairie store was nothing like the stores on the Strait. Burr-net did not greatly differ from Jay-may, but Burr-net didn't run his store; Cakima ran it, and had run it since Burr-net's arrival. Chebansi had told all this to Wedasi earlier. Now he told us that our Bison Prairie kin depended on the gifts in the store, that the Bison Prairie store had powerful enemies, and that Chebansi had pledged himself to help our mother face those enemies. He said the greater enemy was a Cheater and Slaver called Kin-sic, who had installed himself among Kittihawa's kin on the Lakebottom. The lesser enemy was a Redcoat called Petty-song who had opened a store—Burr-net called it a pigsty—on the outskirts of Bison Prairie itself. The aim of each was to draw the flow of gifts and furs away from Bison Prairie, and they were succeeding. Topinbi's last fur load was so meager that he hesitated to carry it to the Strait.

Chebansi and Cakima knew that Kin-sic was the greedier and more powerful, but Burr-net's lifelong hatred of Redcoats blinded him. Burr-net had made common cause with the Lakebottom Slaver and had sent Shandó to join Kin-sic in pouring out barrels of rum that had arrived for Petty-song, on the pretext that the United Scalpers prohibited the rum trade. Shandó hadn't accompanied Topinbi's caravan to the Strait because he'd feared retribution by the Redcoat's allies, and the fear of Redcoats was driving Burr-net into ever closer association with Kin-sic. Meanwhile, Kin-sic was destroying our Lakebottom kin. He had already driven Sandypoint away; he was embroiling our uncles in ugly wars.

Wedasi and I brought our brother nothing. Chebansi's war was not the war Wedasi dreamt of fighting, and I couldn't even follow Chebansi's account. We sought out Bindizeosekwe in the cornfield; her daughters Koyoshkwe, pockmarked, and Wamoshkeshekwe, the marks not visible, were already grown enough to help with the planting. Wedasi joined Bindizeosekwe in waiting for Meteya to return from the hunt; Wedasi hoped Meteya would bring news of his brothers Gizes and Wapmimi, news that differed from Aptegizhek's.

I joined my cousin Mimikwe and waited for Shabeni to return. Mimikwe's son Komenoteya, born shortly before I left Bison Prairie, already used a bow, and hit marks more often than I did. I offered the boy songs and stories but Komenoteya, like Wedasi, had no ear for them. As Mimikwe watched the boy play with his arrows, I saw that she was repelled by his desire to be a warrior.

I thanked Mimikwe for sending our grandmother's bundle to me six springs earlier. Mimikwe thanked me for returning to her lodge. She embraced me, looked deeply into my eyes, and thanked me again. She had feared that I would return with a strange haze in my eyes, but I hadn't; the inner joy, and also the sadness, was still in them; she'd heard Katabwe say that I had our great-grandmother Menoko's eyes. Mimikwe took me to her bed and made my seed flow into her, dementing me with a joy I hadn't yet felt. She told me she yearned for my gratitude, because only I could ease the pain she felt whenever she thought of our grandmother.

Disfigured by the smallpox as a small child, Mimikwe had grown up fearing plagues, wars and war dances. She'd clung to her mother Nogewi to protect her from Katabwe and the other painted dancers; she'd grown up hating and fearing the warrior Katabwe. Mimikwe and her brother Nesoki had both seen their mother disembowelled by the Scalpers who had spread terror and desolation in the Wabash valley during their wars against Kekionga, and Mimikwe had blamed Katabwe's war dances for the Scalpers' rage.

Mimikwe went on hating Katabwe after my birth, when both returned to Bison Prairie. Convinced that Katabwe wanted to turn all her grandsons into warriors, Mimikwe had joined Nashkowatak in his dream lodge to keep the war spirits from visiting him. She had married Shabeni only after he'd convinced her that he had renounced the ways of the warrior, and then she'd tried to discourage Shabeni from counciling with Katabwe. Mimikwe had even been glad of my separation from my warlike grandmother. And not once had she counciled with Katabwe until our grandmother lay dying. Only then did Mimikwe learn that Katabwe had not been singing of war in Bison Prairie, but of regeneration, of a peaceful regeneration such as Mimikwe would have liked to see. Mimikwe learned this from Katabwe's instructions about the bundle, from Katabwe's fondness for the grandson least disposed to kill, the grandson least likely to become a warrior or even a hunter.

A vine grew alongside Mimikwe's lodge, on the spot where Katabwe's lodge had stood. When Mimikwe joined Bindizeosekwe in the cornfield, I sat down next to the vine, as if to council with it; I spread the objects of my bundle between myself and the foot of the vine. And I remembered the day when I first arrived on that spot. Although my memories were given to me only later, I remembered as if I had myself been aware of my first arrival in Bison Prairie, as if the memories were my own.

I knew that my grandmother had come to Bison Prairie to be close to me and her other grandchildren, to get away from the battlefields. My birth cries were drowned out by news of the death of my grandfather, yet she heard my cries as she listened to Sigenak tell of Nanikibi's burial, as she listened to Nawak tell of his father Batí's death at the very gate of the ally's fort. She accepted Nanikibi's bundle from Sigenak, but she did not intend to carry that bundle to any more wars. She intended to pass the bundle to a grandchild whose joy came from the sight of waving cornstalks and bounding deer, from the songs and ceremonies of dancing kin, and not from the fall of enemies in a battlefield. She had taken part in several victories, had seen numerous fields filled with fallen enemies and fallen kin, yet the Beautiful Valley was invaded and Kekionga was destroyed. The deaths were of no avail; they had not stopped the invasion.

Katabwe had become convinced that there were other ways, and that these ways could be found in the bundle she inherited from Nanikibi, on the scrolls Aptegizhek had inherited from Oashi, on the belts Isadór had inherited from Miní, even on the arrowhead Wakaya had inherited from his Redearth grandmother Wagoshkwe. And Katabwe intended to show these other ways to her grandchildren, to her son's Mimikwe and Nesoki and to her daughter's Nashkowatak, Chebansi, Wedasi, Wabnokwe and the newborn. She would try to give her grandchildren what she had failed to give her children.

She knew that her reasons for returning to Bison Prairie were not Topinbi's or Cakima's reasons. She knew that Topinbi and Cakima were not returning to renew a Firekeepers' village that had dispersed to distant battlefields, but to renew a fur trade that had been disrupted by the wars. She knew she'd have to face Cakima's hostility, just as she knew she'd have to face

Mimikwe's fear, Nashkowatak's disorientation, Chebansi's indifference. But she also knew she wouldn't be alone. Sigenak's oldest son Meteya shared her rejection of the warrior's ways and joined the westbound caravan, and Meteya didn't stir from Bison Prairie when his father sent word of the enemy's desire to hold a peace council with the warriors. Topinbi rushed away to that council, as did his cousin Winámek from the Lakebottom, even though neither of them had fought against the Beautiful Valley's invaders.

Topinbi's and Winámek's return from the peace council coincided with my naming ceremony. Aptegizhek came with them, as well as several canoes laden with gifts. Topinbi and Cakima invited kin from nearby villages; Aptegizhek's sisters came from the Lakebottom, as well as Bindizeosekwe.

Three fires were lit, and at their center stood Topinbi and Cakima, the hosts, the Firekeepers who were ready to give out the gifts as compensation for the deaths on the field of fallen trees. But before any gifts were given out, Aptegizhek spoke to the gathering; he began by saying Meteya had been wise to stay away from the council with the enemy, which had not been a peace council but a humiliation ceremony.

Aptegizhek had helped Sigenak spread word of the council because he, like Sigenak and most of the other warriors, had thought that the Invaders meant peace when they said peace. Aptegizhek still thought this when Will-well and Gabinya and the other interpreters repeated the Invaders' words to those who hadn't learned the enemy's language. The agreement was unambiguous: both armies were to disband, Scalper Vain's uniformed soldiers as well as the Kekionga council's warriors, and it was on this agreement that the warriors placed their marks. The first to sign was Sigenak, followed by his sons Gizes, Wapmimi and Wakaya. Nawak signed eagerly. Atsimet signed, and his brother Mowhawa was ready to sign. At that point, to everyone's amazement, people who had not fought against Vain or against any of the Scalpers' armies, began to sign. Topinbi rose to put his mark on the agreement, as did his cousin Winámek as well as Winámek's son-in-law Lashás. Mowhawa asked the interpreters what this meant. He was told that anyone who renounced his claims on the Beautiful Valley was welcome to sign and would be rewarded with a mound of gifts. Mowhawa backed away from the Scalpers' leaf, as did Isadór and Aptegizhek and others who had not yet signed.

It was suddenly clear that the Scalpers used the word peace to mean capitulation, that the warriors agreed to disband while the Scalpers agreed to nothing, that one side severed itself from home and kin while the other poured out beads and whiskey. Aptegizhek who needed no interpreter, told the Scalpers to take their gifts to the other side of the Sunrise Mountains, to feed them to the hungry and the greedy, and to hold a peace council there. Wakaya, who had already signed, covered himself from head to foot with excrement to communicate that the Piqua gathering had not been a peace council but a ceremony of humiliation. Of the signers, only Nawak felt bound by the leaf he marked. The others would wait and see. Mowhawa and Gizes headed to the Wabash, Atsimet to Kekionga, Wakaya and Isadór to the Strait. And when all had turned their backs, Topinbi and his Lakebottom cousin loaded themselves up with beads, cloth and whiskey and set out to compensate their kin with death gifts.

Topinbi and Cakima had been distributing the gifts while Aptegizhek spoke. Katabwe rose, gathered up her share of the gifts and dropped it all into the fire; her kinswoman Shutaha had similarly disposed of earlier gifts.

Only then did Katabwe turn to me. She heard the name thrown at me by Topinbi, the name Wiske, which Topinbi purposely pronounced whiskey, and she threw that name back to Topinbi, saying that one whiskey was enough. She named me Obenabi, one who looks back. Aptegizhek heartily approved, but his sister Shecogosikwe, who had accepted Topinbi's whiskey, asked why Katabwe and Aptegizhek were so concerned to heal earth's wounds; she said the trees, the animals and earth herself seemed altogether unconcerned, almost indifferent. Aptegizhek's younger sister Wagoshkwe didn't share this indifference, and she urged her brother to remain in Bison Prairie or on the Lakebottom. Aptegizhek chose to return to the broken center between the Peninsula and the Valley, to all-but-abandoned Kekionga.

Katabwe burned the gifts, like ancient Shutaha. Also like Shutaha, she bent to the ground to remove obstacles and encumbrances, so that young shoots could grow straight and strong. But after Aptegizhek departed to Kekionga and his younger sister returned to the Lakebottom, Katabwe was alone in her task. Sigenak's oldest son Meteya stayed on in Bison Prairie; he too had renounced the warrior's ways. But he had grown in distant Cahokia among Prairiekin who no longer dreamt, and he stayed out of Katabwe's lodge; he had no ear for her songs. Bindizeosekwe moved in with Meteya after the other visitors dispersed; she had grown with Shecogosikwe among the Lakebottom's crosswearers, and she too remained a stranger to Katabwe. Katabwe had so much to give; she'd thought her grandchildren would be willing to receive it. She was disappointed. I had a name, but I was still too young to grasp her songs. My cousin Nesoki and my brother Chebansi stayed with Cakima in my father's store. Mimikwe shared Katabwe's lodge but hated her grandmother, never once forgetting that Katabwe had lived most of her life as a warrior, and that warriors had disembowelled Mimikwe's mother.

Mimikwe didn't let her hatred show; she cooked for Katabwe, she made sandals and clothes, she warmed the lodge; but when Katabwe sang, Mimikwe joined Bindizeosekwe in the cornfield or the furdressing lodge. Wabnokwe was too young to grasp what she heard, and Wedasi listened to Katabwe only when she told of the wars.

Nashkowatak was the only grandchild who wanted to hear Katabwe. He sought her out. On the Strait, someone had called him a halfbreed and the name rankled in his memory. Unlike Wabnokwe, who grew up proud of belonging to both the Invaders' and the Firekeepers' worlds, Nashkowatak grew up ashamed, thinking he belonged to neither. He wanted Katabwe to show him who he was. He listened to Katabwe's songs and stories, especially those about Pyerwá and Nizokwe and Lókaskwe who were not born among the Peninsulakin but became kin by adoption. And he begged Katabwe to build him a fasting lodge. But as he prepared to dream, Nashkowatak saw himself through the eyes of his friends on the Strait and thought himself ridiculous. He wanted to go to the woods for a reason his friends would have approved, even admired. So he told his cousin Mimikwe he was afraid, and begged her to follow him to the fasting lodge. Unknown to all, Nesoki followed his sister.

Nesoki's mind had been twisted by crosswearers, especially by his aunt Mikenokwe. He ran to Burr-net and Cakima to tell them Nashkowatak was committing carnal sin with Mimikwe. The lovers returned at different times and by separate paths, to no avail; all the villagers greeted them with knowing smiles— all except Katabwe, who was annoyed by her grandson's misuse of his fasting lodge, and Burr-net, who was enraged by his son's carnal sin and incest. Burr-net would not have his sons revert to the old ways; he resolved to send his oldest sons back to the Strait and to keep his younger three away from the old witch, as he called Katabwe. And Cakima, who lit the three fires only to attract furs to her store, treated her mother as a disease, and was determined to sever Katabwe from everyone in Bison Prairie.

Shabeni was one of the hunters who took furs to Cakima. Topinbi hastily befriended the newcomer, seeing in him a fellow-carrier, perhaps even a successor more capable than Shandó, who didn't inspire the trust of hunters. Shabeni had fought with Wakaya and Nanikibi on the field of fallen trees, but he'd grown among carriers, and Topinbi assumed Shabeni was attached to the carriers' ways. Shabeni's eyes often rested on Mimikwe, and Topinbi, during his brief stays in Bison Prairie, removed obstacles that blocked Shabeni's view. Cakima foresaw a union between Bison Prairie's Firekeepers and Leaning Tree carriers, a union that was bound to bring more furs to Burr-net's store. Cakima also thought her mother would be left all alone.

Cakima chose the naming ceremony for Meteya's and Bindi-zeosekwe's firstborn as the occasion for the event. While Katabwe was occupied with the naming, Shabeni was to offer Mimikwe his marriage gift. Topinbi brought loads of gifts. Cakima invited neighboring kin. Three fires were lit. But despite all the scheming and arranging, the intentions went unrealized.

Cakima had underestimated Katabwe, and Topinbi had misjudged Shabeni. Katabwe knew what was intended; she also knew that most of the gathered kin remembered the old ceremonies. Katabwe named Koyoshkwe but didn't stop with the naming. She began the dance associated with the three fires her daughter had so conveniently lit. Katabwe started the renewal ceremony familiar to guests as well as hosts, and she'd done some arranging of her own: her grandson Nashkowatak turned up as long-eared Wiske wearing trader Burr-net's clothes. By the time the expulsion of the hare began, Cakima had fled to her trader's lodge, stung and humiliated. But the sequel upset Nashkowatak's hopes as well. He had hoped Mimikwe would join in the chase of the hare, and would go on chasing him deep into the woods. Mimikwe didn't take part in the chase. Shabeni had sworn to her that he had renounced the warrior's ways, and Mimikwe had already accepted this oath as Shabeni's marriage gift. And then Shabeni did what no one had expected. Instead of pulling Mimikwe to his lodge, he installed himself in Katabwe's. Topinbi had been wrong. Shabeni wasn't attached to the carriers' ways. He had sought to be close to Mimikwe so as to be close to Katabwe. He wanted to be the grandson of the woman who had been a warrior and had renounced war, and he wanted to learn the songs his people had forgotten.

Nashkowatak felt betrayed—by Mimikwe, by Katabwe, by everyone in Bison Prairie. Blinded by desire, jealousy and self-pity, he convinced himself that Mimikwe had chosen the proven warrior, and Nashkowatak resolved to prove himself a greater warrior, on the Strait, in the enemy's army.

My brothers and my sister let themselves be pulled out of Bison Prairie. But Katabwe wasn't left alone. In Shabeni she had a new grandson, more attentive to her than any of her other grandchildren. And by then I was old enough to find my way to my grandmother's lodge.

From the very first time I sat at Katabwe's hearth, I was transported out of myself by the stories she told: I flew over the places I hadn't visited, mingled with beings different from any I had seen. Katabwe's songs and stories carried me to worlds untouched by fur traders, firesticks and plagues. She showed me bones of ancestors who had lived in the water and the feather of an ancestor who had flown; she unrolled the scroll that spoke of the wanderings of Kichigami's first human beings, the common ancestors of all Peninsulakin. I hungered for her songs; I even begged her to build me a dream lodge. But I never asked her for the Firekeepers' bundle; I never even asked to touch the otterskin pouch or any of its contents. I took it for granted that if she ever died, the bundle would be given to self-assured Shabeni, who knew why he listened to her songs, who understood everything she told him. When I begged her for a fasting lodge, she thought me too young. But when I returned to tell her my interrupted dream, she no longer thought me too young. My dream was a sign—for her, not for me.

And then she died, suddenly, right after Shabeni and I left her. She surely died when I was in Mishilimakina, the very moment when I rose from the ground with the power of my own wings and flew above the men carrying corpses out of canoes. She had told me my first dream had not been interrupted by

Topinbi; it had been complete. I hadn't believed her, and it was long before I realized that in my first dream Katabwe-Binesikwe the birdwoman had flown me over a world-to-come. In Mishilimakina, from the moment she died, I had to rise from the ground on my own.

I was still sitting face to face with the vine that had grown on Katabwe's lodge site, my bundle's contents spread out between me and the vine, when Mimikwe returned from the field. The whole day had passed. Mimikwe called me to her lodge, and I panicked. I packed up the contents of the bundle and backed away from Mimikwe's lodge. Mimikwe had sent me the Firekeepers' bundle. Mimikwe had said my eyes were my great-grandmother Menoko's eyes. Mimikwe wanted to be near the bearer of the Firekeepers' bundle, and she wanted the bearer to be as gentle as Menoko. But I suddenly remembered what Katabwe had told me about her mother. Menoko had been gentle and weak, too weak to bear the burden of sorrow and suffering that fell on her, and one night she'd left her burden behind and walked out of her village to die.

I moved to the youth lodge where Shandó was staying, and I waited for Shabeni to return from the hunt. I didn't like Shandó, and I didn't befriend the other youths in the lodge. I moved in with them to escape from Mimikwe. She knew what I had inherited from my grandmother. She knew that the Firekeepers' bundle was not a carrier's nor a trader's nor a hunter's nor a warrior's bundle. And I knew—I had known since the moment Mimikwe had told me I had Menoko's eyes—that I didn't want the Firekeepers' bundle. My two dreams, the dream of the desolate village and the dream of the men carrying corpses, had already told me what the bundle would face. If Katabwe too had recognized Menoko's eyes in mine, why had she given me such a burden?

Meteya returned from the hunt, and Wedasi plied him with questions about Sigenak, Gizes and Wapmimi, but Meteya had heard neither from his father nor from his brothers. Meteya said Shabeni knew more about the prophet's gathering on the Wabash, and Wedasi grew as impatient for Shabeni's return as I was.

At last Shabeni returned, bringing bison meat from the other side of the Long River. I let Wedasi get to him first. I saw and heard a Shabeni who was strange to me, a Shabeni I had briefly glimpsed in the Leaning Tree village. My heart ached for Mimikwe; I knew why she had reached for me. Shabeni had reverted to a warrior. The companions with whom he had hunted the bison were Redearth kin who expected much from the Wabash gathering; they expected a great war against the Scalpers and all their allies. Wedasi at last heard the news he'd been waiting to hear since he was a child.

I reminded Shabeni of his promise to build me a dream lodge. Seven winters had passed since he'd made that promise. He remembered. He became the Shabeni I had known. He told me I had grown old enough to build my own lodge, but if it pleased me, he would live up to his promise.

He led me deep into the forest, far from any villages, to a hill at the turn of a stream. We sang Katabwe's songs as we climbed to the top. At a spot overlooking the stream, we propped a small rain shelter on a lone birch, with the birch's trunk serving as lodge pole. When we were done, I gave him Katabwe's bundle. I told him he too had heard my grandmother's songs, and I had found the bundle too heavy to carry. Shabeni sat down beside me. He wasn't angry at me for having enticed him far into the forest so as to give him my burden. He told me he had even less strength to carry the bundle than I did. He had heard Katabwe—too well, he said. She had renounced the way of the warrior and seen another way. He, Shabeni, had also renounced the way of the warrior but he was a warrior again. He had heard Katabwe, but he hadn't seen what she had seen. He gently set the bundle down next to me, and left.

A storm broke out. The birds who are said to make thunder flapped their wings furiously and drenched the forest with their tears. Leaning on the birch that held up my lodge, I stared at a veined rock perched on the hillside between me and the stream. I thought I saw the stream's level rising, but when I looked again, I saw that it wasn't the stream rising, but the banks themselves turning into water. Looking further, I saw that all the land was becoming water, and then the bases of the trees. Wolves, bears, rabbits and deer were scampering up the hillside toward me as tree trunks turned to water and then the upper branches. The animals huddled around me on a tiny island in the middle of a rising lake. A huge eagle landed next to the birch and flattened its wing against the ground, inviting me to its back. I gratefully patted the feathers nearest me, but stayed where I was, huddling with the forest's refugees while the water kept on rising.

Topinbi and Shabeni

The sky was clear and the sun was high when I heard a familiar voice and crawled out of my flimsy lodge. Looking down toward the peaceful stream, I noticed that there was no veined rock halfway down the hillside, and the ground I crawled on was dry. Meteya and Wedasi helped me to the small hearth where they were warming soup with hot stones. Wedasi had been doing all the talking. Shabeni hadn't come for me.

My brother asked what I had seen, and I told my dream. Uncle Meteya looked at me as he listened. His face told me he doubted that one needed to go to a fasting lodge to see what I had seen; but he said nothing. Wedasi didn't hold his thoughts back. He understood my dream perfectly. The rising flood was the invasion. The eagle was the prophet in Kithepekanu on the Wabash. Listening to Wedasi, I was relieved that Shabeni hadn't come for me, that I was spared from hearing Wedasi's words come out of Shabeni's mouth.

Bindizeosekwe as well as Mimikwe offered to lodge me while I recovered my strength. I preferred to return to the youth lodge, not so as to be with Shandó, but so as to avoid Mimikwe. Shandó talked endlessly of a Redcoat conspiracy to ruin Burr-net and other peaceful traders. He told me that only he and Burr-net were aware of the danger; that everyone else was blind; that neither Cakima nor Chebansi took the conspiracy seriously; and that Wedasi and Shabeni were preparing to join the Redcoats. Shandó left me no peace, but at least he expected nothing from me.

Shabeni stayed away from me; he had told me all he was going to tell me. Mimikwe came to see me. She didn't ask to hear my dream. She told me she knew Shabeni was going to leave her. I kept silent, but I couldn't stop my tears from flowing. I knew that I too was going to leave Bison Prairie. Mimikwe's mere presence made me panic. I knew she had expectations in me, our grandmother's expectations. If even Shabeni couldn't live up to those expectations, how could I?

I was almost well when Topinbi came to see me. Mimikwe's father couldn't have been more unlike his daughter. He laughed, reminded me he had once named me Whiskey, and called me a drunkard. He said my fondness for dreams was similar to his fondness for whiskey, and he recommended whiskey as less of an ordeal. He had grown in the Lakebottom lodge of Katwyn and Nagmo, amidst crosses and furs, among kin who had replaced dream fasts with drinking feasts. Topinbi asked to hear my dream. He laughed at me again and told me he saw the world turn watery whenever he drank enough. He said my dream's eagle was none other than Wiske the gift-carrier, and advised me to do as he had done: hop on and ride.

My strength at last returned, I visited Shabeni to ask him about the conspiracy Shandó feared. Chebansi reminded me that our father had originally come to Bison Prairie so as to escape from the Redcoats, and that Shandó's father had been a Redcoat who had let Namakwe's Batí die at a closed gate, and who had then abandoned Shandó's mother. To Burr-net and Shandó, Redcoat, conspirator and enemy were interchangeable words. Chebansi said there really was a crisis, but this was caused by a Slaver called Kin-sic who was embroiling our Lakebottom uncles Winámek and Nangisi in wars against distant Redearth kin. This Kin-sic had injured our other Lakebottom kin, Kittihawa's children, and driven them to make common cause with the Redearth kin. Fratricidal war could break out. Chebansi and Cakima knew, and Scalper Kin-sic also knew, that such a war would destroy Bison Prairie's fur trade.

When Topinbi prepared to go to the Lakebottom on a peace mission, I begged to go with him, even though I had no interest in Bison Prairie's fur trade or in Scalper Kin-sic or in Shandó's conspiracy. Meteya and Bindizeosekwe also accompanied the peacemaker.

Sandypoint's lodge on the Lakebottom was as large as Piér's on the Strait, with two stories and glass windows. Colorful representations of the lakeshore and the woods, said to have been painted by Sandypoint, hung on all the walls. It was said that Sandypoint himself had been driven away from the Lakebottom by the threats of Slaver Kin-sic, and that this Slaver had also forced the trader Jambatí to abandon Sandypoint's daughter Suzán. I remembered the feats of Reverend Bay-con in the north, and assumed this Kin-sic possessed similar powers.

Bindizeosekwe found her sister Meshewokwe, and together they gathered the Lakebottom's Firekeepers in Sandypoint's lodge. Kin I had never seen greeted me as they entered the great hall. Bindizeosekwe's cousin Topash arrived with Shecogosikwe and their fiery daughter Menashi. I couldn't keep myself from staring at the greenstone pendant that dangled from Shecogosikwe's neck. Little Menashi, at most seven springs old, caught me staring and told me that if I thought her mother beautiful, I would swoon when I saw Suzán. I thought Menashi mean-spirited. The carrier Lalím came with his son Naganwatek. The boy's mother, Wagoshkwe, was in the upper part of the lodge with Suzán, nursing bedridden Kittihawa. The Southbranch woman Wewasikwe came with her newborn daughter Miskokwe. Everyone was there except the people Topinbi had hoped to find there.

Nangisi and Winámek had already departed to the Long River, where they would raid Redearth kin and kidnap children. And when they had left for their raid, Sandypoint's son Kegon had rushed to the Wabash, to Kithepekanu, to join the allies of the Redearth kin. The war Topinbi had wanted to avert was already under way. Topash said he had tried to talk sense to the hotheads, and that Kegon was reasonable, but that Nangisi used his reason only to serve his greed. His mission a failure, Topinbi asked Lalím to bring out a barrel of whiskey to celebrate the good intentions.

I found my way to Kittihawa's room and tiptoed in. The old woman looked like a skeleton. She smiled and motioned me to approach her. She knew who I was; my sister had grown in her lodge. Her hand traced a cross and rested on my hair, blessing me. I wondered if Kittihawa's blessing would help me more than my bundle or my dreams; I doubted it.

As soon as I saw Suzán's face and body, my eyes shifted to her daughter Olalí. I didn't want to be caught staring again, as I would have if Menashi hadn't caught me earlier. I had heard talk of beautiful women but had never before seen one. Suzán's daughter wasn't beautiful; Olalí was older than Menashi, but seemed less self-assured, almost fearful, and not in the least mischievous.

The third woman in the room was Wagoshkwe, Aptegizhek's youngest sister. She was nursing Kittihawa with herbs and songs. She asked if I too was concerned with beaver furs. I told her no, I was concerned with the meaning of my dreams. She had me tell my dream. When I was done, she fixed her fierce eyes on me. She said my dream's eagle was the Invader who had murdered her father Oashi before she was born and her mother Lókaskwe during the Tuscarawas massacre.

She said I had done well to stay on the hillside with my kin. She told me Redearth warriors were waking from a long sleep, but when they rose, they would oust the murderers from the Lakes. I later learned it was Wagoshkwe who sent Suzán's brother Kegon to the Wabash for armed allies. She had no use for the peace Topinbi came seeking. She wanted to live up to her namesake, Kittihawa's mother, my great-grandmother, the Redearth woman Wagoshkwe, as different from my other great-grandmother, Menoko, as fire from water.

The Lakebottom wasn't the place where I wanted to be, and since no peace council could be held, we soon returned to Bison Prairie. That winter I accompanied the silent Meteya whenever Wedasi didn't. Meteya's hunts were more like walks in the woods. He shot only when he knew the meat was expected. Most of the time he tracked animals to their lodges and observed their ways. I could have stayed with Meteya longer, but the melting snows brought a flood of strange guests to Bison Prairie.

Meteya and I heard the war cries long before we could see the lodges. As we approached our village, we saw that the councilground was alive with the motion of dancing warriors. Winámek and other Lakebottom carriers were tied to a post near the central fire. Among the warriors circling the captives, Meteya recognized his brother Wapmimi; I guessed that the youth my age was Shawanokwe's and Wapmimi's son Ojejok, Muns's friend. I moved around the outer circle, trying to learn what had happened. Burr-net and Shandó were in the store, behind barred doors, convinced that the Redcoat conspiracy had arrived. Mimikwe had run to Bindizeosekwe's lodge the moment the warriors had arrived and was determined to stay there until they left.

I learned, mainly from Topinbi, that the raiding party led by his cousins Nangisi and Winámek had been surprised at the Long River. Instead of finding villages with absent hunters, they had found an army. The Redearth warriors had been warned, probably by a messenger sent by Wagoshkwe. Nangisi and several companions had been killed. Winámek and his warriors had retreated all the way back to the Lakebottom.

To avenge his brother's death, Winámek and his warriors had begun to prepare another war party, armed with weapons given to him by Slaver Kin-sic and the Scalpers in the Lakebottom fort. But Winámek had barely begun to recruit warriors when he'd been surrounded and disarmed.

Kittihawa's son Kegon had returned to the Lakebottom accompanied by Prairie and Redearth warriors from the Wabash, including my uncle Wapmimi and my cousin Ojejok. The Wabash warriors had wanted to put a quick end to Winámek's force, but Topash and other Lakebottom Firekeepers had intervened and stopped the outbreak of a fratricidal war. The Scalpers in the fort would have embroiled themselves in such a war, and the Lakebottom village would have been destroyed.

Wagoshkwe wanted such a war because she was sure the Redearth warriors would defeat the Scalpers and their allies. Slaver Kin-sic wanted such a war because he was sure his side would win. But Wapmimi and his companions had followed the advice of Topash and the Firekeepers; they had brought the captives to Bison Prairie, where there was no encampment of armed Scalpers, and where Winámek had no armed allies.

The Wabash warriors had already resolved to kill Winámek. But as soon as the dancing ended and the counciling began, Topinbi and Cakima made their voices heard. Both pleaded for the life of their Lakebottom cousin. Both insisted that Winámek was a kinsman, that the real enemies were the Scalpers and Slavers who armed Winámek and embroiled him in their wars. Most of the Wabash warriors were hostile to these words; there was even talk of including Topinbi among the captives.

Meteya rose and placed himself alongside Topinbi and Cakima. Meteya was immediately joined by Bindizeosekwe, by her Lakebottom cousin Topash, by Chebansi, by almost all of Bison Prairie's Firekeepers, but not by Shabeni or Wedasi. At this point a formidable-looking Redearth warrior called Macataimeshekiakak rose. He said he knew perfectly well who the real enemy was. He enumerated the kin he had lost to that enemy. He said he was preparing to confront the real enemy. But the handful of Scalpers on the Lakebottom were no more than the enemy's nose, and he wouldn't pinch the nose until he was ready to defend himself from the whole body. In order to get ready, he had to remove poisonous snakes from his path. But he had no intention of depriving any villagers of a kinsman as dear to them as Winámek appeared to be.

Wapmimi and others promptly released Winámek. Topinbi assured the warriors that he would urge his cousin to go gift-gathering, something Winámek did well. Winámek himself consented.

Cakima thanked her cousin Wapmimi for having helped to prevent war on the Lakebottom. His task accomplished, Wapmimi could now return to the Wabash or wherever else his prophet sent him. Cakima's voice grew harsh. She said Winámek had been condemned to die because he had kidnapped children of Redearth kin. Cakima was the grandchild of a Redearth woman. So were most of Bison Prairie's Firekeepers. And Wapmimi was kidnapping her kin, even her own son. Did the Wabash prophet condone Wapmimi's doing the very thing for which Winámek had been so righteously condemned?

I knew that Wapmimi had wanted to recruit Meteya. The brothers hadn't been together since before my birth, and Wapmimi couldn't have known how far Meteya had moved from the warrior's path. But Cakima's words were the last words spoken at the council. The warriors prepared to leave Bison Prairie, accompanied by Wedasi and Shabeni. When I parted with Wedasi, I could feel his joy; he had at last found his life's dream. Shabeni wasn't joyful; he pretended not to notice me. His son Komenoteya begged to accompany him, and Shabeni pretended to be all taken up convincing his son to stay in Bison Prairie so as to defend his mother and her kin. When he could put me off no longer, Shabeni told me he had renounced war when he had thought that the world described in Katabwe's songs had broken up into little pieces. He'd thought there was nothing to defend. But now, he said, the pieces seemed to be reconstituting.

Wapmimi insisted that Topinbi and Winámek set out on their gift-giving mission at the same moment as the warriors left Bison Prairie. I asked Topinbi to take me along.

Chebansi came running as soon as he learned of my decision. He gave me talking leaves from Burr-net to Jay-may. He begged me to do whatever Jay-may asked of me. The hostilities had all but ruined Burr-net's fur supply. Burr-net was sending me instead of furs.

I was relieved to leave Bison Prairie before abandoned Mimikwe emerged from Bindizeosekwe's lodge, before she walked toward me and looked into my eyes; the strap that supported the bundle she'd sent me would have cut through my body.

I felt like a migratory bird, returning and leaving again, passing the same familiar places on the way. Topinbi's and Winámek's destination was not the Strait, but Kekionga; Topinbi would go to the Strait later, and only to deliver me.

Winámek had so readily consented to leave with Topinbi because he'd known that the Scalpers would be offering gifts in Kekionga. This would be the first humiliation ceremony since the one held at Piqua the spring I was named. The countless uniformed Scalpers turned the Kekionga councilground into a forest of dwarfed blue-branched trees. Wagons loaded with gifts stood in every clearing. Eastbranch and Southbranch kin, many of them drunk, sat before the entrances of their lodges, waiting for the ceremony to begin.

Aptegizhek, Muns and Pezhki didn't come to the landingplace; I had to seek them out. They had not expected me to arrive in Kekionga in such company, nor for such an occasion. Pezhki showed his hostility by turning his back and walking away from me. Muns looked at me expectantly, like Mimikwe, as if expecting to hear me describe the wonders I intended to accomplish.

Aptegizhek spoke to me, but only to describe to me the purpose of the Kekionga gathering, and to warn me of its consequences. He said all the rumsacks who had ever marked the Invaders' leaves were in Kekionga; the Scalpers called each of them a chief. The headman of the Scalpers' western armies, a landgrabber called Will-hen-garrison, was also present. Our kinsmen Bijiki and Onimush as well as Sigenak's false son Will-well were the landgrabber's interpreters. This Will-hen-garrison wanted the rumsacks to give their consent to the invasion of the Beautiful Valley, the Wabash Valley below Kithepekanu, and the Strait's shore. Such claims were an open declaration of war, since none of the people living in those places had ever consented to let Scalpers invade their lands, and they wouldn't consent after Topinbi and his likes were given wagonloads of whiskey and beads. Will-well fueled the fire by insisting that anyone who resisted the Scalpers' claims was an enemy agent, an ally of the Redcoats.

I could have told Aptegizhek that nothing I said could stop Topinbi from signing the leaf, and nothing I did could avert the consequences of the signing. But all I wanted to tell him was that I didn't want Katabwe's bundle, that he was its rightful heir. But I kept silent. I knew he wouldn't accept the bundle because he didn't consider himself a Firekeeper. And I knew he shared Katabwe's expectations in me.

The only person who was friendly to me was Pezhki's brother Kezhek, Bijiki's younger son. He had been too young to befriend me earlier, had no expectations, and so didn't feel betrayed by me. He told me the Friends who had come to teach Kekionga's men to plant had abandoned their task; I could see that their neat square lodges no longer bounded the fields. But the land had not been reclaimed by the women. Will-well had called on the armed Scalpers in the fort to occupy the fields, forcing Chindiskwe, Mekinges and other Eastbranch women to seek a distant clearing for their beans and corn. And then Will-well, as well as Kezhek's father Bijiki and Muns's father Onimush, had accepted large gifts from newly arrived Invaders and had invited the newcomers to settle on the Kekionga fields. I began to understand the coldness of Muns and Pezhki toward me; they must have thought that I, Winámek's traveling companion, had set out on the path their fathers were following. I didn't know how to tell Muns my real reasons for being there: that I was fleeing from myself, that I had found no path to follow.

I didn't ask Topinbi about the gifts he'd accepted for bowing to the Scalpers' claims to other people's lands. I tried not to hear the jokes he made about the kin closest to me, whom he considered shortsighted and backward-looking; I was relieved that at least he didn't speak of them as enemy agents.

On the Strait, Topinbi led me directly to Piér's house, which had become Jay-may's house since Piér's death. I delivered Burr-net's messages. Topinbi counciled with Jay-may, Witnags and other Cheaters. The council must have been stormy; everyone seemed on edge after it ended. Topinbi gathered a few trinkets and rushed away, eager to rejoin his cousin and his gift-load in Kekionga. Jay-may harangued me about Burr-net's unpaid debts, but the incomprehension and indifference he saw on my face eventually silenced him. He led me to a small room next door to my sister's, threw a trader's costume on the bed and told me to dress like a proper human being and trim my hair. He called me Jeik, Jeik Burr-net; he referred to my sister as Rebekah and my oldest brother as Jeims. He would find me a place on the Strait, he said, but it would not be in his store or anywhere near it.

Chebansi had begged me to do what the Cheater wanted, and I put on the clothes of a proper human being, a Jeik Burr-net. But I kept my hair.

Wabnokwe came to my room at sunset. She kissed me and called me little brother. She looked into my eyes. Unlike

Mimikwe, my sister wasn't attracted by what she saw. She seemed repelled. Noticing the bulge caused by the bundle under my shirt, she asked me, with undisguised contempt, why I didn't put that thing away. She didn't ask about our Bison Prairie kin. She grew enthusiastic when she told me of the school in which she and Beth spent their days. My incomprehension silenced her. I understood that she and Beth were doing to younger children what Misus Bay-con had tried to do to us. I couldn't understand Wabnokwe's enthusiasm. At dinner I saw Margít's three children. The boy, Jim-may, born during the fire, was four. His older sisters didn't welcome me. The oldest, Anna-may, stared past me as if I wasn't there. Greta-may was openly hostile, as if I had injured her.

Margít was recovering from a stillbirth and a painful illness. She had only seen me two or three times, yet she greeted me as if I were a long-absent son. She, too, saw something in my eyes; she said it was music. She told me I should have stayed on the Strait and learned to play an instrument. I told her I wished I had.

Margít told me of the changes I had noticed since my arrival. Downstream from Jay-may's house was the house built by Wit-nags, and further down was an enclosure in which Wit-nags kept horses. The horse-enclosure occupied the space I remembered as the councilground, bounded by the burial hill, the bubbling springs and the forest. There was not a trace of the Firekeepers' village! The kin among whom Wedasi and I had lodged were gone. Nawak, Pamoko and Mikenokwe had been pushed southward, toward the swamp.

When I left Margít, I walked toward the Strait's shore. My ancestors—Shutaha, Miogwewe, Katabwe—had felt empowered to confront such changes. I felt helpless. I had an urge to hurl my bundle into the water and watch it sink.

Jay-may delayed finding a place for me, and I wasn't anxious to occupy the place he found. I wandered along the Strait's shore, away from the rebuilt village, toward the kin who now lodged downstream. But I didn't go far from the house. Margít was right. I was attracted to music the way a moth is drawn to a flame. And there was always music at the house.

As Margít grew stronger, she went to her music box, her piano, and filled the house with melodies and rhythms that made me feel I was floating on clouds. When Margít wasn't playing, her daughter Anna-may was creating an altogether different world of sound with the little instrument across which she pulled a bow. And in the evenings, when Wabnokwe played her bowed instrument, larger than Anna-may's and deeper in tone, I wanted to be nowhere except where I was, entranced by the sound.

I learned from Wabnokwe that Belle-may and Gabinya lived on the Strait with their daughter Anabel, together with Gabinya's first wife Nebeshkwe and her daughter Sukwe—and that Jay-may was on good terms with his daughter's husband. Gabinya pretended his first wife was a servant, even a slave, and the pretence was accepted by all the traders to whom Gabinya carried Kekionga's furs.

I heard talk of marriages and talk of betrayals. Margít's younger sister Moník had betrayed my brother Nashkowatak and would soon marry one of the Strait's largest landholders. Sofí's daughter Felice had betrayed her northern kin and would soon marry a crosswearer called Dasisí, whom I remembered from Misus Bay-con's school. Felice's uncle Jambatí, the man who had abandoned Sandypoint's daughter Suzán and her daughter Olalí on the Lakebottom, would soon marry a crosswearing daughter of Lemond. My school friends Sharlokwe, Rina and their two brothers were no longer on the Strait; their father Lesotér had been pushed out at the time the Firekeepers' village had been pushed out. Marikwe, Lesotér and their children had moved to Mishilimakina, to Agibicocona and the northern Rootkin. Sofí and Felice had gone north with them, but Felice had returned to the Strait with her uncle Jambatí.

I remembered Felice as the snob who had avoided her cousins and been ashamed of her mother. On an impulse, I entered the camp of square lodges to seek her out. I thought, or rather hoped, that she had returned to the Strait for reasons similar to mine. She welcomed me with a smile, a pretty smile; maybe it was my memory of her smile that led me to seek her out. Felice thought I had returned for reasons similar to hers. I grew dizzy listening to her reasons.

Felice told me her grandfather Soli-man originated among people who had been despised and persecuted since the world began, people who had never been crosswearers. Soli-man had crossed the Ocean to be among people who did not despise him. He had found acceptance among the crosswearers, Redcoats and Scalpers of Mishilimakina, not because these Invaders had ceased to despise Soli-man's people, but only because they despised other people more.

Agibicocona's people, the redskinned people of the forests, were the despised people here, they were the persecuted people. Soli-man's son, Will Soli-man, had pretended not to know this, and had married Agibicocona. Soli-man's daughter Sofí had known this, but had persisted in befriending Agibicocona. When Felice was in Misus Bay-con's school, Rev-rend Bay-con was in Mishilimakina, explaining to Felice's uncles Will Soli-man and Jambatí that blackskinned and redskinned people were despicable, unfit for marriages; he severed Will Soli-man from Agibicocona and Jambatí from Suzán.

But Sofí had not forgotten why her father had crossed the Ocean; she persisted in befriending the despised. She came to the Strait with Agibicocona's cousin Lesotér and together they hounded Rev-rend and Misus Bay-con out of Kichigami. When the Scalpers at last succeeded in ridding themselves of Lesotér, Sofí pulled Felice back to Mishilimakina, not to Will Soli-man's proper new family, but to Agibicocona's redskins. But Felice had been told too much about grandfather Soli-man's persecuted people, and she had no desire to be one of them. Felice abandoned her mother and her aunt. She returned to the Strait with her uncle. She resolved to marry the crosswearer Dasisí; she wanted to live among people who were not despised.

I would go on remembering Felice's smile, but not as something pretty. I ran from her house. I stayed away from her marriage celebration, and I also stayed away from the other celebrations. I listened to music, usually alongside little Jim-may, Margít's youngest. And I waited. I heard Wabnokwe and Margít talk of my brother Nashkowatak's desperation after Moník's marriage, of my uncle Isadór's attempts to undo the effects of the treaty signed by Topinbi in Kekionga. I heard that Wakaya's son Poposi, together with other Turtleyouths, raided the enclosure in which Wit-nags penned horses. At last I heard Jay-may tell me he had found a place for me. I was to crop my hair and join Nashkowatak in the uniformed militia.

I removed the proper clothes, folded them and left them on the bed. With my hair untrimmed, and wearing my own clothes, I tiptoed to a corner of the music room. Jim-may was listening. Anna-may and Margít's twin Josét were bowing smaller instruments, Wabnokwe a larger one. Margít looked up from her piano and saw me; she surely knew I couldn't join the uniformed armed men; I didn't have Felice's smile. When the music ended I left the house and rushed into the night.

Song of Udatonte

I headed downstream toward the Firekeepers among whom Wedasi and I had lodged, the kin among whom I was born. Bursts of thunder replaced the music I had been hearing. I thought of the kin I intended to join. I remembered that Pamoko, Mikenokwe and Nawak had trusted the Scalper who had promised to protect the village and its burial grounds, the forest and its trees; their trust in the Scalper's promise had angered their cousins and split the village and driven the Turtlefolk downstream. The Scalper's pledge had been as solid as ice in spring, and the Firekeepers themselves had been driven downstream, though not as far down as the Turtlefolk. The inhabitants of Tiosa Rondion, the people of three fires, were far from home, in two separate villages, hostile to one another, and threatened where they were. I thought of my dream. A flood had driven the forest's inhabitants to seek refuge on top of a hill. A bird had landed on the hilltop and offered... What had the bird offered? Had it offered to raise all of us out of the flood? Had it offered to show me a way out? Or had the bird offered to take me away from my kin, away from the persecuted and the despised?

It began to pour, the path became muddy, and I couldn't go on. Leaning against the trunk of a large tree, I listened to the storm, but Felice's words were repeated by the thunder and the rain and when I looked into the dark, I saw Felice's smile. The forest was drowning and I was trying to reach the kin on top of my dream's hill.

The storm passed with the night, and I went on. The path hardened under the warming sun. I heard galloping behind me and I hid. Three horsemen rode past me; I recognized one of them as Nawak's falsetongued kinsman, Wit-nags; the other two were armed militiamen. I walked on following their tracks. I didn't go far before I heard voices. I stopped. Slowly and noiselessly I made my way to a lookout. Before me, in a small clearing, were four men, Wit-nags and his armed companions and a man I hadn't seen before, a hunter with a bow. Wit-nags was holding the reins of two horses and shouting; the mounted militiamen were pointing their rifles at the hunter. Hearing a slight movement, I turned and saw a young woman at the edge of the clearing, only partially hidden from me by the intervening bushes and trees; she held a dead rabbit in one hand, a rifle in the other. She hadn't seen me; her attention was fixed on the men in the clearing. The militiamen started to tie up the hunter; Wit-nags was about to mount his horse, ready to pull the other horse in tow. The woman raised her rifle and pointed it at Wit-nags. If she shot Wit-nags, the militiamen would find and kill her and probably me as well. I walked into the clearing.

Wit-nags recognized me; he identified me to the armed men as Jeik Burr-net and he told them I would soon be one of them. I said I was heading toward my uncle's village and he urged me to hurry on so as not to delay his recovery of his stolen horse. I stayed put. I had heard how he had acquired the horses in his pen: he and his armed men stopped lone hunters and demanded deeds or titles which no hunters possessed. Wit-nags was lying to me: he wasn't recovering a stolen horse; he was stealing the hunter's horse. I lied too; I told him I knew the hunter, and I also knew the horse to be this hunter's horse. Wit-nags' face turned red. He told the militiamen to arrest me. One of the armed men grabbed me. Suddenly all eyes turned toward a rustle at the edge of the clearing; all saw the barrel of a rifle protuding from a bush. Wit-nags and the militiamen froze, stiffened by fear. They were no longer three against one; they thought they were surrounded. They hastily let go of me, of the hunter and of his horse. Wit-nags mounted, and the three galloped away, in the direction from which they had come. I untied the hunter. He put his hands on my shoulders in gratitude. Then he mounted and galloped away in the opposite direction, without once glancing toward the hidden rifle or the person behind it.

I had never been so close to death. I stumbled toward the nearest tree and fell at its foot, shaking with fear. I didn't hear the woman stir until she stood in front of me. Her face didn't show a trace of fear. She sat down alongside me. I saw that she was only a girl, a spring or two younger than I. Her long black hair hung behind her in a single braid. Her dark eyes were fierce and mischievous, reminding me of my Lakebottom cousin Menashi. She sat silently and examined me. At last she said Udatonte, pointing to herself. How I wished I had learned the language of the Turtlefolk! I pointed to myself and spoke my name. She then pointed in the direction in which Wit-nags had fled, and looked at me questioningly. With words and motions, I assured her I was not one of them. Seeming satisfied, she placed her hand on mine.

At that moment, the whole forest became silent, the Strait's water stopped flowing, the birds stood motionless in the sky. A shiver passed through my whole body, a shiver I had felt before, in fasting lodges and when listening to Margít's music. I knew that my dream spirit had at last come to me, and her name was Udatonte.

She broke my trance by rushing off to her hidingplace to gather up her animal and her rifle. I begged her to stay with me. She spoke and she motioned, but all I understood was the word she said in my language, the word night. She ran across the clearing into the woods, toward the Strait's shore. I heard the swish of a canoe sliding into the water. She was gone.

I remained seated, staring at the empty spot next to me, imagining she was still there. Tears of joy ran down my cheeks, then tears of sadness. I longed for Udatonte's return more than I had longed for a dream spirit in my fasting lodges.

At dusk I crossed the clearing and looked for the path she'd followed toward her canoe. I stumbled toward a tree at the water's edge as fog settled over the Strait. I leaned against a large rock below the tree's branch and waited. I knew she would come for me, but I didn't know if she'd come when the night began or ended, if she'd come on this night or another night. After what seemed like eternity, I heard a sound in the fog. I told myself it was the Strait's water licking the shore, but when I heard it again I knew it was the swish of a paddle. The rhythm of my heart quickened as I made out the outline of a canoe gliding to shore. A hand groped toward mine and pulled me into the vessel. I knelt behind the silent figure and noticed the rifle and a second paddle. I took up the paddle.

We headed downstream, but the fog kept me from seeing either the Strait's islands or the outlines of the villages on shore. When I thought we had reached the Strait's mouth, where Kichigami's waters flow into the Lake of the vanished Ehryes, she headed the canoe westward, into the Peninsula. By the dim light of a fogged sunrise, I saw that we were paddling up a narrow stream, midway between its tree-lined banks. The fog rose, exposing a cloudless blue sky. Udatonte's black braid fell along her back to the bottom of the canoe, reminding me of the black wing extended toward me in my dream.

The rhythm of the paddles stroking the stream's waters made me think of the large bird's flapping wings. I knew I had accepted my dream spirit's offered refuge; I also knew I was not, like Felice, fleeing from my kin. I was fleeing from Felice and her justifications, from Wabnokwe and her accommodations, from Chebansi and his store, from Nashkowatak and his militia, from Wedasi and his warriors. I saw that they were all following one path, and I was on another. I was carrying ancient Wedasi's bundle toward the center of the Peninsula, and my guide was ancient Yahatase's kinswoman. I was filled with gratitude for the clear day, for the beautiful girl who led me, for the bundle my grandmother had sent to me.

We paddled by day and we paddled by moonlit night. Far inland, where the stream was narrow and its water shallow, Udatonte banked the canoe and covered it with brush. She led me to a small clearing, gathering twigs along the way. From her gestures I understood that this clearing was not our final destination.

After starting a small fire, she pulled tobacco out of the pouch and placed it on the flames, singing as the smoke rose to the sky. While we shared dry meat and winter crackers from her pouch, she translated some words of her songs into the language of Rootkin. I understood only parts of stories I had heard before: the world rested on a turtle's back, where furry swimmers had deposited the earth they had scooped up from below the water. I also understood that the Turtleland had been located in the Morningland across the Strait, so that Udatonte's people were distantly related to ancient Yahatase. I knew that the Morningland's Turtlefolk had dispersed in several directions, some fleeing with Yahatase to Greenbay, others to the Peninsula's upper and lower straits, yet others to the lands of the Ehryes. I understood that Udatonte's people had fled to Sandusky Bay on the southern shore of the Lake of the Ehryes.

We didn't rest in the clearing. Udatonte extinguished the fire, dispersed the ashes and removed every trace of our presence. In her eyes and on her moist lips I saw the same joy, the same anticipation that filled my whole body with energy. She took my hand and gently pulled me away from the stream and clearing into a thick forest. She followed a trail I couldn't distinguish, a trail made by wolves or bears or wolverines; she seemed familiar with every bent twig. We came to a more recognizable trail, a deer trail, and her hand clasped mine ever more tightly.

The trail ended at the shore of a lake surrounded by grass. Deer played among sparse trees on green ground that surrounded water as still and blue as the sky. Udatonte led me toward a large tree; together we watched the sun descend into the lake. She removed her clothes and set them alongside her rifle and her pouch at the foot of the tree. I removed my clothes and followed her to the water's edge. Udatonte glided into the darkening water like a canoe pushing off shore. I stood at the water's edge, alone with the full moon. I dipped my head to sip the clear water; and Udatonte's face rose up; her lips met mine. My hand reached for hers, but she vanished in a splash. I slowly crawled into the water after her.

Udatonte and I emerged from the water hand in hand and floated to a grass bed by the root of our tree. Our hands ran over each other's bodies like squirrels along a tree's branches, from ears to neck to thighs and legs and back again. We embraced and rolled over each other like playful cubs, our arms and legs intertwined like vines. At last we lost ourselves in each other, becoming a single body pulsating in rhythm with our beating hearts. We were one with each other, with the grass and the forest and the lake and the moon. I dissolved as I had dissolved once before, in Mimikwe's lodge in Bison Prairie. I didn't remember Mimikwe then; I didn't remember anything. I felt myself turning to water, water that held a dream in its depth the way the lake held the moon's reflection. I was free of my body, free of all limits; I was all and nothing, full and empty; I was a sky that had turned itself to rain. In that moment of eternity Udatonte and I, Turtlefolk and Rootkin, earth and sky married.

We relaxed, embraced again and relaxed again until sleep overwhelmed desire. In a dream I returned to the lake's shore and dipped down to sip the water. A face rose out of the water; its lips kissed mine; as it slipped away I saw that the face belonged to a shell-less turtle with a beaver's head and glistening silvery-grey scales. I woke up terrified and sweating. I found myself in Udatonte's embrace on the grass near the tree's root, our bodies covered by moon-streaks that penetrated through the branches. I slid back into a long dreamless sleep.

We didn't separate and rise from our grass bed until the sun was high. Udatonte knew I had dreamt, and she made me understand that untold dreams fester like unhealing wounds. In the very act of describing the scaly monster to Udatonte, I realized that I was describing Misus Bay-con and her school, Jay-may and his jail, Burr-net and his store. I was describing something with pent-up desire, something I myself could become, something that lashed out against love and freedom, something that swallowed earth's people and animals while imprisoning earth herself in picketed enclosures.

We built a fire, which I enlarged with twigs and fallen wood while Udatonte darted into the forest like a deer. She returned with a skirtfull of roots and berries. After placing stones on the fire, she dug a hole in the ground, lined and sealed it with leaves, and filled it with lakewater. Bringing the berries and crushed roots to a boil with the heated stones, Udatonte prepared our wedding feast. And all the while she sang in her melodious language of a woman who fell through a hole in the sky, of the twins she bore on the turtle's back.

Counciling with each other around our cooking fire on the grass between our tree and the blue lake, we shared songs and stories. I sang the songs Katabwe taught me as I showed Udatonte the contents of my bundle. I sang of ancestors who lived in the water and of ancestors who flew like spirits of birds. I sang of Kichigami before the coming of the plagues, and of the powers of the shell to bring the dead back to life. For the first time in my life, I understood the meaning of the fishbones, the feather, the shell and the scrolls that lodged in my bundle.

Udatonte took a sharp stone, cut a lock from her black braid, and offered me the lock. Between songs, she told me about herself and her people. Until her ninth spring, she thought the world's center was a longhouse in Sandusky, a lodge whose occupants kept the ways of ancient Turtlefolk and shunned the crosses, the whiskey, the beads and the firesticks that cluttered the lodges of their neighbors. From the longhouse grandmother and from her mother, she learned planting ceremonies, healing songs, and the secrets of herbs and roots; from her mother's brother, she learned to track animals.

During her ninth spring, her world was shattered. There were guests in the Sandusky longhouses, numerous girls of Udatonte's age led by two blackrobed women and one man, a kinsman of the Turtlefolk. The guests were fearful; they thought armed men had followed them to Sandusky, and they embarked and fled during the dark of night.

The paddles of the fleeing guests were barely beyond hearing when a band of pioneers stormed into the Sandusky village, their eyes blazing and their mouths twisted with pent-up desire. Not finding the girls they were seeking, the pioneers lunged into the longhouses, emptying the bullets in their rifles and the liquids in their groins into the bodies of the villagers. By the time the Turtlewarriors rallied and removed the Invaders, Udatonte's longhouse, the first one attacked, was a tomb; only the old woman, two aunts and Udatonte were still alive. Udatonte flushed the murderer's juices out of her body, and she broke from the ancient ways. When hunters set out from a neighboring longhouse, she accompanied them, learned to use a rifle and acquired one of her own. She became the meat bringer of her broken longhouse and she rarely parted with her rifle.

No intruders marred our joy at the Grasslake. Our only guests were the deer who played among the sparse trees surrounding the blue water, and the squirrels who ran on the branches of the tree by our marriage bed.

After helping scatter the ashes of our fires, I gratefully gave an offering of tobacco to the spirit of the lake. With Udatonte's hairlock in my bundle, I was overwhelmed with sadness as I looked for the last time at our grass bed, our tree and the blue water. Returning along the same path, I recognized some of the plants, trees and branches that guided us to the hidingplace of Udatonte's canoe. The downstream paddling took no effort, and before long we left the stream's mouth, approached the Isle of White Trees and banked our canoe across from the isle, on the shore of the Strait's Turtlefolk, in Karontaen. We were in the village of Isadór and Wakaya, the village of the Turtlefolk who had left Tiosa Rondion ten springs earlier.

Our arrival wasn't noticed. All the longhouses seemed empty; their inhabitants were gathered in the councilground, around a single fire. I saw Isadór and Wakaya on opposite sides of the fire. Udatonte left me on the councilground and ran to her lodge. I circled the gathering until I recognized one of the painted warriors as Wakaya's son Poposi; I hadn't seen him since he'd been a little boy. Poposi must have known I understood little of what I heard, and at intervals he whispered to me in the language of Rootkin. I learned that Poposi's and my uncles, Wapmimi and Mowhawa, had come to Karontaen with sad news: the village of Kithepekanu on the Wabash had been destroyed by an army of Scalpers. Sigenak had been killed. Wapmimi's daughter Omemekwe and wife Shawanokwe had been killed.

I asked Poposi about my brother Wedasi, about Shabeni, but he knew no more. He told me Wapmimi had urged Wakaya to prepare to avenge their father's death, and Wakaya had been ready. Most of Karontaen's youth had been ready. Only Isadór and the longhouse grandmothers hadn't been ready. Even now, Poposi told me angrily, when the Prairie warriors had forged the greatest alliance since the days of the Kekionga council, Isadór was still insisting that Karontaen's warriors remove their paint and lay down their weapons, insisting on neutrality, as if there were room for a neutral between a hunter and his prey.

Poposi's angry words sickened me. I stumbled out of the circle toward the edge of the woods. The news of the deaths on the Wabash and of the split among Karontaen's Turtlefolk made my head spin. Udatonte found me and led me to a longhouse which stood apart from all the others. The lodge was full of people; none of its occupants were attending the council. I soon learned that I was among Turtlefolk who had come to Karontaen from Ehrye's southern shore, refugees who had wanted to get away from councils of war.

The longhouse grandmother, a wrinkled Turtlewoman fluent in the language of Rootkin, took me to a corner of the lodge where other youths had their mats. She told me I was to pretend not to know Udatonte until the day of my adoption ceremony; only then could we reenact our meeting and marriage. The old woman told me Udatonte had expected me to lodge in another corner of the village until my adoption, but hadn't expected to find the Turtlevillage torn by hatreds and war preparations.

From Udatonte's grandmother I learned that the Ehrye refugees shared Wakaya's hatred of the murderous pioneers but had no desire to take part in war councils, because such councils had torn apart their village in Sandusky Bay. The old woman's people had been attacked and slaughtered by pioneers; Udatonte had already given me some understanding of this attack.

The Sandusky Turtlefolk had armed themselves after the attack, they had counciled, and they had sent out messengers in search of allies. The messengers had returned with alliances that quartered the Sandusky village. Some had found allies among Redcoats who wanted to push the pioneers back toward the Sunrise Mountains. Others found allies among Wabash Prairiekin who shared the goal of the Redcoats. Yet others, grandsons of men allied with bluejacketed pioneers in the age of my great-grandfather Mota, found allies among the Bluejackets. Instead of strengthening the Sandusky village, the councils and alliances tore the village apart. Kin had turned against kin.

The old woman had gathered around her all those who abhorred the fratricidal passions and had fled with them to Karontaen, to be with kin who had seemed impervious to such passions. The old woman said that the war councils and alliances led only to the further decimation of Turtlefolk; she was convinced that the Redcoats and Bluejackets and their likes were so violent that, if left alone, they would soon wipe each other out and leave the world to its original inhabitants.

The Karontaen councils went on, but I didn't wander far from the longhouse of the Sandusky refugees. On the day of the ceremony, Isadór and several others joined the celebrants; Wakaya and his kin stayed away. Dancers with grimacing wooden masks, others with animal heads and horns, frightened me with howls and rattles, cut my flesh, passed me over a fire, and at last showered me with a mound of gifts. I understood that I was to take the gifts to Udatonte, who stood at the lodge entrance waiting.

Udatonte and I relaxed in a prepared sweatlodge, bathed in the cold water of the Strait, stuffed ourselves with meat, berries and corn until we thought we'd burst, and entered the longhouse together. I lay down on the soft mat; Udatonte sat alongside me and sang, almost in a whisper, of the twins born to the woman who fell from the sky. When she lay down beside me and our arms and legs intertwined, all the deaths and war councils became a bad dream I could no longer remember.

Separation

I avoided the councilground and the war preparations; I lived in a world apart, a world that consisted of Udatonte and her Sandusky kin. But I didn't live there long. Udatonte's grandmother died, and before her burial ceremony ended, her own longhouse filled with the fratricidal passions from which the old woman had fled. The youth of Udatonte's longhouse joined the youth of other longhouses, painted themselves and sang of war. Heated to boiling point by their own shrieks and leaps, the young warriors then confronted me.

The Turtleyouth who faced me were led by Wakaya's son Poposi and by another whom I recognized as Wapmimi's son Ojejok. I hadn't known that Wapmimi and his son were in Karontaen again. I longed to ask Ojejok how my brother Wedasi was faring, how my cousin Shabeni, where they were. But the youths would hear no questions from me. They only wanted answers. Was I a warrior like my uncles Wakaya, Wapmimi, Gizes, Mowhawa? Or was I a cowardly neutral like Isadór? There was no council, no deliberation, no ceremony. I was to spit out my answer as if I were a rifle spitting out a bullet as soon as the trigger was pressed. The longer I put off answering, the tighter their circle around me. Suddenly the circle broke up; the youths dispersed as soon as they saw Wakaya approach; they knew this was not how he wanted his warriors recruited. Only Ojejok stayed behind, and only long enough to spit on me. I realized that the impatience of the youths had been roused by Ojejok who had lost his sister, mother and grandfather in Kithepekanu.

Udatonte was at my side as soon as the youths dispersed. She had seen the confrontation, but didn't think me a coward for refusing to bow to the young warriors. Udatonte had prepared a food pack, baskets and blankets; she was eager to leave war-torn Karontaen. With her rifle and my bow, with our pouches and bundles, we walked into the woods in search of a camp.

Alone among leaves and birds, we sang to each other of the first beings. Udatonte particularly liked to hear of the ancient Turtlewoman Yahatase who had turned her back on the stone lodges of crosswearers, and of the ancient Firekeeper Wedasi who refused to kill animals with a rifle. When we hunted together, Udatonte insisted that I confine myself to the ceremonies of gratitude and the songs addressed to the rabbits, deer and moose we stalked. I showed Udatonte the herbs and roots my aunt Pamoko had taught me to identify. We knew we were reversing the ways of our kin villages. Udatonte and I told each other we were first beings, we were a new beginning. Neither of us could imagine how near the end was.

While preparing our camp, Udatonte and I rarely separated. We stalked animals together, dried meats and dressed furs together. Only rarely did she leave to hunt by herself. But one morning when I was occupied lighting the fire,

Udatonte noticed fresh moose tracks at the edge of our camp, and she bounded off with her rifle.

I was still feeding my fire when I was surrounded by armed men whose uniforms I recognized as those of the Strait's militia. Leaving the fire burning, the armed men pulled me away from my camp, away from Udatonte. They half pushed and half carried me toward the Strait's shore, into a huge encampment of uniformed men. They threw me into a wooden cage. They handled me with a hatred I couldn't explain to myself; what had I ever done to them? Their treatment of me led me to fear I would be beaten or tortured or scalped, or all three. And I feared that Udatonte would follow the tracks of my captors and find herself surrounded by hundreds of armed Scalpers.

After an eternity of fears, I was released from the cage and pushed toward the camp's headman, who was addressed as Loos-gas. This headman asked how many we were and what weapons we carried, and an interpreter repeated the question. I answered the headman in his own language. Loos-gas slapped my face, called me a lying halfbreed, and repeated the question. Commotion kept me from repeating the same answer. It was announced that one of the militiamen recognized the lying halfbreed as his brother. Soon Nashkowatak was at my side, acknowledging our kinship. Loos-gas repeated his question yet again. But when I again answered that there were only two of us, my bride and I, and that she had been away with the rifle, Loos-gas laughed; soon all the men in the camp were laughing, and Nashkowatak was filled with shame.

Nashkowatak was told to lead his halfbreed brother to a prison upstream while the rest of the army followed Loos-gas downstream. Nashkowatak was given a bundle of messages for the Strait's big men.

My first emotion toward my brother was boundless gratitude, but as soon as we were alone I could think only of Udatonte, and I begged him to let me rejoin or at least find her. Nashkowatak was enraged. He told me he had saved my life twice, first by admitting his relationship to me, then by saying nothing of my desertion from the militia. These were times when deserters were being killed without as much as a hearing. As for my bride, he told me I would have helped her more if I had joined the militia and defended her village from the enemies who were overrunning it. What angered Nashkowatak most of all was having to accompany me, being separated from his armed companions. He had anticipated confronting armed enemies for the first time in his life, and I kept him from his first chance to prove himself a warrior. I wondered if he was still proving himself to his childhood love, his cousin Mimikwe, and if he knew, if he had ever known, that his ambition would only have repelled Mimikwe.

Nashkowatak delivered me as well as some of his messages to the house I had fled from, Jay-may's, and not to the fort. I knew without his telling me that my brother was saving my life for the third time. With my own clothes, with my bundle, with my hair uncropped, I would not have been left alive in the fort.

The whole Strait, particularly the armed men, seemed to be affected by some sort of hysteria. Felice had told me of similar outbreaks of hysteria on the other side of the Ocean; the mere sight of one of the despised provoked desires to torture, to maim, to kill. Even Wabnokwe, my own sister, greeted me with murderous glances. Jay-may wasn't kind, but at least he wasn't hysterical; perhaps the kindly Margít swayed him from his preferred course. Jay-may told me what Nashkowatak had told me, that deserters were shot. But he didn't hand me over to the fort. He had bars installed on the windows of my former room and kept me behind a locked door. I realized that in Jay-may's eyes I was an enemy, a Redcoat, since only an enemy would have run away from his militia.

I tested my strength against the strength of the window bars. I looked for cracks in the wall. I thought only of rejoining Udatonte.

Margít brought me food; she was again big with child. She always left the door ajar. When she was alone in the house with young Jim-may, she invited me to the music room to listen. Jim-may played the small bowed instrument. Margít said he played it almost as well as my aunt Pamoko, whose playing I had never heard. I took the hairlock out of my bundle. The music of the instruments fused with Udatonte's melodies and I was transported to the Grasslake; I could almost feel Udatonte's touch. I was free to run out on the only two people who cared for me, but I could not have carried my bundle, nor could I have faced Udatonte with such a betrayal behind me.

One day I heard angry shouts in the councilroom and recognized the voice of horse-snatcher Wit-nags. Margít later told me that Wit-nags' brother had been killed in a battle near Karontaen, and Wit-nags, like Greta-may, wanted me handed over to the armed men in the fort, as if I had been one of his brother's killers. I wondered who else was killed in the battle near Karontaen, and by whom. Margít was confined to her bed. My sister brought me food but told me nothing of what was happening. One day Jim-may, who had no key, whispered to me through the door. He told me the enemy, the Redcoats, had invaded the Strait and occupied the fort, and not a shot had been fired against them. Jim-may was only repeating what he'd heard; the implications of the event were as impenetrable to him as they were to me.

I learned nothing more until Margít resumed her visits to my room. She showed me her new baby girl, Carrie-may, born on the day of the Redcoat occupation. She told me my cousin Poposi and his companions had once again raided Wit-nags' horse-pen; this time the youths had succeeded in releasing all the horses.

Suddenly I was released. Jay-may unlocked the door and told me I was free to go wherever I pleased. The Redcoats had released some of their prisoners; I was one of the prisoners released by the other side, in exchange. Jay-may asked me to do only one thing before I left, to attend that evening's council and listen carefully to Jay-may's guest. He said what I heard would help me choose my path intelligently.

I stayed for the council. Everyone was in the room, Margít's family as well as Jozét's; Nashkowatak was there. He told me our father, Burr-net, had been killed on the Lakebottom, and that Burr-net's fellow-trader Kin-sic was about to tell us how our father died. Kin-sic and our cousin Shandó had been captured by the Redcoats and taken to the Strait's fort. Jay-may had exchanged Kin-sic's release for mine.

I had never seen the Slaver from the Lakebottom, the man my brother Chebansi and our mother Cakima had feared. A cold chill ran through my body as soon as Kin-sic began to speak. He told of himself, together with Burr-net and other peaceloving traders, being surrounded by a shouting horde of savages. The savages were Redcoat agents; he also called them cannibals. He said Burr-net's own son was among the savages, painted black as night and shouting hellish obscenities. Burr-net tried to calm the demons but only provoked them to greater fury. One of the savages who had an account to settle with Burr-net settled it then and there, by splitting the trader's skull with a tomahawk. This act gave the signal for a general massacre of the peaceloving men in the fort and fur post. Little children were smacked against posts, women were raped while they were scalped, men were shot and skinned. Kin-sic's allies at last arrived from Kekionga, but they arrived too late; they were themselves massacred; their headman was scalped and quartered; the cannibals removed his heart and ate it . . .

Kin-sic grinned as he told of the deaths and tortures. I backed out of the room, stumbled to the Strait's shore, and vomited. What sickened me was Kin-sic's grin, the contempt in his voice. I knew that Kin-sic derived pleasure from telling his tale, and that Jay-may enjoyed hearing it. His every word was a Scalper's knife. I could feel Kin-sic twisting a knife in my chest and grinning while he twisted. I knew that something horrible had happened on the Lakebottom, and I wondered which of my kin had really died, and how.

Margít ran out to look for me. She gave me a food bundle. She knew I would not return to her house. She also knew that Kin-sic's tale was the massacre, his words were the tortures.

I hadn't walked for so long that my strength gave out when I reached the fence of Wit-nags' empty horse-pen. I leaned against a tree by the Strait's shore and fell asleep. I dreamt that I was leaning against a huge rock under the tree's overhanging branch. Fog had settled over the Strait. I heard a sound in the fog, like a swish of a paddle through the water. Through the fog I saw an arm move toward me, a hand reaching for mine. I woke with a start and stared into the dark, looking for the hand, the body, the long black braid. I heard the sound again: the Strait's waters were lapping the shore. Groping for the hairlock in my bundle, I clutched it in my hand and fell asleep again. I heard Udatonte's voice, singing faintly, from far away, and then I heard nothing but the mocking voice of the Slaver becoming ever louder, coming at me from every direction, repeating: the cannibals removed his heart and ate it.

The next day I reached the spot to which the Firekeepers had moved their village across from Turkey Isle. I recognized only the shapes of the abandoned lodges. I had never visited Pamoko, Mikenokwe or Nawak in that village. I looked for signs that might tell me what had happened, where they had gone. My search was cut short. Armed men leapt from behind the lodges and surrounded me. I thought I was reliving the moment of my separation from Udatonte. But I quickly saw that the men surrounding me this time were Southbranch hunters. Their tension left them as soon as I told them I was alone, unarmed, and seeking my bride. They told me the Strait's Firekeepers and Turtlefolk had fled in several directions; they had themselves crossed paths with people fleeing southward, toward Sandusky Bay. I thought it likely that Udatonte would have rejoined her Sandusky kin.

The hunters were on their return voyage to the Beautiful Valley. They told me there were few animals to hunt in the vicinity of their own village; pioneers more numerous than mosquitoes in summer had killed off the animals in some places, destroyed the forest in other places. The Southbranch men said the Sandusky village was not far from their homeward path. They seemed as grateful for my songs and stories as I was for their guidance and protection. I was under the impression that the hunters never slept. Whether we walked or rested, they were continually on the lookout for traps and ambushes, for pioneers or uniformed men armed with long knives, scalping knives or rifles.

My heart ached when I entered the Sandusky village. The Turtlefolk were unfamiliar to me, and they were all crosswearers. The only kin from the Strait were the Firekeepers, among them Mikenokwe and her brother Nawak, as well as Likét's brother José and his wife Rose. I realized that Udatonte would not have stayed in the Sandusky village even if she had returned there. Likét's brother wore a black robe and conducted continual ceremonies in the largest of the longhouses, the crosswearers' lodge.

I remembered that my uncle Nawak had not been a lover of crosses when Wedasi and I had known him, and I asked him if he had been converted. I also asked him if he might know where the Strait's Turtlefolk had gone.

Nawak welcomed me warmly. He was glad to have a bundle-carrying Firekeeper as a companion. He told me he had not been led to Sandusky by his love of crosses, and even his sister Mikenokwe had not come only to be close to crosswearers. The Strait's militia had passed through Nawak's village and had forcefully recruited several Firekeepers, including Dupré. Under cover of night, Dupré fled from his captors, returned to Pamoko and his son Jon Dupré, and the three crossed the Strait to the Morningland, begging Nawak and Mikenokwe to accompany them. Nawak was suspicious of Dupré's destination, and his suspicions were confirmed when he learned that Karontaen's Turtlefolk were crossing to the Morningland to seek the protection of the Redcoats.

Nawak and Mikenokwe had no desire to be protected by Redcoats; they bitterly remembered the type of protection their father Batí had received on the field of fallen trees. But they couldn't stay in their village which was located halfway between the Bluejackets in the Strait's fort and the warriors from the Wabash who were gathering in Karontaen. Nawak learned from Southbranch hunters, the very ones who later accompanied me, that the Strait's Firekeepers would be welcomed in Sandusky. The Sandusky Turtlefolk had dispersed in several directions. Those who rejected the crosswearers' ways had not returned from the Strait; they had crossed to the Morningland. Those who sympathized with the Wabash prophet had left Sandusky to join the prophet's warriors. The only Turtlefolk left in Sandusky were people whose ancestors had been crosswearers since the first Blackrobes arrived in the Morningland, people who had fought alongside northern carriers but never alongside Redcoats or Bluejackets. The Strait's Firekeepers moved to Sandusky to join kindred spirits.

I surmised that Udatonte had either fled by herself further into the Peninsula, perhaps even to the Grasslake, or else had accompanied the Turtlefolk who had crossed to the Morningland. I hoped to join another group of hunters heading toward the Strait. Nawak assured me that I would wait long; he told me the way to the Strait was blocked up by armed men who cluttered every landingplace, traversed every path and clashed at every intersection.

I didn't want to believe Nawak. I kept on waiting for a band of hunters heading northward. I prepared to set out alone, but Nawak convinced me that even if I were able to find my way, I was not a scout and would not be able to avoid the traps and ambushes. The battles raged ever closer to Sandusky, sometimes so close that we could hear the gunshots and smell the smoke.

No hunters moved, either northward or southward. A Turtlewoman gave me a bow and arrows but I had no use for them. The village men stopped venturing out, even in search of squirrels or rabbits. The women didn't go in search of herbs. Soon the women became afraid of going to their cornfields. There was little food to eat, there were no furs to dress. The only activity was the song and prayer in the crosswearers' lodge. The Sandusky village was surrounded by armed men; it became a prison.

Blue-uniformed armed men entered the village. Everyone except me gathered in the crosswearers' lodge to council with the intruders, to ask when this war would end. The council with the Bluejackets was no more appealing to me than the prayers of the crosswearers. I leaned against the wall of Nawak's lodge. Clutching the hairlock, I tried to imagine myself by the edge of the Grasslake listening to Udatonte's song. But all I could hear was the mocking voice of Kin-sic drawling, the cannibals removed her heart and ate it.

Nawak told me the headman of the Bluejackets, Will-hen-garrison himself, had been one of the guests. The headman had promised to protect the Sandusky villagers, but had imposed a heavy condition. The Bluejackets were ready to advance toward the Strait, and they didn't want any warriors to remain behind them. They wanted all warriors—which meant all men and boys except the Blackrobe—to accompany the rearguard of Will-hen-garrison's army. If any of the warriors remained in the village, they would be burned out.

I was eager to return to the Strait, but not in the rearguard of an army of Scalpers, not wearing a blue jacket and trousers. I could have escaped. The Scalpers didn't watch us closely, although they did keep count and others would have had to answer for my absence. I moved with the rearguard, staying close to Nawak. I did want to reach the Strait. I told myself I would escape as soon as I reached a place where I was likely to find my bride. I did not intend to carry the Firekeepers' bundle into another battlefield.

With Nawak's help, I kept my bearings so long as we traversed places familiar to me. I knew we had moved along the Ehrye's western shore toward the mouth of Kekionga's river. We waited to cross on rafts. We crossed at night. The crossing took long, far too long, and when we landed I no longer knew where I was. From the trees, Nawak guessed that we were on the Isle of Birches, the isle that had given refuge to our Tiosa Rondion ancestors during an earlier dispersal. I tried to walk to the shore to listen for the swish of a paddle. I was stopped. I was to stay where I was put. Now our every move was being watched.

I was roused from sleep by men who pushed and pulled me as they shouted incomprehensible instructions, the sense of the shouts being drowned by the general din. Something horrible was about to happen, and all knew it; every face was marked by fear.

I managed to stay by Nawak during another raft crossing, during the walk through woods to a river's edge, and then along the river's bank. On one side of us as on the other were armed men who never let up watching us, ready to kill any who might try to run toward the woods or the river. I sickened and fell but was immediately lifted up and forced to go on. The sun rose ahead of us, and I knew we had been following the Morningland's river inland.

We reached the river's fork. Arrows flew toward us. A bullet grazed Nawak's shirt. We were not in the rearguard at all! The bluejacketed Firekeepers and Turtlefolk and Eastbranch warriors were the front line; no one and nothing stood between us and the bushes from which the bullets and arrows came. Nawak forced me down to the ground, behind a clump of grass. I felt my bow drop from my right arm and suddenly felt a sharp pain.

The main force of Will-hen-garrison's army was behind us, shooting round after round of bullets over our heads toward the bushes. I saw objects floating in the river and turned away when I recognized them as bodies; none of the floating bodies were clothed in red coats. Nawak parted the grass in front of us, and I saw the barrel of a rifle protruding through the bushes. I imagined a long black braid falling on the rifle's handle. I tried to rise, to run toward the bushes, but Nawak kept me down.

There was a short lull, and suddenly the armed men behind us began running past us, shooting into the bushes as they ran. The bushes no longer responded. The people of the lakes and valleys were silent. Instructions and names were shouted all around me, names of the victors, names like Jon-sin, Loos-gas, May-jerk Whip-o, End-sin Tip-tin and Will-hen-garrison. One boasted his belt was full of hair. I could no longer rise. My arm felt as if it were on fire. I vomited and couldn't raise my face out of my own pool.

I knew that Nawak was no longer beside me, that the whole army had run past me, that I was among the dead, alone, in the rearguard. I felt myself dying. Yet I still heard the voices. One with a drawl as thick as Kin-sic's shouted: I'll skin this yaller cheef fur me yunguns. Another shouted, cant ya see sur t'ant no cheef but a yaller skwa—nuthin but a yaller skwa? I heard a slash, like a knife cutting through flesh and bones, and at the end I heard the sound of gushing liquid, the sound of four streams gushing from a source, increasing and diminishing with the rhythm of a heart's beat.

Interlude

Obenabi told all these things to me, Robert Dupré, his nephew, in August of 1851. The last event he described, the war of the Bluejackets against the people of the forests, lakes and valleys, had taken place almost forty years earlier. He had been sitting, leaning against the jailroom wall, talking continuously, barely pausing to eat or sleep. His whole body was drenched with sweat, as was mine. The heat was killing him. The Detroit jailhouse was built in such a way that it intensified the August heat and allowed no relief at night.

While he had spoken, he had seemed to disregard the heat, but when his story was done, he turned from me, vomited and collapsed on the jailroom floor. Two jailers rolled him onto a plank and carried him out. Some days later the jailers came for me. They said my uncle was dying on them, drying up, and the doctors didn't know what to do for him. They took me to the hospital room, which was identical to the jailroom and just as hot. They told me to use witch medicine to keep him alive; they didn't want him to die before the trial. I told them the only medicine he needed was the shade of a tree by the edge of the lake. That suggestion made the jailers and doctors laugh. They pushed me toward him. The room stank of vomit and urine.

I barely recognized my uncle. He was skinny, shrunken; with his eyes closed he looked like a corpse. His arms pressed his bundle to his chest; the jailers or doctors must have tried to take it from him. He heard me approach and opened his eyes, those strange sad eyes that always seemed to be looking elsewhere, seeing things that weren't there. He sat up with strength that seemed to come from somewhere outside his frail body. His hand groped for the strap that supported his bundle. He raised the strap over his head and passed it over mine, after first opening the bundle and removing from it a lock of black hair. His face turned toward mine, but his eyes, although aimed toward mine, were looking at things that were far away. He spoke quickly, as if he feared being cut off before his tale was done.

He started by telling me a dream, as he had the first time, and I again couldn't tell when the dream ended and the events began. To him it was all dream, the things he had actually done as well as those he had dreamt. He told me he had dreamt this dream in the village of the Leaning Tree. I knew he had been in that village twice, the first time as a boy, in 1800, the second time in 1831, the year I was born. He clutched the hairlock as he spoke.

Chapter 9.

Obenabi's second journey

The last council fire

I arrived at the Leaning Tree village with my nephew Mikínak, Wedasi's son. The council Mikínak had wanted to attend was already under way. As soon as we banked our canoe, Mikínak turned his back to me and headed toward the part of the circle where the Redearth warriors sat. I saw Shabeni on the opposite side of the circle and sat down near him.

I listened to one after another Redearth warrior urge the listeners to prepare for war. I listened to the speakers on my side—old Firekeepers, northern Rootkin, Leaning Tree carriers, Shabeni among them—decline the invitation to war, ridicule the Redearth speakers, warn of the prospects of such a war. My head agreed with the councils spoken from my side, but my heart went across the fire to the Redearth warriors.

I stared at the ground; I felt no pride from sitting near Shabeni. I felt like rising, not to speak but to dance, and to scatter shells while dancing. Only my eyes rose; they wandered across the fire toward the Redearth warriors; they came to rest on the face of a woman. The face, framed by long and straight black hair, was terribly familiar. Fierce eyes, lit by the fire and the full moon, appeared to be looking directly into mine. I tried to rise and cross to the other side, but the ground under me started shaking, the people across from me started spinning, the fire crackled and sent bullets and arrows flying over my head. The pain in my arm returned and my strength oozed out of me. I lay on the ground limp, powerless, my face in a pool, drowning. The last thing I heard was a drawling voice asking: Cant ya see sur t'ant no cheef but a yaller skwa—nuthin but a yaller skwa.

When I could hear again, I was sure I was in the land of the dead. I heard speech in every language familiar to me, and in several I had never before heard. Hesitantly opening my eyes, I saw that I was on a blanket-covered floor of an enormous longhouse. The men and women who moved among the corpses were recognizable as Southbranch and Eastbranch kin, as Firekeepers and Turtlefolk. The blankets themselves were covered by what seemed like corpses which were awakening, as I was, and all of them had things to say, either to each other or to those moving among them.

People who must have been Turtlefolk of the eastern Woodlands spoke to Turtlefolk of the Lakes in the language of the Redcoats; Firekeepers from the Strait spoke to Redearth and Plains people in the language of Lemond. Eastbranch kin who lived in Morningland spoke to Southbranch kin from the Beautiful Valley in the completely unintelligible language of the Brethren who had once lodged on the Tuscarawas. I caught familiar words, but their meanings passed me by. The chaos of languages dizzied me. I closed my eyes and tried to shut my ears.

I remembered becoming dizzy from a similar chaos when I was a boy, in Mishilimakina. The din had become rhythmic, like the flapping of wings, and the wings had become my own, enabling me to rise above the din. I began to feel as I had then, like an eagle, but when I began to flap my wings, I cried out from pain. My right arm felt as if it were on fire.

I was aware that someone was sitting on the blanket beside me; I opened my eyes, sure that I would see the northern medicinewoman, Agibicocona. Staring at the sticks tied up with my arm, then at the arrowhead dangling in front of my face, I cried out again. The arrowhead moved away, and I saw the face of the person who wore it. The face wasn't Agibicocona's; it was my uncle Wakaya's. I asked him if he, too, had died on that terrible battlefield by the Morningland River's fork. He looked sad. He told me many of our kin had died on that battlefield. But he said that he and I were alive.

I gradually realized that the people moving among the blankets were healers, and those on the blankets were not awakening corpses but injured and sick women, children and men. I noticed that the healers avoided my blanket; only Wakaya came to me. He told me my arm would recover, but I didn't want to hear about my arm. I wanted to hear about my bride. I begged Wakaya to tell me if Udatonte had returned to Karontaen after my separation from her.

Wakaya told me that Udatonte could not have returned to Karontaen, because the same armed men who had captured me had caused the dispersal of the village. Wakaya had known the Strait's armed men would move against Karontaen; he and his brother Wapmimi and warriors from Kithepekanu had intercepted a messenger and captured talking leaves which spoke of the Bluejackets' intentions.

As soon as he learned that the Strait's armed men were moving downriver, Wakaya rushed to Karontaen to urge the villagers to flee. While I was being captured, Karontaen's Turtlefolk were dispersing in three directions. Some accompanied Wakaya and his family to the Morningland shore, others joined Wapmimi and the Wabash warriors, and the rest went with Isadór to urge the Bluejackets to respect Isadór's peace belts.

By the time Wakaya rejoined Wapmimi and the other warriors, Karontan was a burial ground. The armed Bluejackets had not stopped to council with Isadór about the contents of the ancient peace belts; they had massacred Isadór and his peace party and left the belts in pools of blood. Scouts had carried news of this massacre to Wapmimi and the Wabash warriors, who promptly prepared to ambush the approaching Bluejackets.

It occurred to me that Nashkowatak's having to accompany me upriver while his companions were ambushed had probably saved his life. I remembered the fuss raised by Wit-nags, whose brother was killed in that ambush. Frightened by the ambush, or thinking themselves outnumbered, the Bluejackets on the Strait did not fire a shot when Wakaya, Wapmimi and their allies occupied the Strait's fort. Wapmimi's son Ojejok and Wakaya's Poposi could then raid Wit-nags' horses with impunity. When Wit-nags set out to kill the horse-raiders, Wakaya and his allies imprisoned Wit-nags. Shabeni arrived from the Lakebottom with other prisoners, among them Shandó and Kin-sic.

The Bluejackets had been ousted from all their strongholds on the Great Lakes. Many of the Wabash warriors returned to their villages to hunt. And while the victorious warriors were dispersing, the Bluejackets were gathering a vast revenge-seeking army in the Beautiful Valley. By then I was in Sandusky.

Wakaya told me he and his companions could have held on to the strongholds and the landpaths if their allies, the Redcoats, had held on to the waterways. But the Redcoats lost their ships and immediately prepared to retreat from the Strait. Wakaya rushed to the Morningland shore to evacuate his kin, to move them inland, toward the village of Brethren's converts at the river's fork. Many of the Strait's Turtlefolk and Firekeepers had already found refuge in the Brethren's village.

Wakaya didn't know if Udatonte was with the refugees because he didn't stay with them. He rejoined the warriors who were covering the Redcoat retreat. The Redcoats retreated past the fork, past the Brethren's village, and went on retreating to the easternmost edge of the Morningland.

Wakaya, Wapmimi and the remnant Wabash warriors took their stand at the river's fork, at the threshold to the Brethren's village. And there most of them died. They were outnumbered, their ammunition was soon exhausted. Wakaya feared the Bluejackets would not stop at the fork; he hastened to the Brethren's village to evacuate the refugees further east, behind the Redcoats.

The village was already under fire. Peace-seekers friendly to the Bluejackets, among them Pamoko's man Dupré, had approached the Bluejackets with a white flag, and all had been shot. On learning of this, most of the refugees had fled eastward, but some had grabbed weapons and gone to face the murderers. Pamoko attached herself to Wakaya and begged him to accompany her to the battlefield; her young son Jon Dupré was among those who had gone to face the Bluejackets.

Wakaya and Pamoko hid in the forest and saw the Bluejackets destroy and burn the Brethren's village, then mangle the dead bodies on the battlefield. At night, while the Bluejackets celebrated their victory, the shadows of survivors emerged from the forests. Wakaya, his brother Wapmimi, my cousin Shabeni and the Redearth warrior Macataimeshekiakak buried the dead, lest the bodies be further mangled by day.

They buried Wakaya's son Poposi, Wapmimi's son Ojejok, Bijiki's son Pezhki and Pamoko's man Dupré. They buried Wakaya's brother-in-law Cod-well, a Redcoat who had stayed with the warriors; they buried Gabinya's brother Mowhawa; and before the sun rose they buried those whose bodies had been mangled, scalped, skinned.

Pamoko found her son, slightly injured and pretending to be dead. And Wakaya found me, with a bullet in my arm but breathing. Wakaya carried me to Morningland's eastern edge, to a healing lodge in a village of Turtlefolk of the eastern Woodlands. My aunt Pamoko and other healers dressed my arm, but reluctantly. My blue jacket identified me as one of the murderers of their kin, and I deserved to die.

Wakaya removed the arrow pendant from his neck and placed it on mine. He told me that as a boy he'd thought the arrow had once belonged to a fierce Redearth warrior called Lamina. But Aptegizhek had later told him that the arrow came from a man who had not wanted to shoot a moose with a rifle. Wakaya still remembered me from the days when Wedasi and I accompanied him on a hunt; I had not wanted to hold a rifle.

I rejected Wakaya's gift. I reminded him I had come to the Morningland with the Bluejackets; I was his son's murderer. Wakaya smiled; he told me he had seen my bundle of unused arrows beside me on the battlefield; it had been full.

I was separated from Wakaya when armed men herded me out of the infirmary and penned me up with men who wore blue uniforms. Wakaya had told me that Redcoats and Bluejackets had agreed to exchange prisoners, and he had warned that I would not be treated well, but I wouldn't be killed. We were treated like cattle. Lines of armed Redcoats shouted, pushed, kicked, locked us in boxes, then released and pushed us further. My arm wound filled with pus and I became delirious. When I woke up, I thought I was dreaming again. I was in another infirmary, and the healers were familiar to me: they were my sister Wabnokwe and her friends Beth, Likét and others I hadn't seen since we were children in Misus Bay-con's school. My sister was alongside me as soon as I woke. She asked if I had really fought alongside the Bluejackets, or if I had found my uniform after the last battle. She'd heard that Wakaya had returned to Karontaen wearing a blue uniform, so as to get past the border guards, and kin who knew which side he'd fought on were now calling him Bluejacket.

Wabnokwe seemed to have changed; the contempt I had once seen in her eyes was no longer there. She told me the absence of the Turtlefolk and of the other corngrowers had caused a famine on the Strait, that the infirmary was full of children suffering from hunger, and that the renewal of Karontaen's cornfields was the medicine the children needed. The child on the mat next to mine, a little girl called Sue, was the granddaughter of Sofí, daughter of snobbish Felice.

With my right arm in a sling and my bundle under my blue jacket, I left my mat to a hungry child and accompanied my sister to Jay-may's house. A feast was prepared to celebrate my return. Jay-may was actually warm toward me, and praised me for having come to my senses. He didn't look at my face, but only at the blue uniform, and he didn't probe into my heroic deeds. His daughters Anna-may and Greta-may also saw only the uniform. Margít as well as her son Jim-may, already a youth, smiled conspiratorially; they assumed my blue jacket was a mere disguise.

As soon as my arm was out of its sling, Wabnokwe and I went to seek our brother, Nashkowatak. Wabnokwe had told me that Nashkowatak had returned soon after the last battle, and that he had avoided her and Jay-may and all his former companions. Wabnokwe hadn't known of Nashkowatak's return until he turned up at Jay-may's to demand that our cousin Shandó be released from prison. Shandó had been imprisoned by the Redcoats, and when the Redcoats were ousted, Shandó was left in prison. Jay-may had tried to explain that Shandó was dangerous, that he had tried to shoot his uncle, but Nashkowatak had shouted that the only reason Shandó was still in prison was because he was a halfbreed, like

Nashkowatak himself. Agreeing with Nashkowatak, Wabnokwe had recruited her friends to help her pressure Jay-may and the jailers into releasing Shandó.

We found Nashkowatak together with Shandó in a drinking lodge. Nashkowatak almost leapt out of his skin when he saw my blue clothes. He slapped me on the back, laughed cynically, and said he welcomed his pure and gentle brother to the society of kin murderers. He didn't ask what I had done. He asked if I too had been betrayed by my kin, if I too had longed to avenge the betrayal, if I too had gotten my fill of revenge.

He set out on a tirade. He had missed the first battle because his little brother had been caught tending a bridal fire on the battlefield. But he hadn't missed any of the subsequent battles. He had joined the Bluejackets in the Beautiful Valley, and he had been in the front line of every attack. His resentment of a childhood betrayal had grown with every attack. He had shot, stabbed and scalped those who had betrayed him, telling himself they were vicious, numerous and powerful. He had remained hot with rage until after the last battle, until he returned to the Strait and found Shandó still imprisoned.

Suddenly he knew why he had always been in the front line. Suddenly he remembered that he hadn't once confronted an armed warrior or a Redcoat, that all the attacks had been aimed at villages with no warriors or even hunters in them.

Sandusky had been attacked after the warriors had been lured out with promises. On the outskirts of Kekionga, Nashkowatak had taken part in the slaughter of several of our own Lakebottom kin who had found refuge there. And the same men were always with him in the front line; they were all men who were called halfbreeds by the Bluejackets behind them; they were all kin of the people they slaughtered. The war had been aimed against our kin and against ourselves.

Nashkowatak saw that I was nauseated and told me to save my vomit until after I'd heard all there was to hear. He reminded me of Slaver Kin-sic's description of the savages who ate human hearts, and then asked Shandó to tell me why he and Kin-sic had been imprisoned, and why Shandó had been left in prison.

Shandó told of two Redcoats who arrived in Bison Prairie to arrest him for having spilled the whiskey of a trader called Petty-song. One of the Redcoats was the brother of Shandó's father, the Redcoat who had abandoned Mikenokwe after the battle at the fallen trees. Shandó, encouraged by Burr-net, shot at his uncle and drove the Redcoats out of Bison Prairie.

Soon after this incident, Kin-sic turned up in Bison Prairie and announced that Redcoats were invading the Lakebottom. Most of Bison Prairie's Firekeepers accompanied Kin-sic to the Lakebottom and quickly learned that the Redcoat invasion was a lie. The Lakebottom's fort and Kin-sic's store were surrounded by angry Firekeepers and Redearth kin; only one Redcoat was among them. Kin-sic and his Bluejacket allies were preparing to attack the Lakebottom Firekeepers and their allies, and were waiting for reinforcements from Kekionga. Only Shandó and Burr-net persisted in believing Kin-sic, and they went on believing him until the Kekionga Bluejackets led by Will-well were in sight.

Burr-net woke up to what was happening only when Kin-sic distributed the ammunition destined for fur hunters to the Bluejackets in the fort. Burr-net ran out of the fort toward the Kekiongans, to warn Will-well of Kin-sic's plot. Kin-sic and the fort's headman ordered their armed men to shoot at the Redearth kin, who immediately responded in kind. The approaching Kekiongans thought the bullets were aimed at them, and they shot and killed Burr-net as they scattered for cover. A Redearth warrior shouted to the Bluejackets, calling for a truce and a council. Kin-sic and the headman ordered their men to leave the fort shooting, hoping that Will-well's Kekiongans would back them up. But the Kekiongans abandoned Will-well and he as well as the fort's Bluejackets were killed during their blind charge.

Shandó had stayed inside the fort with Kin-sic and the headman. When the battle was over, the three were surrounded by hostile warriors. That was when Kin-sic began to speak of cannibals; he was sure the warriors intended to eat his heart. But Kin-sic wasn't even harmed. Shabeni, the Redearth warrior and the Redcoat called Cod-well accompanied the fort's headman and his family to Bison Prairie, and they escorted Kin-sic and Shandó to imprisonment on the Strait.

Kin-sic was released during an exchange of prisoners, and then Kin-sic saw to it that Shandó be kept in jail because Shandó knew too much about Burr-net's death. During the Redcoat occupation, Kin-sic made much of Shandó's attempt to shoot his redfrocked uncle, and after the occupation he pretended that the halfbreed Shandó had been one of the cannibals.

I didn't vomit when Shandó finished his tale. I told Wabnokwe that I would not return to Jay-may's house with her. I knew that Nashkowatak and Shandó intended to go to Bison Prairie. I decided to go with them.

Shandó went by way of Sandusky where his mother Mikenokwe still lived. Nashkowatak and I went by way of Kekionga. Nashkowatak hoped our Kekionga kin would torture and kill him, since they all knew he had been among the attackers who had murdered their kin. Muns avoided us; his aunt Chindiskwe had been one of the victims. Aptegizhek's sister had been another. She had fled to Kekionga after her younger sister Wagoshkwe had been killed by Kin-sic's Bluejackets on the Lakebottom. Yet Aptegizhek came to me, welcomed me, urged me to hold on to the Firekeepers' bundle. Nawak had stopped in Kekionga on his way back to Sandusky and had told Aptegizhek that I had died in the last battle; Nawak had blamed himself for dragging me to the Morningland battlefield.

Meteya's village

Nashkowatak and I set out toward Bison Prairie as soon as Shandó joined us. Shandó had not been well received in Sandusky, even by his mother. My beautiful aunt Suzán and her daughter Olalí had fled to Sandusky after the massacre of their kin in their Kekionga refuge, and Suzán had told her hosts of Shandó's collaboration with the Slavers on the Lakebottom.

I filled with apprehension as we approached Bison Prairie; the familiar landmarks saddened me. Katabwe, Mimikwe and my bundle had made me think of Bison Prairie as the Firekeepers' center. But I wanted to be heading toward another center, toward a blue lake surrounded by grass and sparse trees. I was not eager to see my Bison Prairie kin, and I was sure they were no more eager to see me or Nashkowatak or Shandó.

At first glance, I was wrong about the coolness of our kin toward us. Topinbi and his son Nesoki, Cakima and Chebansi welcomed us as if we were hunters returning with boats full of furs. They warmed sweat lodges, feasted us and lit three fires. But the joy, as in all of Topinbi's and Cakima's pagentry, was all on the surface. Topinbi and Cakima used the old ceremonies the way they used beads, to decorate and disguise, and to Topinbi the ceremonies were nothing more than occasions for opening whiskey barrels.

Topinbi himself revealed the wounds below the surface as soon as he started drinking. His daughter Mimikwe was dead. She from whom I had fled, to whom Nashkowatak had wanted to prove himself, had been murdered by a band of Bluejackets. Our brother Wedasi was crippled; he lodged with peaceful Meteya and spoke of nothing but revenge. Cakima and Chebansi wanted only peace, so as to resume the fur trade, first of all with the Lakebottom's hunters. But a group of Lakebottom Firekeepers, among them Topash, had moved to Bison Prairie to get away from the Lakebottom's warriors and fur hunters, and Topash's camp was as hostile to Cakima's aims as to Wedasi's. Topinbi as much as admitted that his three fires did not unite four peoples, they did not even unite the Firekeepers themselves, who were split into three mutually hostile camps.

Cakima expected Nashkowatak and me to join Chebansi and Nesoki in the store, to replace Burr-net. She told us she wanted to lure the Lakebottom furs away from Kin-sic, who had returned to the Lakebottom and swallowed Sandypoint's fur post. She had thought Topash would help her, but Topash broke his links with the hunters when he'd moved to Bison Prairie. Some of the Lakebottom furs were carried to Bison Prairie by Naganwatek, whose mother Wagoshkwe and father Lalím had both been murdered by Kin-sic. But Cakima wanted more; she wanted Nashkowatak and me to seek brides on the Lakebottom.

Neither Nashkowatak nor I intended to replace our dead father; we disappointed Cakima and Chebansi. Nashkowatak walked out on Cakima before she was done pleading; I walked out with him. Nashkowatak headed toward the lodges of the Lakebottom refugees, and went directly to Topash's. I didn't share all of Nashkowatak's guilt but I was as anxious as he to expose the wounds so they wouldn't fester.

Topash left his lodge as soon as we entered. He recognized Nashkowatak as Shecogosikwe's murderer, as one of the

Bluejackets who had attacked the Lakebottom's Firekeepers in their Kekionga refuge. Topash's daughter Menashi also recognized her mother's murderer, but she didn't leave. She confronted us with eyes as fierce as Udatonte's. Menashi was no longer the mischievous little girl who had caught me staring at her mother's greenstone pendant in Kittihawa's lodge. The mischief was still in Menashi's eyes, but the face and body were those of a beautiful woman. I couldn't keep my eyes from staring at the greenstone pendant, ancient Shutaha's pendant, suspended above Menashi's breasts. She didn't seem aware of my staring. All her attention was on her mother's murderer. She watched his every move, the way a fox watches a duck just before pouncing. She was stalking prey. Nashkowatak had come for a beating, and she yearned to beat him. She wanted not only revenge but also compensation and Nashkowatak offered her both. She would not allow Nashkowatak to leave her lodge. Sensing that I was between a huntress and her prey, I rushed out of Menashi's lodge.

Still wearing the blue jacket, I made my way to Meteya's knowing that a band of Bluejackets had murdered Bindizeosekwe and crippled Wedasi. I found Meteya's brother Gizes counciling with Wedasi. Gizes was on his way toward Mishigami's other shore where he hoped to rejoin Shabeni and the Redearth warriors. Gizes and his daughter Damushkekwe had stayed in the Morningland, near the Redcoats, until the Redcoats began to starve them. Damushkekwe, whose mother had been murdered on the Wabash, had accompanied Gizes to all the battlefields, but wanted to travel no further.

Meteya was away hunting or stalking. His older daughter, pockmarked Koyoshkwe, greeted me with silence. The younger, Wamoshkeshekwe, told me she admired Cakima and let me know she was willing and ready to be my bride. Wedasi was hostile. Hobbling on one leg, supporting his weight with a stick, he quickly let me know that he considered me a coward, Shandó and Nashkowatak traitors, and that the war against traitors wasn't over.

Wedasi's urge to tell the reasons for his rage was greater than the rage itself, and I soon knew more than I wanted to know.

I had last seen Wedasi when he had painted himself and left Bison Prairie with Wapmimi and the other Wabash warriors. He accompanied the warriors to Kithepekanu, where he lodged with Shawanokwe, Wapmimi, their son Ojejok, their daughter Omemekwe, and grandfather Sigenak, the old warrior, Nanikibi's brother. Wedasi devoted his days to war dances and preparations with Ojejok's grandfather and uncles; he devoted his nights to Ojejok's sister Omemekwe, who soon grew large with Wedasi's child. Everyone in Kithepekanu expected war, but no one was ready when scouts brought word of a large army of Bluejackets led by headman Will-hen-garrison moving up the Wabash.

Wedasi joined the warriors who rushed to confront the approaching Bluejackets; the warriors lunged against the uniformed armed men with no heed to their own lives, but the Bluejackets kept on moving. The enemy had called no council, announced no conditions, stated no terms for negotiation; they simply invaded the lands of the Prairiekin and moved to exterminate everyone in and near Kithepekanu; they burned every lodge, set fire to all the weapons and all the food. This was the only battle in which Wedasi fought. When it ended, pregnant Omemekwe and Wedasi's unborn child were dead; Omemekwe's mother Shawanokwe and grandfather Sigenak were dead.

The survivors rebuilt Kithepekanu on the ashes, as a war camp. Wedasi, Wapmimi and Ojejok lodged briefly with Gizes and his young daughter Damushkekwe. When Wapmimi and Gizes set out toward the Strait, Wedasi joined Shabeni and the other warriors who headed toward the Lakebottom. They had been told of the Lakebottom Scalpers' ravages by Sandypoint's son Kegon, who did not survive to return to his kin. Wedasi and his companions reached the Lakebottom after the battle was over, the ground already stained.

Those responsible for the bloodshed—the fort's headman, the Slaver Kin-sic and Shandó—were still alive, and Wedasi joined his voice to the voices of the angry Redearth kin who wanted the enemies killed. Shabeni and the Redearth warrior Macataimeshekiakak restrained Wedasi, said enough blood had been shed, and insisted on transporting the enemies to the Strait. The headman was ill from fright; he was left in Bison Prairie and Mimikwe nursed him back to health. Wedasi was also left in Bison Prairie; Shabeni insisted that Wedasi stay behind to protect Mimikwe, her son Komenoteya and the remaining villagers.

When Wedasi's chance came, he failed. A band of Bluejackets surrounded Mimikwe and Bindizeosekwe in Bison

Prairie's cornfield, maltreated the two women and then murdered them. Wedasi ran for his rifle; he and Komenoteya pursued the killers until Wedasi's leg was shot off. Wedasi was carried to Meteya's lodge; he was nursed by Koyoshkwe, who shared her mat with my crippled brother, fed him, and helped him learn to walk with a stick. Wedasi's worst humiliation came when Shabeni returned to Bison Prairie after burying the kin who died in the last battle. For several days Shabeni wept for Mimikwe. Then, without once greeting or looking in on Wedasi, Shabeni and his son Komenoteya left Bison Prairie and headed west.

I felt as out of place in Meteya's lodge as I had in Cakima's and Menashi's. Gizes, his daughter Damushkekwe and Wedasi filled the lodge with talk of battles, deaths and revenge. Koyoshkwe tended the cooking fires, gathered berries and herbs, prepared sweat baths, and never said a word. Wamoshkeshekwe insistently offered herself to me, seeing me as the trader's son, expecting me to be her gate to the trader's lodge, hoping I would turn her into the trader's wife. I had been afraid of Mimikwe's expectations; I was repelled by Wamoshkeshekwe's.

Gizes stayed in Bison Prairie until Meteya returned from the hunt. Gizes councilled with Meteya to learn his brother's attitudes and to give news of their brothers Wapmimi and Wakaya; and he prepared to leave. I left with Gizes. I wanted to see Shabeni, and I wanted to get away from Wamoshkeshekwe's expectations.

We circumvented the Lakebottom village and followed a path once used by Redearth kin on their treks between the Long River and the Strait. I had never before visited the other shore, the land of lakes and forests that had sheltered and fed my great-grandmother's people. Shabeni's village was at the edge of a lake which, Gizes told me, lay halfway between Mishigami and the Long Lake.

Shabeni and the Redearth warriors greeted Gizes as a brother and me as a curiosity. They had seen me among the corpses on the Morningland battlefield and were surprised I was alive. Mimikwe's son didn't greet me; Komenoteya saw only the blue jacket, the uniform of his mother's murderers.

Shabeni was more anxious to council with Gizes about the whereabouts of their companions than with me about my grandmother Katabwe. He granted me a brief council, but only to tell me that when he'd returned to Bison Prairie after burying his companions and learned that Mimikwe was dead, he had repudiated me and my bundle and my grandmother and all the dream spirits. With tears in my eyes I asked him to explain why. Shabeni answered. He told me that something more powerful than our bundles, spirits and old songs had risen out of the ashes on the Wabash. After Kithepekanu was burned, after Sigenak and Shawanokwe and Kegon and the other dead were buried, the survivors regrouped and rebuilt a new village, a new center that was not a gathering of Firekeepers, Prairiekin, Redearth kin and other people, but a center of a single people with a single goal and a single army. The army of this people born on the ashes of Kithepekanu, captured the enemy's ships, cut supply lines, captured the impregnable fortresses on Mishilimakina and on the Strait, emptied all the lesser forts, and cleared the Invaders out of all forests, lakes and villages between Cahokia and the Peninsula's Northern Strait. But at that point, instead of strengthening their unity, the single people decomposed. The single army reverted to an alliance of warrior bands, and the bands decomposed into hotheads like Wedasi and bundle-carriers like me, into hunters and dreamers who quickly dispersed, one to settle a petty revenge, another to seek spirits, a third to dance. As a single people they had recovered the world from the Invaders, as hotheads and bundle-carriers they couldn't even protect Mimikwe from a band of bluejacketed plunderers.

I sought no further councils with Shabeni. I accompanied a band of eastward-bound hunters out of his village. Shabeni's answer angered me. I had never before had a standpoint from which I could think of someone as a traitor. Shabeni had built my dream lodges; he had been my cousin, guide and companion. But I knew that his single people with a single army had not been born on the ashes of Kithepekanu, but had been carried across the Ocean on the ships that brought firewater, rifles and plagues.

The hunters with whom I returned to Mishigami's shore, men named Lashás, Laframboáz, Lemé and Lepetí, were my distant cousins, sons-in-law of Nangisí and Winámek. Our kinship was a thin bond. I tried to speak with them of common ancestors and met only indifference and ridicule; the only ancestor they remembered was Wabskeni, the manhunter, and he was their Wiske, the founder of their village.

Bison Prairie was half empty when I arrived with Naganwatek and the furs of the Lakebottom hunters. Topinbi and Cakima had led a caravan to a council in Kekionga; Nashkowatak, Menashi and Wamoshkeshekwe were among those who had left with the caravan. I learned that Menashi had given birth to a child just before the caravan's departure, a boy with trader Burr-net's yellow hair and blue eyes; Cakima had named her first grandson Wimego, the name that was given to Burr-net when he was adopted by Bison Prairie's Firekeepers.

Wedasi was still at Meteya's but he no longer shared his mat with Koyoshkwe, who had nursed him and taught him to walk with a stick. Wedasi spent his days and nights with Damushkekwe, the warlike daughter of Gizes; the two filled the air with talk of past and future battles, and of the day when Kithepekanu had risen on top of ashes. They had briefly shared a lodge in the re-risen village; Wedasi had been a hotheaded warrior, she an admiring little girl. My heart went out to abandoned Koyoshkwe, who treated Damushkekwe as a sister, Wedasi as a brother, and let no trace of sadness or anger show on her face or in her movements.

Bison Prairie came alive with feasts, celebrations, misused ceremonies and drinking orgies when Topinbi, Cakima and their train returned with canoe-loads of gifts. Wamoshkeshekwe returned as Shandó's bride. Menashi and Nashkowatak seemed estranged. Nashkowatak sought me out. He carried a whiskey pouch to a place away from the other celebrants, and harangued me as he drank. He asked about the contents of the Firekeepers' bundle and he told me to do whatever I was going to do with my bundle, and to do it quickly. He bitterly told me that he had never known who he was, but he wanted his newly-named son to grow among people who knew who they were.

The Kekionga gathering had shown him that our kin no longer knew who they were. He called our mother and our uncle Topinbi prostitutes, and said they had gone to Kekionga to give away their own people and their lands for a few cartloads of beads and whiskey. They had sold themselves to Nashkowatak's one-time militia chief Loos-gas, who was now the headman of all of Kichigami's Invaders. Our uncles Onimush, Bijiki and Gabinya had served Loos-gas as interpreters; Nashkowatak called them pimps.

Without consulting Aptegizhek or Muns or Mekinges or the other Eastbranch Rootkin who lodged in Kekionga, the pimps and the prostitutes gave Loos-gas all the land of Kekionga and of the Wabash valley—all but tiny parcels. The parcels were reserved for the children of traders, whom Loos-gas called children of the three fires by birth or marriage. Cakima received titles to such parcels, one for each of her sons and daughter. Aptegizhek tried to stop his kin; he carried a fistful of earth to Loos-gas and begged to be given a title for it. Aptegizhek was disregarded. All eyes, including Menashi's were on Cakima, the person who had acquired the biggest load of gifts, enough to revive Bison Prairie's trade and to lure furs away from the Lakebottom's trader Kin-sic. Menashi had carried little Wimego to Cakima's councils with Loos-gas to acquaint herself and her son with the behavior of people who no longer knew who they were.

Nashkowatak drank until he was numb. Koyoshkwe stepped out of the shadows; she too had heard his harangue. Koyoshkwe helped me carry him to Menashi's lodge. Taking my hand, she led me to Meteya's, to her mat. She spoke only with her eyes. She didn't know what I could do, and she had no expectations; she wanted me to know that she would help me.

Koyoshkwe let me know she had shared her mat with several men, all of them had abandoned her, and she expected no more; she said she knew she could bear no children, and she knew she was pockmarked. My love grew with my admiration for her; there was nothing she could not do, and she never tired. My love did not help me forget Udatonte, but it did make that spring, the third since my return to Bison Prairie, my happiest spring there.

I was especially happy when, shortly after Damushkekwe gave birth, Wedasi asked me to arrange his newborn child's naming ceremony. My brother wanted the old ceremony, our grandmother's. I was overjoyed to be asked, but I didn't know how to begin. If Koyoshkwe hadn't gathered masks and wood and food, if she hadn't sent her father and cousins running with invitations, I would have been lost. I didn't ask Koyoshkwe where she had learned all the things I didn't know; I assumed that her mother Bindizeosekwe and my cousin Mimikwe had carried on the old ceremonies after Katabwe's death, and that Koyoshkwe had silently watched and listened. She left me nothing to do but rehearse the songs and dances and prepare the other participants. I named Damushkekwe's round and healthy son Mikínak, turtle, in memory of the generous animal who supported our Yahatase's and my Udatonte's world.

Word of the ancient naming ceremony was carried to other quarters, and soon Koyoshkwe's aunt Meshewokwe invited me to the Lakebottom to name her newborn son. Most of my Bison Prairie kin set out for the Lakebottom when Koyoshkwe and I did, not to take part in the naming ceremony, but in another. Cakima had at last succeeded in pushing one of her sons into a marriage with one of the daughters of the Lakebottom hunters. Chebansi had agreed to marry Nangisi's granddaughter Notanokwe. The naming preceded the marriage. The baby, my cousin Naganwatek's son, was the grandson of Wagoshkwe, great-grandson of the bowlmaker Lókaskwe. I named the boy Shawanetek for the Southbranch kin with whom Lókaskwe shared joys and sorrows.

Chebansi's marriage was a cold affair which revolved around three hearths that had no meaning, and principally around Topinbi's mounds of gifts and barrels of whiskey. Cakima had what she wanted: a direct link to the Lakebottom's Lashás, Laframbóaz, Lemé, Lepetí, and she expected Kin-sic's fur post to decompose soon after Naganwatek began carrying all of the Lakebottom furs to Bison Prairie. Chebansi's bride accompanied us to Bison Prairie and joined Cakima in the store, but not happily. Notanokwe, a crosswearer, seemed to dislike everyone in Bison Prairie, especially Chebansi.

Topinbi and Shandó set out toward the Strait with the largest fur caravan that had left Bison Prairie since before the Bluejackets' war. They returned with Shandó's mother Mikenokwe and with frightening news. Crosswearing Mikenokwe told us she had been hounded out of Sandusky by evangelists who had bewitched the villagers, including my aunt Suzán, with their messages and visions. She had joined her sister Pamoko in Karontaen, but only long enough to see Karontaen's kin driven from the Strait by landgrabbers who invoked titles given to them by Topinbi and Cakima in Kekionga.

Wamoshkeshekwe gave birth to a son. I knew that she as well as Shandó wanted to ask me to arrange the naming ceremony. But Mikenokwe would not allow her newborn grandson to be exposed to a pagan ceremony. Mikenokwe recruited Chebansi's bride Notanokwe as well as my cousin Nesoki to help her arrange an affair with crosses and incense and murmured prayers, the first crosswearers' ceremony in Bison Prairie since my great-grandmother's days. The child was named Pogon.

Topinbi brought the frightening news that the Invaders' headman Loos-gas intended to hold a gift-giving council on the

Lakebottom. Topinbi and Cakima thought only of the gifts, but most others knew what such a council would bring. That fall and winter, Wedasi and Damushkekwe resumed their talk of war and revenge against traitors, and Wedasi sent runners to nearby villages. Youth arrived from many quarters and painted themselves; the preparing warriors pledged themselves to kill anyone who ceded the Peninsula's land to the Invaders. Koyoshkwe was alarmed, as was her father Meteya, who concerned himself with the affairs of the village only when fratricidal war threatened to break out. Too many of our kin had died in fratricidal wars. Koyoshkwe and Meteya sent out messages urging Firekeepers to converge on the Lakebottom so as to dissuade their kin from signing the Invaders' leaves and to disarm the hotheads in their midst. Koyoshkwe begged me to carry such a message to our Kekionga kin.

I accompanied Topinbi's and Shandó's spring caravan out of Bison Prairie. In view of the message I was carrying, I traveled in strange company. Topinbi, of course, knew why I was going to Kekionga, and my mission didn't bother him in the least; he told me he sympathized with the resisters, he did not want the Peninsula's lands to go to the Invaders. The reason he signed the treaties, he told me, was because he was convinced that the landgrabbers would come on the day they were ready to come whether or not Topinbi signed their treaties, and landgrabbers who arrived with signed treaties were less violent than those who arrived with nothing but their rifles.

Topinbi and Shandó went on to the Strait. I stayed in Kekionga. My insides ached when I saw the village. The only reminders of the village I had known were the traders' lodges. Invaders were everywhere. The only kinsman I found was Aptegizhek. He told me the last Eastbranch kin had been pushed out. Already before the treaty council, Invaders had been downing trees, killing animals, fencing fields, so that every winter the villagers had starved.

Too weak to oust the Invaders from the hunting grounds and fields, the villagers had at last abandoned their home and fled westward toward Eastbranch kin who had fled earlier. My friend Muns and his mother Mekinges were among the starvelings who set out in search of fields and forests untrampled by Invaders. It was a sad sight. Aptegizhek mourned, and then gave away the scrolls which told of the earlier wanderings of the Eastbranch Rootkin. He gave the scrolls to one who promised to bury them in the east, by the Oceanshore, at the place where the earlier wanderings of the Eastbranch kin had ended.

Aptegizhek had not accompanied either his kin or his scrolls; he had stayed in Kekionga with the few Eastbranch kin who preferred starvation over migration. He told me the Invaders named the place Fort Vain, after the headman who had killed my grandfather at the fallen trees, but the place remained Kekionga so long as any Rootkin lived in it. He told me his cousin Onimush had married a daughter of an Invader as soon as Mekinges and Muns were gone. His cousin Bijiki had married an Invader's daughter already earlier. Bijiki's son Kezhek had fled to Piqua in search of Wapmimi and the few Southbranch kin who still lived in the Beautiful Valley.

Aptegizhek was cheered by my mission. He said he hoped the Firekeepers were stronger than the Eastbranch kin. He agreed to go to the Lakebottom with me. We left Kekionga and followed the caravan that carried headman Loos-gas and his signers, interpreters, gifts and whiskey toward the Lakebottom. My uncle Topinbi was the caravan's guide. Aptegizhek's cousins Onimush and Bijiki traveled with my uncles Gabinya and Atsimet near the head of the caravan.

The Lakebottom teemed with more people than I had ever seen gathered in one place. The Invaders' headman and his agents were welcomed by trader Kin-sic, who installed them in lodges and stores that had once been Sandypoint's. The Invaders and their wares were like a tiny island in a turbulent sea; the Lakebottom plain was crowded with hearths and tents extending as far as an eye could see. Firekeepers from every corner of the Great Lakes had responded to the call; I was told that kin from seventy-four villages were gathered on the Lakebottom.

I accompanied Aptegizhek from one hearth to the next. His sadness left him when he saw Menashi's son Wimego, the grandson of Shecogosikwe, and when he saw Naganwatek's son Shawanetek, the grandson of Wagoshkwe. The grandchildren would not grow up in a decomposing world. At every hearth we felt the determination of kin who knew that the land could not be ceded, that earth could not be bargained away. There was no need for Wedasi's threats or war dances. The mere presence of so many kin kept Topinbi and other gift-seekers from offering their signatures to the landgrabbers.

A flood or earthquake could not have caused greater shock than the news that suddenly spread from hearth to hearth.

Unable to coax any Firekeepers into signing his treaty, headman Loos-gas had filled his leaf with the names of his own agents and interpreters. Gabinya and Atsimet, Bijiki and Onimush, Wit-nags and Kin-sic and others with the faintest of links to the Peninsula's Rootkin had signed the leaf as children of Firekeepers by birth or marriage. The signers had been rewarded with gifts and with titles to sections of the Peninsula. When Aptegizhek learned of this, he covered himself with earth, removed the bandana from his head, and went to the traders' camp, to his cousins Onimush, Bijiki and the others, displaying his scalped head, his body reduced to dirt.

The Firekeepers began to disperse, knowing that the gift-seekers among them were not the snakes in the grass, that their show of determination to hold on to the land had not stopped or even delayed the Invaders, that the treaty councils were neither treaties nor councils. And as soon as the gathered Firekeepers dispersed, Cakima and Topinbi rushed to the headman's camp for their share of the gifts and sections.

Nashkowatak later told me that Menashi accompanied Cakima and pretended to display yellowhaired Wimego to his kinsmen; her real intention was to display herself. Invited to return alone for private councils with Bijiki, Gabinya, Wit-nags and headman Loos-gas himself, Menashi left Wimego with Wamoshkeshekwe and returned to the Invaders. She emerged from her councils with more gifts and sections than all the others put together; Menashi became the first among the prostitutes.

Shandó later told me that his mother Mikenokwe had also counciled with headman Loos-gas, not to acquire gifts and land sections, but to request that a Blackrobe be sent to Bison Prairie. Mikenokwe and other crosswearers wanted to put an end to the ancient renewal ceremonies that were still remembered by the Firekeepers.

I looked for Aptegizhek during the general dispersal. I found him sitting by the lake's shore, away from the commotion, his body covered with dirt, his head unbound. He was as thin as a stick. He looked at me but didn't see me. His eyes were blood red and spoke of intense pain, as if he had been scalped, not on the Tuscarawas forty summers earlier, but on the Lakebottom the previous day. I sat down by him and looked across the lake toward the Peninsula. His nephew Naganwatek later guided him back to Kekionga.

In Bison Prairie all eyes, including mine, turned toward Menashi. She seemed to be driven by the spirit of the greenstone pendant that had once been Shutaha's, the pendant that always dangled prominently between Menashi's breasts like an angry, defiant and misplaced eye. Shutaha had used her powers to transform sick strangers into healthy Turtlefolk. Menashi seemed bent on transforming everyone around her into moths that revolved around her fire.

Returning from the Lakebottom with several canoe-loads of blankets, clothes and whiskey, Menashi eclipsed Cakima and Topinbi as Bison Prairie's gift-bringer. She did not return to Topash's lodge with Nashkowatak and Wimego, but installed herself alongside Cakima in the store, and soon hunters, rum-carriers, even Bluejackets veered away from their paths and entered Bison Prairie seeking the woman with the green pendant. The visitors became demented the moment they set their eyes on the greenstone. They arrived with blankets, coins, powder, rifles, food; they left Cakima's lodge with nothing but their shirts. Chebansi's censurious Notanokwe tried to oust Menashi from Cakima's lodge and recruited Mikenokwe to help her, but Chebansi as well as Cakima held on to Menashi. The store prospered; its gifts were luring all of the Lakebottom's furs away from Kin-sic. Chebansi and Topinbi were turned into arrangers and sustainers of Menashi's encounters.

Koyoshkwe and I kept our distance from the trading lodge, but our paths kept crossing Menashi's. Nashkowatak, abandoned by Menashi, brought little Wimego to Meteya's to play with Wedasi's son Mikínak. Nashkowatak and I took the boys to the fields or herb-gathering with Koyoshkwe, on walks into the woods with Meteya. Koyoshkwe and I enacted ancient planting ceremonies before the boys, singing the old songs and losing ourselves in fragments of old dances. But Menashi let us know, with glances and sometimes with words, that Wimego was her son, and that he was with us only because she wasn't yet ready to take him from us.

Menashi's effect on Damushkekwe created daily war in Meteya's lodge. Disappointed that her and Wedasi's war councils had not led to bloodshed on the Lakebottom, Damushkekwe cast envious eyes toward Menashi, considering Menashi's fleecing of guests a greater feat than any warrior's. Damushkekwe grew ever more contemptuous of warrior Wedasi, ridiculing his disability, calling him a do-nothing who warred only with his mouth, even threatening to move to Cakima's and to take Mikínak with her.

Great commotion was caused by the coming of the Blackrobe requested by Mikenokwe. A man called Ma-caynin arrived with his family, several assistants, and with cartloads of furniture; it was obvious that he intended to stay. Mikenokwe and Chebansi's frustrated Notanokwe prepared an elaborate welcome. Ma-caynin let it be known that he did not tolerate prostitution any more than he tolerated whiskey. Koyoshkwe and I thought the crosswearers had been given a powerful ally and that Menashi would become entangled in a tug of war with the crosswearers and would leave the rest of us in peace. But it was Mikenokwe who lashed out against the newcomer. She complained that headman Loos-gas had sent the wrong type of crosswearer, that Ma-caynin was an evangelist like those who had hounded Mikenokwe out of Sandusky, that he wasn't a proper Blackrobe. And as soon as Mikenokwe turned against the newcomer, Menashi drew him into her net; she placed herself between Ma-caynin and the things he needed from Cakima's store, and she promised to fill Ma-caynin's missionlodge with converts and his schoolhouse with children of Firekeepers.

Adoption of Wimego

Koyoshkwe was a wonder. She led the children to fields and clearings, showing them herbs, singing them ancient songs. Wedasi's son, eager to learn his father's warrior skills, did not open himself to Koyoshkwe's gifts but wide-eyed Wimego drew in all she gave him and asked for more. And Koyoshkwe's gifts amazed me. She took up a song or story only after I started it, but once she began, she went to realms where I had never been.

She sang, with a conviction I lacked, of our kinship with swimmers, flyers and crawlers, of the migrations of our ancestors over the land of ice to the woodlands of Kichigami, of the wars among Kichigami's four peoples and their peace at the council of three fires. She had never seen the contents of my bundle but was familiar with the meaning of everything in it except the hairlock. Koyoshkwe was the true heiress of Shutaha's pendant, not Menashi. Koyoshkwe created the healthy ground out of which shoots could grow unhampered. She expressed her gratitude to me, but it was she, not I, who rekindled a fire that had been faltering. Nashkowatak, Topash and even Topinbi visited our lodge seeking the warmth of the rekindled fire.

But my cousin Menashi had set out to extinguish every fire but one. She turned up at Meteya's lodge. Everyone thought she'd come to fetch Wimego away from me and Koyoshkwe. I placed myself between the boy and his mother, ready to protect Wimego from Ma-caynin's mission and school. Menashi walked past everyone, straight toward me, her dark eyes burning into mine. Below the fierce eyes dangled the greenstone pendant. My eyes were drawn to it, my heart beat like a duck's wings, my prepared words bunched up in my throat. A hand came toward me, and I saw the hand as Udatonte's reaching for mine through fog.

I placed my hand into hers, and when she pulled, I followed, ready to be drawn into Udatonte's canoe. She pulled me past Koyoshkwe, Meteya, Topash and Nashkowatak, past the councilground and the furthest lodges, along the riverbank, into the forest. Dressed in a glistening dress made of Invaders' cloth, she stretched out on a grass bed, her eyes inviting me to lie beside her. I knew I was not with Udatonte. I was not filled with love. I was filled with desire. I was entranced. I had seen a beautiful woman, my aunt Suzán, only once and only for an instant. Menashi's dark eyes, her parted lips, her black hair, her firm body pushed all other thoughts out of my head. I let her guide my hand to her breast, her stomach, her thighs, my head toward the pendant, my mouth to her bosom. I burned with desire and still she played, entangling her arms and legs in mine and disentangling as we rolled over each other on the grass until, both of us panting, naked and covered with sweat, we lunged at each other and joined.

I'd had a sensation of fullness with Udatonte. I felt completely empty, dry, when Menashi led me back through the village to Cakima's lodge. I followed like a loyal dog. She put me in a room with a wide bed, and I stayed in the room as if the windows were barred and the door locked; I writhed with longing for Menashi's return. My mind had no room for thoughts of betrayed Koyoshkwe, of betrayed Nashkowatak, of abandoned Wimego, of the Firekeepers' bundle which I had left on the grass in the forest.

Menashi's room was no Grasslake, and I soon came to hate its bare walls, but still I remained in it, longing for nothing but her return. I knew that she bedded with other men in other rooms, but I feared only that she wouldn't return to me. I was Menashi's prisoner, a fish caught in her net.

I gradually became aware that there were other fish in her net, that she had set out to enmesh all persons susceptible to her powers and to isolate those who were impervious. She lured Damushkekwe away from Wedasi, installed Damushkekwe in a room with a wide bed, and led Wedasi's son to Ma-caynin's school. She lured Wamoshkeshekwe away from Shandó, and installed her in another room, and tried unsuccessfully to pull the boy Pogon away from his crosswearing grandmother Mikenokwe. She pulled her own Wimego away from Koyoshkwe and installed him in the school.

The store filled with trade-gifts, the mission filled with schoolchildren, and Bison Prairie prospered. The whole village glowed with a light that emanated from Menashi. Cakima and Chebansi were her ablest accomplices. Cakima had always wanted Bison Prairie's children to be transformed into traders by the Invaders' schools and she could not but admire Menashi's success. Chebansi, obsessed by the desire to gather all of Mishigami's furs, didn't care how the gifts or the furs were lured to Bison Prairie's store.

I remained obsessed, demented by my desire for Menashi, although after two seasons in her room, shame alone would have kept me from leaving the room and facing my kin. The passage of seasons increased Menashi's beauty, but not her power. Menashi was a greedy huntress, but she was not Wiske; her powers were great, but limited. After a summer, fall and winter, the fur post's prosperity collapsed. Menashi told me little, but I learned much from Wimego who spent his time away from school alongside me, waiting for his mother.

Wimego told me Topinbi and Shandó were back from the Strait with nothing in their canoes but the paddles. They had set out with more furs than had ever been sent out of Bison Prairie in a single caravan, had been ambushed by armed Invaders, and had been fortunate to escape with their lives and their canoes. Chebansi was desperate; he had no gifts to offer the hunters for their furs; the only gifts left in the store were those offered by Menashi, Damushkekwe and Wamoshkeshekwe: their wide beds.

From Wimego I learned of my uncle Gizes's arrival in Bison Prairie with a band of hunters from the western Plains. Wedasi and Topinbi counciled with the westerners. Wedasi's son Mikínak ran from Ma-caynin's school to hear the councils. Gizes told of paths untrodden by Invaders, of buffalo herds so populous they blackened the horizons, of forests where no trees had been killed. Gizes no longer lived with Shabeni; he lived with Shabeni's son Komenoteya and with the warrior Macatai-meshekiakak in a village of Redearth and Plains kin on the western shore of the Long River.

My brother Wedasi was so impressed by Gizes's descriptions of the lands beyond the Long River that he urged his son Mikínak to leave the mission school and take up the bow and the rifle. Wedasi was ready to become the trainer of a new generation of warriors; he apparently expected his leg to grow back while he crossed the Long River. Wimego told me my uncle Topinbi was also impressed by Gizes's words. The aging Topinbi probably saw himself as ancient Nangisi, the first carrier of Invaders' gifts to kin who had not yet seen them.

Gizes came and went. More seasons passed. I accompanied Chebansi to the landingplace and helped unload canoes, but I strayed no further from Cakima's lodge, from Menashi's room. Menashi returned to her room ever less frequently; her son visited ever more frequently, occasionally with his cousin Mikínak.

Wimego remembered the songs Koyoshkwe and I had sung to him; he wanted to know about the dream-spirits; he even begged me to build him a fasting lodge. I remembered myself at the same age begging the same favor of Shabeni. But I found excuses not to stir. I told myself the boy was timid; he feared Menashi; he would be frightened to death by a dream-spirit. Mikínak was strong enough to fast, but Mikínak's head was full of Wedasi's words; he wanted to kill, not to sing or dream. I found excuses and I stayed where I was. I told myself I was no longer the Firekeepers' bundle carrier. I was free. But I felt empty. I lived for the moments Menashi spared me, and when she left I felt yet emptier.

I almost left my prison on the day when Wimego ran into the room hysterically seeking Menashi, his eyes red with fear, his body trembling. I tried in vain to calm him until Menashi came; Wimego felt safe only when he buried his face in Menashi's bosom. At last Wimego said between sobs that Mikínak had been carried into the mission with his arm bleeding blood and that Wedasi had been hung by Invaders. I was ready to run out but Menashi held me; she already knew what had happened.

Mikínak and Wedasi had gone with Koyoshkwe to a place in the forest where she gathered herbs. Wedasi was showing Mikínak how to ambush an army of Bluejackets when three armed men surrounded him and his son. Three others surrounded Koyoshkwe, beat her, pounced on her, emptied their juices into her, while Wedasi, pinned to a tree by two of the armed men, Mikínak by the third, helplessly watched. Thinking they had killed Koyoshkwe, the men released Wedasi and Mikínak and rushed away. Wedasi reached for his bow and shot an arrow through one of the men's shirt sleeves. All six turned and shot their rifles, missing Wedasi, grazing Mikínak's arm with a bullet. Mikínak ran into the village screaming for help; Ma-caynin and two of his mission assistants returned to the spot with the boy. The men had captured lame Wedasi and were ready to hang him from a tree. Ma-caynin spoke to the men of Hell and Damnation until they let Wedasi go. Mikínak and Wedasi fainted and had to be carried to the mission. Koyoshkwe was carried to her lodge. No one had died.

I heard the hardness in Menashi's voice. I wanted to run to Koyoshkwe. But still Menashi held me. She told me the crosswearers Mikenokwe, Notanokwe and their convert Nesoki were standing guard in front of Koyoshkwe's lodge; they didn't let even Wamoshkeshekwe go to her sister's side, howling that Koyoshkwe's rape was the Lord's punishment for the daily sins of Wamoshkeshekwe, Damushkekwe and Menashi. I stayed where I was. I could have faced the crosswearers' howls no better than Wamoshkeshekwe did, and when the shock left me I told myself I could not have faced Koyoshkwe either.

Menashi's hardness initially surprised me; in time it started to repel me. Menashi was frustrated and she was angry, but her anger was not directed at the six pioneers who had assaulted Koyoshkwe. She was angry because she thought the six armed men would have sought Menashi's gifts in the trading lodge if they had not found Koyoshkwe in the field. She was angry at Wedasi for his failure to block access to Koyoshkwe. She was angry because Koyoshkwe's availability debased the value of Menashi's gifts. Menashi had begun to reason about her gifts the same way Chebansi and Cakima reasoned about theirs.

The next time Wimego burst in on me panting with fear, I didn't wait for Menashi to return and calm him. I bolted out of my room and hurried toward the gathering crowd. Shandó, staggering, was leading two horses to the village, one laden with beaver furs, the other carrying the dead body of Topinbi. Cakima had her brother's body carried to her lodge by Chebansi and Nashkowatak. Cakima's face was a mask of sorrow. She and her brother had been closer to each other than either had been to anyone else; they had mirrored and supported each other's lifelong commitment to Wiske's ways. I had never before seen Cakima weep.

Shandó collapsed. Ignoring the howls and wails let loose by his crosswearing mother and her friends, I stayed by Shandó's side while Koyoshkwe revived him. Everyone in the village gathered on the councilground to hear his tale.

Topinbi and Shandó had set out with missionary Ma-caynin toward the Firekeepers' villages north of Bison Prairie. Topinbi went to collect furs and also to convince Ma-caynin that Wedasi was not the only young Firekeeper eager to leave the Peninsula and move west. Along the way, Topinbi showed Ma-caynin the complexes of mounds in ancient burial grounds; the sheer size of the mounds impressed Ma-caynin who admitted that he had considered only his fellow-Invaders capable of such feats. Topinbi had said that Firekeepers would repeat and surpass such feats if only they found a place where their very existence wasn't threatened.

In the villages, Topinbi introduced the missionary to every Firekeeper who wanted to leave the besieged Peninsula. Ma-caynin was convinced; he promised to ask the headman on the Strait for the supplies needed for such a trip, and he said he was willing to set out with Topinbi and Shandó in search of a suitable place. Others accompanied Ma-caynin back to his mission while Topinbi and Shandó gathered their last furs.

Along their return, Topinbi and Shandó crossed paths with a party of land measurers who were girdling trees—elm, ash and birch as well as sap-dripping maple. Topinbi approached the tree-girdlers and told them they were destroying the food and shelter of people who still lived in those woodlands, and begged them not to invite unnecessary anger and possible violence. The land measurers listened calmly, but when one of them turned vicious, they all did. They tied Topinbi and Shandó to two girdled trees near the land measurers' night camp. In the morning they returned the horses but not the furs. They carried the bound captives to the horses' backs and shot into the air. The horses bolted and Topinbi was thrown to the ground. Seeing that Topinbi was dead, the men abandoned the fur load and fled.

Firekeepers from seventy villages gathered in Bison Prairie for the burial. Few among them had accepted gifts for dead beavers, but all of them had known Topinbi. Nashkowatak drank himself to senselessness. Wedasi hid inside the mission, humiliated by his failure as a warrior, too ashamed to face Mikínak and the other revenge-seeking youths. Chebansi and Cakima begged Shandó to go to the Strait and demand the reparations repeatedly offered by Loos-gas for murders perpetrated by his agents.

Shandó had been afraid to go to the Strait since the time his caravan was ambushed, and he was more afraid now. I offered myself. I knew the way. Cakima prepared the horse and the furs. Chebansi gave me his talking leaves and missionary Macaynin ran to me with leaves for headman Loos-gas. Mikenokwe told me to be sure to ask Loos-gas to send a proper Blackrobe. I looked for Menashi but she was not where I could see her. Wimego came to me, his wide eyes pleading. I promised to build him a fasting lodge as soon as I returned. Just before I left, Koyoshkwe came toward me. Saying nothing, she hung the Firekeepers' bundle around my neck.

Reunited with the bundle of my ancestors, I set out for the Strait, following the path that carriers had taken for generations. Though the horse carried furs and I bore messages for the Invader, I was making this journey in the hope of finding the means of maintaining the Firekeepers' ways, whether it be in Bison Prairie or west of the Long River. As I traveled east, my thoughts were sad as I observed the ever-wider swath of destruction along the route.

Memories and longings caused me to leave the wide path and revisit the shore of the Grasslake where fifteen years earlier I had spent the joy-filled days and nights with Udatonte. Spreading the lock of black hair, the feather, the fishbones, the shell and the scroll fragments in front of me, I was renewed and strengthened. The surroundings brought me peace and I remained by the tree on the shore of the lake singing of things I had heard and seen.

But not even songs about love and dreams were possible by the Grasslake. An intruding pioneer interrupted my songs, scattered my memories. His firestick permitted him to treat me as the intruder. I returned to the path leading to the Strait and found my way to the lodge of my sister Wabnokwe and our kin.

Before reaching the lodge I was greeted by a group of playing children, most of them born since I had left the Strait eleven springs earlier: Wabnokwe's twin daughters Molly and Marti, aunt Margít's Benjy-may and her granddaughter Marianne Brooks. Among them was a young woman Mendideti, with a long black braid, who spoke in Udatonte's tongue. I eagerly sought her eyes, expecting to encounter the fierce gaze of my lost bride. Instead I found eyes like my cousin Mimikwe's, eyes that seemed to be looking elsewhere. The hair, too, differed from Udatonte's, being wavy rather than straight. I felt sudden shame for appearing here as a carrier and I wanted to explain to the black-braided girl that I had not journeyed to the Strait for the Invaders' objects, but in order to seek a way of retaining the harmony between earth and all her creatures. The arrival of aunt Margít and Wabnokwe prevented me from even beginning to explain that I was not what she saw.

I told Wabnokwe I had come with messages from our Bison Prairie kin and asked her to assemble a council so I could carry out the task entrusted to me. I told her I would sleep and feast only after I had counciled with our kin.

The warmth that greeted my arrival was abruptly shattered by the screech of pain and the black smoke of a floating island that moved in the Strait. The ugly intrusion of this machine on the waters next to the graves of our grandmothers was so painful that I grew confused, asking myself why I had come to this place, this place which remained strange to me, asking if my grandmothers could forgive me for accepting the transformation of their Tiosa Rondion.

Wabnokwe and Jim-may led me into the house, both seeming to share my pain at the sight of the floating object. Jim-may had grown to manhood since I had last seen him. Except for his pensive eyes, he resembled his father Jay-may so closely that I thought perhaps he would discuss matters of trade. I saw I was mistaken when instead of account books, Jim-may pulled out instruments and assembled players. The echoes of the unnatural, intruding machine were replaced by the wondrous sounds brought into this world by the four instruments and their players. The music restored my sense of having a place among my kin on the Strait.

As the room filled with those coming to council, the music ended. I prepared a pipe and when it had been passed around the circle, I told about Topinbi's and Shandó's visit to the lands beyond the Long River and about Topinbi's murder. I spoke of the uncertainty and divisions among our kin in Bison Prairie. Some, like Wedasi and Shandó, wanted to take their families to the western lands. Others, like Cakima and Chebansi, refused to consider abandoning Bison Prairie. Our mother's life engagement had the fur post as its center and she and our brother were resolved to continue it.

I told of the constant fear that lurked in all quarters of Bison Prairie. Invaders and their weapons were ever more numerous. The forests and fields of our ancestors were no longer safe for Rootkin and many of us saw hope for our people's renewal only in a distant place. I asked my sister, cousins and kin if they could consider joining those planning to journey to a new place.

Their angry responses burst forth like a torrent. Black-haired Mendideti's response was expressed in Udatonte's tongue and came as questions. She asked if the Firekeepers were prepared to see themselves as Invaders, prepared to occupy the prairies that bison hunters roam, prepared to make their home on the riverless plains which are so unlike the Peninsula's woodland shelters. She asked if the uprooted kin could find a path when the Invader followed them across the Long River and brought into their new home the fears they were now fleeing. I could not answer the questions posed by the black-braided girl but they made me see myself as I was seen, and again I felt shame.

The sudden anger of aunts Margít, Jozét and Moník, of cousins Lisa, Beth and Likét and of Wabnokwe was countered by Jay-may's, Wit-nags' and Killer Brooks's sudden interest. They were indifferent to uncle Topinbi's death, but talk of Rootkin abandoning the Peninsula brightened their faces and their words. To them, the prospect of more woodlands and meadows accessible to land measurers, tree cutters and fence-builders seemed a matter important enough for a council with headman Loos-gas. Mendideti's comment which likened these men to birds of prey only briefly interrupted their enthusiasm. After chasing Mendideti from the room, they resumed their talk. Dismayed by how my news had been received, I followed the children who left with Mendideti.

I stumbled toward clear air, to a spot overlooking the now calm river. In the dusk, the children appeared to be reenacting the scene inside; Benji-may sat like his father while Mendideti extended her arms and sang of greedy vultures circling their prey. But the children's version changed the outcome. When Benji-may rose to attack Mendideti, the attacker was pinned down by the girls; and Mendideti's black hair, loosened from her braid by the captive's flailing arm, fell over the boy's chest like drooping branches of a willow. The song and the heaving torso entranced me and I rested my heavy head on the trunk of the tree at the water's edge. Fog enveloped me, the tree and the water.

I wonder if this is the ninth moonless night by the round rock and the tree overhanging the water of the Strait. There's a sound in the fog which I first take for water lapping the shore, but when I look into the water I see Udatonte's face rising up; her lips meet mine. My hand reaches for hers and I crawl into the water, becoming liquid, full, unbounded. Water with a dream in its depths, a dream that love-play of sun and moon rouse, rupturing the unity. Desire emerges on winged fragments oscillating between land and water, undecided. Turning the water into her body's blood, earth decorates her moistened flesh with hair and welcomes the silvery-grey turtle spawning on its surface. The parent turns on the children and swallows the offspring. They give themselves—but only when they can't avoid being eaten. Some of us fly into the air, others crawl under rocks, yet others walk to dens.

Our scales fall off on our journey beyond sand's end. We flee the cold slush that swallows our cousins and wander into woodlands bounded by seas of sweet water. We find the tree split by a great rock that stands on the shore of Kichigami's waters. When a raven lifts me on her wings I share the flight of my Oceanshore grandmother and we merge with Yahatase who scatters seeds and sings the longhouse songs of earth's regeneration. We offer ourselves to earth and discover ourselves in Miogwewe, expelling Wiske. We share the songs and dreams of Rootkin as Katabwe, as the warrior-woman who turns away from killing. We rejoice at the splendor of earth's gifts. Udatonte's love causes our limbs to grow light; the joy is followed by grief at our loss. With amazement we see, through a tent of transparent hair, four gushing streams of liquid, each shaped like an arch. On the spot where one of the gushing arches reaches ground, a sapling emerges; where a second stream hits ground an egg cracks, a tiny bird emerges; a third jet lands on a worm and elongates it into the writhing body of a snake; the fourth stream showers the body of a furry animal that rises on its hind legs like a bear. Trembling, we hear a baby's cry that reaches us through the fog.

Even before opening my eyes, I knew I was in the room where I had been locked up fourteen summers earlier, after I had been separated from Udatonte. Now the windows weren't barred and the door wasn't locked. I walked to the music room, drawn to the sound like a bee to flowers. The music stopped. Wabnokwe led me out of the house to vent her anger. I had excited and upset everyone with my announcements and intentions, and had then gone to sleep for three days in a hidingplace by the Strait's shore. She had arranged for the council I had wanted with headman Loos-gas and had postponed it because she couldn't find me.

I told Wabnokwe that I hadn't slept. I had learned who I was. I hadn't known who I was when I had expressed a desire to leave the Peninsula. I held the medicine bundle of the Peninsula's Firekeepers and I wouldn't move until the Peninsula itself moved. I would council with Loos-gas, but only to deliver other people's messages. My most urgent desire was to return to Bison Prairie. The only person I wanted to see again was the girl with the long black braid because she reminded me of someone I had known. I was disappointed to learn that the girl had left the Strait while I dreamt; she had accompanied Wabnokwe's daughters on a voyage toward the Oceanshore.

Wabnokwe begged me not to vanish again before I counciled with the headman. I did visit the spot on shore once again. I didn't see the great rock or the double-trunked tree, but I knew they were there. All I saw was a denuded shore, square lodges, a fort upstream, a road, smoke-spewing ships in the water; I knew that these were all a bad dream.

I counciled with headman Loos-gas wearing my bundle outside my shirt. Loos-gas, a big man, grinned and bowed as he lit his tobacco tube. He told me he'd heard that Bison Prairie's chief To-pin-a-bee, as he called my uncle, had killed himself by falling off a horse when he was drunk. He must have heard this from the land measurers responsible for Topinbi's death. I handed him the talking leaves from Chebansi and Ma-caynin. Loos-gas frowned; he said he would himself go to Bison Prairie to compensate Topinbi's kin.

His grin returned after he examined Ma-caynin's leaf. He said that the Firekeepers who wanted to leave the Peninsula were sensible, and that he would urge missionary Ma-caynin to find them a suitable place in the western Plains. He asked me if I too was eager to leave. I told him that I would cross the Long River after I died, and I asked him if he and his people were sensible enough to return to the east. Loos-gas frowned. He told me I had spoken his language better the last time he had seen me. He thought I was Nashkowatak, who had once been a soldier in this headman's army. When I prepared to leave he told me, still frowning, that Wabnokwe and I and our brothers possessed titles which no one could violate, that we could stay on the Peninsula as long as the sun kept rising.

I returned to Jay-may's lodge for the horse and the meager gifts. I had nothing more to say to Wabnokwe or Margít or her children. I headed to Kekionga, to Aptegizhek's lodge on the fringes of a vast encampment of Invaders. Aptegizhek was a skeleton with a bandana on top. He couldn't see well enough to hunt. He told me his cousin Onimush brought him food. I stayed with Aptegizhek through the winter. He rarely left his small lodge, but his mind still roamed over Kichigami and the Beautiful Valley. I told him I had been with Yahatase, Miogwewe and Katabwe. My story cheered him, as I knew it would.

The path from Kekionga westward was littered with signs of pioneers. The dead trees, cleared paths reverting to forest, fields of stunted cover and abandoned makeshift lodges marked the arrival and departure of people who made no sense to me. The signs accompanied me to the very edge of Bison Prairie.

I looked for Wimego as soon as I entered the village; I was ready to build his fasting lodge. I wasn't prepared for the news that greeted me when I delivered the horse and gifts to Cakima and Chebansi. Cakima told me I had carried out my mission well. Headman Loos-gas had left the Strait soon after I had councilied with him and had called Bison Prairie's Firekeepers to a gathering in Kithepekanu. Loos-gas had showered Cakima with gifts to compensate her for the death of her brother, had promised to stop in Bison Prairie on his return journey to confirm Cakima's titles and to grant her more, and had sent all of Bison Prairie's children to a distant school.

Dismayed by Cakima's words, I rushed to Meteya's lodge. Nashkowatak greeted me warmly, with none of the animosity I anticipated since the day I had followed Menashi to the forest. He told me he remembered that he had once separated me from my bride, and he asked me to forgive him for separating me from Udatonte and also from Koyoshkwe. Nashkowatak told me that after Menashi's and Wimego's departure, he had moved to Koyoshkwe's mat. Koyoshkwe, grateful to anyone who asked her for anything, had not turned him away.

Nashkowatak was surprised that I didn't know what had happened to the children. He thought I had made the arrangements to remove the children from pioneer-encircled Bison Prairie. Ma-caynin had received word of the Wabash gathering and had carried word to Cakima and Menashi. Cakima had begged Nashkowatak to accompany her to Kithepekanu because Chebansi refused to leave the store and Wedasi refused to budge from the mission. Menashi and Ma-caynin dragged the children to the Wabash; Nashkowatak wasn't told why. The aim of headman Loos-gas was to deprive the Wabash Prairiekin of their lands. Nashkowatak's aim was to drink as much whiskey as he could lay his hands on. Everything was over before Nashkowatak learned what had happened.

After concluding his treaty with the Prairiekin, Loos-gas told the Firekeepers that he had councilied with Burr-net's son, meaning me, and that he was ready to fulfill the promises he had made to me. He gave traveling supplies and elaborate promises to Menashi, Damushkekwe and others who were willing to accompany him to the western shore of the Long River; he gave compensation gifts to Cakima; and he had the children sent to a school called an academy far south of the Beautiful River. Shandó's son Pogon, Wedasi's Mikínak and Nashkowatak's Wimego were among the children led away to the distant academy.

I told Nashkowatak that I had met with the headman, but had asked for nothing and approved nothing. Nashkowatak told me Loos-gas had used me the way he used the signatures on his treaties, as a cover for his next move. Loos-gas wanted us to consent to every wound he inflicted on us, and he recruited our fears and our greed to squeeze that consent out of us. Menashi and Damushkekwe were rewarded with a mound of gifts for every child sent away. Shandó was promised a refuge away from ambushes and murders. Cakima favored the schooling of the children. Crosswearing Mikenokwe would have raised a cry to stop the kidnapping of her grandson Pogon, but Menashi and Shandó had been careful not to forewarn Mikenokwe, and she hadn't gone to the Wabash gathering. Nashkowatak couldn't have stopped the kidnapping. Even if he'd known that Loos-gas was using me, and if he'd been sober, he could not have coped with Shandó's fear or Menashi's greed.

Menashi was gone. Nashkowatak spoke cruelly of her. He said she had gone to found her own house of prostitutes—he named it Menashi's sunset whorehouse—in a place where the monopoly of sexual favors would be guaranteed by the headman's troops; Damushkekwe was her first recruit. I shared much of Nashkowatak's resentment, and I was dismayed by Menashi's sacrifice of her son. But I also pitied her. Beautiful Menashi wore Shutaha's pendant and she knew how to wield Shutaha's powers. In different circumstances she might have repeated or even surpassed Shutaha's feats. I also pitied Damushkekwe, a girl-warrior like my grandmother Katabwe, reduced to stalking and attacking the enemy with her sexual organ.

I knew that Menashi and Damushkekwe had done no more than they had seen Cakima do. It was from Cakima that they learned to honor greed above kinship. Cakima saw nothing in their departure but a diminution in the store's gifts. With Topinbi dead and Shandó too fearful to replace him, Bison Prairie's fur trade shrank to the few furs Naganwatek still brought from the Lakebottom and the few gifts Wamoshkeshekwe still received for her favors. But Wamoshkeshekwe without her two friends was ever less willing to receive the store's guests and ever more receptive to the reproaches of crosswearing Notanokwe and Mikenokwe.

Cakima's trading post was dying; she and Chebansi looked forward to Loos-gas's council in Bison Prairie to resuscitate their ailing store.

Kin from various villages, especially from the Lakebottom, began to gather in Bison Prairie long before the council with the

Invaders. Naganwatek and his family moved into and alongside Meteya's lodge; his woman Meshewokwe was Koyoshkwe's aunt; their son Shawanetek, whom I had named, was already old enough to want a fasting lodge. Meshewokwe's niece Miskokwe arrived large with child, and she gave birth to a son almost as soon as she reached Koyoshkwe's offered mat. I was asked to name the boy.

I resolved to confront the fear and the greed, to celebrate the child's beginning as a new beginning of Bison Prairie. Koyoshkwe knew what I had in mind before I spoke to her. Nashkowatak was eager to help, as were Meteya and Topash. I approached Chebansi, thinking that the collapse of the fur trade might have led him to seek something else, but found him hostile; he thought the ceremony would make bad air for the coming council. Wedasi and Shandó were just as hostile; both of them clung to missionary Ma-caynin, waiting only for the day when he would lead them westward. Wedasi said Bison Prairie was no longer a place where people could grow, either as dreamers or as warriors.

Koyoshkwe kept herself so much in the shadows that everyone thought I was the arranger of the ceremony. Yet it was Koyoshkwe who sent word of the celebration to everyone except the crosswearers. She saw to the gathering of food and firewood. She gathered the masks of the spirit-impersonators, marked out the spots for the three fires, and rehearsed those unfamiliar with the ceremony. I merely took Miskokwe's child, laid him on the ground between the fires, and named him Oki or earth, land, soil. Koyoshkwe stayed in the shadows during all the renewal dances around the three hearths; she emerged only when the long-eared Trickster, the bringer of fear and arouser of greed, impersonated by Nashkowatak, broke through the circles to extinguish the fires. Koyoshkwe was foremost among the women who took up sticks and chased the Invader away from the Firekeepers' circles.

Suicide of Wimego

The dancing mood stayed with us. Soon after the naming of Miskokwe's child, Koyoshkwe threw herself into preparations for the planting ceremony; she drew out of me songs I had heard as a child but never sung. By the time headman Loos-gas and his train entered Bison Prairie we—those of us who had danced— were able to face him without fear and without greed; we knew who we were and what we wanted.

Headman Loos-gas arrived from the west with a train of Lakebottom hunters and carriers. Notanokwe's brother Wiske Lashás and her cousin Shishibinqua Robin-sin served him as scouts and guides; Miskokwe's brother Billy Cod-well served him as interpreter. I learned that the Lakebottom's trader Kin-sic had died and that the landgrabbers and coinseekers who replaced Kin-sic had killed what remained of the Lakebottom's fur trade.

Deprived of the gifts and gunpowder they couldn't live without, the grandsons of Nangisi and Winámek had grasped at the promises offered to them by headman Loos-gas: their scouting and interpreting would be rewarded with gifts and powder and also with titles to land sections in the western Plains. They guided Loos-gas from the Wabash to the western shore of the Long River where, near a village of Redearth kin, the Lakebottom hunters helped Loos-gas gather signatures on leaves that spoke of all the lands on Mishigami's other shore. I was told that my cousin Shabeni had also helped gather the signatures. The last task of the scouts and guides was to lead Loos-gas eastward, to Bison Prairie, to help him oust the Firekeepers from the Peninsula.

With all his guides and interpreters, headman Loos-gas did not find what he sought in Bison Prairie, maybe because his ablest assistant Topinbi was no longer with us, or because we had strengthened ourselves before his arrival. The headman's arrival from the west coincided with the arrival, from the east, of a caravan that included many of the Strait's traders as well as Onimush and Aptegizhek from Kekionga.

The traders came for grants of land sections to children of Firekeepers by birth or marriage. Aptegizhek, a skeleton that walked and talked, came to warn us not to sign away any land, no matter how distant from us, but to insist we were all children of Firekeepers by birth or marriage and to demand titles to our lands. This was precisely what we did. Nashkowatak and I, as well as Mikenokwe, also demanded the return of Bison Prairie's kidnapped children. Loos-gas found no allies in Bison Prairie other than missionary Ma-caynin and those who, like Wedasi and Shandó, were driven by humiliation and fear. Loos-gas pretended to give in to our demands, and he gave Ma-caynin and the Lakebottom hunters supplies for the western journey.

As soon as Loos-gas and his train left Bison Prairie, the Lakebottom hunters filled themselves with firewater supplied to them by a whiskey peddler left behind by the headman. The drinking feast turned into a brawl and two men were killed; one of the victims was Miskokwe's man Sogun, who had not wanted to accompany his cousins to the west.

Koyoshkwe, Meshewokwe and I helped Miskokwe arrange the burial ceremony. The Lakebottom hunters left Bison Prairie during the burial. Ma-caynin and Shandó left with them, to see the Plains and to look for a place similar to Bison Prairie. Young Shawanetek longed to leave with his cousins Katwyn Cod-well, Pezhenkwe Robin-sin, Wabskeni Lashás and little Nagmo Lepetí, but Shawanetek's mother, Meshewokwe, had no desire to leave Koyoshkwe's lodge. And the boy's father Naganwatek, who had once loved Menashi, was preparing to depart in the opposite direction, to accompany Aptegizhek back to Kekionga.

After the Lakebottom's hunters set out to decimate the beaver in its next refuge, neither beavers nor peace returned to Bison Prairie. The whiskey peddler left behind by Loos-gas, a man called Bar-trend, did not follow the headman eastward nor the hunters westward. Bar-trend stayed in Bison Prairie and raised a whiskey tent on the path from Topash's lodge to the river. The whiskey tent attracted youths who fancied themselves warriors when the liquid burned their brains, and who threatened all nearby villages.

When Topash and Nashkowatak asked Bar-trend to move his whiskey tent elsewhere, he waved a leaf in their faces. Nashkowatak recognized the leaf as the title to Menashi's land section which stretched from the heart of our village to Boatmaker's abandoned fort at the rivermouth. Menashi had apparently exchanged her Bison Prairie title for a title to western lands, and Loos-gas had given her title to the whiskey peddler.

Topash called for a council of Firekeepers. Cakima was irate at the man's presence in our village, although as a girl she had brought a similar man, my father, to Bison Prairie. Wedasi, predictably, called for a war dance, but Topash and Meteya insisted on a peaceful confrontation and convinced most others. I accompanied the group that set out to expel the whiskey peddler. Bar-trend knew of the council's resolve and fled. Several drunken youths guarded the whiskey tent, and when we approached, they shot at us. Young Shawanetek was wounded. Meteya was shot in the heart.

Nashkowatak and I carried the injured boy to Meteya's lodge; there, Meshewokwe and Koyoshkwe applied salves to the wound and sang to the boy's spirit. Koyoshkwe left Shawanetek in his mother's care and threw herself into preparations for Meteya's burial. Koyoshkwe shed no tears, showed no visible sorrow; she could have been arranging a child's naming, but I knew that Koyoshkwe's insides were torn. She had loved her father as much as one person can love another. She had considered Meteya her guide. She shared his shyness of talk, his love of trees and animals, his loneliness. The mere sight of her tearless face filled my eyes with tears; I was too sad to help her.

I went to share my sorrow with Wedasi, who had lived most of his life alongside Meteya. Wedasi too shed tears, but his were tears of humiliation. He spoke of himself as Damushkekwe had spoken of him, as a warrior with his mouth only, as a warrior who had not stopped a single abuse or a single murder. And he again spoke of Bison Prairie as a place where people could no longer live. His only thoughts were on Shandó's and Macaynin's return with news of the west.

Koyoshkwe's sister Wamoshkeshekwe wailed so the entire valley could hear. She wore a black dress given to her by Chebansi's untouched bride Notanokwe, and she displayed her sorrow wherever people could see and hear her. Season after season Wamoshkeshekwe had listened to Notanokwe and to Shandó's mother telling her that her sinful life was to blame for the rape of Koyoshkwe, for the death of Topinbi, for the kidnapping of Pogon. Now she was to blame for the murder of her father. Wamoshkeshekwe made a show of moving out of Cakima's lodge and into Mikenokwe's, alongside Notanokwe. Her guilt led her to grieve in the crosswearers' way, so showily that she made tearless Koyoshkwe seem hardhearted.

Cakima shed no tears for her dead cousin Meteya. Her main concern was the whiskey peddler, who had moved his post to the rivermouth after the shooting. Cakima and Chebansi were convinced that Loos-gas had left Bar-trend among us as a replacement for Kin-sic, to ruin Cakima's post, to reduce us to misery, so as to make us beg to exchange our titles for food and supplies. Cakima spoke to Naganwatek as he prepared to leave with Aptegizhek. She asked Naganwatek to go further than Kekionga, to replace Topinbi and be her emissary to the Strait, to demand that Menashi's title be returned to Menashi's kin and to seek compensation for the murder of Meteya.

On the eve of Aptegizhek's departure with Naganwatek, the skinny old man went to the bedside of Naganwatek's son and placed small shells on Shawanetek's wound and on the boy's chest. Aptegizhek then scattered shells in other corners of Meteya's lodge, near the entrances to other lodges and on spots where no lodges stood.

With the aid of Aptegizhek's shells, Meshewokwe's compresses, Koyoshkwe's herbs and songs, Shawanetek soon recovered. I sang to the boy of ancient days when Rootkin regained their strength after encounters with monsters more powerful than drunken youths, and of the spirits who guided and protected those of us who could see them. At first the boy put a wall between himself and me. He said he wanted only to rejoin his cousins, Nangisi's youngest descendants Nagmo, Wabskeni and Katwyn. But Aptegizhek had left a mark on the boy.

The skinny granduncle who had lived a long life after being scalped, who seemed to defy death, impressed Shawanetek. When the snows melted, he accompanied Meshewokwe and Koyoshkwe to the cornfields and into the forest to gather herbs, and he began to sing Koyoshkwe's songs. At last he told me he too wanted what Aptegizhek surely had: a protector, a spirit-guide.

The joy of the new spring was on the faces of Meshewokwe and Koyoshkwe the morning I set out with Shawanetek. I led him deep into the forest to a hill at the turn of a stream, the same hill to which Shabeni had led me over twenty springs earlier. Shawanetek helped me prop a small rain shelter on an ancient birch overlooking the stream. When I got back to the village, I found Koyoshkwe and Meshewokwe already preparing to celebrate Shawanetek's return from his fast. The void left in Koyoshkwe by Meteya's death was partially filled by young Shawanetek; and in her aunt Meshewokwe, the youth's mother, Koyoshkwe found something she hadn't known before, loving friendship.

The celebration of Shawanetek's dream was marred by the clamorous return of Shandó and Ma-caynin from the west. Ma-caynin announced that he and Shandó had found the promised land and that he had a title to it. Nashkowatak and I rushed to the mission to hear the good news. Ma-caynin's voice drowned out all others, but the more he spoke the more evident it became that he wasn't speaking of an actual place.

Ma-caynin said we could all reach the promised land if we kept reaching for better things; he said all people were beasts by birth, and all could grope their way from bestiality to civility. He reminded me of my childhood teacher, Misus Bay-con. Yet Wedasi was entranced by the man's words; he seemed to have forgotten our animosity toward Misus Bay-con; he behaved as if the empty words annulled his life's humiliations and restored his missing leg.

Nashkowatak and I separated Shandó from his mentor and pressed Shandó to speak of the place he had visited. Shandó admitted that the place was dry the year round, with no connected lakes through which to paddle bark canoes and no birches with which to make the canoes; the animals and the plants were not those that had sustained our ancestors, and there were no sap-bearing maples; traders were established wherever paths intersected, and uniformed armed men guarded the posts; the original inhabitants of the place were being driven toward the Sunset Mountains to make room for the newcomers, and armed Invaders were crossing the Long River in hordes, denuding earth of her cover.

Yet after all his admissions, Shandó persisted in speaking of the place as the promised land, which he also named Caynin. I remembered that as a boy I had been warned of the Invaders' powerful sorcery. In Misus Bay-con's school I hadn't been impressed. Now I was impressed. Ma-caynin had bewitched Shandó and Wedasi. He gave them everything they lacked: full villages of kin, powerful spirit-guides and healthy limbs. But his gifts lodged only in his head; they were mere words—words which emptied Shandó and Wedasi while seeming to fill them.

Naganwatek's return from the Strait in a house on wheels brought everything in Bison Prairie to a standstill. We all thought Naganwatek had brought five Invaders into Bison Prairie when we saw the strangely dressed occupants of the rolling lodge, two of them with yellow hair. Only gradually did I recognize the minister-like youth in black as Shandó's son

Pogon, the two youths in traders' clothes as my nephews Wimego and Mikínak, the two women, one in a red dress that clashed with her yellow hair, the other in black, as my sister Wabnokwe and her friend Likét. My eyes fixed themselves on the object suspended from Wimego's neck, on Menashi's greenstone pendant; it seemed misplaced in front of the trader's jacket, below the yellow hair.

Nashkowatak was the first to recognize the guests. He greeted our sister by asking if she had come to rejoin her kin, or only to show them to her friend. Cakima backed away embarrassed, as if she were ashamed to be one of us. Cakima's composure returned when she turned to her grandson Wimego, who was not as shockingly foreign to her. The youth's clothes, his blue eyes, his shyness surely reminded her of her first view of trader Burr-net.

Nashkowatak persisted in his rudeness. Instead of inviting the guests to the chairs in Cakima's councilroom, he announced that since the guests were not really guests but Firekeepers returning to their kin-village, the place to greet them was the councilground. From their very manners Nashkowatak knew that the guests had been accepted among the Invaders as he had not been, and his rudeness was his way of questioning their need to return to their kin-village during its last days. I was afraid he would stretch his inappropriate offers to the point of asking Koyoshkwe to prepare a sweat lodge and me to start a dance, but he stopped with his invitation to the councilground. Shandó's mother, incensed by Nashkowatak's invitation, pulled her grandson Pogon and also Likét away from the rest of us, toward the crosswearers' lodge.

Wabnokwe and the two youths accepted the invitation to the councilground; Koyoshkwe and I lit a fire. Wedasi hobbled out of the mission house. Chebansi came out of the store. Wabnokwe told us she and Likét had come to Bison Prairie to urge us not to leave the Peninsula, and to help us stay if they could. The three youths had returned for reasons of their own, although their coming together was less than a coincidence.

I was under the impression that headman Loos-gas was honoring his promise to us by returning the youths to us. Wedasi's son quickly disabused me of this impression. Mikínak told us Loos-gas intended to forcefully remove all the free villagers who still hunted and danced on our side of the Long River, and he had begun to carry out his intention by recruiting the youths in the southern academy into his armies. Mikínak and Wimego had not been recruited because their trainers had known they would turn their rifles in the wrong direction as soon as they were given rifles. Pogon had not been recruited because he had become the minister's favorite and during all his five years at the academy, Pogon had learned only to pray, not to shoot. When the academy broke up, the minister gave Pogon a purse of coins with which to return to his people so as to teach them the Word of God, and it was thanks to Pogon's purse that the three youths were able to travel on the Invaders' paths.

Mikínak spoke without an accent, but his manner was foreign, and he punctuated his statements with foul expressions in the Invaders' language. He was what Wedasi had wanted him to be, a warrior, but Wedasi looked ill at ease beside him, and when Mikínak was done speaking, Wedasi hobbled back to the mission. The contempt with which Mikínak spoke of Pogon was heard by everyone. I saw that the youth looked at me with unmistakable contempt. Wedasi fled before his son turned to him and called him a powerless cripple.

When the council ended, I saw Shawanetek approach Wimego and Mikínak to invite them to lodge with him at Koyoshkwe's. Both youths turned their backs to Shawanetek as someone unworthy of their attention. Wimego accompanied Wabnokwe to Cakima's lodge; he had undoubtedly become used to raised beds, chairs and plates. Mikínak asked where the whiskey was kept and made his way to the whiskey peddler's post.

A few days later, Nashkowatak and I visited our sister to learn what truth there was in Mikínak's description of the Invaders' intentions. We found Cakima in a death-like trance and Chebansi incapacitated by a trembling fit. Wabnokwe told us that the Strait's trader Jay-may was dead, that his successors would not have given anything to Topinbi, and would not even open their door to Naganwatek. Wabnokwe and her friends had succeeded in arranging a council between Naganwatek and the headman, but to no avail. The headman's response to Chebansi's messages had been that the government owed Burr-net nothing, neither a title nor compensation, and the headman had spoken of Bar-trend as the owner of Menashi's land section. Wabnokwe thought Chebansi ought to prepare another appeal to the headman, and offered herself as messenger.

Another brawl had broken out and Shawanetek was injured again. For several nights Mikínak had been joining the drunken youths at Bar-trend's whiskey post. Mikínak had excited the youths with talk of war until at last they had all set out in search of enemies. Shawanetek, still trying to befriend Mikínak, had approached the demented youths. Mikínak had called Shawanetek the son of a traitor, had referred to me as a sorcerer and to Nashkowatak as an enemy agent. Shawanetek had replied that the only traitors in Bison Prairie were the drunkards who had murdered Meteya. Mikínak and his confederates responded to Shawanetek's accusation by surrounding and beating the younger boy. Koyoshkwe overheard the exchange, fetched Meshewokwe and Topash, and saved the boy from serious harm.

I ran to Koyoshkwe's. The boy wasn't there. Meshewokwe was in tears. Shawanetek had refused to let Meshewokwe or Koyoshkwe treat his bruises, and had joined his father and the others who were ready to leave Bison Prairie.

Koyoshkwe accompanied me to the dismantled mission. Rev-rend Ma-caynin and his assistants were done packing, and were waiting for Shandó to return from his last visit with his mother, wife and son. Wedasi was ready to leave without parting words for anyone. Naganwatek and his son were alongside Wedasi. Naganwatek told me Meshewokwe had found Koyoshkwe and no longer needed him. He was a carrier and he had once loved Menashi; he had wanted to go west ever since Menashi had left; now that there would be no more carrying to or from Bison Prairie, he had no reason to stay, and the beating of his son made him eager to leave quickly. Shawanetek, still bleeding from untended bruises, defiantly told me he'd had better friends on the Lakebottom than he'd found in Bison Prairie, and he wanted only to rejoin his friends. When the caravan began to move, Shawanetek thanked me for helping him find his dream-spirit; he did not thank Koyoshkwe, and he did not give me a parting word for Meshewokwe.

My cousin Nesoki, dressed in black, was at the head of the departing caravan, alongside Rev-rend Ma-caynin. Ma-caynin had pulled Nesoki away from Mikenokwe and the other crosswearers by addressing him as chief To-pin-a-bee and speaking of him as the son and heir of the former chief, as the spokesman of Kichigami's Firekeepers, as the savior who led his people to the promised land. Ma-caynin knew that Nesoki had never been so important, and that Nesoki's rebirth as Christ and Wiske would turn Nesoki into a pliant tool, useful for Ma-caynin's dealings with other Invaders in the promised land.

The leaves fell from the trees and soon snow covered the tracks of those who had departed. Nashkowatak and Topash left to hunt. Koyoshkwe and Meshewokwe tied the ribs of snowshoes and sang songs of mourning. In midwinter Wimego entered our lodge, only to visit, he said, but he stayed on. He let Koyoshkwe and me know that he had not returned to Bison Prairie to do what his grandmother Cakima expected of him. With Lókaskwe's yellow hair and Burr-net's blue eyes, Wimego could have become trader Burr-net in any of the Invaders' camps along the way from the southern academy to the Strait.

He told us he no longer knew who his kin were, and had returned to seek them. He remembered that Menashi had been his refuge, that he had trustingly accompanied her to the Wabash, and that she had given him away to the academy's recruiting agent in exchange for a purse and a promise. He remembered that Nashkowatak had also been on the Wabash, too drunk to protect or even recognize his own son. On the eve of his departure, he had run to Menashi and buried his face in her bosom. She had pushed him away, hung Shutaha's pendant around his neck, and told him the greenstone would help him learn the Invaders' ways.

Wimego didn't want to learn their ways; he feared the Invaders. He had not forgotten what they had done to Koyoshkwe and Topinbi. But his mother pushed him away, and the boy felt rejected, alone and kinless. He gave himself to his trainers as completely as Nashkowatak had once done. He cropped his hair, wore clothes that kept the sun from his skin, carried his snot in his pocket and his sweat in his underclothes. He imprisoned his neck in a stiff collar and his feet in leather boots. He learned how to read from paper while forgetting how to read from branches and animal tracks. He learned how to sleep on a raised bed, comb his shorn hair, eat with a fork, use a toilet, pray to the savior and shoot a rifle, while forgetting how to give and share. He learned to ridicule and despise his kin for their inability to eat with forks or read from paper. Like his cousin Mikínak, he learned to think of his mother as a prostitute, his father a drunkard, his uncles a pimp, a cripple and a sorcerer. But he did not lose his fear of the Invaders; he never forgot that their likes had raped Koyoshkwe and murdered Topinbi. His trainers knew he hated them, and when they began to recruit youths into their army, they rejected Wimego for the same reason they rejected Mikínak, as untrustworthy.

Koyoshkwe, Meshewokwe and I could not keep our eyes dry; we were saddened as much by Wimego's story as by the manner in which he told it. He spoke as if he felt nothing, as if he were empty, as if his heart had been removed. He asked nothing of us, seemed to want nothing from us.

Remembering my own return after my years of schooling on the Strait, I reminded Wimego that I had promised to build him a fasting lodge. Wimego looked at me with the same contempt I had seen in Mikínak's eyes, and said that any fool who fasted long enough would see things that weren't real.

When Nashkowatak returned, Wimego spoke not a word to his father. But when the ground softened, Wimego appeared to soften too. He accompanied Koyoshkwe and Meshewokwe, he followed Koyoshkwe to the forest to gather herbs, he questioned Koyoshkwe about the uses of the barks and roots.

When he asked me to guide him to a fasting lodge, I thought his heart was returning, I thought he wanted to become one of us. I delayed as long as I could because he learned none of the songs, did not give signs of even hearing me. But I remembered my own frustration at having my dream deferred, and I gave in to his request.

Koyoshkwe was uneasy when Wimego and I left her lodge and headed toward the forest. I sang, unaccompanied, along the trail to the hillside where Shawanetek and I myself had dreamt; Wimego followed, silent. I repaired Shawanetek's rain shelter unaided, and left Wimego in it.

Remembering Topinbi's interruption of my first dream, I resolved to leave Wimego alone for a fortnight. But only two or three nights after we had set out, I had a bad dream, and the following morning I prepared to return to the hillside, not to interrupt but only to see.

As I stepped out of the lodge, I saw Mikínak and his painted companions enter the village carrying a body. Villagers gathered around the youths. Mikínak announced that he and his companions had been scouting and had seen a band of Scalpers surround and murder Wimego. Mikínak urged the village men to arm themselves and follow him in pursuit of the enemy. Koyoshkwe screamed as if she'd just waken from a nightmare and ran toward the body, Nashkowatak and I close behind her.

Koyoshkwe pushed Mikínak and his friends aside, took the dead body in her arms, examined the eyes, the mouth. With a trembling hand she gave me the greenstone pendant. Between sobs she said that Wimego had questioned her only about poisonous roots. Wimego had not been surrounded or murdered. He had eaten the root of a mayapple.

I did not join Nashkowatak in drowning the pain with whiskey, but I was as dazed as he, and Koyoshkwe made all the burial arrangements unaided. Except for Mikínak, who confined himself to Bar-trend's post at the Rivermouth during the burial, everyone in the village, even the crosswearers, took part in Koyoshkwe's ceremony. Numerous unrealized and conflicting expectations went into the ground with the yellowhaired youth.

Mikínak did not return to the village until a band of visitors arrived from the west, and then he returned painted, armed and defiant, making no apologies for his lie about Wimego's death. The visitors were young Redearth warriors, and Mikínak entered the village as one of them. I stared with amazement at the painted face of one of the warriors; the eyes were frighteningly familiar to me. I approached him and learned he was Shabeni's son Komenoteya, small like his mother and with Mimikwe's distant and sorrowful eyes, the eyes that I too had gotten from my great-grandmother Menoko.

Komenoteya came to us with a message from his wife's father, the Redearth warrior Macataimeshekiakak. He told us that greedy stoneseekers were on Mishigami's other shore, digging in sacred places, gouging in mountains and burrowing into ancestral grounds. They were killing all who stood between them and their stones, driving the other shore's villagers to seek refuge among the Redearth kin on the western shore of the Long River.

The refugees were angry; they were painting themselves and dancing; they were resolved to put an end to the extermination of the other shore's Rootkin. Many, among them Komenoteya's father Shabeni, thought that Rootkin were too few to paint themselves and dance, too few to face the Invaders on yet another battlefield. But Macataimeshekiakak and other Redearth warriors, including Shabeni's son, were sure that the Peninsula's Rootkin, victims of so many incursions and murders since the days of the first plagues, would make common cause with the Redearth kin, and then the warriors would not be too few. The message was a call to gather at the Leaning Tree village for a war council with kin from both shores.

Bison Prairie's Firekeepers listened to the Redearth messengers, many with deep sympathy, but they agreed with Shabeni that we were too few to confront the Invaders with weapons in hand. Only Mikínak and his drinking companions committed themselves to attending the war council at the Leaning Tree. But after the messengers had moved on to recruit in neighboring villages, when Mikínak prepared to set out, his companions lost their courage. They were as ready to boast as they were to defend their whiskey supplier from unarmed men and boys, but they were not ready to go to war.

Mikínak severed his friendships and prepared to depart alone. Koyoshkwe begged me to talk to the hotheaded youth, to show him the Firekeepers' bundle, to keep him in Bison Prairie, but to go with him if I couldn't keep him from going. She begged me to return with him, and with Mimikwe's son if I could. Bison Prairie was half empty. Koyoshkwe feared that a war would bring complete desolation.

But talking to Mikínak was beyond my powers. I sang and I spoke, but Mikínak did not say a word to me during the entire journey. He knew I was with him only to restrain him, just as Shabeni had once restrained Wedasi. Mikínak's father had admired Shabeni. Mikinak hated me; he tolerated my company only because I knew the way.

The council was already under way when we beached our canoe. Mikínak promptly turned his back to me and headed toward Komenoteya and the other Redearth warriors. I saw Shabeni on the opposite side of the circle and sat down near him. I listened to one after another Redearth warrior urge his listeners to prepare for war. I listened to the speakers on my side decline the invitation to war, ridicule the childish rashness of the Redearth speakers, warn of the prospects, accuse the warriors of wanting to hasten our demise.

I knew I was seeing the last great councilfire on the Great Lakes, and my eyes filled with tears. My thoughts agreed with those of Shabeni and the other peacemakers, but my sympathies were with Mimikwe's son and the Redearth warriors. To me, the Firekeepers and carriers on my side, even Shabeni, seemed similar to the boasters who gathered at Bar-trend's whiskey post. They praised the feats of ancient warriors but accepted gifts, powder and whiskey from the present enemy.

I had an urge to rise, to dance, to scatter the shells that would revive the ancient Peninsulakin. I didn't rise, but my eyes wandered across the fire and came to rest on the face of a woman, a familiar face framed by straight black hair. Fierce eyes, lit by the fire and the full moon, looked directly into mine, made my head spin, entranced me. I sank to the ground and I dreamt of my near-death on the Morningland battlefield, of my inability to find Udatonte, and of my attempts to stray from and then to stay on the path of a bundle-carrier until it led me to the village by the Leaning Tree, where I thought I was about to rejoin Udatonte.

The sun was rising when I woke from my dream. The last council was over, the fire was all burnt out, most of the warriors were gone. A few people still sat at various points along the broken circle; the sun in my eyes kept me from seeing their faces. I rose from the ground and walked past the burnt-out fire. I saw that the people who remained were old women and men who stared at the still hearth or dozed. I leapt forward when I saw that the woman with the black hair and fierce eyes was still there—and then I stopped. The eyes weren't fierce; they were distant and tortured. The hair was black and straight, and it hung down to the ground like a tent, but the face it framed was as wrinkled as bark.

Epilogue

I kept on staring, waiting for the face to turn smooth, to take on the features I remembered so well. But the longer I stared, the less did that face look like Udatonte's. My head swam as I slowly grasped that I was staring at an unfamiliar, old, blind woman, and I started to fall. An old man rose from the broken circle; his powerful hand gripped my arm and kept me from falling. He asked if I needed a sweat, a swim or an herbal potion; he called me nephew. I told him my dizziness had already passed. I studied his face but failed to recognize him. He saw my confusion and told me he was Wakaya, my uncle Meteya's brother. He said he had not recognized me either; he had recognized the arrowhead that dangled from my neck.

Leading me slowly away from the councilground, he told me he had come to the Leaning Tree gathering, as he guessed that I had, in order to throw water on the fire, in order to cool down the warriors. He said our warriors had been too few at the field of fallen trees, too few at the river fork in the Morningland, and they were even fewer now. But he had not sat on Shabeni's side of the circle. He said he too was Lamina's descendant, he too was made of red earth and if the council had resolved to stand and fight until the last warrior fell, he had been ready to stand with them.

The council had not resolved to fight, and Wakaya was relieved. He had weathered sixty winters and he longed to return to his children and grandchildren. As we walked along Mishigami's shore, I asked him if a young woman had returned to his village after the last battle in the Morningland, a woman with straight black hair and fierce eyes.

Wakaya remembered that she had been one of the Turtlefolk from Sandusky. He told me she had not returned. But when he looked into my eyes he became excited, as if he had seen something in them. His own eyes told me he was remembering things he had not thought about. He said that just before he had found me on the battlefield by the fork, he had hurried to the Brethren's village to urge its inhabitants to evacuate.

His cousin Pamoko was holding a newborn child given to her by a young Turtlewoman who was unknown to Pamoko; the child's mother had rushed to the battlefield armed with a rifle. The child was taken to Karontaen, lodged and nursed by Pamoko. Wakaya had considered the child Pamoko's daughter and had not given the child much thought.

The girl befriended my sister Wabnokwe's daughters, moved in with them, and eventually left the Strait altogether, so that Wakaya lost all contact with her. He remembered the girl's wavy black hair, something uncommon in Karontaen. But he said her eyes were not fierce. Wakaya remembered having looked into her eyes once, and having thought that the girl's sorrowful, distant eyes were not like those of anyone in Karontaen; they were like the eyes of the nephew Wakaya had nursed in the Morningland infirmary.

I gratefully placed my hand on Wakaya's. I now knew that I had not been looking into Udatonte's fierce eyes when I had seen the four gushing streams of black rain that regenerated the trees, the fliers, the crawlers and the walkers. I had been looking into the tortured eyes of . . .

The old man's voice was so weak that I barely heard his last words. His eyes were still open, but he no longer saw me or anything else in the hospital room. I was exhausted from keeping my ear next to his moving lips listening to sounds so faint they seemed to come from the land of the dead.